Today's Essentials of Governmental and Not-for-Profit Accounting and Reporting

Susan W. Martin
Professor of Accounting
Provost and Vice-Chancellor
The University of Michigan–Dearborn

Ellen N. West
Governmental Finance Consultant

WAVELAND
PRESS, INC.
Long Grove, Illinois

For information about this book, contact:
    Waveland Press, Inc.
    4180 IL Route 83, Suite 101
    Long Grove, IL 60047-9580
    (847) 634-0081
    info@waveland.com
    www.waveland.com

BRIEF CONTENTS

CONTENTS

PREFACE

This is an all-new text in governmental and not-for-profit accounting that fully integrates the new governmental financial reporting model and GASB Statements through No. 38. Many governmental and not-for-profit accounting texts organize chapters by fund type and add new GASB Statements in separate sections, inserts or chapters as editions are updated. This text does not organize material into chapters by fund type. *Today's Essentials of Governmental and Not-for-Profit Accounting* offers a completely fresh approach to governmental and not-for-profit accounting and financial reporting with a new organization of topics. The text logically builds the student's understanding of basic concepts like accountability, typical transactions like recording budgets and property taxes, and carries those concepts through to the detailed production of annual financial statements and conversions to produce government-wide financial statements. *Putting it together* examples walk students through the process of analyzing and entering typical transactions and developing financial statements. As part of their development process, the authors have class-tested their chapters, assignments, and test bank items. They have written not only the text content and assignments but also all of the supporting materials to ensure accuracy and complete integration with the module.

Highlights of *Today's Essentials of Governmental and Not-for-Profit Accounting* include:

- An original, up-to-date text that fully integrates the new financial reporting model for governmental entities through GASB Statement No. 38.
- A fresh approach that organizes the content around topics and financial statements, rather than funds, introduces concepts in a logical flow.
- Clearly explained essentials that the authors carefully gleaned from thousands of pages of authoritative documents.
- Sufficient, yet not burdensome, detail that enables students to understand complex topics and transactions.

- *Putting it together* examples reinforce the concepts of the chapters and illustrate basic transactions through preparation of financial statements.
- A continuous governmental problem starts in Chapter 3 with budgetary transactions and funds, continues in Chapter 4 with recording typical transactions and year-end closing entries, and then in Chapter 5 produces both fund financial statements and government-wide statements according to the new financial reporting model prescribed in GASB Statement No. 34.
- Student-tested end-of-chapter materials: 30 multiple choice items for each chapter and additional exercises and problems that include Internet research. No AICPA examination materials are used as these are readily available to students elsewhere.

Chapters are organized around the assets, liabilities, and net assets that flow into the Statement of Net Assets and the revenues, and expenditures or expenses that flow into the operating statements. The adjustments necessary to convert governmental fund statements to government-wide are illustrated in detail and organized into a logical six-step approach.

Chapter 1 provides an introduction to governmental and not-for-profit organizations, standard-setting bodies, a brief history of the development of generally accepted accounting principles (GAAP) for governmental and not-for-profit organizations, and the Hierarchy of GAAP. *Chapter 2* introduces the basic governmental fund categories and types, budgets and budgetary accounting, and illustrates basic budgetary journal entries for governmental units. *Chapter 3* covers typical governmental transactions and illustrates the recognition and recording of revenues (exchange and nonexchange transactions), expenditures or expenses, other financing sources and uses, and reciprocal and nonreciprocal interfund transactions. *Chapter 4* illustrates governmental transactions that affect the Statement of Net Assets or Balance Sheet accounts of Assets, Liabilities and Equity or Fund Balance. *Chapter 5* illustrates the GASB Statement No. 34 financial reporting model including a detailed explanation of the components of the new financial statements as well as a detailed example of how to put the statements together and convert the governmental fund statements to the government-wide statements. *Chapter 6* explains basic accounting concepts for not-for-profit organizations, including types of funds, unique revenue and expense transactions such as accounting for contributions including gifts-in-kind, split-interest agreements, contributed services, and special events and fund-raising activities, as well as the basic financial reporting model of FASB Statement No. 117. *Chapter 7* covers unique aspects of health care and college and university accounting and reporting including sample transactions and illustrations of GASB Statement No. 35 financial statements. Chapter 7 also includes a basic coverage of the single audit act and generally accepted governmental (and not-for-profit) auditing principles (GAGAS).

This is an elementary text yet it provides in-depth up-to-date coverage through *GASB Statement No. 38.* The text is suitable for use in an advanced accounting course or a one-credit course in governmental and not-for-profit accounting or for a supplementary text in advanced accounting. The evolving draft text was pilot-tested for two semesters in a 3-credit senior-level course in governmental and not-for-profit accounting. Many refinements and improvements were made based upon student feedback and edits. Sample syllabi will be included in the instructor's manual for a one-credit course, an advanced accounting module of 5 weeks, and a 3-credit course utilizing the *GASB Codification of Governmental Accounting and Financial Reporting Standards.*

Excerpts from GASB Statement No. 33, *Accounting and Financial Reporting for Nonexchange Transactions*, No. 34, *Basic Financial Statements—and Management's Discussion and Analysis—for State and Local Governments*, and No. 35, *Basic Financial Statements—and Management's Discussion and Analysis—for Public Colleges and Universities* are copyrighted by the governmental Accounting Standards Board, 401 Merritt 7, P.O. Box 5116, Norwalk, Connecticut 06856-5116, U.S.A. Portions are reprinted with permission. Complete copies of this document are available from the GASB.

We extend special thanks to:

The following reviewers, who provided helpful suggestions and constructive criticisms as the chapters were being developed:

Laurel Berry, Bryant & Stratton
L. Charles Bokemeier, Michigan State University
Sam Lanzafame, Bryant & Stratton
Don Pagach, North Carolina State University

- The Grand Valley State University students who provided suggestions and edits while pretesting the draft text
- The Governmental Accounting Standards Board and the American Institute of Certified Public Accountants for their support and assistance in permitting information to be utilized in this text
- Stephen Gauthier of the Government Finance Officers Association and Michael "Mickey" Miller of the City of Orlando, Florida, for sharing their understanding of the conversion from governmental to government-wide financial statements
- Kathy Goralski and Carolyn VanValkenburg for their assistance in the production of the text material, PowerPoint® slides, and instructor/solutions manual
- Walt Zarnoch and Sara Wilson for their continued encouragement and enthusiasm for this project
- Our immediate families for their patience and understanding during the writing of this text. The project became much larger than either of us ever imagined; yet we remained friends to the end

We have enjoyed writing this text and strived to integrate the large amount of new GASB material in an understandable yet challenging text for students. We invite your suggestions and comments to improve the teaching and learning of governmental and not-for-profit accounting from this text. Please email comments to martins@gvsu.edu or ellenwest@qwest.net.

Sue Martin and Ellen West

ABOUT THE AUTHORS

Susan Work Martin is a Professor of Accounting and Provost and Vice-Chancellor of Academic Affairs at the University of Michigan–Dearborn. Susan has been appointed to serve four terms from 1989 to 2007 as Chair of the State of Michigan Hospital Finance Authority, which issues tax-exempt bonds for Michigan health care facilities. Susan was also appointed to serve on the Internal Revenue Service Electronic Tax Administration Advisory Board from 1998 to 2000 to advise the IRS on e-filing issues. Susan served from 1997 to 2000 on the Tax Executive Committee of the American Institute of CPAs (AICPA), which issued enforceable professional standards for tax practice in 2000. Prior to joining Grand Valley State University in 1988, Susan worked over 10 years for the State of Michigan as Commissioner of Revenue, Deputy State Treasurer in charge of the Local Government Bureau, and as an Assistant Auditor General.

Susan is a member of the Government Finance Officers Association, AICPA, Michigan Association of CPAs, Association of Governmental Accountants, and the American Accounting Association. She has published in a variety of professional publications on tax and governmental accounting topics.

Sue developed a study-abroad program in international accounting at Kingston University in England and has also been active in Poland since 1991 attending professional conferences and leading study-abroad programs at the Cracow University of Economics. Dr. Martin is a CPA, CMA, CIA and Certified Government Financial Manager (CGFM). Dr. Martin received MBA and Ph.D. degrees from Michigan State University and a B.S. degree from Central Michigan University. Susan is a Master Gardener and loves to garden and walk her golden retriever named Lucky. Susan grew up on a dairy farm in Michigan and attended a one-room school for grades K–8.

Ellen West has a diverse background in government finance and public sector portfolio management. She worked with many public entities as Vice President, Client Services, for MBIA Municipal Investors Service Company. She served as Treasurer and Executive Vice President of American Money Management Associates, Inc., an investment advisory firm that specialized in the development of customized investment management programs for public entities and merged with MBIA Municipal Investors Service Company in 2000. She has worked with numerous public entities and her areas of expertise include public sector investment accounting and reporting, cash flow forecasting, the development of investment policies, and the documentation of investment management programs. Her experience includes four years as Assistant to the Executive Director of the Government Finance Officers Association of the United States and Canada, where she was responsible for the administration of member service programs. She also served as Finance Officer for the Village of Grosse Pointe Shores, Michigan for ten years.

Ms. West is a frequent instructor of public sector investment management topics and she has presented sessions for the Municipal Treasurers Association of the US and Canada, the Southwest School of Governmental Finance at Texas Tech University, and many professional organizations. She is a past president of both the Michigan Municipal Finance Officers Association and the Colorado Treasury Management Association. She also served as a member of the Governmental Accounting Standards Board's advisory committee for the development of the *Guide to Implementation of GASB Statement 31 on Accounting and Financial Reporting for Certain Investments and for External Investment Pools.* Ms. West holds the designation of Certified Cash Manager through the Association of Finance Professionals. She graduated Summa Cum Laude with a degree in General Studies from Wayne State University and has attended numerous conferences and training sessions on government finance topics throughout her career. She enjoyed travel with her husband and mentor George Nielsen.

*This book is dedicated to the memory of George A. Nielsen,
husband and mentor, and Samuel M. Work, father and friend.*

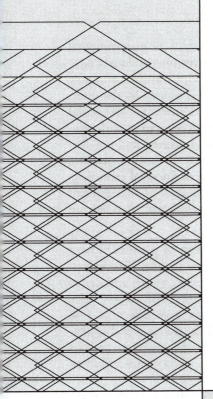

CHAPTER 1

THE FOUNDATION OF GOVERNMENTAL AND NOT-FOR-PROFIT ACCOUNTING

LEARNING OBJECTIVES

- Describe similarities and differences between governmental and not-for-profit organizations
- State the hierarchy of generally accepted accounting principles (GAAP)
- Explain the concepts that form the basis for governmental accounting standards
- Demonstrate an understanding of the concepts of fund accounting and governmental and business-type activities
- Describe the concepts of basis of accounting and measurement focus
- Outline the evolution of governmental and not-for-profit accounting standards

THE GOVERNMENTAL AND NOT–FOR–PROFIT ENVIRONMENT

Accountability is a key theme you will find throughout the study of governmental and not-for-profit accounting. Unlike a for-profit business, governments do not have customers who voluntarily choose to buy products or services. Governments and not-for-profit organizations do not have a product or service that is judged by the commercial marketplace or bottom-line profits to shareholders. Rather, governmental entities and not-for-profit organizations are organized by constituents to provide specific services. Governments are supported in large part by various taxes, and not-for-profit organizations are supported by grants and donations. In both instances, **accountability** for how the funds are used is the primary focus of financial reporting.

Three key factors in the governmental environment that influence accounting and financial reporting standards are described in the Governmental Accounting Standards Board's (GASB)[1] Concepts Statement No. 1[2]:

1. **The representative form of government and separation of powers.** There are three branches of government: executive, legislative, and judicial. The executive branch submits a proposed budget to the legislative branch, which authorizes an appropriation of governmental resources to fund the approved budget. The appropriation, or authorization to spend, has the force and effect of law. Expenditures made by the executive branch must be within limits of the appropriation. Failure to operate within the appropriation could result in judicial enforcement. This relationship has a significant budgetary and control influence in the accounting standards for governmental operations.
2. **The federalist system of governmental and intergovernmental revenues.** The flow-through and sharing of governmental resources between governmental units requires a high level of accountability for such funds.
3. **The relationship of taxpayers (or lack of) to services received.** There is not always a direct relationship between taxes paid and services received. Citizens who pay no taxes may receive services, and citizens who pay a high amount of taxes may receive little service. Taxpayers demand a high level of accountability and scrutiny over resources and services.

GASB Concepts Statement No. 1[3] sets forth five key characteristics of governmental units that impact financial reporting objectives:

1. **Taxpayers are involuntary resource providers.** They are not free to choose whether or not to pay taxes. They are legally required to provide these resources to the government.
2. **The amount of taxes paid seldom bears a direct relationship to the services received.** Property taxes are based upon the value of the home. Income taxes are based upon income. Individuals do not receive governmental services in proportion to the taxes paid.
3. **No "exchange" relationship exists between services received and resources provided.** Governments generally have several types of taxes that are pooled to

---

[1]The Governmental Accounting Standards Board (GASB) establishes accounting and financial reporting standards for state and local governmental entities and some not-for-profit organizations.
[2]GASB Concepts Statement No. 1, *Objectives of Financial Reporting*, paragraph 13.
[3]Ibid, paragraph 17.

support a budget of programs and services. Citizens who provide these resources do not receive coupons for a certain amount of fire or police protection. There is no "matching" of revenues provided with services received.

4. **Governments often monopolize certain services.** A good example would be public safety—police and fire protection. This does not mean that citizens can't purchase private police or fire protection, but the government has a natural monopoly for this service, making it difficult to measure the efficiency in providing the services.

5. **It is difficult to measure the optimal quantity or quality of service.** Benchmarking is a relatively new practice where governments seek to use benchmarks (average amounts of services provided by similar size governments) to establish optimal services.

The characteristics of governments are very different from corporations that are selling a product or service. For-profit corporations are measured by concepts such as matching revenues to expenses to determine the net profit and earnings per share. Governments do not measure profits, nor can they establish the services per resident as a meaningful measure.

Similarly, not-for-profit organizations receive large amounts of resources from donors, grants, and a variety of sources. These providers of resources do not necessarily expect any services in return. Not-for-profit organizations are, by their very nature, created to solicit revenues for purposes that benefit the public. There are no profits or returns on investment for not-for-profits.

Corporate accounting practices focus upon measuring profits, return on investment, and earnings per share. Because goals are different, these accounting practices would not be meaningful or applicable for governments or not-for-profits where the focus is on collecting resources to provide services deemed important for the public good. As a result, different accounting practices that will demonstrate accountability are required to report on governmental and not-for-profit operations.

The GASB groups the primary users of governmental financial reports into three types: 1) citizens that the government is primarily accountable to, 2) legislative bodies, governing boards, and oversight bodies that represent citizens, and 3) investors and creditors[4]. Governments often issue bonds or borrow funds to finance projects, and, therefore, need to be accountable to the investors who purchase the bonds or creditors who provide short-term financing. Accountability for these users is found by comparing budgeted to actual results and in assessing financial condition, legal compliance, and evaluating efficiency and effectiveness.

Governmental accounting standards

In June 1984, the **Governmental Accounting Standards Board** (GASB) was created and the authority to establish GAAP for state and local governments (including counties, cities, school districts, special districts and other public authorities) was transferred from the NCGA to the GASB. The **Financial Accounting Foundation** (FAF) provides funding for the GASB and appoints members of the GASB Board. The GASB is based in Norwalk, Connecticut. The GASB now has seven members; one full-time and six part-time, and the assistance of a full-time professional staff. The

---

[4]Ibid, paragraph 30.

GASB's first Statement No. 1 affirmed that all existing NCGA Statements would remain in effect until superseded by future GASB pronouncements, in effect, saying **current GAAP remains GAAP until the GASB changes it.** The *Codification of Governmental Accounting and Financial Reporting Standards,* published by the GASB, is an organized compilation of GASB Statements, which provides the primary source of GAAP for state and local governments.

For-profit accounting standards

Just as GAAP for state and local governments or governmentally related units (the public sector) is established by the GASB, GAAP for business enterprises (the private sector) and nongovernmental not-for-profit organizations is established by the **Financial Accounting Standards Board** (FASB). Like its counterpart the GASB, the FASB is funded by the Financial Accounting Foundation (FAF), which also appoints its Board members. The FASB shares offices with the GASB in Norwalk, Connecticut.

Not-for-profit accounting standards

Some not-for-profit organizations are covered by GASB standards and others fall under FASB standards, depending upon the characteristics of the organization. The FAF made a jurisdictional determination on November 30, 1989, defining the split of standard-setting responsibilities between the GASB and the FASB. This FAF determination clarified that the GASB will set standards for governments and governmental-type not-for-profits.

What is a **not-for-profit organization?** A not-for-profit organization is one that has "predominantly nonbusiness characteristics that heavily influence the operations of the organization."[5] Not-for-profit organizations are different from business enterprises and similar to governmental units because they possess the following characteristics:

- No direct relationship between resources provided and goods or services provided or created by the organization
- Operating goals and purposes that are not profit-based
- Absence of defined ownership interests

Not-for-profit organizations include human service organizations, churches, foundations, private nonprofit hospitals and schools, and other organizations that receive a significant portion of their revenues from sources other than the sale of goods or services.

There are four categories of not-for-profit organizations: Health Care, Colleges and Universities, Voluntary Health and Welfare Organizations (VHWO), and Other Not-for-Profit Organizations. Health Care organizations and Colleges and Universities have some unique characteristics and transactions, which are discussed in Chapter 7. The key characteristic that distinguishes a VHWO from an Other Not-for-Profit Organization is that the VHWO has some public health and welfare

---

[5]Financial Accounting Standards Board (FASB) Concepts Statement No. 4, *Objectives of Financial Reporting by Nonbusiness Organizations,* December 1980.

purpose as a primary mission or activity of the organization. For example, the American Red Cross would be a VHWO, and a local museum would be an Other Not-for-Profit Organization. Harvard University would be a private not-for-profit university, and the University of Michigan would be a public governmental university. Columbia HCA is a publicly-traded health care corporation, and Ascension Health system is a not-for-profit health care hospital system.

What criteria determine if the not-for-profit is *nongovernmental*? First, "nongovernmental organizations are all organizations other than governmental organizations."[6] Governmental organizations include municipalities or governmental corporations created to administer public affairs, instrumentalities created by the state, and organizations that have the power to levy taxes and issue tax-exempt debt directly. Not-for-profit organizations are considered to be governmental if they have one or more of the following characteristics[7]:

- Popular election of officers or appointment (or approval) of a controlling majority of the members of the organization's governing body by officials of one or more state or local governments;
- The potential for unilateral dissolution by a government with the net assets reverting to a government;
- The power to enact and enforce a tax levy; or
- The power to directly issue tax-exempt debt.

There may be cases in which it is difficult to determine the nature of the organization. Is the organization a business or not-for-profit organization? Consider a private hospital that receives a significant portion of its revenue from the charges for services provided to patients yet also receives donations and is registered with tax authorities as a not-for-profit institution. This private hospital exhibits characteristics of both business and nonbusiness organizations. A not-for-profit organization does not have key financial indicators of performance like earnings per share or return on investment as a business organization would have. Not-for-profit organizations often are not subject to direct competition. Yet, nonbusiness organizations may sell goods or services. In some cases, they may provide these goods or services below cost or for free. In other cases, they may provide goods or services that are in such demand that the price is raised to subsidize other activities in the nonbusiness organization. College athletics is a good example where higher ticket prices for men's football or basketball revenues may support all other student athletics at the university.

Throughout this text, the reader may presume the term **not-for-profit** means a nongovernmental not-for-profit organization and that **governmental** includes governmental-type not-for-profit organizations.

Not-for-profit organizations are not subject to direct competition in the marketplace, so it is important to have budgets and donor restrictions on the use of resources to ensure compliance and performance.

Not-for-profit organizations generally qualify under Section 501(c)3 of the Internal Revenue Code to have a tax-exempt status due to their goals and objectives to serve a public purpose. Most not-for-profit organizations are required to file an annual information return on Form 990 with the Internal Revenue Service unless

---

[6]Ibid, Paragraph 1.03.
[7]American Institute of Certified Public Accountants (AICPA), *Professional Standards*, Section AU411.

their gross receipts are less than $25,000. If the not-for-profit organization regularly engages in trade or business activities that are not substantially related to its tax-exempt purpose, then any profits from those activities will be subject to a Federal Unrelated Business Income Tax (UBIT).

HIERARCHY OF GAAP

The FAF's 1984 GASB Structural Agreement set forth a **hierarchy of GAAP** for governmental entities. The hierarchy, or ordering, designates GASB Statements and Interpretations as the first and primary source of GAAP and lists in order of ranking what other sources should be used for guidance. The American Institute of Certified Public Accountants (AICPA) Auditing Standards Board issued Statement 69 *The Meaning of "Present Fairly in Conformity with Generally Accepted Accounting Principle" in the Independent Auditor's Report*, which implements the FAF decision and sets forth a hierarchy of GAAP shown in Exhibit 1-1. This exhibit also presents the parallel hierarchy for nongovernmental entities, which follow the FASB guidelines.

In effect, the AICPA and the FAF have agreed on a structure (hierarchy) for practitioners to find GAAP. Because governmental and not-for-profit accounting standards only began to be issued as Statements in 1979 by the NCGA, some topics remain that have not been addressed in a GASB Statement or Interpretation. Facing a topic not covered in GASB Statements, the hierarchy of GAAP provides a clear road map of the path to search for guidance starting at the top with "GASB Statements and Interpretations" and proceeding down the list through "other accounting literature."

The AICPA issues *Audit and Accounting Guides for Not-for-Profit Organizations* and for *Health Care Organizations* and updates these annually to maintain them in accordance with current FASB and GASB standards. The National Association of College and University Business Officers (NACUBO) has played an important role in setting accounting and financial reporting standards for colleges and universities just as the Government Finance Officers Association (GFOA) has for governmental units. NACUBO practices are reflected in the NACUBO *Financial Accounting and Reporting Manual for Higher Education* and also in the *AICPA Audit and Accounting Guide for Not-for-Profit Organizations*. The *AICPA Audit and Accounting Guides* are useful tools for the CPA engaged to audit the not-for-profit or health care organization and are second in the hierarchy of GAAP.

The hierarchy of GAAP shows that FASB is the primary source of GAAP for accounting and reporting standards for nongovernmental not-for-profit organizations and that GASB is the primary source of GAAP for governmental organizations. FASB issued Statements 115, 116, 117, and 124 to establish new accounting and financial reporting standards for not-for-profit organizations. These FASB Statements are applicable to all four types of not-for-profit organizations except for those that are governmental not-for-profit organizations. GASB issued Statements No. 33, 34, and 35 to establish new accounting and financial reporting standards for governmental organizations. Governmental not-for-profit organizations will continue to use fund accounting and issue financial reports following GASB Statement No. 34 as illustrated in Chapter 5. Not-for-profit organizations will issue financial reports as illustrated in Chapter 6. Governmental colleges and universities will issue financial reports following GASB Statement No. 35 as illustrated in Chapter 7.

EXHIBIT 1-1 GAAP Hierarchy Summary[8]

Authority Level	State and Local Governments and Governmental Not-for-Profit	Not-for-Profit Organizations and For-Profit Businesses
	Established Accounting Principles	
1	**GASB Statements and Interpretations,** plus AICPA and FASB pronouncements if made applicable to state and local governments by a GASB Statement or Interpretation	FASB Statements and Interpretations, APB Opinions, and AICPA Accounting Research Bulletins
2	**GASB Technical Bulletins,** and the following pronouncements if specifically made applicable to state and local governments by the AICPA: **AICPA Industry Audit and Accounting Guides** and **AICPA Statements of Position**	FASB Technical Bulletins, AICPA Industry Audit and Accounting Guides, and AICPA Statements of Position
3	**Consensus positions of the GASB Emerging Issues Task Force** and **AICPA Practice Bulletins** if specifically made applicable to state and local governments by the AICPA	Consensus positions of the FASB Emerging Issues Task Force and AICPA Practice Bulletins
4	**Implementation Guides** and **Questions and Answers** published by the GASB staff, as well as industry practices widely recognized and prevalent	AICPA Accounting Interpretations, Questions and Answers published by the FASB staff, as well as industry practices widely recognized and prevalent
	Other Accounting Literature	
5	**Other accounting literature,** including GASB Concepts Statements; pronouncements in the categories above when not specifically made applicable to state and local governments; FASB Concepts Statements; AICPA Issues Papers; International Accounting Standards Committee Statements; pronouncements of other professional associations or regulatory agencies; AICPA *Technical Practice Aids;* and accounting textbooks, handbooks, and articles	Other accounting literature, including FASB Concepts Statements; AICPA Issues Papers; International Accounting Standards Committee Statements; GASB Statements, Interpretations, and Technical Bulletins; pronouncements of other professional associations or regulatory agencies; AICPA *Technical Practice Aids,* and accounting textbooks, handbooks, and articles

● **INTERPRETIVE EXERCISE**

A small rural village with a lake is "discovered" by a developer who plans a summer home development. The village negotiates with the developer, and they agree on a $300,000 fee that the developer will pay the village for water and sewer system tap-in fees and for development of the water and sewer connections for the summer homes. The village accountant looks in GASB and FASB standards but cannot find any guidance on how to account for this $300,000 fee. The accountant does not know whether to capitalize the fee or book it as revenue in the current fiscal year. Where should the accountant look for guidance next in the hierarchy of GAAP? Why?

---

[8]Ibid, Section AU 411.16, 2000, page 720.

Accounting standards for the federal government

The federal government and its agencies are not covered by the reporting standards of either the GASB or the FASB. The **Federal Accounting Standards Advisory Board** (FASAB) was established by the Department of Treasury, the General Accounting Office (GAO), and the Office of Management and Budget (OMB) to develop recommended accounting standards for federal entities. Through the efforts of the FASAB, a degree of uniformity in the reporting practices of federal agencies has been established. This text will not cover federal accounting and reporting.

GOVERNMENTAL ACCOUNTING AND FINANCIAL REPORTING

GASB Concepts Statement No. 1 sets forth two primary concepts that must guide accounting and financial reporting standards: 1) accountability, and 2) interperiod equity. **Accountability** is considered the "cornerstone" of financial reporting[9]. Governments are accountable for public resources to provide public services, and their primary constituent is their citizenry. Legislative and oversight bodies also check to ensure that the government is accountable for proper and efficient use of these resources. Investors and creditors hold the government accountable to repay borrowed resources in a timely manner. **Interperiod equity** is a more difficult concept to understand. Simply put, interperiod equity means that the government should pay for current services with current resources and should not postpone payment to burden future budgetary periods[10]. For example, if a government fails to properly fund pensions that will be due in future periods, it burdens the future periods with the need to obtain enough money to pay the debt. This practice of underfunding pensions will decrease interperiod equity because it results in a large liability that future citizens will have to provide resources to pay. Payment of this liability in the future could even force a cutback of important public services. The underlying premise of interperiod equity is that budgets should be balanced to ensure future resources are not diverted to pay for past services.

Another measure of accountability in financial reporting is encompassed in the concept of **service efforts and accomplishments** (SEA)[11]. SEA reporting is intended to provide information to users about services provided and accomplishments and then use measures to link the two together. The relationship between service efforts and accomplishments should provide citizens and other users valuable information about governmental performance and provide information to hold managers accountable.

The influence of the budget on governmental accounting

Budgeting is another method to enhance accountability. Governmental entities adopt a budget to govern the spending of available resources for services. GASB Concepts Statement No. 1[12] notes that the budget is the most important financial document of the governmental unit because it expresses public policy, financial intent, control

---

[9]GASB Concepts Statement No. 1, paragraph 56.
[10]Ibid, paragraph 61.
[11]GASB Concepts Statement No. 2, Service Efforts and Accomplishments Reporting, paragraphs 1–5.
[12]GASB Concepts Statement No. 1, paragraph 19.

Should citizens grade their city management?

The 35 cities with the largest revenues in the United States were given an overall grade by researchers at Syracuse University and also individual grades in five categories: Finances, Capital, Personnel, Information, and Managing. The top city with an overall grade of A based on four A's and one A– was Phoenix, Arizona. Phoenix encourages its workers to innovate and manage for results. Phoenix monitors performance every month with a detailed report on performance on hundreds of measures. Some of these measures, for example, tell how long citizens must wait for services. Of course, the goal is to cut these waiting times and improve services. Phoenix has found that by making its citizens happy they are, in turn, helpful and volunteer in many ways to improve services. A survey of 35,000 residents is done annually to get input on services and how to improve them. City workers are very satisfied with 97%, rating Phoenix as a good place to work.

(Source: *USA Today*, January 31, 2000)

---

usually with the force of law, and a basis for evaluating performance. Governmental resources are public monies that cannot be spent without legal authority. It is extremely important to control and monitor the budget throughout the fiscal year to ensure that the estimated resources are coming in as expected and that the expenses are not exceeding the authorized amounts. A government cannot quickly raise its "price" of services by increasing taxes, so it must carefully live within the budgeted levels. The importance of the budget has a pervasive influence in the accounting standards for governmental units. The accounting methods and reporting formats were not developed to measure profits; they were **developed to monitor, control and measure budgetary performance.** As a result, governmental accounting methods are different from corporate accounting methods.

GASB Concepts Statement No. 1 sets forth financial reporting objectives for assessing accountability. These objectives indicate that financial reports should enable users to determine if resources were sufficient to pay for the current budget year's services and whether those resources were used in compliance with the adopted budget and other relevant laws.

Fund accounting and governmental and business-type activities

The use of funds in governmental accounting provides another mechanism for accountability and control over public monies.[13] **Funds** are self-balancing sets of accounts that are established to keep track of budgetary appropriations and the cost of providing specific services. The GASB defines three fund categories for governmental entities: **governmental funds, proprietary funds, and fiduciary funds.** Governmental funds account for the **governmental activities** of the entity that encompass general activities, such as administration and public safety. Proprietary funds account for any **business-type activities** of governments such as water and sewer services that are supported by fees charged to users of the services. Fiduciary funds account for **monies the government holds on behalf of others** such as

---

[13]Ibid, paragraphs 21–22.

pension funds that cannot be used to support other government programs. The GASB has established different accounting and reporting standards for governmental and business-type activities to reflect the nature of the activities and to provide appropriate related financial information. Funds and fund accounting are explained further in Chapter 2.

Basis of accounting

The **basis of accounting**[14] determines *when* transactions or events are recognized in the accounting system. Under the **accrual** method of accounting, revenues are recognized when earned and expenses when incurred, regardless of when cash is received or paid out. For-profit organizations covered by the FASB accounting standards use the accrual method of accounting whereby a corporation will strive to match revenues with expenses. Business-type activities of governments also use the accrual method of accounting.

The accrual method of accounting has been modified to account for governmental activities. This **modified accrual** method states that revenues will be recorded when they are "susceptible to accrual" or "measurable and available." Available is interpreted as meaning that the resources will be available in time to pay the expenses of the current budgetary period. In other words, if the government will not receive the resources in time to pay the current budget year operating expenses, it should not be recorded as revenue. Under modified accrual, governments record expenses when they are incurred if measurable or an obligation against the *current* budgetary resources is made. The modified accrual method is yet another example of the profound impact that the budgetary focus has upon governmental accounting and financial reporting.

In Statement No. 33, *Accounting and Reporting for Nonexchange Transactions*, the GASB has adopted changes that shifted the measurement of governmental resources more closely to accrual accounting. The details of how resources and expenses are measured under modified accrual and Statement No. 33 will be more fully explained with example transactions in Chapter 3.

Measurement focus

The concept of **measurement focus** refers to *what* is being reported upon or measured in the financial statements. The **current financial resources measurement focus** concept suggests that revenues and expenses should be recorded when they flow in as financial resources to the budgetary period and when they flow out to be used to pay for services during the budgetary period. This method of reporting is used with the modified accrual basis of accounting. For example, property taxes can be accrued at fiscal year-end (FYE) if they will be collected within 60 days after FYE. This is *not* cash basis or accrual basis accounting.

The **economic resources measurement focus**[15] states that revenues, expenses, gains, losses, assets, and liabilities of exchange transactions are recorded when the

---

[14]National Council on Governmental Accounting (NCGA) Statement 1, *Governmental Accounting and Financial Reporting Principles*, paragraphs 57–70.
[15]GASB Statement No. 34, *Basic Financial Statements—and Management's Discussion and Analysis—for State and Local Governments*, paragraph 16.

exchange takes place and that nonexchange transactions are recorded as prescribed in GASB Statement No. 33. This method of reporting is used with the accrual basis of accounting. In an **exchange transaction,** the governmental entity gives and receives approximately equal values in the transaction. For example, a city charges $35 to play 18 holes of golf on the municipal course. In **nonexchange transactions,** the government receives (or gives) resources without giving (or receiving) resources that are approximately equal in value. For example, when a city charges a 3% sales tax, the purchaser of goods does not receive a direct equivalent value in city services in return. The details of how and when to record exchange and nonexchange transactions will be covered in Chapters 3 and 4. Chapter 5 will explain how the types of measurement focus and basis of accounting are utilized in creating governmental financial reports.

GASB Statement No. 34 changes the measurement of government-wide operations from the flow of financial resources concept (current financial resources measurement focus) and modified accrual basis of accounting to the economic resources measurement focus and accrual basis of accounting. One example of the difference between the old and new methods of accounting is in capital assets. Under the modified accrual method, a fire truck would be charged to expense when purchased rather than depreciated because it was budgeted at full cost and resources flowed out during the budgetary period. Under the accrual method, the fire truck will be capitalized and charged off over its useful life in depreciation expense. This is one of many changes in the new model and perhaps one of the more controversial. Another controversial change is that under accrual, governments will account for all of their assets including infrastructure (examples include streets, sewers, and streetlights). Some governmental finance professionals wonder if the cost of obtaining such information about capital assets will exceed the benefit of the information obtained. That is certainly an interesting public policy question to evaluate as these new accounting and reporting changes are implemented. GASB 34 will be phased in by size of government over the years 2001–2004 for financial accounting and reporting.

Not-for-profit accounting concepts

Not-for-profit organizations use accrual accounting and have some unique approaches in financial reporting to enhance accountability to the providers of their resources. For example, voluntary health and welfare organizations have a functional expense classification between program and administration that enables donors to quickly see how much of their resources are actually going toward the agency's program and how much is spent just to run the agency in administration.

FASB standards prescribe an accrual-based accounting and financial reporting model that departs from the governmental model with its budgetary and modified accrual focus. FASB Statements 115, 116, 117, and 124 changed many aspects of accounting and financial reporting for not-for-profits. Accounting and reporting for not-for-profit organizations is covered in Chapters 6 and 7.

Evolution of governmental accounting standards

The founding of the **Municipal Finance Officers Association** (MFOA) in 1906 marked one of the first attempts to establish uniform governmental accounting standards. The purpose of the Association was "to improve methods of public finance." To do that, the MFOA worked to develop procedures of accounting, budgeting, and financial reporting for state and local governmentsand to encourage adoption of common principles and presentations. Today, the MFOA, now known as the **Government Finance Officers Association** (GFOA), continues to provide guidance and training on governmental finance, accounting, and reporting topics.

Over the years, the MFOA has sponsored and published the works of several groups dedicated to developing governmental accounting standards. The first group, the **National Committee on Municipal Accounting** (NCMA), issued Bulletin No. 6, *Municipal Accounting Statements* in 1936. This book, commonly referred to as the "blue book" because of its blue cover, became the early source of **generally accepted accounting principles** (GAAP) for governments. Governmental GAAP sets minimum requirements for fair presentation of financial data in external financial reports to help assure comparability in financial reporting among different governments.

The NCMA was eventually replaced by the **National Committee on Governmental Accounting** (NCGA). In 1951, the NCGA issued Bulletin No. 14, which was published by MFOA as *Municipal Accounting and Auditing*, the second version of the blue book. The next major revision of accounting standards came in 1968 when the NCGA issued the third blue book, *Governmental Accounting, Auditing and Financial Reporting (GAAFR)*.

The *GAAFR* blue book continues to be updated and published by the GFOA, most recently in 2001. Although the *GAAFR* is no longer considered a source of GAAP for state and local governments, the blue book is an excellent reference for common accounting topics, recommended practices, sample journal entries, and sample financial reports.

In an effort to encourage compliance with GAAP standards, the MFOA initiated the Certificate of Achievement for Excellence in Financial Reporting program in 1945 to recognize governmental units that prepared financial statements in accordance with GAAP. This Certificate was suitable for publication in the next fiscal year's financial report so that the government could publicize its excellence in accounting and compliance with GAAP. The program continues today, with over 70% of the U.S. cities with populations in excess of 50,000 participating in the program.[16] Until the 1970s, compliance with GAAP standards, as outlined in the blue book was generally a voluntary matter for governments. Several events in the 1970s gave the movement for uniformity in governmental accounting and financial reporting a boost.

In 1974, the **American Institute of Certified Public Accountants** (AICPA) issued an audit guide *"Audits of State and Local Governmental Units."* The audit guide referred to the 1968 *GAAFR* as the source of generally accepted accounting principles for governmental units, which made the *GAAFR* an authoritative standard. In order to receive an unqualified opinion on their audited financial statements, governments were now required to follow the guidance provided in the 1968 *GAAFR*.

In the mid-1970s, the near failure of New York City to pay principal and interest on long-term bonds focused national attention on accounting and financial reporting standards for governmental units. Critics wondered how New York City could not be aware of how weak the city's financial position was before this financial crisis occurred. It soon became obvious that financial reporting practices for governments provided no clear overall picture of a government's finances. A bill was introduced in Congress to provide for federal oversight and establishment of governmental accounting practices. In response, the MFOA acted upon the need to improve governmental

---

[16]See web site for information on the GFOA Certificate of Achievement for Excellence in Financial Reporting (CAFR program) at http://www.gfoa.org/gfoa2000/gfoaawrd.htm.

accounting and financial reporting and created a standard-setting body of 25 part-time board members called the **National Council on Governmental Accounting** (NCGA) as a successor to the National Committee on Governmental Accounting. NCGA Statements and Interpretations replaced the 1968 *GAAFR* as the source of GAAP for governmental entities. The NCGA issued Statements 1 and 2 in 1979 to define the organization of governmental funds and a financial reporting model to combine fund types into an overall financial report.

After the issuance of the NCGA's first Statements 1 and 2, Standard and Poor's rating agency issued a "Policy Statement on Municipal Accounting and Financial Reporting," which required governments to conform with NCGA Statements 1 and 2 (GAAP) and produce audited financial statements within 6 months after fiscal year-end. If governments did not comply, the Standard and Poor's policy statement indicated that a negative downgrade of the bond rating or failure to rate could occur. This action by a bond rating agency was a powerful incentive for governments to take action to issue financial reports in compliance with NCGA Statements 1 and 2. GASB took over standard setting from NCGA in 1984.

EXHIBIT 1-2 Evolution of Generally Accepted Accounting Standards for Governments

1934	National Committee on Municipal Accounting (NCMA) issues Bulletin No 6. *Municipal Accounting Standards.*
1951	National Committee on Governmental Accounting (NCGA) issues *Municipal Accounting and Auditing.*
1968	National Committee on Governmental Accounting (NCGA) issues *Governmental Accounting, Auditing and Financial Reporting (GAAFR).*
1979	National Council on Governmental Accounting (NCGA) Statements and Interpretations replace 1968 *GAAFR.* as source of GAAP for governmental units.
1984	Governmental Accounting Standards Board (GASB) is created and assumes authority to establish GAAP for state and local governmental units.

The most recent evolution in governmental accounting has been the move to a more business-like financial reporting model utilizing accrual accounting on the government-wide financial statements. This new financial reporting model is detailed in GASB Statement 34, Basic Financial Statements—and Management's Discussion and Analysis—for State and Local Governments that was issued in June, 1999. Statement 34 defines basic financial statements and required supplementary information for governmental entities. The new reporting model is intended to give a clear picture of an entity's overall financial position including an objective narrative of the government's financial activities. This new reporting model provided yet another level of accountability for financial reporting.

SUMMARY

Chapter 1 had the following learning objectives:

- Describe similarities and differences between governmental and not-for-profit organizations
- State the hierarchy of generally accepted accounting principles (GAAP)
- Explain the concepts that form the basis for governmental accounting standards

- Demonstrate an understanding of the concepts of fund accounting and governmental and business-type activities
- Describe the concepts of basis of accounting and measurement focus
- Outline the evolution of governmental and not-for-profit accounting standards

Governmental and not-for-profit entities are sufficiently different from for-profit entities to require different accounting standards to evolve over time. Governmental and not-for-profit accounting standards reflect the need for enhanced accountability for tax dollars and donated funds. Recent pronouncements in the 1990s by the GASB and the FASB have produced new financial reporting models and accounting standards. Accountants have to rely upon the hierarchy of GAAP established by the AICPA to determine who is the proper standard-setting authority for governmental and not-for-profit organizations.

Governmental and not-for-profit institutions have a public purpose and have developed different concepts such as accountability to reflect their core purpose. The strong budgetary influence is reflected in modified accrual accounting and in the financial reporting methods for governmental units. Governments are shifting from a modified accrual and current financial resources measurement focus toward accrual and economic resources measurement focus. Both governmental and not-for-profit units have conceptual goals to measure their service to citizens, the public, and resource providers with information to investors and creditors as a secondary goal of importance. There is much that is unique and unusual for the student of corporate accounting to learn about governmental and not-for-profit accounting and financial reporting.

This chapter was an introduction to the history, underlying concepts, and some basic principles of governmental and not-for-profit accounting. In the next chapter, fund accounting and funds will be described. Subsequent chapters will explain the actual accounting requirements, in detail, for typical transactions and accounts and illustrate the required financial reports.

QUESTIONS

1. What are some of the ways accounting information can assist citizens in grading their government?
2. What is meant by the term GAAP? What is the relationship between GAAFR and GAAP?
3. What criteria would you use to determine whether a not-for-profit university is covered by GASB or FASB accounting standards?
4. If you needed information about a governmental accounting topic not covered by GASB Statements, what other sources of information could you turn to for guidance?
5. What are the three key factors in the governmental environment, as described in GASB Concepts Statement No. 1, that influence accounting and reporting standards?
6. Describe the major differences between governments and corporations that create the need for different accounting standards.
7. Describe the modified accrual basis of accounting and how it differs from the accrual basis of accounting.
8. Describe the difference between the flow of financial resources measurement focus and the economic resources measurement focus.
9. Explain what interperiod equity means and provide an example.
10. What is the cornerstone of governmental financial reporting? Why?
11. What role did the rating agencies play in improving governmental financial reporting?

12. What is the service efforts and accomplishments model for financial reporting?
13. What is the importance of the jurisdictional agreement between the FASB and the GASB?
14. Is governmental financial reporting moving toward or away from the accrual for-profit model of financial reporting?
15. What role does the budget play in influencing governmental accounting?
16. Explain what the hierarchy of GAAP means and why it is important.
17. What relationship generally exists between the taxes paid by a citizen and the services received in return?
18. What relationship generally exists between the price paid to a corporation and the goods or services received?
19. Who are the primary users of governmental financial reports?
20. What impact did the New York City financial crisis have upon financial reporting?

EXERCISES

Exercise 1-1

Multiple Choice—Select the best answer for each of the following:

1. Accounting and reporting standards for state and local governments are established by:
   a. Generally Accepted Accounting Standards
   b. Financial Accounting Standards Board
   c. Government Finance Officers Association
   d. Governmental Accounting Standards Board
2. Accounting and reporting standards for the federal government are set by:
   a. Financial Accounting Standards Board
   b. Governmental Accounting Standards Board
   c. Federal Accounting Standards Advisory Board
   d. American Institute of Certified Public Accountants
3. Which of the following is *not* true? The GASB sets standards for governments and not-for-profits if they have one or more of the following characteristics:
   a. ability of the governing body to enact legislation by a majority vote
   b. power to adopt and enforce a tax levy
   c. appointment of a majority of the governing body by officials of the governmental unit
   d. power to directly issue tax-exempt debt
4. Which standard-setting body would have jurisdiction over a private sector not-for-profit university?
   a. Governmental Accounting Standards Board
   b. Financial Accounting Standards Board
   c. National Association of College and University Business Officers
   d. College Accounting Standards Board
5. In the hierarchy of GAAP for state and local governments, which of the following should be consulted first?
   a. GASB Technical Bulletins
   b. GASB Statements
   c. GASB interpretations
   d. Both b and c
6. In the hierarchy of GAAP for nongovernmental organizations, which of the following should be consulted first?
   a. AICPA accounting interpretations
   b. GASB Statements
   c. FASB Statements
   d. Consensus positions of the FASB

7. The term *business-type activity* includes:
   a. property taxes
   b. green fees paid at a city golf course
   c. income taxes
   d. police services
8. The term *governmental-type activity* includes:
   a. government selling power to external users
   b. direct exchange of fee for services
   c. city firefighters providing service to a resident
   d. green fees paid at a city golf course
9. As set forth in GASB Concepts Statement No. 1, the primary concepts that should guide accounting and financial reporting standards are:
   a. modified accrual basis of accounting and interperiod equity
   b. flow of financial resources and modified accrual basis of accounting
   c. hierarchy of GAAP and accountability
   d. interperiod equity and accountability
10. The modified accrual basis of accounting:
    a. strives to match revenues with expenses
    b. records revenues when they are earned and measurable
    c. records revenues when they are measurable and available to pay expenses of the current budget period
    d. is also known as the corporate method of measuring resources

Exercise 1-2

Multiple Choice—Select the best answer for each of the following:

1. Under what method of reporting are revenues, expenses, gain, losses, assets, and liabilities of exchange transactions recorded when the exchange takes place?
   a. Economic resources measurement focus
   b. Budgetary focus
   c. Flow of financial resources focus
   d. Interperiod equity focus
2. With the implementation of GASB Statement No. 34, the measurement of governmental operations changes from:
   a. the modified accrual basis of accounting and flow of financial resources focus to the accrual basis of accounting and economic resources focus
   b. the accrual basis of accounting and flow of financial resources focus to the modified accrual basis of accounting and the economic resources focus
   c. the modified accrual basis of accounting and the budgetary focus to the accrual basis and flow of financial resources focus
   d. the modified accrual basis of accounting and the matching of revenues and expenditures focus to the accrual exchange and non-exchange focus
3. If the federal deficit was increasing across time, this would mean that:
   a. interperiod equity was increasing
   b. the federal government needs to print more money
   c. interperiod equity was decreasing
   d. taxes should be increased
4. The Governmental Accounting Standards Board has:
   a. eight board members
   b. five board members
   c. ten board members
   d. seven board members

5. The NCGA Statements 1 and 2 provided a model to:
   a. name all of the funds
   b. issue a financial report of individual fund statements
   c. organize the funds into categories and a financial report
   d. record tax revenue
6. The GFOA is an organization that:
   a. prepares and publishes the "GASB Code"
   b. publishes books to establish professional accounting standards for governments
   c. audits governments
   d. invests government monies
7. Categories of funds for governmental entities include:
   a. proprietary
   b. account groups
   c. governmental
   d. both a and c
8. The economic resource measurement focus requires:
   a. cash basis accounting
   b. modified accrual accounting
   c. accrual basis accounting
   d. none of the above
9. Taxpayers are involuntary resource providers. This means that taxpayers must:
   a. sell their home to pay property taxes
   b. pay taxes by borrowing money
   c. pay extra withholding in income taxes to get a refund
   d. provide resources to the government by paying taxes as legally required
10. Under modified accrual, revenue is recognized when it is:
    a. received in cash
    b. measurable and earned
    c. measurable and available
    d. time to send bills to taxpayers for late taxes

PROBLEMS

Problem 1-1

Internet Research: GASB Board

Visit the GASB web site at http://www.gasb.org or access the site through the text's web site at http://advanced.swcollege.com. Find out the name of one of the seven board members and read their biographies. How does each board member's background prepare him/her to handle the responsibility of issuing governmental accounting standards?

Problem 1-2

Internet Research: Organizations

Visit the web site at http://www.taxsites.com or access the site through the text's web site at http://advanced.swcollege.com. This handy site maintains a current set of links for tax and accounting sites. Under "Accounting Sites," select the "Gov & NFP" link. A list of links to web sites for governmental and nonprofit organizations will appear. Select one and describe what this organization does and what helpful information you can find at this site.

Problem 1-3

Internet Research: GFOA Certificate Program

The Government Finance Officers Association (GFOA) web site at http://www.gfoa.org (or access the site through the text's web site at http://advanced.swcollege.com) contains information about its Certificate of Achievement for Excellence in Financial Reporting Program. Prepare a report that describes the certification and the requirements to obtain and keep it.

Problem 1-4   **Internet Research: Standard Setting**

From the GASB web site (at http://www.gasb.org or access the site through the text's web site at http://advanced.swcollege.com), find out about the organization's mission statement, how it intends to accomplish its mission, and other key facts about the GASB. Prepare a report, in your own words, that explains these facts. Then, describe the due-process procedure GASB uses to establish governmental GAAP.

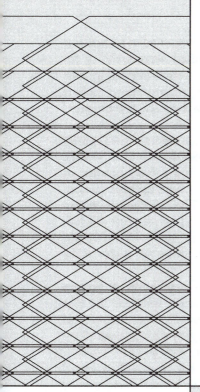

CHAPTER 2

THE BASICS OF
FUND ACCOUNTING

FUNDS AND FUND ACCOUNTING

The fund accounting systems used by governmental and governmental-type not-for-profit entities have evolved as a method of providing detailed accountability for resources. Throughout the text, references to "governmental" accounting will include governmental-type not-for-profit organizations. Not-for-profit organizations include those that are nongovernmental-type. Funds are a means of tracking the revenues and expenditures related to providing specific services.

A **fund**[1] is a self-balancing set of accounts. It is considered a separate fiscal entity in governmental accounting that is set up to segregate resources dedicated to specific activities of a government. Each fund has assets, liabilities, and a fund balance or equity section. Funds with a governmental purpose will have a fund balance section, and funds with a business purpose will have an equity section. The difference between fund assets and liabilities will equal fund balance or fund equity. This parallels the balance sheet for a for-profit company. For example, if the fund has assets of $10,000 and liabilities of $2,000, the fund balance will be $8,000 representing the net assets of the fund.

A basic history lesson learned in elementary school is the separation of powers between the three branches of government: legislative, executive, and judicial. In a democracy, governments are created by their citizens to provide common services such as police protection and garbage removal. The process begins with citizens electing representatives to form a legislative branch of government, such as a city council, house of representatives, or senate to make decisions about what taxes will be levied (charged) to provide the desired level of services. The legislative branch decides what taxes must be charged to citizens and what services will be provided through the adoption of the budget and the appropriation of funds. Depending on the structure of the government, the legislative branch might appoint or the citizens might elect someone, such as a governor or mayor, to head the executive branch. This branch oversees the operations of the entity and is responsible for the implementation of the decisions of the legislative branch.

For example, the city council (legislative branch of government) might decide to give the fire chief (part of the executive branch of government) $200,000 to run the volunteer fire department. The citizens have decided to volunteer and provide their own labor for fire services so they can pay lower taxes to fund fire protection. The $200,000 appropriation from the city council will pay for expenses such as maintenance of the fire truck and uniforms. The legislative body wants to make sure the $200,000 is spent for fire protection services. So, it authorizes the transfer of $200,000 to a bank account and, in this very simplified example, hands the checkbook to the fire chief. In this way, the council can be sure that the funds it has authorized to be spent for fire protection will be segregated from other monies and will be spent only for fire protection. Likewise, the police chief is also given a separate bank account for police protection services. The concept of separate funds for separate appropriations is a simplified form of internal and budgetary control to ensure that monies are spent for the intended purpose. The concept underlying fund accounting is that a fund, as a separate accounting and fiscal entity, is created for each purpose that the legislative body has authorized the spending for. This authorization is called an **appropriation.**

---

[1]NCGA Statement 1, paragraph 2.

The fund accounting system was created to provide segregation of monies and to be a form of budgetary control by the legislative arm of government over the executive branch or bureaucrats who expend the monies.

Fund accounting systems were created to track the spending of appropriated monies for the provision of services. These systems are clearly grounded in the budgetary base of governmental provision of services. The funds are intended to reflect major categories of spending and to track activity throughout the fiscal year. This fund system creates a control over spending.

How many funds should a governmental unit have? In the early days of financial reporting, some governmental financial reports were as thick as phone books. Because a new fund was created for every new spending category, hundreds of funds might exist for a large government. Currently, the GASB recommends that governments establish the *minimum number of funds* consistent with legal and operating requirements.[2] Minimizing the number of funds makes the financial report more understandable and less complex. In practice, however, some funds may be legally required by State statutes or grant provisions and others may be desirable to track a specific activity of government operations. Thus, there are important reasons why some governmental entities must retain certain funds.

GOVERNMENTAL AND BUSINESS-TYPE ACTIVITIES

Governmental entities are organized to provide many different types of programs and services, which are referred to as *activities* in governmental accounting. Activities are further categorized as governmental and business-type. **Governmental activities** encompass the general activities of a governmental entity, such as general administration and police protection. Governmental activities are primarily supported by taxes, funding from other governmental units, and other nonexchange transactions. These are all accounted for in the **governmental funds.** Governments and not-for-profit entities also engage in **business-type activities** that are supported by fees and charges to the users of the services in exchange transactions. Examples include water and sewer services and a book store run by a public university. Business-type activities are accounted for in **proprietary funds.** The type of activity determines the fund category that will be used for accounting and reporting purposes. Governmental-type activities are accounted for in the governmental funds, and business-type activities are accounted for in proprietary funds.

Funds, functions, and activities

To provide more control over revenues and expenditures, GAAP defines additional classification levels for reporting the detail of activities within each of the funds.[2] These classification levels are used when adopting the annual budget and preparing the organization's annual financial report. Revenues are classified within the funds by major source, such as taxes, charges for services, or investment earnings. There are several levels of classifications for expenditures within each fund:

---

[2]Ibid, paragraph 4.
[3]Ibid, paragraphs 109–116.

Function or program: A function is comprised of activities related to providing a major service or regulatory program, such as general government or public safety. A program is similar to a function except the focus is on a specific purpose or objective of the government such as public welfare. In the government-wide financial report, functions are the minimum level of reporting.

Organizational unit: An organizational unit is generally a department or unit responsible for one or more activities of the government.

Activity: An activity is a specific service performed by one or more organizational unit. For example, police protection could be an activity of the public safety **function.**

Object: An object is a detailed expenditure within an activity such as salaries, fringe benefits, or supplies. Many governmental or not-for-profit organizations have a chart of accounts and object codes for expenditures. For example, equipment would have a particular object code.

It is important to understand the concepts of funds and activities. A fund can be used to account for more than one activity. For example, the general fund can be used to account for police activities and general administration activities. An activity category can be accounted for in more than one fund. For example, general administration activities that include payroll and billing could be reported in both the general fund and a proprietary fund. This is because general administration supports the activities of both funds, and proprietary funds need to report all expenses related to providing the business-type activities.

Fund categories for governmental entities

The Governmental Accounting Standards Board defines three fund categories for governmental entities and governmental not-for-profits: governmental funds, proprietary funds, and fiduciary funds. **Governmental funds account for the governmental activities of the entity and use the modified accrual basis of accounting. Proprietary funds account for any business-type activities and use the accrual basis of accounting. Fiduciary funds use the accrual basis of accounting and account for monies that the government holds on behalf of others that cannot be used to support other government programs.** Some entities may not need to utilize all of the fund types, depending upon the types of activities they engage in. A chart of the fund categories for governmental entities, shown in Exhibit 2-1, is followed by descriptions of the fund types within each category.

Prior to the adoption of GASB Statement No. 34, governmental units did not utilize permanent funds or private-purpose trust funds. Nonexpendable trust and expendable trust fiduciary funds were used instead. The only difference between nonexpendable and expendable trust funds is that the principal must remain intact in nonexpendable trust funds.

Two account groups were used under the pre-GASB Statement No. 34 fund structure to account for long-term assets and long-term debt of the governmental funds: General Fixed Assets Account Group and General Long-Term Debt Account Group. In practice, many governmental units may continue to use these account groups within their accounting system after implementing GASB Statement No. 34 but will not display the account groups in their financial report.

EXHIBIT 2·1   Fund Categories and Types
(as defined by GASB Statement No. 34)[4]

Governmental fund category (emphasizing major funds):
(1) General fund
(2) Special revenue funds
(3) Capital projects funds
(4) Debt service funds
(5) Permanent funds

Proprietary fund category:
(1) Enterprise funds (emphasizing major funds)
(2) Internal service funds

Fiduciary fund category:
(1) Pension (and other employee benefit) trust funds
(2) Investment trust funds
(3) Private-purpose trust funds
(4) Agency funds

Governmental fund category

There are five governmental funds that contain the accounting information for the general operating (governmental) activities of a governmental unit: general, special revenue, capital projects, debt service and permanent funds. These funds are primarily supported by taxes or funding from other governmental units. Governmental funds use the *current financial resources measurement focus and the modified accrual basis of accounting*. Modified accrual reflects the available resources and expenditures when incurred to finance the budget during the fiscal year. Governmental funds have a budgetary focus. It is important to understand the nature of the economic activity or transactions that is accounted for in each fund.

General fund. All of the general operating activities of a governmental unit are recorded in the general fund. This is where most of the action takes place! The collection of tax revenues (or donations for governmental not-for-profit entities) and the payment of most governmental employees would be accounted for within this fund. It is not uncommon to see governmental units receive and record a majority of their incoming monies in the general fund and then transfer money as needed to other funds for designated purposes. The general fund is used to account for any resources that are not required to be accounted for in other funds. Governmental units can establish only one general fund; however, the general fund can account for many different activities.

Special revenue funds. Resources that have legal restrictions on their use are recorded in the special revenue funds, except for those monies that are restricted to trust or capital project purposes. GAAP standards do not require that special revenue funds be used unless they are legally mandated. For example, if a condition of a grant requires that the monies be segregated in a separate fund, a special revenue fund must be used. Again, the concept is that use of a separate fund will provide internal control and safekeeping of the monies. Normally the restriction that requires a special revenue fund is from law, contract, grant, or some external party. Resources that have *internal* restrictions on their use are not generally set up in a special revenue fund.

---

[4]GASB Statement No. 34, paragraph 63.

Capital projects funds. General government major construction and renovation projects and the acquisitions of major capital facilities are recorded in capital projects funds. A capital projects fund would be created at the beginning of a building project and closed at the end of construction. Any monies left over at the end of the project would either be transferred according to any legal restrictions on their use (if the money was borrowed, excess monies may be required to be set aside for debt repayment) or returned to the general fund for future use. The capital projects fund does not account for capital projects financed by proprietary funds such as power plant construction or fiduciary fund projects. Examples of typical projects that would be accounted for in a capital projects fund are the construction of a fire station. Do not confuse major construction or major renovation with upkeep and repairs. Repair of the roof of the fire station would be an expenditure in the general fund and would not require a capital projects fund to be created. If there is no legal requirement for a capital projects fund, the project can be recorded in the general fund.

Debt service funds. The debt service funds contain the accounting for the resources set aside for and the repayment of principal and interest on general long-term debt obligations. GAAP standards do not require that the debt service funds be used. However, legal restrictions on long-term debt often requires the monies for debt repayment be segregated in a separate fund. It is common to find a separate debt service fund for each general long-term debt obligation. Again, the bond market and bondholders gain some comfort from knowing that monies for repayment are in a separate fund. The underlying concept is that a separate fund creates a greater likelihood of repayment of the long-term debt. Creating a separate fund, of course, has no effect on the financial ability of the governmental unit to repay. The use of a debt service fund is also required if the governmental unit accumulates funds to pay debt service, principal, and interest in future fiscal years.[5] The government may account for all general long-term debt service within the general fund if there are no legal requirements to use debt service funds.

Permanent funds. Permanent funds contain the accounting for resources that are legally restricted resources so that only the earnings that are generated from investing the money can be spent. The principal cannot be spent; and the income must be used to benefit the government or its citizens.[6] If the resources are intended to be used to benefit a different government, private organizations, or specific individuals, a private-purpose trust fund would be set up instead. For example, a wealthy individual donates money to a town and specifies that only the investment income can be spent for public park and recreation programs. A permanent fund would be created to account for the investment earnings to be spent on public park and recreation programs that benefit the citizenry. The private-purpose trust fund is explained in the Fiduciary Fund section of this chapter.

In summary, there are five governmental funds that focus upon accounting for general governmental resources. The general fund contains the accounting for most governmental activity and any resources not required to be reported elsewhere. The special revenue and debt service funds contain the transactions concerning monies with legal restrictions on their use. The capital projects fund is used for transactions involving major, general government building and acquisition projects. The permanent fund reflects the accounting for both the principal resources that cannot be spent

---

[5]NCGA Statement 1, paragraph 30.
[6]GASB Statement No. 34, paragraph 65.

and the monies earned from investing that principal if those earnings are to be used for a public purpose or the benefit of citizens.

Proprietary fund category

There are two proprietary funds that account for the business-type activities of governmental units: enterprise and internal service funds. The key distinction between these two funds is that enterprise funds charge fees for goods or services to external users and internal service funds charge fees for goods or services to governmental departments, agencies, component units (related government agencies), or other governmental units. Proprietary funds use the *economic resources measurement focus and accrual basis of accounting*, and have equity accounts.

Enterprise funds. Enterprise funds *may* be used for any activity for which a fee is charged to *external users* for goods or services or if a fee is expected to be charged in the near forseeable future. Enterprise funds are **required** to be used if *any* of these criteria are met[7]:

- Debt is issued that is secured *solely* by a pledge of the revenues from fees and charges of the enterprise activity (these are generally called revenue bonds).
- Laws or regulations require the enterprise's costs of providing services (including capital costs such as depreciation or debt service) be paid by fees and charges rather than by taxes.
- Pricing policies of the enterprise establish fees and charges that are intended to recover all costs (including capital costs such as depreciation or debt service).

A common example of an enterprise fund is a city power plant or city water service that provides a service and sets fees that are charged to the recipients of the power or water service. These fees are generally set at a break-even level, which is sufficient to recover all costs including capital costs (depreciation on fixed assets or debt service on long-term debt).

● **INTERPRETIVE EXERCISE**

Revenue bonds of $10 million are issued to build an addition on the city power plant.
Would the debt service fund pay principal and interest on the revenue bonds?

Internal service funds. Internal service funds may be used to record transactions relating to activities that provide goods or services to *other departments within the government or to other governmental units* on a fee basis for cost reimbursement.[8] An internal service fund can only be used if the reporting government is the predominant participant in the activity. The goods or services are generally provided on a cost-reimbursement basis. In other words, the fees or prices are set at a level that enables the government to break even on the provision of such services. Examples of services that are often provided in this manner are central data processing or information technology services. Common efficiencies can often be achieved for the governmental unit as a whole by pooling the information technology employees and equipment in one

---

[7]Ibid, paragraph 67.
[8]Ibid, paragraph 68.

unit, which then provides services throughout the governmental unit on a cost-reimbursement basis. Motor pools are sometimes found in governmental units. A motor pool is a pool of vehicles that is available for use by governmental employees in the discharge of their duties. These vehicles are maintained in a central garage and checked out by employees. The employees' department is charged for the use of the vehicle. This is more efficient than having each department maintain vehicles for employee use.

Internal service funds are also used for activities that charge a fee for goods and services provided by the primary government to *a component unit (related governmental entity) or other governmental unit* provided that the primary government is the main participant in the activity. For example, a county government might process property tax bills for a small city or village and charge a fee for this service. GAAP does not require use of internal service funds, and they are eliminated in government-wide statements.

In summary, there are two proprietary funds that account for business-type activities within the governmental unit: enterprise and internal service funds. These two funds are differentiated by one simple question: does the fund charge fees to *external* users or do they only charge fees to *internal* users or other governmental units? If they charge external users, it is an enterprise fund. If internal users are the predominant participants in the activity, it is an internal service fund. In both cases, the enterprise fund and internal service fund are usually charging fees on a *break-even basis* to recover costs.

● **INTERPRETATIVE EXERCISE**

A city has a recycling project that charges a small fee for disposal of toxic materials such as oil-based paints and car batteries but accepts other recycling materials free of charge. The fees are legally restricted to support recycling and are recorded in a special revenue fund. The city also has a historic site that attracts visitors from all over the nation and charges an entrance fee of $10. These entrance fees are recorded in an enterprise fund established for all business activities (such as gift shops) related to the city's historic sites. Why are these two activities accounted for in different funds?

Fiduciary fund category

There are four types of fiduciary funds: pension and other employee benefit trust funds, investment trust funds, private-purpose trust funds, and agency funds. These funds contain the accounting for the monies held by the government on behalf of others in a trustee or agency capacity. These resources cannot be used to support the government's programs. Fiduciary funds use the *economic resources measurement focus* and the *accrual basis of accounting*.

Pension (and other employee benefit) trust funds. Pension trust funds record the transactions related to monies held in trust on behalf of employees' and beneficiaries' future pensions or benefits.[9] These resources usually represent monies set aside to fund future payments for beneficiaries of defined benefit pensions, defined

---

[9]Ibid, paragraph 70.

contribution pensions, other post-employment benefits such as health insurance, and other employee benefit plans. The resources are invested. The earnings are usually legally restricted to be retained in the trust fund until the benefits are paid to the qualified individuals. A separate trust fund should be established for each pension plan or benefit trust.

Investment trust funds. Investment trust funds account for the external portion of investment pools by the sponsoring government.[10] These pools are created when governments join together to invest excess cash. For example, a State treasurer is in charge of an investment pool that invests State monies and monies of any participating local governments within the state. The monies are combined into one investment portfolio. The external portion of the investment pool is the portion that belongs to the other governments (counties, cities, towns, villages, etc.). The monies that belong to other governments should be reported in an investment trust fund of the sponsoring government. The portion of the investment pool trust that belongs to the sponsoring government is reported as assets of the contributing funds. The other governments that participate in the pool would report their investment in the pool as an asset of the contributing fund, not in an investment trust fund. Sometimes governments will manage the investments of other legally separate entities in a separate non-pooled portfolio called an individual investment account. The government that manages the individual investment account would report the assets in a separate investment trust fund.[11]

Private-purpose trust funds. Private-purpose trust funds record transactions involving resources that do not have a public purpose or do not belong to the government. As noted above, the private purpose of the monies (both principal and interest) held in trust will be to benefit individuals, private organizations, or other governments.[12] One example would be **escheat property,** which is property that is returned to the government. Unclaimed property, such as a bank savings account that has had no deposits or withdrawals for several years, is transferred to the state escheats division where the money will be held for a specified period while efforts are made to notify the owner of the account. These escheated moneys would be held in a private-purpose trust fund. As another example, assume a wealthy resident donated $500,000 to provide benefits to the widows of firefighters. Since the funds benefit only certain individuals, it would be a private-purpose trust fund.

Agency funds. Agency funds are used for the accounting of transactions involving monies held by the governmental unit on behalf of others in a custodial capacity.[13] These monies are often collected on behalf of other governmental units. In many cases, the governmental unit is providing a service for other governmental units. For example, property taxes that are collected from homeowners are recorded into a county's agency fund and then redistributed to the school district, the library, and the city.

In summary, there are four fiduciary funds that focus upon resources that are held by a government in a fiduciary capacity. The resources are held in either a trust or a custodial capacity by the government.

As you move forward through the chapters, keep in mind that the governmental funds reflect transactions tied to the general operations of the government or

---

[10]GASB Statement No. 31 *Accounting and Financial Reporting for Certain Investments and for External Investment Pools*, paragraph 18.

[11]Ibid, paragraph 20.

[12]GASB Statement No. 34, paragraph 72.

[13]Ibid, paragraph 73.

governmental-type not-for-profit entity, the proprietary funds reflect transactions related to business-type activities, and the fiduciary funds reflect transactions involving monies the government holds on behalf of others.

Prior to the implementation of GASB Statement No. 34, governmental units maintained two **Account Groups** to record the general fixed assets and general long-term debt. Many entities will retain these accounts within the accounting system to track the related information on long-term capital assets and long-term debt of the governmental funds.

As a student of fund accounting, you must learn the fund names and understand how to identify the appropriate fund in which specific economic transactions should be recorded.

Is the recreation center a governmental or proprietary activity?

Many cities are building large recreational complexes with a combination of public funding from tax revenues and user fees. Middleburg Heights Community Center opened in June 2000 at a cost of $17 million and has indoor and outdoor pools, two gyms, fitness center, community hall and classrooms, and two concession stands. Dearborn, Michigan, is building a $43 million recreation and performing arts center with annual family fees of $660 per year. This $660 fee provoked criticism that tax dollars were used to construct a recreation facility that working-class families cannot afford to join. Jefferson County, Colorado, opened a $25 million Apex Center with two NHL-size ice rinks, aquatic park, three gyms, teen computer center, rock-climbing wall, and European cafe. The Jefferson County Center was funded by bonds that will be repaid by property taxes and user fees. Middlebury Heights Community Center is funded by a payroll tax and user fees. These recreational center projects have elements of governmental activities for the public health and welfare and also business-type activities in user fee charges as well as businesses such as cafes and concessions run by the government.

All of these recreational centers were created to serve the public of those communities and promote the general health and welfare of their citizens. Therefore, it makes sense that they are financed by long-term debt that will be paid over time from general tax revenues. It also seems reasonable that these recreational facilities are supported by user fees for specific activities to encourage respect for the facility and to provide revenues for expected maintenance required by the level of usage.

(Source: *USA Today*, August 7, 2000, *"Not your parents' recreation center,"* page 3A. *Detroit Free Press*, "New civic center grows—so does controversy," page B1.

BUDGETARY ACCOUNTING[14]

The **budget** serves as a master blueprint for **planning, control, and evaluation** of governmental, proprietary, and fiduciary fund financial operations. The GASB states that every governmental entity should adopt an annual budget that estimates revenues and expenditures. Often, state or local statutes detail the type of budget(s) that must

---

[14]NCGA Statement 1, paragraphs 76–98.

be prepared. GASB standards require the consistent use of terminology and classifications in the budget and financial reports.

The budgetary process generally begins when the executive branch develops a proposed budget. The legislative body adopts and enacts the proposed budget with an appropriation of funds. This document becomes the **original budget.** The **appropriation** is a legal authorization setting the *maximum amount* of monies the executive branch can expend for designated purposes. This authorization to spend (appropriation) is normally an annual budget for the fiscal period. Generally, the appropriation *lapses* (expires) at the end of the annual fiscal period. Governments may prepare **long-term budgets** to plan projects that span several fiscal years. For example, a capital budget to plan spending to construct a city hall extends beyond the annual fiscal period because it will take two years to build.

The budgetary control process of accounting focuses upon the governmental fund category (general, special revenue, capital projects, debt service, and permanent funds) where **fixed budgets** are adopted for specific dollar amounts. Governmental funds can only expend public monies that are *available* during the annual fiscal period or collected soon enough thereafter to pay the expenses. Proprietary funds should adopt **flexible budgets** that can increase or decrease spending in response to the demand for the goods or services they provide on a fee basis. Because fiduciary fund spending is controlled by legal restrictions upon the monies held in trust or on behalf of others, budgets generally are not necessary for control purposes.

Budgets can be adopted with various levels of detail. For budgetary control purposes, the minimum level of detail for governmental funds is generally revenues by fund and source and expenditures by fund and function or program. For example, general fund property tax revenues or general fund public safety expenditures provides sufficient detail to identify the fund (general), source of revenue (property tax) or expenditure by function (public safety).

Budgetary controls are needed because governmental funds cannot increase resources available if spending exceeds the appropriated levels. A deficit could occur if spending exceeds the appropriation. However, the legislative branch can reduce the appropriation during the annual fiscal period to bring the budget into balance if revenues are not being received or expenditures are exceeding the levels that were estimated in the budget. Many governmental fund services such as police and fire protection cannot be easily or quickly reduced if taxes are not received at the budgeted amount. Therefore, it is imperative that the governmental fund budget(s) be monitored and controlled throughout the fiscal period to ensure proper accountability for public monies. Conversely, appropriations can be increased if additional revenues are received. The **final budget** incorporates all of the changes to the original budget that are made during the fiscal year. Information about how actual revenues and expenditures compare to the original and final budgets are included in the budgetary reporting section of the financial statements that are covered in Chapter 5. The budgetary accounts capture information in the accounting system that enables governmental managers to monitor the budget during the fiscal period.

Budgets must be prepared in accordance with legal requirements even though they may be different from GAAP requirements. In that case, the governmental unit must maintain adequate financial records to permit the annual financial report to be prepared in accordance with GAAP at the end of the fiscal period. Budgets can be prepared on the cash basis but often reflect the modified accrual basis of the governmental funds, which focuses on resources available to finance the budget, and the accrual basis of the proprietary funds, which recognizes revenues when earned.

Budgetary accounts in governmental funds

Budgetary accounting is a tool used to maintain a high level of *accountability and control* over governmental funds during the annual fiscal period. **Budgetary accounts** are used and integrated into the accounting system for general, special revenue, and other governmental funds that have a significant number of transactions to record revenues, expenditures, and transfers for general government operations. In contrast, a debt service fund may not require the use of budgetary accounts because it only accounts for the legally mandated payment of principal and interest on general long-term debt. Proprietary funds and fiduciary funds normally do not use budgetary accounts. However, if a proprietary fund is legally required to adopt a fixed budget, the use of budgetary accounts would be appropriate.

Most computerized accounting systems have the capability of recording budgeted revenue and expenditure amounts and producing reports throughout the fiscal year of budgeted versus actual amounts. This enables governmental managers to monitor the budget throughout the fiscal year.

Budgetary accounts include: Estimated Revenues, Revenues, Appropriations, Encumbrances, Expenditures, Other Financing Sources, Other Financing Uses, Estimated Other Financing Sources, Estimated Other Financing Uses, and Budgetary Fund Balance. These accounts are used to record amounts related to the current fiscal year's budget. Therefore, these accounts start each fiscal year with a zero balance and must be closed to a zero balance at fiscal year-end. Details of Estimated Revenues and Appropriations (estimated expenditures) are maintained in subsidiary ledgers for each fund that adopts a budget.

Estimated revenues are the projected revenues that will become available to pay expenditures of the current budget during the fiscal period. The estimated revenues are the basis for granting spending authority in appropriations.

Revenues are increases in net financial resources and should be recorded when received or available, whichever occurs first, under modified accrual or when earned under the accrual basis of accounting.

Appropriations are legal authorizations to spend public funds. The appropriations reflect spending authority granted in budgets adopted by the governing body.

Encumbrances are commitments to spend such as a purchase order or contract. If the accounting system records an encumbrance when a commitment to be paid in the future from budgeted funds is made, it helps to monitor spending levels during the fiscal period.

Expenditures are decreases in net financial resources and should be recorded when incurred on the modified accrual basis of accounting. Expenditures are recorded in governmental funds, and expenses are recorded in proprietary funds. The expenditures and expenses are recorded to reflect that the monies are *no longer available* for use.

Other Financing Sources and **Other Financing Uses** are two accounts that reflect the *unusual, nonrecurring* sources of revenue and expenditures. If these unusual items can be predicted in advance of the fiscal period, the estimates for these items would be recorded in **Estimated Other Financing Sources** (a form of revenue) and **Estimated Other Financing Uses** (a form of expenditure) in the entry to record the budget. Examples of other financing sources would be the issuance of long-term debt or the sale of capital assets. Examples of other financing uses would be the escrow of monies for advance refunding of long-term debt or discount upon issuance of long-term debt. At the individual fund level, transfers to or from other funds would be included as other financing uses or sources. Interfund transfers are eliminated in government-wide financial reports.

Budgetary Fund Balance is the net of Estimated Revenues, Estimated Other Financing Sources, Appropriations, and Estimated Other Financing Uses at the *beginning* of the budgetary accounting cycle. At the end of the fiscal year, the remaining balance in the Budgetary Fund Balance is closed out to the Unreserved Fund Balance Account.

Accounts	Descriptions
Estimated Revenues	Revenues expected in budget year
Revenues	Revenues reflect resources
Appropriations	Authorized spending for budget year
Expenditures	Actual spending during
Encumbrances	Commitments to spend
Other Financing Sources	Unusual, nonrecurring revenue
Estimated Other Financing Sources.	Expected unusual, nonrecurring revenue
Other Financing Uses	Unusual, non-recurring spending
Estimated Other Financing Uses	Expected unusual, non-recurring spending
Budgetary Fund Balance	Budgetary account that is a surrogate for Unreserved Fund Balance

Recording the budget

The journal entry to record the general fund budget of a governmental unit is illustrated by the example below:

Estimated Revenues	5,000,000	
Estimated Other Financing Sources	20,000	
Appropriations		4,800,000
Estimated Other Financing Uses		10,000
Budgetary Fund Balance		210,000

In this example, the government estimates that it will receive $5 million in general revenue sources. The government also estimates that it will receive $20,000 from proceeds from the sale of surplus equipment. This disposal of equipment is an unusual, nonrecurring transaction, so it is recorded as an Estimated Other Financing Source. The legislative body of the government decides to grant spending authority of $4,800,000 to the executive branch of the government to provide public services. In addition, the legislative body estimates that it will spend $10,000 to settle a lawsuit, so it estimates this as Estimated Other Financing Use. The difference between the amount estimated to become available within the fiscal period in resources and the amount appropriated for spending in the fiscal period is credited or debited to Budgetary Fund Balance. A credit increases Budgetary Fund Balance just as it would for an equity account in a for-profit corporation. A debit decreases Budgetary Fund Balance just as it would for an equity account in a for-profit corporation.

Recording revenues and expenditures

Revenues and expenditures are recognized as they become available or are incurred throughout the fiscal year. The following journal entry illustrates a simple example where revenues of $4,900,000 that are available to finance expenditures of the current budgetary period are collected throughout the fiscal year.

Cash	4,900,000	
Revenues		4,900,000

Expenditures for governmental operations of $2,000,000 would be recorded as paid throughout the year as follows:

Expenditures	2,000,000	
Cash		2,000,000

Surplus equipment is sold for $22,000 and recorded as follows:

Cash	22,000	
Other Financing Source—Disposal of Asset		22,000

These examples are illustrations of a few very basic journal entries. The journal entries to record transactions for governmental activities are illustrated further in Chapters 3 and 4.

Recording encumbrances

Throughout the fiscal year, major commitments to spend should be recorded as encumbrances when a purchase order or contract commitment is entered into. For example, the governmental unit issued a purchase order for $800,000 to buy a fire truck that was included in the original $4,800,000 in appropriations. The journal entry[15] to reserve a portion of the available fund balance is illustrated below:

Encumbrances	800,000	
Budgetary Fund Balance Reserved		
for Encumbrances		800,000

This estimate of the expenditure reserves a portion of fund balance, and the funds are no longer available to appropriate. This reserves a portion of fund balance so that the expenditure will be charged against the current budget if it is paid after fiscal year-end. When the actual invoice ($780,000) and fire truck arrive, the estimate ($800,000) for this bill previously recorded as an encumbrance must be removed. The original encumbrance journal entry is simply reversed to remove it. The expenditure is then recorded. An account called Vouchers Payable or Accounts Payable is often used to reflect the liability to pay a bill while the payment approval process takes place. A voucher is a document that is processed through various approval levels to authorize payment to the vendor. Voucher systems are intended to provide internal control over public expenditure before disbursement. When the voucher is approved, the payment is made to the vendor and the Vouchers Payable entry is reversed and cash is credited. If the vouchers payable account is not used, cash (or a subsidiary checking account) is credited when the Expenditures account is debited.

---

[15]Students who do not have a familiarity with basic journal entries should refer to Appendix 1 at the end of the text.

Budgetary Fund Balance Reserved for Encumbrances	800,000	
Encumbrances		800,000
Expenditures	780,000	
Vouchers Payable		780,000
Vouchers Payable	780,000	
Cash		780,000

The governmental unit issues other purchase orders throughout the year totaling $1,995,000, and $575,000 of these encumbrances remain outstanding at fiscal year-end.

Encumbrances	1,995,000	
Budgetary Fund Balance Reserved for Encumbrances		1,995,000

Goods and services are received in the amount of $1,420,000. In this simple example, the orders received were invoiced at the same amount that they were estimated ($1,420,000).

Budgetary Fund Balance Reserved for Encumbrances	1,420,000	
Encumbrances		1,420,000
Expenditures	1,420,000	
Vouchers Payable		1,420,000
Vouchers Payable	1,420,000	
Cash		1,420,000

The Encumbrances account is unique to governmental fund accounting and reflects the primary emphasis of these funds on budgetary control. Note that $575,000 ($1,995,000 less $1,420,000) remains in the Encumbrances and Budgetary Fund Balance Reserved for Encumbrances accounts.

Budgetary control

The budgetary accounts enable the governmental manager to control the budget by monitoring if revenues are actually becoming available as originally estimated and also if spending is staying within approved levels. Most accounting systems permit budget amounts to be allocated throughout the fiscal year on a periodic (often monthly) basis to better control and monitor the budget.

At any point in the fiscal year, Estimated Revenues – Revenues (actually received) = Revenues not realized and resources not yet available to expend. For example, if only $2 million of revenues had been received halfway through the fiscal period, the government's management could compare the $5,000,000 estimated revenues to the $2,000,000 actually received so far and available. (Note that the final total amount of revenues collected by the government may not equal the original $5,000,000 estimated.) Resources not yet "available" to expend would equal $3,000,000. This $3,000,000 estimate has not yet been received, and prudent governmental managers would monitor this to be sure that actual revenues are being received throughout the fiscal period in line with the estimated revenues that were the basis of the appropriated spending authority in the budget. If an economic downturn occurred and the revenue forecast was drastically changed during the fiscal period, then the governing body might have to cut back the spending authority previously granted in appropriations to curtail spending. Likewise, the governmental financial manager can monitor spending using these budgetary accounts: Appropriations – (Expenditures + Encumbrances) = uncommited or available appropriation (spending authority left for remaining fiscal year). For example, $4,800,000 appropriations – ($2,780,000 expenditures for governmental operations + $1,995,000 in other encumbrances) = $25,000 remaining in available spending authority in the appropriation for the fiscal year.

Recording all major commitments made for future spending in the encumbrances account enables quick monitoring of spending levels. The total of expenditures and encumbrances can be subtracted from the authorized appropriation to reveal the remaining budgeted funds left to fund operations. At fiscal year-end, a portion of the current year appropriation will be reserved to pay the encumbrances related to the current budget. As stated earlier in this simple example, that amount is $575,000. This reservation of fund balance protects and preserves the funds needed to pay for commitments already made to provide current services. It enables effective planning for the next year's budget as well by setting aside monies to pay for those bills when they arrive in the next fiscal year.

Closing the budget

At the end of the fiscal year, actual revenues and expenditures have been recorded in the governmental funds as revenues became available and expenditures were incurred. These revenue and expenditure accounts must be closed to a zero balance at fiscal year-end as the budget year draws to a close. The entries to close the budgetary accounts at fiscal year-end compare the actual revenues to estimated revenues and also compare actual spending and commitments to the authorized appropriation. The journal entries to close the budgetary accounts of a governmental unit are illustrated by the examples that follow.

Assume for the fiscal year the government had received $4,900,000 in Revenues and a $22,000 Other Financing Source from the sale of surplus equipment. The journal entry to close the revenues would be:

Revenues	4,900,000	
Other Financing Source—Disposal of Asset	22,000	
Budgetary Fund Balance	98,000	
Estimated Revenues		5,000,000
Estimated Other Financing Sources		20,000

Since the actual revenues of $4,900,000 were less than the estimated revenues of $5,000,000, the Budgetary Fund Balance account must be decreased by $100,000. However, proceeds from the sale of equipment were $22,000, which exceeded the estimate of $20,000 by $2,000. The net effect of closing the actual Revenue and Estimated Revenue accounts decreases Budgetary Fund Balance by $98,000 ($100,000 decrease and $2,000 increase).

The government's actual expenditures were $4,200,000 plus $575,000 still outstanding in encumbrances at fiscal year-end. The $10,000 lawsuit was still unsettled. The next entry to close the Expenditures, Appropriations, and Estimated Other Financing Uses accounts follows.

Appropriations	4,800,000	
Estimated Other Financing Uses	10,000	
Expenditures		4,200,000
Budgetary Fund Balance		610,000

The actual expenditures ($4,200,000) are $600,000 less than the appropriation of $4,800,000. This would increase the Budgetary Fund Balance account by $600,000. The appropriation law also estimated $10,000 would be spent to settle a lawsuit, but the case was still pending at fiscal year-end, resulting in an additional $10,000 increase in the budgetary fund balance. As a result of closing of the budgetary accounts, the Budgetary Fund Balance account increases by $610,000. Spending and commitments of $4,200,000 was $610,000 less than the $4,810,000 expected.

The Budgetary Fund Balance account must also be closed at the end of the fiscal year to a zero balance. The first entry to record the budget (see **Recording the budget**) increased Budgetary Fund Balance by $210,000. The journal entry to close the revenue components of the budget decreased Budgetary Fund Balance by $98,000. The journal entry to close the spending components of the budget increased the account by $610,000. Thus, the Budgetary Fund Balance account has a $722,000 credit balance ($210,000 + $610,000 – $98,000) at fiscal year-end as a net result of the budgetary activity for this fiscal year. This budgetary account must be closed. The journal entry for this closing entry transaction is illustrated below.

Budgetary Fund Balance	722,000	
Unreserved Fund Balance		722,000

As a net result of recording this year's budgeted activity, the unreserved portion of this government's fund balance increased by $722,000. The Encumbrances budgetary account still has a balance of $575,000 and must be closed as illustrated below:

Budgetary Fund Balance Reserved for Encumbrances	575,000	
Encumbrances		575,000

If the government intends to continue the remaining commitment originally recorded in the Encumbrances account, then a portion of Unreserved Fund Balance should be reserved to indicate funds are committed and cannot be appropriated.

Unreserved Fund Balance	575,000	
Fund Balance Reserved for Encumbrances		575,000

The Unreserved Fund Balance account is an equity account reflecting available net assets in the governmental fund. The government has $575,000 set aside in Fund Balance Reserved for Encumbrances to pay the outstanding purchase orders when the goods arrive.

The government can maintain budgetary accounts in governmental funds during the fiscal period. These accounts are closed at the end of the fiscal year. If the governmental-type activities are not recorded in accordance with GAAP, the government will have to reconcile these differences in the annual financial report. The financial reporting model will be illustrated and explained in Chapter 5.

SUMMARY

Chapter 2 had the following learning objectives:

- Demonstrate an understanding of the basics of funds and fund accounting
- Explain the difference between governmental and business-type activities
- Describe the categories and types of funds for governmental entities
- Explain the role of the budget and the use of budgetary accounts

Funds are a self-balancing set of accounts and are fiscal entities. Funds contain assets, liabilities, and a fund balance or equity account. Funds and fund accounting evolved to create an accounting system that would provide greater accountability over public or donated monies. Governmental funds have a budgetary focus. This chapter focused upon an introduction to the categories and funds for governmental entities. Governmental funds are used to record the governmental-type activities, and proprietary funds are used to record business-type activities. Fiduciary funds are used to record monies held in trust by the government on behalf of others. The budget and basic budgetary transactions of governmental funds were introduced and illustrated. Fund accounting and the use of budgetary accounts both provide a high level of accountability. The heart of the governmental funds is to keep track of the current year's budget, and the accounting reflects that focus. Accounting for transactions of governmental entities as well as the financial reporting model will be discussed in Chapters 3, 4, and 5.

QUESTIONS

1. What is the purpose of a fund?
2. What is the basis of accounting that is used in the governmental funds?
3. What is the basis of accounting that is used in the proprietary funds?
4. What type of activities will be accounted for in the two proprietary funds? Why are proprietary funds needed?
5. What type of activities will be accounted for in the five governmental funds?
6. What type of activities will be accounted for in the four fiduciary funds? Why are fiduciary funds needed?
7. What fund would account for lottery revenues restricted by law to be used solely for education?
8. How does the use of funds and fund accounting relate to accountability?
9. What is the difference between permanent funds and private-purpose trust funds?
10. In what fund should the transactions related to capital assets purchased by a city-owned power plant be recorded?
11. Where should you record transactions related to the construction of a police station for a governmental unit?
12. Where should you record payment of a firefighter's salary?
13. What type of activity is recorded in an agency fund?
14. Where should you record transactions involving the monies accumulated to repay principal and interest on general long-term debt for a city?
15. Where should you record the receipt of a federal research grant made to a city?

EXERCISES

Exercise 2-1   **Multiple Choice—Select the best answer for each of the following:**

1. Funds are:
   a. not fiscal entities
   b. only used for governmental-type activities
   c. self-balancing sets of accounts
   d. eliminated by GASB Statement No. 34
2. Fund accounting systems provide budgetary control by:
   a. segregating monies for debt repayment
   b. accounting for the budget
   c. ensuring monies remain in the right bank account
   d. none of the above
3. GASB recommends that governments should:
   a. maximize the number of funds
   b. have a separate fund for every project
   c. minimize the number of funds
   d. have one fund for governmental operations
4. A city receives a federal transportation grant to build a major bridge. This grant will be accounted for in the:
   a. general fund
   b. private-purpose trust fund
   c. special revenue fund
   d. capital projects fund
5. A chemist in a State Department of Agriculture receives a federal grant for research on contamination of animal feed. The grant specifies segregation of the funds. Transactions related to this grant will be recorded in the:
   a. general fund
   b. private-purpose trust fund
   c. endowment funds
   d. special revenue fund
6. A central supplies warehouse of a State government bills a State department for office supplies purchased. This bill will be recorded in the state's:
   a. enterprise fund
   b. internal service fund
   c. general fund
   d. internal service fund and general fund
7. A county sets up an investment pool for investment of cash of several other local governments. Transactions related to the monies belonging to the other local governments participating in this investment pool will be recorded in the county's:
   a. agency fund
   b. enterprise fund
   c. investment trust fund
   d. general fund
8. A state collects taxes that are designated for repayment of general long-term debt. These monies available to repay this debt will be recorded in the:
   a. debt service fund
   b. special revenue fund
   c. private purpose trust fund
   d. agency fund

9. A township decides to construct a township hall. Economic information about this project will be recorded in the:
   a. general fund
   b. debt service fund
   c. capital projects fund
   d. special revenue fund

10. A court awards a judgment of $100,000 to a plaintiff who charged the police department with improper arrest and imprisonment. This judgment will be paid from the:
    a. police pension trust fund
    b. general fund
    c. agency fund
    d. special revenue fund

Exercise 2-2

Multiple Choice—Select the best answer for each of the following:

1. Jenny Rose donates $500,000 to be kept in trust with investment earnings designated to create and maintain rose gardens in city parks. These monies will be recorded in the:
   a. permanent fund
   b. private-purpose trust fund
   c. special revenue fund
   d. general fund

2. Fred donates land for a practice field for local youth adjacent to the city park. This donation will be recorded in:
   a. the general fund
   b. the permanent fund
   c. the capital projects fund
   d. none of the above

3. The City Council sets aside $500,000 for future expansion of the downtown fire station. These monies would be recorded in the:
   a. permanent fund
   b. general fund
   c. private-purpose trust fund
   d. agency fund

4. Central City issues revenue bonds to be repaid by fees from water and sewer services. These bonds and fees will be recorded in the:
   a. debt service fund
   b. enterprise fund
   c. special revenue fund
   d. agency fund

5. Culver City collects taxes and pays police and fire salaries. These transactions will be recorded in the:
   a. general fund
   b. enterprise fund
   c. agency fund
   d. pension trust fund

6. The State of Arkansas centralized its data processing and information technology functions into one department. These services are provided to other governmental departments and are billed to them. This activity would be recorded in the:
   a. enterprise fund
   b. private-purpose trust fund
   c. internal service fund
   d. general fund

7. The Village of Berrygate receives a donation that is restricted by the donor to be invested and held in trust to produce investment income. This income will be used to provide healthcare for migrant workers. These monies would be recorded in the:
   a. private-purpose trust fund
   b. endowment fund
   c. general fund
   d. special revenue fund

8. The city golf course bills patrons green fees for use of the public golf course. These fees would be recorded in the:
   a. general fund
   b. golf fund
   c. enterprise fund
   d. internal service fund

9. The library receives a donation to construct a new library. This donation will be recorded in the:
   a. special revenue fund
   b. capital projects fund
   c. private-purpose trust fund
   d. permanent fund

10. Income taxes of $2,000,000 are received by the city. These monies will be recorded in the:
    a. permanent fund
    b. private-purpose trust fund
    c. general fund
    d. agency fund

Exercise 2-3

Multiple Choice—Select the best answer for each of the following:

1. A governmental-type activity would be:
   a. a golf course charges public players green fees
   b. a public museum charges an admission to cover operating costs
   c. a police officer arrests a burglar
   d. a crowd protests government sale of public lands at public auction

2. A business-type activity would be:
   a. a firefighter puts out a warehouse fire
   b. a police officer visits an elementary school class
   c. a city power plant bills customers for power used
   d. a free city fireworks display is held on the Fourth of July

3. The legal authorization to spend is recorded as:
   a. an Amendment to the Constitution
   b. an appropriations
   c. an expenditure
   d. an expense

4. The account Budgetary Fund Balance is closed into:
   a. Appropriations
   b. Unreserved Fund Balance
   c. Retained Earnings
   d. Expenditures

5. The budget authorizes Appropriations of $2,000,000, and the estimate of revenues is $1,800,000. The entry to record the budget will:
   a. increase Budgetary Fund Balance
   b. decrease Appropriations
   c. decrease Revenues
   d. decrease Budgetary Fund Balance

6. Appropriations were authorized at $1,200,000. At the end of the fiscal year, the total Expenditures are $1,000,000, and Encumbrances are $100,000. The effect of closing these three accounts to zero will:
   a. increase Unreserved Fund Balance
   b. decrease Unreserved Fund Balance
   c. decrease Revenues
   d. increase Retained Earnings

7. A police car was ordered and estimated to cost $22,000. The $22,000 estimate was recorded as an encumbrance. Upon receipt of the police car with an invoice for $21,000, the encumbrance account will:
   a. be debited for $21,000
   b. be credited for $22,000
   c. be credited for $1,000
   d. not change

8. At the end of the fiscal year, the Revenues account balance is $800,000. Estimated Revenues at the beginning of the year were $900,000. The entry to close these two budgetary accounts at the end of the fiscal year will have the effect of:
   a. increasing Unreserved Fund Balance
   b. decreasing Unreserved Fund Balance
   c. increasing Revenues
   d. decreasing Other Financing Sources

9. At the end of the fiscal year, the Appropriations account balance is $1,000,000, Encumbrances is $200,000, and Expenditures is $750,000. The entry to close these three budgetary accounts at the end of the fiscal year will have the effect of:
   a. increasing Unreserved Fund Balance
   b. decreasing Unreserved Fund Balance
   c. increasing Encumbrances
   d. decreasing next years' Appropriations

10. At the end of the fiscal year, Revenues were equal to Estimated Revenues. Expenditures exceeded Appropriations by $100,000. This will result in:
    a. Authorized spending to increase next year
    b. Revenues being reduced
    c. Unreserved Fund Balance to increase
    d. Unreserved Fund Balance to decrease

Exercise 2-4

What fund would be appropriate for recording the following activities?

a. A police officer issues a parking ticket.
b. A citizen donates a historic building to serve as a visitor center.
c. A city council approves the general operating budget.
d. A citizen pays a water bill received from the city.
e. A dog owner pays the county dog license.
f. Principal and interest on general long-term debt is paid.
g. Construction begins on a new fire station.
h. A citizen donates cash for general operations.

Exercise 2-5

What fund(s) would be appropriate for recording the transactions listed below?

a. collection of property taxes
b. payment of city finance officer's salary
c. payment of debt service on general long-term debt
d. payment of debt service on revenue bonds
e. payment of pensions to retirees
f. federal grant for provision of medical services to indigent children
g. cash receipts from city's 100 parking meters
h. cash receipts from city golf course
i. income tax revenues

PROBLEMS

Problem 2-1   **Conceptual: GASB vs. FASB accounting focus**

Why do governmental units need fund accounting, budgetary accounts, and modified accrual? Wouldn't it make sense to consolidate GASB into FASB and eliminate fund accounting, budgetary accounts, and modified accrual to operate governments on a business-like basis with business accounting standards? Explain your reasoning.

Problem 2-2   **Conceptual: Accounting for mixed-use facilities**

Refer to "Is the recreation center a governmental or proprietary activity?" on page 28. How should the governmental units account for these "mixed-use" recreational centers that clearly have a public purpose and are funded, in part, from public revenues yet retain a business-type character with user fees related to the level of usage and related maintenance required?

Problem 2-3   **Conceptual: Trust funds**

GASB has created a permanent fund that accounts for endowments and is classified as a governmental fund instead of a fiduciary fund like the private-purpose trust fund. Why are monies held in trust in a permanent fund held as governmental funds instead of fiduciary funds?

Problem 2-4   **Other financing sources and uses**

A city has an increase in crime and decides to issue general long-term bonds in the amount of $5,000,000 to upgrade its crime-fighting equipment, lease and equip neighborhood mini-police stations, and purchase a new fleet of police cars with integrated computer technology. The city included the issuance of bonds and sale of equipment in the original budget. It sells its old police cars for $200,000 and issues bonds for the anticipated amount. What budgetary accounts would be used when these transactions are recorded in the city's accounting system?

Problem 2-5   **Trust funds**

Joe decided to donate $500,000 to his local city library with the condition that the monies will be held in trust. Joe specifies that the library board can determine how to spend investment earnings from the $500,000 for the library. In which fund should these monies be recorded? In which fund should the spending of the investment earnings be recorded?

Problem 2-6   **Governmental or business-type activity**

Ernie gets elected mayor. Ernie decides to privatize city garbage collection and charge residents a fee for pickup of garbage. Garbage collection was previously paid for from the general budget. In which fund should the new garbage fees be recorded? Which fund previously paid for the budgeted garbage collection services?

Problem 2-7   **Investment pool**

A city creates an investment pool to invest the excess short-term cash of neighboring smaller governments. This will help the city increase its own investment yield by having a larger pool of funds to invest short-term and will benefit the smaller governments by increasing their yield as well. Where will the city record the monies received to invest from the neighboring smaller governments? Where will the city record the monies it invests from its own funds?

Problem 2-8 — Journal entries

a. A city adopts the general fund budget. The budget estimates that $2,000,000 in property taxes will be received and authorizes spending for operating activities of $1,900,000 and also anticipates $80,000 will be spent during the year to settle an outstanding lawsuit. Prepare the journal entry to record the budget.

b. The city completes its fiscal year. The city received property tax revenues of $1,900,000, and the remaining balance will not be received until 90 days after fiscal year-end. The city settled the lawsuit for $75,000. The city spent $1,750,000 during the fiscal year and still has $80,000 in encumbrances outstanding. Prepare the entries to close the budgetary accounts (use the information from a. above as needed).

Problem 2-9 — Encumbrances

The city orders a fire truck estimated to cost $140,000. The fire truck arrives with an invoice of $138,000. A voucher is processed and paid 2 weeks later. Record the journal entries for these transactions.

Problem 2-10 — Budgetary accounts

What is the "normal" balance for the following accounts?
a. Other Financing Sources
b. Encumbrances
c. Cash
d. Budgetary Fund Balance
e. Expenditures
f. Estimated Revenues
g. Appropriations
h. Other Financing Uses
i. Revenues

Problem 2-11 — Journal entries

Record the following transactions:
a. The city orders a police car estimated to cost $22,000.
b. The police car arrives with an invoice of $25,000. The invoice is processed for payment.
c. The invoice is paid.
d. The police car is destroyed in a crash and is sold for scrap of $1,000.

Problem 2-12 — Conceptual: Budgetary accounts

Reflect upon the transactions in 2-11 above. Why does the governmental fund charge the full amount of the police car to expenditures in the year of purchase rather than capitalize the asset in the fund? Why does the government record an other financing source for the destruction of the asset rather than record a loss of $24,000?

Problem 2-13 — Internet Research: Accounting for activities

Visit the Denver International Airport web site and select a recent Annual Report at http://flydenver.com/z404.html or access the site through the text's web site at advanced.swcollege.com. You may have flown through and read about the new Denver International Airport, which has the famous peaked roof and opened in the late 1990s. Is the Denver International Airport a governmental-type or business-type activity, and what type of fund would account for this activity? Is the Denver International Airport part of the City of Denver, and if so, how is it accounted for? http://www.denvergov.org/ is the web site for the City of Denver for additional information. You can also access the site through the text's web site at advanced.swcollege.com.

Problem 2-14

Internet Research: Budgets

Visit the Federal Office of Management and Budget web site for the Federal Budget at http://www.gpo.gov/usbudget or access the site through the text's web site at advanced.swcollege.com. Scroll down to the link for the "Citizen's Guide to the Federal Budget." Use the easy-to-follow explanation of the budget process contained in the Citizen's Guide and explain what the primary sources of revenues and expenditures are in the Federal Budget. Also note anything that particularly surprised you in reviewing this information about the Federal Budget.

Problem 2-15

Internet Research: Budget

Search the Internet to find a governmental unit in your local community. Review the most recent financial report available on the web site and then compare that to the current operating budget. Many governmental units have financial reports and budgets posted on their web sites. Evaluate the impact of last year's financial operations on this year's operating budget. Prepare a brief report of conclusions and the basis for those findings.

GOVERNMENTAL OPERATING ACTIVITY

- Illustrate the recognition and recording of revenue sources
- Explain accounting for exchange and nonexchange transactions
- Illustrate the recognition and recording of expenditures and expenses
- Illustrate recording of interfund transactions

OPERATING ACTIVITY OF GOVERNMENTAL ENTITIES

Recall from earlier chapters that governmental units and governmental-type not-for-profit entities must follow the statements and other guidelines of the GASB. This chapter explains some of those guidelines for recording transactions, as set forth by the GASB Statements No. 33, 36, and other pronouncements.

The governmental unit will record a budget at the beginning of the fiscal year and then record operating activity as transactions occur throughout the year. This chapter illustrates how to record operating activity transactions that affect Revenues, Expenditures or Expenses, Other Financing Sources and Other Financing Uses and interfund transactions. These operating activities are reflected at fiscal year-end in the government-wide Statement of Activities or in the governmental fund Statement of Revenues, Expenditures and Changes in Fund Balance or the proprietary fund Statement of Revenues, Expenses and Changes in Fund Net Assets. Chapter 4 illustrates how to record many transactions that affect the Statement of Net Assets or Balance Sheet accounts: assets, liabilities and fund balance or equity. Chapter 5 illustrates the financial reporting model and how to put together the government-wide financial statements.

This chapter uses accounts that record in each fund the operating activity that results in revenues, expenses, expenditures, and other financing sources or uses during the fiscal year. At the end of the fiscal year, these accounts are closed out to create financial statements, and the difference between revenues and expenses is recorded as an increase or decrease in the fund balance or net assets.

The basis of accounting determines *when* transactions or events are *recognized* in the accounting system. The **accrual basis of accounting** recognizes revenues when they are *earned and measurable* and expenses when they are incurred if measurable, regardless of when the cash is received or paid out. Proprietary funds and most fiduciary funds use the accrual basis of accounting. The **modified accrual basis of accounting** recognizes revenues when they are *measurable and available* (expected to be received in time to pay expenses of the current budgetary period) and expenditures when they are incurred if measurable or an *obligation* against *current* budgetary resources. Governmental funds use the modified accrual basis of accounting. Proprietary and fiduciary funds use the accrual basis of accounting.

EXCHANGE AND NONEXCHANGE TRANSACTIONS[1]

The GASB provides additional guidance for *when to record* certain types of transactions in Statement No. 33. The statement categorizes transactions as either exchange and exchange-like transactions or nonexchange transactions. In **exchange transactions,** the government gives and receives approximately equal values in the exchange. For example, a municipal utility would bill customers for the amount of electricity that is used. In **exchange-like transactions,** the government gives and receives similar but *not* equal values in the exchange. Examples of exchange-like transactions would include fees for professional or regulatory licenses, tap fees, and developer fees. Revenue from exchange and exchange-like transactions is generally recognized at the

---

[1]GASB Statement No. 33, *Accounting and Financial Reporting for Nonexchange Transactions.*

time the exchange takes place and the revenue is earned, unless it is subject to the "available" provisions of the modified accrual basis of accounting.

In **nonexchange transactions,** the government receives (or gives) resources without providing (or receiving) resources that are approximately equal in value. GASB Statement No. 33 classifies nonexchange transactions into four categories: **derived tax revenues, imposed nonexchange revenues, government-mandated nonexchange transactions, and voluntary nonexchange transactions.** Each category has specific rules governing the accounting for and recognition of assets, liabilities, revenues, and expenditures. It is important to note that *only the timing of the recognition of revenue* in nonexchange transactions is impacted by the basis of accounting used by the fund reporting the transaction.

A common feature of all nonexchange transactions is that they are "governed by legislative or contractual requirements (or both)."[2] The government must fulfill these legislative or contractual requirements in order for a transaction to exist. If the government does not fulfill these requirements, it will have no claim on the resources (asset or receivable) and the provider will have no obligation to pay (liability or payable).[3] For example, a tax on property is authorized by constitutional and legislative requirements. The government must fulfill the requirements to assess (value) the property and levy the tax in order for a transaction to exist. Sometimes fulfillment of the requirements is sufficient for recognition of revenues and expenses, and at other times, additional requirements such as time restrictions may delay recognition.

Time and purpose restrictions[4] frequently occur in nonexchange transactions. A **time restriction** limits the use of the resources to a particular point or period in time when the resources must be used or when use can begin. A timing restriction will affect the recognition of the revenue. If the funds are not available due to a timing restriction on their use, these resources cannot be recognized as revenue until the time specified occurs. A **purpose restriction** limits the use of the resources to a specific purpose. A purpose restriction will not affect the timing of the recognition of revenues. The resources will simply be restricted net assets until the purpose restriction is met by expending the funds for the specified purpose.

Derived tax revenues are taxes levied (charged) on an underlying exchange transaction. The main characteristic of derived tax revenues is the fact that the tax is charged to the person or entity that acquires a product, service, or income in an exchange transaction. Governments sometimes place purpose restrictions on derived tax revenues.

A sales tax is a derived tax revenue because a flat percentage tax is collected at the point of sale when goods are purchased. The exchange of goods for monies (or a promise to pay) triggers the recognition of the tax revenue. For example, a student purchases a $100 textbook for her college accounting course, and a 5% sales tax is collected at the point of sale. The student pays $100 and receives a $100 textbook in exchange. The sales tax revenue of $5 is also collected at the point of sale and remitted by the bookstore to the government periodically as required by law. This $5 sales tax is derived from the underlying exchange between the student and the bookstore. In theory, the government recognizes the $5 sales tax when the purchase transaction occurs. (In practice, a government may estimate monthly collections and adjust the revenue recognized when it is reported by the bookstore.)

---

[2]*Ibid*, paragraph 58, Appendix B, Basis for Conclusions.
[3]*Ibid*, paragraph 60, Appendix B, Basis for Conclusions.
[4]*Ibid*, paragraph 12.

Income taxes are also derived tax revenues. An employee provides labor and services to an employer and is paid a salary in return. An income tax is assessed upon the employee's income and is derived from the underlying exchange between the employee and employer. The income tax is recognized as governmental revenue at the time the employee is paid and the underlying exchange occurs. (Again, in practice, the government can estimate the amount of tax but cannot fully determine the amount to recognize until it receives the report from the employer and the tax returns from the employees.)

Motor fuel taxes are also derived tax revenues. A driver pulls into a gas station and fills the car's tank with gasoline. The driver pays the gas station for the gasoline. The motor fuel tax is included in the price of the gasoline, and the gas station remits it to the governmental unit periodically. In theory, the governmental unit recognizes the motor fuel tax revenue at the time that the underlying exchange between the driver and the gas station occurs. (In practice, revenue is recognized periodically.) Often, motor fuel taxes have purpose restrictions for use on the maintenance of streets and highways.

The general rule for revenue recognition of derived tax revenues is to recognize these resources as revenue *net of estimated refunds* at the time of the exchange or when the resources are received, whichever event occurs first. In the case of sales, income, and motor fuel tax revenues, the underlying transaction will normally occur before the taxes are transmitted to the government, so they would be recognized at the time the underlying exchange occurs because it occurs first. When the modified accrual basis of accounting is used, the resources also should be "available."

Sales taxes withheld by the seller at the point of sale or income taxes withheld by the employer at the time the employee is paid are generally due at a later date, often the 15th of the month following the sale or payroll. The governmental unit can estimate the amount expected to be remitted at the time of the sale or payroll based upon historical experience. The time lag between collection and remittance to the government, in effect, compensates the seller or employer by permitting them the "use" of the funds for a short period of time to earn and retain any short-term investment income. Since the exact amount of revenue is not known until the taxes are periodically remitted to the government, monthly estimates of revenue are recorded and then adjusted when actual amounts are available.

Imposed nonexchange revenues are assessments by governments on nongovernmental entities that have no underlying exchange transaction. They include property taxes, fines, and forfeitures imposed by governments. The main characteristics of imposed nonexchange revenues is that the assessment is imposed on an act that is committed or omitted such as owning property or not obeying a law. These revenues are recognized in the first period that the resources are permitted or required to be used and may also have purpose restrictions.

A classic example of an imposed nonexchange revenue is property tax, which is a common and significant source of local governmental revenues. The tax is imposed by the governmental unit on property that is valued according to local laws. The property tax provides revenue for governmental services and is based upon the value of the property. There is no underlying exchange as a basis for this tax, and it is clearly an imposed tax established by law.

Government-mandated nonexchange transactions occur when one government provides resources to another government and requires that those resources be used for a specific purpose. Time restrictions may also be imposed. The main characteristics of government-mandated nonexchange transactions are that the government providing the resource mandates that the recipient provides a service or facilitates its performance by another entity and certain eligibility requirements must be met for the transaction to occur. Revenues are recognized in the period when all eligibility requirements have been met. For example, the federal government allocates monies to state governments for shelter and assistance programs for the homeless. Half of these monies is to be used by the state, and half is to be passed through to large cities (over 500,000 population). The federal government is mandating the program. The state must fulfill the eligibility requirement by identifying and passing through monies to cities of a certain size and spending the funds on the specified program. The state and cities will recognize the award as a revenue but because it has a specified purpose, the monies will be classified as restricted net assets until spent on the program.

A **voluntary nonexchange transaction** occurs as a result of legislative action or other contractual agreements entered into willingly by the parties. The government voluntarily agrees to receive the resources specified in the legislation, grant, donation, or other contractual agreement, often with eligibility or purpose restrictions. The main characteristics of voluntary nonexchange transactions are that they are not imposed on either party (provider or recipient) and that eligibility requirements must be met for the transaction to occur. Revenues are recognized in the period when all eligibility requirements have been met. For example, a donor agrees to provide $5,000,000 for a new library if the city can obtain a matching amount of $5,000,000 in funding. The city must fulfill the requirement to obtain $5,000,000 for a new library in order to recognize a transaction. If the city does raise $5,000,000 to match the donor's $5,000,000, it can then recognize the receivable and revenue for the donor's contribution. The $5,000,000 donation will be restricted until it is used for the new library (purpose restriction). Note that there is no legal requirement forcing the city to accept the donor's offer.

Eligibility requirements generally must be met to receive the resources with government-mandated and voluntary nonexchange transactions. Eligibility requirements include one or more of the following:[5]

a) **Required characteristics of recipients.** The recipient (or secondary recipient) has the eligibility characteristics detailed by the provider.

b) **Time requirements.** Any time specification by the provider of the resources has been met.

c) **Reimbursements.** The government is eligible to seek reimbursement from the provider for allowable costs for a certain program. The government is required to have incurred allowable costs before the resources will be provided.

d) **Contingencies.** The provider requires the government to perform a certain action in order to receive the funding (this is considered a voluntary nonexchange transaction). For example, the provider requires the government to raise funds from third parties or provide their own monies to fund a program.

As explained above, GASB Statement No. 33 classifies governmental transactions into two categories: exchange or exchange-like and nonexchange transactions. Time restrictions will delay recognition of revenue until the restriction is met. Purpose restrictions will not delay revenue recognition but will cause the resources to be restricted net assets until expended for the restricted purpose. Exhibit 3-1 describes the four categories of nonexchange transactions.

---

[5]*Ibid*, paragraph 20.

EXHIBIT 3-1   Classes and Timing of Recognition of Nonexchange Transactions[6]

Class	Recognition
Derived tax revenues Examples: Sales taxes, shared sales taxes, personal and corporate income taxes, motor fuel taxes, and similar taxes on earnings or consumption	**Assets*** Period when *underlying exchange has occurred* or when resources are received, whichever is first. **Revenues** Period when *underlying exchange has occurred.* (Report advance receipts as deferred revenues.) When modified accrual accounting is used, resources also should be "available." Statement No. 33, paragraphs 16 and 30a.
Imposed nonexchange revenues Examples: property taxes, shared property taxes, most fines and forfeitures	**Assets*** Period when an enforceable legal claim has arisen or when resources are received, whichever is first. **Revenues** Period when *resources are required to be used* or first period that use is permitted (for example, for property taxes, *the period for which levied*). When modified accrual accounting is used, resources also should be "available." (For property taxes, apply NCGA Interpretation 3, as amended.) Statement No. 33, paragraphs 17, 18, 30b, and 30c.
Government-mandated nonexchange transactions Examples: federal government mandates on state and local governments **Voluntary nonexchange transactions** Examples: certain grants and entitlements, most donations	**Assets* and liabilities** Period when *all eligibility requirements have been met* or (for asset recognition) when resources are received, whichever is first. **Revenues and expenses or expenditures** Period when *all eligibility requirements have been met.* (Report advance receipts or payments for use in the following period as deferred revenues or advances, respectively. However, when a provider precludes the sale, disbursement, or consumption of resources for a specified number of years, until a specified event has occurred, or permanently [for example, permanent and term endowments], report revenues and expenses or expenditures when the resources are, respectively, received or paid and report resulting net assets, equity, or fund balance as restricted.) When modified accrual accounting is used for revenue recognition, resources also should be "available." Statement No. 33, paragraphs 19 through 25 and 30d.

*If there are purpose restrictions, report as restricted net assets (or equity or fund balance) or, for governmental funds, as a reservation of fund balance.

---

[6]*Ibid*, Appendix C Summary Chart, and GASB Statement No. 36, *Recipient Reporting for Certain Shared Nonexchange Revenues.*

● **INTERPRETIVE EXERCISE**

A state shares sales tax revenues with local governments according to a formula established in the State Constitution. The state also provides grants to local governments who submit applications to establish new recreation programs in urban neighborhoods. What class of nonexchange revenues would the local government categorize each of these monies received from the state? Would there be any difference in the revenue recognition criteria for the state shared revenues as compared to the state grant program?

RECOGNITION AND RECORDING OF COMMON SOURCES OF GOVERNMENTAL REVENUE

There are many common sources of governmental revenue: taxes, licenses and permits, fines and forfeitures, special assessments, grants, entitlements, government shared revenues, donations, and charges for services. Revenues that are received by governmental-type activities will normally be recorded in the governmental funds on the modified accrual basis. Revenues that are received by business-type activities will normally be recorded in the proprietary funds on the accrual basis. Fiduciary funds record revenues based upon related restrictions for the monies. Each common source of governmental revenue will be discussed below.

Taxes

Taxes are the primary source of revenue for most governments. The revenue recognition criteria vary depending upon the type of tax. Most taxes are nonexchange transactions. Common taxes are discussed individually below.

Property taxes. Property taxes are received in a nonexchange transaction and are an imposed tax revenue. The property tax is normally recorded in the general fund on the modified accrual basis of accounting. Property tax is an **ad valorem tax** (a tax assessed upon a valuation) that is assessed in **mills** (commonly referred to as millage). A mill equals $1 per $1,000 of a property's assessed valuation. Note that assessed value is usually less, sometimes significantly less, than the fair market value of the property at the time of the assessment. For example, assume that for tax purposes a property is assessed at 50% of fair market value, which is $100,000. The assessed valuation would be $50,000 ($100,000 × 50%). If the property tax is 30 mills, the tax would be $1,500 [$30 × ($50,000 ÷ $1,000)].

The property tax is *levied*, and bills are sent to each owner noting the legal due date. If the property owner does not pay the property tax on or before the due date, the government can often impose late penalties and interest. If the property owner fails to pay for an extended period of time (often 3 years) the government will file a lien against the property and may even sell this lien to other parties. The **lien** is a legal instrument that will prevent sale and transfer of title for the property without payment of the back taxes. Each of these actions by the government—the levy, assessing penalties and interest, filing a lien and receiving payments—are transactions that must be recorded and are prescribed by law. The revenue recognition flows from the underlying law that the tax is based upon.

"Property taxes should be recognized as revenues in the period for which they are levied."[7] In the case of property taxes, they are deemed to be available if they will be received within 60 days after the fiscal year-end for which they are levied.[8] The GASB created a "cutoff," in a sense, to determine how and when to recognize property tax revenue, which is a primary source of funding for local governments. As a practical matter, most governments are able to record an accurate amount at year end because the books are kept open for at least 60 days.

The journal entries to record property tax transactions are illustrated below. First, a property tax of $3,000,000 is levied (bills are sent to owners) and 1% is estimated to be uncollectible. The levy occurs in the fiscal budget period in which the tax is intended to be used. This levy is for funding of general operations and is recorded in the general fund.

Property Taxes Receivable - Current	3,000,000	
Allowance for Uncollectible		
Property Taxes - Current		30,000
Property Tax Revenues		2,970,000

Property taxes of $2,900,000 are collected.

Cash	2,900,000	
Property Taxes Receivable - Current		2,900,000

The due date for current property taxes passes and the remaining uncollected portion becomes delinquent. The original levy was $3,000,000 and $2,900,000 has been collected, so $100,000 must become delinquent. The Allowance account must also be changed.

Property Taxes Receivable - Delinquent	100,000	
Property Taxes Receivable - Current		100,000
Allowance for Uncollectible Property Taxes -		
Current	30,000	
Allowance for Uncollectible Property Taxes -		
Delinquent		30,000

Interest and penalties of $4,000 are charged as soon as the taxes become delinquent. The interest and penalties charged are recorded as a deferred revenue because it is uncertain whether they will be received in time to be used in the current fiscal period.

Interest and Penalties Receivable - Property Taxes	4,000	
Deferred Revenue - Interest and Penalties		4,000

Delinquent property taxes of $80,000 and $3,200 of interest and penalties are received from the property owners.

---

[7]GASB Statement No. 33, Appendix B, Basis for Conclusions, paragraph 84.
[8]GASB Interpretation No. 5, Property Tax Recognition in Governmental Funds.

Cash	83,200	
Property Taxes Receivable-Delinquent		80,000
Interest and Penalties Receivable -		
Property Taxes		3,200

The deferred revenue can now be recognized in an amount equal to that received above.

Deferred Revenue-Interest and Penalties	3,200	
Interest and Penalties Revenue		3,200

The Allowance account is now overstated because only $20,000 ($100,000 – $80,000) remains uncollected, so it must be adjusted. The original estimate for uncollectible property taxes was $30,000, but only $20,000 remains uncollected. Therefore, $10,000 of property tax revenue must be recognized.

Allowance for Uncollectible Property Taxes-		
Delinquent	10,000	
Property Tax Revenues		10,000

The delinquent property taxes remain unpaid. The date passes when the government now must attach a lien to the property to ensure that these delinquent property taxes will eventually be paid. The government has the right to sell the property to pay off the tax lien (generally at public auction or bid). The receivable and allowance account can be reclassified from delinquent to liens. In practice, many governmental units legally record tax liens against the properties that are delinquent and leave the amount owed in a Property Taxes Receivable - Delinquent account. The amount of Interest and Penalties outstanding would be added to the tax liens receivable (or delinquent receivable if the tax liens receivable is not used).

Tax Liens Receivable	20,800	
Interest and Penalties Receivable		800
Property Taxes Receivable - Delinquent		20,000

The allowance account is reclassified as an allowance for tax liens and reduced to an estimate of 10% uncollectible of the remaining balance due ($20,000 × 10% = $2,000).

Allowance for Uncollectible Property Taxes -		
Delinquent	20,000	
Deferred Property Tax Revenue - Tax Liens		18,000
Allowance for Uncollectible Tax Liens -		
Property Taxes		2,000

The uncollected tax lien is recorded as deferred revenue because it is unlikely to be collected in time to pay budgetary costs of the current fiscal year. This completes the entire property tax collection cycle. Each fiscal period will have another similar cycle of property tax collection that proceeds from initial levy to final liens. It is common for the property tax cycle to "cross" fiscal years. For example, the property tax cycle often is on a calendar year basis, whereas the governmental unit has a July 1 to June 30 fiscal year. As a result, the governmental funds will recognize property tax revenue as "available" if it is to be received within the fiscal period or 60 days after fiscal year-end regardless of which calendar year property tax cycle it relates to unless the ordinance specifically relates the property tax collection to a specific period.

Sales taxes. Forty-five states, the District of Columbia, and about 7,600 local governments[9] impose a flat rate sales tax on an exchange transaction between consumers and merchants. The consumers purchase goods. The merchant collects payment for the goods and also collects the sales tax to be remitted at a later date to the government. The sales tax is a nonexchange derived tax revenue. The sales tax is derived from an underlying exchange between consumer and merchant. The sales tax is recognized at the time that the underlying exchange occurs. If the sales tax is to be used to fund governmental-type activities, it must also be "available" in time to fund current fiscal year expenditures. The journal entry to record the estimate of sales taxes in the hands of merchants not yet remitted would be done periodically. The government estimates the $2,000,000 monthly sales tax revenue currently in the hands of merchants at month-end (not due until the 15th of the next month).

Sales Tax Receivable	2,000,000	
Sales Tax Revenue		2,000,000

The government should recognize the sales tax revenue when the underlying exchange event occurs. This will require the use of reasonable estimates as the sales taxes will still be in the hands of the merchants who collected them at the time the exchange occurs. The revenue is recognized at this point of sale because it is "available" to finance the budget of the current fiscal period and a legally enforceable claim exists.

How should governments develop reasonable estimates of sales tax revenues?

States and localities can require merchants to collect sales taxes at the point of sale when the merchant has a "physical presence" in the state or locality. If the merchant has a warehouse or retail store located in the State or local government region, then the merchant must collect the sales tax and remit it to the governmental unit. The growth of e-commerce by remote sellers (sellers who do not have a physical presence in the taxing region of the buyer) poses a threat to collection of sales tax revenues. The General Accounting Office (GAO) recently estimated the State and local sales tax losses for all remote sales (home shopping network, mail-order, Internet, etc.) and for Internet sales alone. The estimated State and local sales tax losses for all remote sales was as high as $9.1 billion in 2000 and could reach $20.4 billion in 2003. The estimated State and local sales tax losses for Internet sales alone was as high as $3.8 billion in 2000 and could reach $12.4 billion in 2003. Clearly, the GAO estimates serious erosion in State and local sales tax revenues due to the increased popularity of remote sellers and Internet sellers.

(Source: U.S. GAO Report to Congress OCE-00-165 *SALES TAXES Electronic Commerce Growth Presents Challenges; Revenue Losses Are Uncertain.* June, 2000)

---

[9]U.S. GAO Report to Congress OCE-00-165, *SALES TAXES Electronic Commerce Growth Presents Challenges: Revenue Losses Are Uncertain.* June, 2000, page 5.

Income tax. Income taxes are nonexchange derived tax revenues that tax employee income paid by an employer (the underlying exchange). Income taxes are paid to the government on behalf of employees by employers who withhold taxes from employees and in quarterly estimates by self-employed individuals. Income taxes that flow in and become available during the fiscal period may also be subject to a liability for estimated refunds. Income taxes should be recorded as revenue at the time the underlying exchange takes place. As a practical matter, the government will periodically estimate withholding plus quarterly estimates and net expected refunds to arrive at a reasonable income tax revenue that will be "available" within the current budgetary period. The journal entry to record income taxes of $4,000,000 with an estimated $500,000 likely refund of such taxes would be:

Income Taxes Receivable	4,000,000	
Income Tax Refunds Payable		500,000
Income Tax Revenues		3,500,000

Hotel taxes. Many cities that attract conventions have a hotel tax on each hotel room nightly rental to fund improvements such as a convention center. For example, the convention center construction would be paid for by issuing long-term debt. The principal and interest payments on the long-term debt would be paid by revenues generated from the hotel tax. The local government is often predicting that there will be increased hotel utilization due to the construction of a convention center.

The hotel tax is a nonexchange derived tax revenue with an underlying exchange between hotel guest and hotel for the room rental, which will include a charge for the tax. The hotel will remit the tax to the government at a later date. The government should recognize the hotel tax at the time the underlying exchange takes place. It will not be feasible or practical for the government to recognize each hotel room rental's tax on an individual basis. The government will develop a reasonable estimate of hotel tax revenue that will be available within the current budgetary period and record it periodically in the governmental funds. The journal entry to record the estimated $200,000 hotel tax would be:

Hotel Tax Receivable	200,000	
Hotel Tax Revenues		200,000

Licenses and permits. Governments issue various licenses and permits in exchange (exchange or exchange-like transaction) for an annual fee. A dog license is an example. A dog owner must pay the local government an annual license fee. Licenses and permits are recorded on the cash basis at the time of the exchange of cash for the license in the governmental funds. If proprietary funds were to issue licenses or charge tap or developer fees, these revenues would be recorded on the accrual basis as revenues when they are earned. Generally, licenses and permits are issued by governmental funds. The journal entry to record $5,000 in licenses and permit receipts in a governmental fund would be:

Cash	5,000	
License and Permit Revenues		5,000

Government-mandated programs

Government-mandated (federal mandate to state, or state mandate to city) programs are common. The federal government may mandate (require) and fund a state or local government program. Likewise, a state government may mandate and fund a local government program. There is no underlying exchange. The mandated program usually specifies certain eligibility requirements for the funding such as: 1) required characteristics of recipients, 2) time requirements, or 3) reimbursements for allowable cost. The revenues will be recognized when the eligibility requirements are met for it is then that a transaction has occurred. Until the eligibility requirements for the funding are met, no transaction has occurred. For example, a state might provide funding for local governments to provide health care and food to pregnant women with incomes below a specified level. The local government will record revenue when the pregnant women who are eligible have been identified and a reasonable estimate of resources ($50,000) to be received and expended can be made. The restriction to spend the estimated resources to be received on health care and food for the identified pregnant women is a purpose restriction that does not require a delay in recognizing the estimated revenues. However, when the asset cash is received, it will be restricted until it is spent for the intended purpose.

The journal entry for the state government would be:

Expenditures	50,000	
Due to City of Kent		50,000

The journal entry for the local government would be:

Due from State of Iowa	50,000	
Women's Health Program Revenues		50,000

This is a good example of an intergovernmental program that has mandated (required, often by law) funding by one level of government and mandated services provided or performed by another level of government.

Food stamps.[10] are a unique government-mandated nonexchange transaction. GASB Statement No. 24 specifies that food stamps must be recognized at face value as revenues and expenditures in the general or special revenue fund. The expenditure should be recognized when the food stamp benefit is distributed to the recipient by the government or its agent and the revenue is recognized at the same time. This is to provide accountability for the public benefit flowing through the governmental unit to qualified food-stamp recipients. The governmental unit recognizes revenues in an amount equal to expenditures for distributions of food stamps to qualified recipients. The journal entry in the general or special revenue fund to recognize distribution of $50,000 in food stamps to qualified recipients would be:

Expenditures	50,000	
Food Stamp Revenues		50,000

---

[10]GASB Statement No. 24, *Accounting and Financial Reporting for Certain Grants and Other Financial Assistance*, paragraph 6.

If food stamps are held by the government prior to distribution to qualified recipients, they should be accounted for as an asset and equal amount of deferred liability. For example, if the government received $500,000 in food stamps but had not yet distributed them to qualified recipients, the following journal entry would be recorded in the general or special revenue fund:

Food Stamps	500,000	
Deferred Food Stamp Revenues		500,000

The governmental unit distributing food stamps must recognize a revenue for the amount of food stamps at the time of distribution and an equal amount of expenditure. If the food stamps have been received but not distributed, the food stamps are recorded as an asset and an equal amount of deferred revenue is recorded as well.

Grants and entitlements

Grants and entitlements are legislative, legal, or contractual agreements that provide funding to governmental units. In most cases, grants are provided for governmental funds. A grant occurs when funding is provided from an agency, an individual, a foundation, another government, or other source for a specific purpose to a governmental unit. This is a voluntary nonexchange transaction. The grantor does not have to provide the funding, and the governmental unit does not have to accept the grant and the restrictions that accompany it. The grantor chooses to provide the resources, and the governmental unit voluntarily chooses to accept it. The grant will be recorded in the appropriate fund depending on its purpose. If a grant was received for general operating purposes, it would be recorded in the general fund. For example, if a $5,000,000 grant is received to construct a town hall, it would be recorded in a capital projects fund as follows:

Cash	5,000,000	
Grant Revenues		5,000,000

The cash will be a restricted net asset until the town hall is constructed due to the purpose restriction.

An **entitlement** is a federally funded program in which a government can voluntarily participate. If the state or local government meets the eligibility requirements for the federal funding specified in the entitlement law, the state and local government is entitled to the funding. The federal government must provide resources at whatever level is necessary to fund the eligible programs under the entitlement.

Eligibility requirements for the grant or entitlement must be fulfilled in order for a transaction to occur that requires revenue recognition. A grant of $500,000 from the State of Missouri to the City of Metropolis to provide job-training programs during the current fiscal years of both governments should be recorded in journal entries as follows:

State:

Expenditures - Grants to Cities	500,000	
Due to City of Metropolis		500,000

City:

Due from State of Missouri	500,000	
Job-Training Program Revenues		500,000

These two entries presume the following facts: 1) both parties (state and city) voluntarily agreed on the conditions of the grant: state provides $500,000 to city and city provides $500,000 in job-training programs to eligible recipients as specified by the grant conditions, 2) the state will provide the resources within the current budgetary period, 3) the city will accept these resources. The city does not have to perform the services in order to recognize the revenue, as that is a purpose restriction. The purpose restriction does not delay revenue recognition but merely causes these resources to be classified as restricted net assets until the funds are expended for the designated purpose. However, if the state specifies that the services must be provided within a certain time period, that will cause the city's revenue recognition to occur in the same time period as services are required to be performed.

Should state funding formulas for schools be based on "need"?

The State of New York formula for funding schools is based upon a calculation that determines the "combined wealth ratio," which includes the property value and average family income for each student. This formula is designed to reveal what the school district can "afford" to pay and then determine what it "needs" beyond that amount. In addition, textbook expenses and other operating expenses are considered. The theory behind this formula is that the state funding should result in the "neediest" districts receiving aid. However, the state formula also provides that no district will ever get less money than it did the year before even if "needs" decline and 330 "wealthier" school districts benefit and get more than the formula provides. In turn, 302 "poor" districts get less because the formula also prohibits districts from getting a lot more than they did the year before even if "needs" increase sharply. Strange anomalies result from the formula limitations based upon the "combined wealth ratio" calculation. This caused the State of New York to cut $572 million off the formula to the 302 "poorer" districts and add $161 million in excess of the formula to the 330 "richer" districts. In essence, the formula is resulting in a New York State funding method that enables the rich school districts to get richer and the poor school districts to get poorer based upon "need." A New York State court judge overturned the formula indicating it does not provide enough money to schools in New York City to provide a "sound, basic education."

(Source: *The New York Times*, February 14, 2001.

Shared revenues

The two most common types of **shared revenues** between governmental units are nonexchange derived sales tax revenues and imposed property tax revenues.[11] One government assesses and collects the tax revenues and then shares the revenues with another government. GASB Statement No. 36[12] amends GASB Statement No. 33 and illustrates guidance for recording shared revenues.

Example 1: A state shares a sales tax with local governments who may use the money for any purpose and a continuing appropriation is presumed by state law. Local governments can presume the eligibility requirements are met due to the continuing, rather than annual, appropriation of the shared revenues. The local governments would recognize the shared sales tax revenue when the underlying exchange takes place, net of

---

[11]GASB Statement No. 36, *Recipient Reporting for Certain Shared Nonexchange Revenues*, paragraphs 1–2.
[12]*Ibid*, Appendix C.

expected refunds, as a derived tax revenue. The state government would recognize sales tax revenues and sales tax receivables and also record payables for the shared revenues due to local governments and an equal amount of expenditure or expense at the time that the underlying sales exchange transaction occurs. The journal entries would appear as follows in a case where a state government recognizes an estimated net of expected refunds of $50,000,000 of sales tax revenue when the underlying sales exchanges have occurred. The state will be required to share 60% of this revenue with local governments under a continuing appropriation. The revenue will be recorded as follows:

State government:

Sales tax receivable	50,000,000	
Shared revenue expenditure	30,000,000	
Sales tax revenue		50,000,000
Due to local governments		30,000,000

Local governments (aggregated transaction for all recipients; each government would actually record only its specific share of the revenue):

Due from state government	30,000,000	
Shared sales tax revenue		30,000,000

Example 2: The facts are the same as Example 1 above except there is no continuing appropriation. The state annually appropriates the shared sales tax revenue to local governments. In that case, the same journal entries would be recorded on the first day of the fiscal year that an appropriation is in effect for the shared revenue.

Example 3: A state fuel tax is shared with local governments who are mandated to accept and use the monies for highway repair and improvement. This is a government mandated nonexchange transaction. If there is a continuing appropriation, it would be recorded as illustrated in Example 1 when an estimate of the fuel tax from underlying exchanges is recognized by the state net of expected refunds. If the state shared fuel tax must be annually appropriated, it would be recorded similar to Example 2 at the beginning of the fiscal year that the annual appropriation takes effect.

Example 4: A local sales tax is collected at the point of sale along with a state sales tax. Both sales taxes are remitted to the state each month. The state then remits the local government share of the sales taxes collected on a quarterly basis. This is not a state sales tax revenue being shared; it is a local tax revenue collected by the state. The local government will recognize the local sales tax revenue on an estimated basis at the time of the underlying sales exchange. This is a derived tax revenue. The state is acting as a collection agent for the local government and does not recognize revenue or expenditure for the local sales tax that is simply passing through the state. The state can record a monthly collection of $2,000,000 in local sales taxes in an agency fund. The local government will periodically record a receivable from the state and estimates the approximate amount of local sales tax revenue at the time of the underlying exchange to be $1,900,000 in a month.

State government agency fund:

Cash	2,000,000	
Due to local government		2,000,000

Local government general fund:

Due from state government	1,900,000	
Sales tax revenue		1,900,000

In the final example, only the local government will recognize an estimate of the local sales tax revenue at the time of the underlying exchange.

Donations and endowments

A **donation** is a voluntary nonexchange transaction. The donor expects nothing in return, so it is clearly voluntary. There is no exchange because it is a donation with no expectation in return. The donation may have time or purpose restrictions, but that does not imply that it is not voluntary. If the donation specifies eligibility requirements, they must be satisfied before any revenue recognition for the donation may occur. However, if the donation only restricts purpose, then it may be recognized as revenue when pledged or received. Time restrictions by the donor can delay revenue recognition accordingly to correspond with the time specified by the donor. The donation will be recorded in whatever fund is appropriate given the purpose of the donation and if there is any permanent restriction of the funds.

An **endowment** is a permanent dedication of funds by a donor who may specify how the investment earnings will be utilized (time or purpose restrictions may be specified). An endowment means that the donor has "endowed" the institution (government or not-for-profit) with a permanent "endowment" of funds. The endowed funds may generate earnings from their investments to be used for whatever purpose the donor has specified. An endowment may be recorded in the Permanent Funds if the proceeds are to be used for general governmental purposes, but the Private-Purpose Trust Funds may be more appropriate if a specific purpose that does not benefit all citizens is intended or specified by the donor. For example, a local citizen dies and the will specifies that the estate valued at $4,000,000 will be donated to the city to be held permanently in trust with earnings to be used however the city council sees fit. The journal entry to record the donations would be as follows:

Permanent Trust fund:

Cash	4,000,000	
Net Assets held in trust		4,000,000

It is a permanent trust fund because the principal cannot be spent and the investment earnings from the cash donation is to be used freely by the city council for any purpose they deem appropriate. The cash will be shown as restricted net assets in the city's financial report. The Fund Balance could be shown as reserved or restricted, which indicates that it is not available for expenditure.

Donations of works of art or historical treasures.[13]   A governmental unit can receive a donation of a work of art or historical treasure such as a monument. This would be classified as a voluntary nonexchange transaction. Works of art or historical treasures, or similar assets should be recorded at their historical cost or estimated fair value at the time of donation. Exhaustible items should be depreciated over time but inexhaustible items should not be depreciated. The GASB has established criteria whereby an entity can elect not to capitalize a collection. All of the following conditions must be met for a collection to have an exemption from being capitalized:[14]

---

[13]GASB Statement No. 34, *Basic Financial Statements—and Management's Discussion and Analysis—for State and Local Governments*, paragraphs, 27–29 and 343.

[14]*Ibid*, paragraph 27.

a. Held for public exhibition, education, or research in furtherance of public service, rather than financial gain.
b. Protected, kept unencumbered, cared for, and preserved.
c. Subject to an organizational policy that requires the proceeds from sales of collection items to be used to acquire other items for collection.

Collections already capitalized at June 30, 1999, should remain capitalized, and all additions to such collections must be capitalized even if they meet the conditions that permit an exemption.

If the asset is *not capitalized*, then the value of the work of art or historical treasure should be recognized as revenue and an equal amount of program expenditure or expense. This may seem strange, but it provides accountability for the donation to record it as being donated revenue and then a corresponding amount of expenditure or expense is shown to offset the revenue, as if the government had used cash donated to purchase the work of art. For example, a donor gives a painting valued at $200,000 to a city museum, and the city does not capitalize its collection because it has policies in place for collection assets to hold, exhibit, and protect the assets or, if sold, use the proceeds to purchase other items for its collection. The journal entry to record the receipt of the donated painting in the museum enterprise fund (they charge fees for admission and memberships) reflects the $200,000 of value as revenue and an equal amount of expense as if the museum had actually purchased the painting:

Expense	200,000	
Revenue from Donations		200,000

If the city decided to capitalize the painting, an asset account would be debited instead of expense.

▮ **CONCEPTUAL QUESTION AND REFLECTION**

Should donated works of art and historical treasures be capitalized?

Should a state capitol building be capitalized and depreciated as a fixed asset? Should any revenue be recognized for the donation of a Picasso painting to a city museum? If valued as a fixed asset, should such assets be depreciated and charged to governmental operations over time? Some of the arguments against recording works of art and historical treasures as fixed assets are: 1) the valuation process alone to hire an appraiser for the capitol building or Picasso painting is an unnecessary expenditure to establish a value to record the asset; 2) works of art or historical treasures should not be depreciated since they often appreciate in value over time as the Picasso painting does; and 3) recording the fair market value of donated works of art or historical treasures as revenue in the financial statements would distort the financial status to external users, making it appear that large amounts of revenue were received that are not actually "available" to support general governmental operations. Arguments for recording works of art are: 1) full accountability for all public assets must be maintained and disclosed; and 2) some works of art and historical treasures are eroding or "wasting away" with time and should be depreciated.

Special assessments

Special assessments are charges that are made against properties for services that normally would be funded by taxes and are part of general governmental such as garbage collection and snowplowing. **Service-type special assessments** became popular among governmental units as a way of financing general government services without raising taxes. The services provided by these special assessments are part of general governmental operations, so the special assessment revenues should be accounted for in the governmental fund that would normally provide the service. In most cases, this will be the general fund. For example, an annual special assessment fee of $50 is charged against each property owner in the governmental unit for recycling. The following journal entries reflect the general fund billing of $100,000 (2,000 properties × $50) and the subsequent collection of a portion of these fees ($80,000).

Special Assessments Receivable	100,000	
Recycling Assessment Revenue		100,000
Cash	80,000	
Special Assessments Receivable		80,000

The special assessment "attaches" to the property assessed just as a property tax lien would and must be paid before the property can be sold or title can be transferred.

    Capital-improvement special assessments are assessments against property owners for capital improvements such as sidewalks, curbs and gutters, or street lighting. The revenue would be accounted for in a capital projects fund. If long-term debt is issued to finance the capital improvements project during the period that the assessments are being collected from property owners (often 5 or 10 years) and the governmental unit is obligated in some manner, it will be accounted for as a long-term liability of the governmental unit. The long-term debt principal and interest would be repaid in a debt service fund.

Charges for goods or services

A charge for goods or services is an exchange transaction. Charges for services include exchange and exchange-like revenues as well as nonexchange fines and forfeitures.[15] Most charges for goods or services in governmental entities are related to the business-type activities that are recorded in the Proprietary funds (enterprise and internal service). Proprietary funds record transactions on an accrual basis and would recognize revenue when the service has been provided and the related revenue has been earned. For example, a governmental unit may charge citizens for water consumed at a rate directly related to the amount of water used. The revenues that the business-type activity receives for water fees will be recorded in an enterprise fund as operating revenue on the accrual basis as it is earned. The journal entry to record billings of $300,000 by an enterprise fund for water fees with 5% estimated uncollectible would be recorded as follows:

Accounts receivable	300,000	
Allowance for uncollectible accounts receivable		15,000
Operating revenues		285,000

---

[15]GASB Statement No. 37, *Basic Financial Statements—and Management's Discussion and Analysis—for State and Local Governments: Omnibus*, paragraphs 50–54.

If the water enterprise fund charges customers a refundable deposit when service is initiated, the enterprise fund will have to account for the cash as a restricted asset and create a corresponding liability account for the amount that must be repaid to customers when they terminate service. A customer deposit of $300 to initiate service would be recorded as follows:

Customers' Deposits Cash	300	
Customers' Deposits Payable		
from Restricted Assets		300

In some cases, the enterprise fund will invest these customer deposits and return the investment earnings to these customers at termination of service. The investment earnings would increase the restricted asset account Customers' Deposits Cash and also the liability account Customers' Deposits Payable from Restricted Assets until the deposit is returned to the customer. If the customer is not entitled to receive a refund of the deposit when service is terminated, the deposit would become a revenue of the fund and the transaction would be recorded as follows:

Customers' Deposits Payable from		
Restricted Assets	300	
Revenue from Forfeited Deposits		300

Fines and forfeitures. Fines and forfeitures are imposed by governments and are classified as imposed nonexchange revenues. Common examples of this type of revenue would be a parking fine or a forfeiture of unclaimed property (escheat). Escheat property is reported as an asset in the fund that ultimately received the proceeds from sale or disposal of the escheated property. Any escheat revenue reported should be reduced for an estimate of the amount expected to be reclaimed and an equal liability should also be recorded.[16] Escheat property being held for reclaim should be reported in a private-purpose trust fund or agency fund and should not be included in the government-wide statements.

Fines and forfeitures are normally recorded in governmental funds, so they would be recognized as revenue when they become "available" to finance expenditures of the current period. In most cases, fines and forfeitures are recorded as revenue when the cash to pay the fine is received or the property is forfeited by law to the government. Since the timing and amount of fines and forfeitures are difficult to predict, governments generally do not estimate these revenues. The journal entry to record fines ($5,000 in parking fines) and forfeitures ($5,000 in property forfeitures) as they occur would be:

Cash	10,000	
Parking Fines Revenues		5,000
Forfeited Property Revenues		5,000

Although fines and forfeitures are a nonexchange revenue, they are reported as part of charges for services in the financial report.

---

[16]*Ibid*, paragraphs 3–6.

RECOGNITION AND RECORDING OF EXPENDITURES OR EXPENSES

Expenditures reflect decreases in net financial resources in governmental funds. Expenditures are recorded in governmental funds using the modified accrual method of accounting to reflect that these monies are no longer available for use. **Expenses** reflect outflows or the using up of assets in proprietary funds. Expenses are recorded in proprietary funds using the accrual method of accounting. The journal entries below illustrate the accounting for spending for a governmental or proprietary fund. In both cases, $20,000 has been spent on appropriate and authorized items.

Governmental:		
Expenditures	20,000	
Cash (or Vouchers Payable if unpaid)		20,000
Proprietary:		
Operating Expenses	20,000	
Cash (or Accounts Payable if unpaid)		20,000

The governmental-type activities and governmental funds utilize expenditures to indicate the monies are no longer available in the budget. The business-type activities and proprietary funds utilize expenses to indicate that monies have been used and relate to profit-earning activities. Both expenditure and expense accounts are very similar, and both account for spending activities within the governmental unit. The accounts normally have a debit balance until closed at the end of the fiscal period.

On-behalf payments for fringe benefits or salaries.[17] Employee fringe benefits (pension plan contributions, employee health and life insurance, salary supplements, etc.) can be paid by one governmental unit for another. Revenue and expenditure/ expense recognition depends upon whether the government is or is not legally responsible for payment. If the governmental unit is not responsible (doing some other government a favor, in a sense), then it just recognizes revenue and expenditure/ expense as the resources are received and flow through for the payments. For example, a local governmental unit might send a police officer for 6 months training in a large metropolitan city. The local government may transfer resources to the large metropolitan city to pay their police officer's salary at the training site. The large metropolitan city would recognize a revenue and expense as the money was received from the local government and paid to the police officer.

If the government is legally responsible, then the governmental unit recognizes revenue or expenditures just as it would for any other transaction in that fund. A governmental fund would use modified accrual, and a proprietary fund would use the accrual basis of accounting. For example, some states are required by law to fund the retirement benefits for public school teachers in that state. The state would record an expense for retirement benefits when funding to the pension plan was due.

OTHER FINANCING SOURCES AND OTHER FINANCING USES

The Other Financing Sources and Other Financing Uses accounts are used in the governmental funds to record unusual or nonrecurring activity that is not part of

---

[17]GASB Statement No. 24, paragraph 7.

normal operating activity. These accounts are budgetary accounts that will be closed at the end of the budgetary period. The Other Financing Sources and Other Financing Uses accounts are intended to account for transactions that should not be recorded as normal operating activity Revenues or as Expenditures in the governmental funds. For example, the sale of long-term bonds or sale of fixed assets should be recorded as Other Financing Sources in the governmental funds. For example, the transfer of resources to the debt service fund for payment of principal and interest is Other Financing Uses in the general fund and an Expenditure in the debt service fund to prevent "double-counting" of the expenditure. Sample transactions for Other Financing Sources and Other Financing Uses will be illustrated in the next section.

INTERFUND TRANSACTIONS[18]

GASB Statement No. 34[19] requires interfund activity between the governmental, proprietary, and fiduciary funds to be reported in one of two categories:

1. **Reciprocal activity**—exchange or exchange-like transactions between funds. Interfund loans (loans or advances) and interfund services (quasi-external transactions) provided and used are in this category. The interfund loans should be reported in the financial statements of the respective funds as interfund receivables and payables in the balance sheet. The interfund services sold or purchased should be reported as revenues in the seller funds and expenditures (or expense) in the purchasing funds.
2. **Nonreciprocal interfund activity**—nonexchange transactions between funds. These transactions are transfers or flows of assets or reimbursements. Other Financing Use - Operating Transfers Out and Other Financing Source - Operating Transfers In are the accounts used to record these nonreciprocal items, and they are reported below nonoperating revenues and expenses in the financial statements. Reimbursements are not reported in the financial statements.

Reciprocal interfund activity

Funds of a governmental unit may borrow or loan one another money. Funds of a governmental unit may buy or sell goods or services to one another. In both cases, there is an exchange or reciprocal transaction.

Loans or advances. Loans from one fund to another are common. Fund X that loans monies will record the amount in an asset account Due from Y Fund, and the borrowing Fund Y would record an equal amount in a liability account Due to X Fund. Items extending beyond one budgetary or fiscal year can be recorded as Advances to or Advances from the appropriate fund.

[18]NCGA Statement No. 1, *Governmental Accounting and Financial Reporting Principles*, paragraphs 99–108.
[19]GASB Statement No. 34, paragraph 112.

Quasi-external transactions. A city may do business with itself. For example, a city power plant may bill other customers $3,000,000 and bill the general fund $400,000 for electrical power. These journal entries record the transactions:

Enterprise Fund:

Accounts Receivable	3,000,000	
Due from General Fund	400,000	
Operating Revenues		3,400,000

General Fund:

Expenditures - Electric	400,000	
Due to Enterprise Fund		400,000

Quasi-external means that the transaction should appear as if it happened outside the governmental unit. The enterprise fund could have sold the power to other users, so it should record this as an operating revenue. The general fund could have purchased power elsewhere, so it should record this as a normal operating expenditure.

Nonreciprocal interfund activity

Operating Transfers In and **Operating Transfers Out** are expenditures (governmental funds) or expenses (proprietary funds) to pay or receive resources from other funds in the governmental unit. For example, the general fund authorizes payment of $10,000,000 principal in long-term debt and $500,000 in interest. The journal entries to record this are:

General Fund:

Other Financing Uses - Operating Transfers Out	10,500,000	
Cash		10,500,000

Debt Service Fund:

Cash	10,500,000	
Other Financing Sources - Operating Transfers In		10,500,000

Cash flows out of the general fund and into the debt service fund to satisfy the legally required debt service.

Transfers of capital. Governments can make permanent transfers of assets between funds. For example, a government decides to create a central web design team that will be available to all departments but centralized so as to enhance efficiencies. The start-up costs of creating this high-tech hub of talent that will charge fees for services to other departments, will require hardware, software, office partitions, etc. The governing body (city council) decides to authorize a onetime grant of $300,000 for start-up costs for this technology hub. This is a residual equity transfer of assets from one fund to another and would be recorded as follows:

General Fund:

Other Financing Uses - Operating Transfers Out	300,000	
Cash		300,000

Internal Service Fund:

Cash	300,000	
Other Financing Sources - Operating		
Transfers In		300,000

At fiscal year-end, the Other Financing Source and Other Financing Use will be closed into and increase Unreserved Fund Balance for the fund receiving the capital and decrease Unreserved Fund Balance for the fund disbursing the capital.

Reimbursements. Reimbursements are expenditures made by one fund that should have been paid or recorded in another. In essence, a correction is being made here. Reimbursements are not displayed in the annual financial statements.

● INTERPRETIVE EXERCISE

Record the entries in both funds for a) an initial transfer of capital (equity) of $50,000 from the general fund to establish an internal service fund, and b) a billing by the internal service fund for services provided to the general fund in the amount of $50,000.

PUTTING IT ALL TOGETHER

This example illustrates basic transactions for a small village's governmental operations that are recorded in the general fund. The following events occurred during the fiscal year:

1. The village council adopts a budget that estimates revenues of $500,000 and authorizes spending of $480,000.
2. The village levies property taxes of $400,000 and estimates that 5% will be uncollectible.
3. The village is notified by the state that a state revenue sharing grant for general operating purposes of $120,000 has been awarded and will be distributed in 1 month.
4. The village orders supplies estimated to cost $50,000.
5. The village collects property taxes of $390,000 during the fiscal year.
6. The remaining property taxes become delinquent, and the estimate of uncollectible delinquent taxes is 2% of the balance outstanding.
7. The village pays employees $330,000 during the fiscal year.
8. The village receives the supplies ordered with an invoice of $55,000.
9. The village pays the invoice for the supplies.
10. The state revenue sharing grant is received.
11. The village signs a contract for playground equipment and improvements to be made to the village public park for $90,000.
12. The village fiscal year ends, and the budgetary accounts are closed.

The following journal entries correspond by number to the above transactions.

1.	Estimated Revenues	500,000	
	Appropriations		480,000
	Budgetary Fund Balance		20,000

2.	Property Taxes Receivable - Current	400,000	
	Allowance for Uncollectible Property Taxes - Current		20,000
	Property Tax Revenues		380,000
3.	State Grant Receivable	120,000	
	Grant Revenue		120,000
4.	Encumbrances	50,000	
	Budgetary Fund Balance Reserved for Encumbrances		50,000
5.	Cash	390,000	
	Property Taxes Receivable - Current		390,000
	Allowance for Uncollectible Property Taxes - Current	10,000	
	Property Tax Revenues		10,000
6.	Property Taxes Receivable - Delinquent	10,000	
	Property Taxes Receivable - Current		10,000
	Allowance for Uncollectible Property Taxes - Current	10,000	
	Allowance for Uncollectible Property Taxes - Delinquent		200
	Property Tax Revenues		9,800
7.	Salary Expenditures	330,000	
	Cash		330,000
8.	Budgetary Fund Balance Reserved for Encumbrances	50,000	
	Encumbrances		50,000
	Expenditures	55,000	
	Vouchers Payable		55,000
9.	Vouchers Payable	55,000	
	Cash		55,000
10.	Cash	120,000	
	State Grant Receivable		120,000
11.	Encumbrances	90,000	
	Budgetary Fund Balance Reserved for Encumbrances		90,000
12.	Appropriations	480,000	
	Expenditures		385,000
	Budgetary Fund Balance		95,000
	Grant Revenues	120,000	
	Property Tax Revenues	399,800	
	Estimated Revenues		500,000
	Budgetary Fund Balance		19,800
	Budgetary Fund Balance	134,800	
	Unreserved Fund Balance		134,800
	Budgetary Fund Balance Reserved for Encumbrances	90,000	
	Encumbrances		90,000

As a result of the budgetary activity in this small village during the fiscal year, the Unreserved Fund Balance in the general fund will increase by $134,800. The original budget authorized spending of $20,000 less than the estimate in revenues that increased Budgetary Fund Balance. The actual spending and commitments was $475,000 ($385,000 + $90,000) as compared to the authorized spending of $480,000. The actual revenues available for the budgetary year were $519,800, exceeding the estimate by $19,800, which increased Budgetary Fund Balance. Budgetary Fund Balance has a credit balance of $134,800 ($20,000 cr. + $95,000 cr. + $19,800 cr.) and will be closed by a debit of $134,800 to create a zero balance. The Unreserved Fund Balance is increased by $134,800 as a result of the fiscal year's activities.

SUMMARY

Chapter 3 had the following learning objectives:

- Illustrate the recognition and recording of revenue sources
- Explain accounting for exchange and nonexchange transactions
- Illustrate the recognition and recording of expenditures and expenses
- Illustrate recording of interfund transactions

There are many sources of funding for governmental and business-type activities and operations. Transactions must be classified as exchange or nonexchange transactions to determine the proper revenue recognition. There are four types of nonexchange revenues: derived tax revenues, imposed nonexchange revenues, government-mandated nonexchange transactions, and voluntary nonexchange transactions. The examples above illustrate many basic revenue and expenditure (or expense) transactions that are at the heart of accounting for governmental operating activity. Interfund transactions frequently occur and must be properly accounted for so they are not confused with normal operating activity and external transactions. The next chapter will develop the balance sheet accounts for a governmental unit.

QUESTIONS

1. The state enacts a statewide business tax to fund general governmental operations. Will collection of the tax be an exchange or nonexchange transaction? Explain your reasoning.
2. The state adopts a fee for admission to state parks and a separate fee for camping overnight in these parks. Is collection of the admission fee an exchange or nonexchange transaction? Explain your reasoning.
3. Explain the difference between exchange and nonexchange transactions.
4. Describe how the impact of a timing restriction is different from the impact of a purpose restriction on the recognition of revenue.
5. What is the key difference between a derived tax revenue and an imposed nonexchange revenue?
6. Describe the four categories of nonexchange transactions. Provide a new example (not given in the chapter) for each of these categories.
7. What are the common types of governmental taxes? Do they all recognize revenue using the same criteria? Explain your answer.
8. When is a property tax considered "available"? Explain your answer.
9. Food stamps are distributed by governments to qualified recipients. Why do governments have to account for food stamps as an expenditure and revenue? Explain your answer.
10. Describe the difference between a grant and an entitlement.
11. Explain what an endowment is and the related accounting for it.
12. Describe the criteria that are used to determine whether a donation of a work of art or historical treasure should be capitalized.
13. What is a service-type special assessment? Provide a new example (not given in the chapter) of this kind of assessment.
14. What fund records operating revenue? Explain why it is logical for this account to be used in this fund.
15. Describe the two categories of interfund transactions.

EXERCISES

Exercise 3-1   **Multiple Choice—Select the best answer for each of the following:**

1. Property taxes are considered
   a. a derived tax revenue
   b. a mandatory nonexchange revenue
   c. a voluntary nonexchange revenue
   d. an imposed nonexchange revenue
2. Sales tax is collected by a merchant at the time of sale. When can the government recognize the sales tax revenue?
   a. When the sale transaction takes place
   b. When the merchant remits the tax
   c. On the legal due date for the merchant to remit the tax
   d. Either a or b, whichever is earlier
3. A government issues bonds to pay for construction of a capital asset. The bond proceeds will be reported as an:
   a. Appropriation
   b. Other Financing Use
   c. Other Financing Source
   d. Asset
4. A citizen donates a valuable painting to the State of Montana. The state places the property on exhibit in the state historical museum, which has a policy that all donated property can only be sold if the proceeds are used to add to the collection. The donated painting will:
   a. be recorded as a donation and a capital asset
   b. not be recorded as a capital asset
   c. be recorded in the general fixed asset account group
   d. be recorded as donations revenue
5. A purpose restriction on governmental resources will:
   a. cause donations to be recorded as deferred revenue
   b. cause donations to be recognized as revenue when spent for the purpose
   c. not have an effect on the timing of recognition of revenue
   d. do none of the above
6. A timing restriction on governmental resources will:
   a. cause property taxes to be deposited only after they are levied
   b. cause a delay in revenue recognition in all cases
   c. cause property taxes collected in advance to be recognized revenue
   d. affect the timing of revenue recognition
7. Income tax withholding paid by Goldman Sachs for an employee working in New York City to the State of New York is an example of a(n):
   a. exchange transaction
   b. derived tax revenue
   c. imposed nonexchange transaction
   d. mandatory nonexchange transaction
8. If the federal government provides resources for and mandates a program for state governments to administer, the revenue is:
   a. recorded in the permanent fund
   b. recognized when all eligibility requirements are met
   c. recognized when the resources are received
   d. either b or c, whichever is first

9. A farmer donates land for a public park and nature trail system. This donation is an example of a(n):
   a. exchange transaction
   b. derived tax revenue
   c. voluntary nonexchange transaction
   d. mandatory nonexchange transaction

10. Sally spends the day at her favorite stores buying bargains. Upon returning to her car, she finds a parking ticket for $25 from Carville City. Carville City will recognize the $25 revenue from Sally's ticket when:
    a. she drives away, ticket in hand
    b. she throws the ticket away, vowing never to pay
    c. her husband pays the ticket at Carville City Hall
    d. the ticket becomes past due and delinquent

Exercise 3-2

Multiple Choice—Select the best answer for each of the following:

1. Sam pulls into a gas station, fills up his car's tank with gasoline, and pays state motor fuel taxes of $1.50 as part of his total $22 fill-up. When will the $1.50 be recognized as revenue by the state?
   a. When Sam pays the gas station
   b. When the gas station remits the taxes to the state
   c. When the state chooses between a or b
   d. None of the above

2. Sam buys a pack of cigarettes while paying his fuel bill at the gas station. The state cigarette tax is $1 of the $4 per pack total price. The state will recognize the cigarette tax revenue when:
   a. Sam pays the gas station for the cigarettes
   b. the gas station remits the taxes to the state
   c. Sam smokes the cigarettes
   d. Sam quits smoking

3. Joe stays in a hotel on a business trip. Joe notices that he is charged $20 for each night's stay in local hotel taxes. When will the local government record revenue for Joe's hotel taxes?
   a. each night as the taxes are posted on Joe's bill
   b. when Joe checks out of the hotel and pays his bill
   c. when the hotel remits the taxes to the local government
   d. when Joe makes the reservation to stay at the hotel

4. Property taxes are assessed on December 1. The fiscal year ends December 31, and only half of the property taxes are collected by that date. The government will collect another 30% within 60 days after fiscal year-end. The government will recognize revenue on December 1 when the taxes are levied in the amount of:
   a. 50% of the property taxes levied less an allowance for uncollectible
   b. 30% of the property taxes levied less an allowance for uncollectible
   c. 100% of the property taxes levied less an allowance for uncollectible
   d. 80% of the property taxes levied less an allowance for uncollectible

5. The amount of income taxes that the state expects to refund should be recorded as:
   a. Income tax revenue
   b. Income tax receivable
   c. Income tax refunds payable
   d. Cash

6. The state collects $300,000 annually in hunting and fishing licenses. When will this revenue be recognized?
   a. When the hunting and fishing season begins
   b. When the licenses are sold
   c. When cash is remitted to the state by stores
   d. Either b or c

7. A donor gives the city art museum a painting valued at $100,000 at the time of donation. The art museum sells the painting 6 months later for $105,000 to pay staff salaries. The art museum will:
   a. choose whether to recognize revenue for the donation or not
   b. be required to recognize revenue of $105,000 at the time of donation
   c. be required to recognize revenue of $100,000 at the time of donation
   d. not be required to recognize any revenue from the donation except the $5,000 gain at time of sale

8. The general fund transfers cash to the debt service fund to pay principal and interest on long-term debt. This will be recorded in the general fund as:
   a. Other Financing Sources - Operating Transfers In
   b. Revenue
   c. Expenditure
   d. Other Financing Uses - Operating Transfers Out

9. The enterprise fund bills the general fund $30,000 for monthly water use. The enterprise fund will record this billing as:
   a. Revenue
   b. Other Financing Sources - Operating Transfers In
   c. Due to General Fund
   d. Accounts Receivable

10. A reciprocal interfund activity would be:
    a. a transfer from the general fund to the debt service for principal and interest
    b. a loan between the general fund and capital projects fund to start construction
    c. a reimbursement by the general fund to the enterprise fund
    d. a donation of capital from the general fund to start up an enterprise fund

Exercise 3-3   **Multiple Choice—Select the best answer for each of the following:**

1. The state pays income tax refund claims. This will require a:
   a. credit to Income Tax Revenues
   b. credit to Income Tax Refunds Payable
   c. debit to Income Tax Revenues
   d. debit to Income Tax Refunds Payable

2. Which of the following events occurs first in the property tax collection cycle?
   a. lien
   b. levy
   c. delinquency
   d. penalty

3. Which of the following activities would be a service-type special assessment?
   a. assessment is charged to citizens for snowplowing
   b. fee is charged for overdue library book
   c. fee is charged to citizens for water used during the period
   d. assessment is charged to citizens for curbs and gutters on their property

4. Which of the following activities would be a capital improvement special assessment?
   a. bonds are sold to finance construction of a new city hall
   b. assessment is charged to citizens for garbage collection and recycling
   c. assessment is charged to citizens for sidewalks on their property
   d. fee is charged for delinquent taxes

5. Which of the following interfund transactions is a quasi-external transaction?
   a. loan between funds
   b. sale of power from enterprise to general fund
   c. equity transfer from general to enterprise fund
   d. reimbursement from enterprise to general fund
6. Which of the following interfund transactions is nonreciprocal?
   a. sale of power from enterprise to general fund
   b. loan between funds
   c. transfer of monies for debt repayment from general to debt service
   d. reimbursement from special revenue to general fund
7. The general fund transfers equity to establish an internal service fund. This transaction will require the general fund to record a:
   a. debit to Cash
   b. credit to Unreserved Fund Balance
   c. debit to Contributed Capital
   d. debit to Other Financing Uses - Operating Transfers Out
8. A citizen donates land for a public park but retains a life interest to use the property for personal purposes until her death. When would the government record this donation?
   a. When the donation is made
   b. When the citizen dies
   c. When the public park opens
   d. None of the above
9. A citizen donates land for a public park and transfers title to the city at the time of the donation. When would the government record this donation?
   a. When the donation is made
   b. When the public park opens
   c. When the land is sold by the government
   d. None of the above
10. A citizen donates $500,000 to be held in trust in perpetuity and specifies earnings can be used for any general governmental purpose. The journal entry to record this transaction would include a:
    a. debit to General fund Cash
    b. credit to Permanent Trust fund Cash
    c. credit to Permanent Trust fund Unreserved Fund balance
    d. credit to Permanent Trust fund Reserved Fund balance

Exercise 3-4   **Review of basic accounts**

Is the "normal" balance of the following accounts a debit or a credit?
   a. Estimated Revenues
   b. Other Financing Sources - Operating Transfers In
   c. Appropriations
   d. Property Tax Revenues
   e. Deferred Revenue
   f. Budgetary Fund Balance
   g. Unreserved Fund Balance
   h. Accounts Payable
   i. Cash
   j. Estimated Other Financing Sources
   k. Expenditures
   l. Fund Balance Reserved for Encumbrances

Exercise 3-5	**Exchange vs. nonexchange transactions**

For each of the following governmental transactions, indicate if it is an exchange transaction or type of nonexchange transaction:
- a. a citizen puts $2.00 in change in a parking meter
- b. a citizen purchases a dog license
- c. a citizen pays the city for metered water and sewer services
- d. a citizen pays property taxes
- e. a citizen donates a rare book to the city library
- f. a citizen pays sales tax on a purchase
- g. a citizen has income tax withheld from his gross pay
- h a citizen pays green fees to play 18 holes at the city golf course
- i. a citizen fills her gas tank and the charge includes motor fuel taxes

Exercise 3-6	**Exchange vs. nonexchange transactions**

The State provides highway improvement money to local governments who apply for the funds to repair local streets. A local government applies and is granted funding. The state and local government have the same fiscal year, and the grant and street repairs will both occur during the fiscal year.
- a. Is this an exchange or nonexchange transaction?
- b. If nonexchange, what type is it?
- c. When would the state record the expenditure?
- d. When would the local government record the grant revenue?

Exercise 3-7	**Accounting for revenue**

The Gates Foundation provides Millenium scholarship funding to a state university to be distributed to eligible applicants. Explain what type of revenue this scholarship funding would be for the university and when it would be recognized as revenue.

Exercise 3-8	**Accounting for revenue**

Gold Star Cola pays the local public school district $500,000 for signing a 5-year contract that stipulates that only Gold Star Cola products can be sold on the campuses of the public school district. Explain what type of revenue this payment would be for the public school district and when it would be recognized as revenue by the district.

Exercise 3-9	**Sales tax revenue**

How can states and localities develop reasonable estimates of sales tax revenue given the increased popularity of buying goods online and from remote sellers who are not required to collect sales tax? What relationship does this have to the budget?

Exercise 3-10	**Income tax revenue**

What effect would it have upon the governmental budget if income tax refunds were not required to be recorded as a liability (Income Tax Refunds Payable) at the time that income tax withholding payments from employers were received?

Exercise 3-11	**Escheats**

Fred Jones deposits $100 in a savings account for his grandchild Johnny upon his birth. Unfortunately Johnny's parents move frequently during his childhood and eventually they lose track of this account and forget about it. The state escheats the bank account, which has grown to $122 due to inactivity for the past 7 years (no deposits or withdrawals). What type of revenue is this and how would the state record this transaction?

Exercise 3-12   **Special assessments**

A local government assesses property owners for new sidewalks. The local government also assesses property owners for garbage collection. What are the two categories of special assessments? Classify each of the above transactions into the two categories.

PROBLEMS

Problem 3-1   **Exchange vs. nonexchange transactions**

The City of Anchor received notification that it would receive $14,000,000 in state-shared revenues during the fiscal year, and the first payment of $1,200,000 was simultaneously received. The City of Anchor also collected $300,000 in local sales taxes and $10,000 in parking fees and fines. The City of Anchor landfill received $100,000 in dumping fees. Classify each transaction as exchange or nonexchange and record the transactions in journal entries.

Problem 3-2   **Exchange vs. nonexchange transactions**

Classify each transaction below as exchange or nonexchange. If it is a nonexchange transaction, classify it in one of the four categories of nonexchange transactions. Explain your answer.

  a. Merchant collects state cigarette tax on sale of pack of cigarettes.
  b. State reimburses schools for costs related to special education of handicapped children. The school must verify eligibility of the children.
  c. State fines for hunting illegally on protected state wildlife preserve.
  d. City property taxes are paid by owner.
  e. Hotel tax is collected at checkout.
  f. Donor provides $300,000 to a city homeless shelter and specifies $100,000 may be spent each year.
  g. County landfill collects fee from citizen dumping trash.
  h. Income tax is withheld from an employee's paycheck.
  i. A business donates cash for scholarships to a public university and specifies the scholarships must be for study abroad.
  j. A corporation makes a grant to a public university to conduct research on genetic coding, and the university agrees to give the corporation all patent rights on results of the genetic coding research.

Problem 3-3   **Exchange vs. nonexchange transactions**

Determine *when* the governmental unit should *recognize revenue* from the transactions listed above in Problem 3-2.

Problem 3-4   **Time vs. purpose restriction**

Determine *when* the governmental unit should *recognize revenue* for each transaction below.

  a. The federal government makes a grant to the city for highway construction.
  b. The federal government makes a grant to the city for general operating purposes during calendar year 20x3.
  c. A citizen donates an antique car to the city historical museum to be protected, preserved, or displayed.
  d. A citizen donates $1,000,000 for public recreation and specifies that no more than $200,000 can be spent in any one fiscal year over the next 5 years.
  e. Oil is discovered on state park land, and it is estimated that future revenues for general operations could be as much as $100,000,000 over the next 20 years.
  f. The state mandates a remedial reading program for public schools and grants $100,000 to each school for this purpose.

g. A citizen donates a Frank Lloyd Wright home to the city to be opened to the public for tours after his death. The citizen retains a life estate in the home and resides in the home.

Problem 3-5

Accounting for property taxes

Property taxes in the amount of $10,000,000 are levied, and 2% are estimated to be uncollectible. Property taxes in the amount of $9,900,000 are collected. The remaining property taxes receivable are reclassified as delinquent, and 5% are estimated to be uncollectible. Record these events in journal entries.

Problem 3-6

Accounting for revenues

Record the following transactions in journal entries for the state:
  a. Escheated property is sold at public auction for $300,000.
  b. Oil and gas leases to drill on state land are sold at public auction for $500,000.
  c. State police officers issue and collect $30,000 in speeding tickets.
  d. Income tax refunds in the amount of $300,000 are paid.
  e. Property tax fines on delinquent taxes are received in the amount of $20,000.
  f. Sales tax revenues of $1,000,000 are collected but not yet remitted by merchants.
  g. Federal food stamps of $3,000,000 are received but not distributed.
  h. Federal grant for highway improvements of $10,000,000 is awarded but not yet received.

Problem 3-7

Food stamps

Record the following transactions in journal entries:
  a. Food stamps in the amount of $5,000,000 are received by the state
  b. Food stamps in the amount of $2,500,000 are distributed by the state

Problem 3-8

Interfund transactions

Record the following transactions in journal entries in each fund:
  a. The general fund loans the capital projects fund $100,000 to hire an architect.
  b. The general fund donates $300,000 to start up an internal service fund.
  c. The enterprise fund bills the general fund $50,000 for power.
  d. The general fund transfers $50,000 to the debt service fund to pay principal and interest on general long-term debt.

Problem 3-9

Interfund transactions

Interfund transactions are reciprocal or nonreciprocal. Prepare journal entries to record the following interfund transactions:
  a. The General fund loans the Capital Projects fund $200,000 to hire an architect to start planning a building.
  b. The Enterprise fund bills the General fund $30,000 for electrical power provided.
  c. The General fund pays the Enterprise fund power bill of $30,000.
  d. The General fund permanently transfers $200,000 in capital to an Enterprise fund to help it with start-up expenses.
  e. The General fund transfers $25,000 to the Debt Service fund to pay principal and interest on long-term debt.

Problem 3-10

Putting it all together

Prepare journal entries for the following basic transactions:
  a. The budget is adopted. Estimated revenues are $5,000,000 and appropriations are $5,100,000.

   b. Property taxes in the amount of $5,000,000 are levied, and 5% are estimated to be uncollectible.
   c. Purchase orders in the amount of $2,300,000 are issued.
   d. $4,800,000 in property taxes are collected.
   e. The remaining property taxes are reclassified as delinquent.
   f. The goods ordered on the purchase orders above in (c) arrive with invoices for $2,200,000.
   g. Employee salaries are paid in the amount of $2,700,000.
   h. Office supplies in the amount of $30,000 are ordered but do not arrive before fiscal year-end.
   i. The vouchers for the invoices above in (f) are paid.
   j. The fiscal year ends, and the budgetary accounts are closed.

Problem 3-11

Putting it all together

Prepare journal entries to record the following transactions for a city:

   a. The budget is enacted into law permitting $3,000,000 in spending, and estimating $2,950,000 in revenues will be received.
   b. Property tax revenues of $2,800,000 are levied during the fiscal period, and 5% are estimated to be uncollectible.
   c. Employee salaries are paid totaling $1,900,000 during the fiscal period.
   d. Purchase orders are issued totaling $1,000,000 during the fiscal period.
   e. All goods are received from the purchase orders with invoices of $990,000.
   f. Property taxes are collected in the amount of $2,700,000.
   g. Property taxes become delinquent, and 2% of the delinquent taxes are estimated to be uncollectible.
   h. License, permit, and fine revenues of $100,000 are received during the fiscal period.
   i. The vouchers payable outstanding are paid.
   j. Office supplies are ordered just before fiscal year-end (but not received) for $20,000.
   k. The budgetary accounts are closed at fiscal year-end.

Problem 3-12

Internet case: food stamps

Food stamps can be distributed in the traditional manner as an actual paper document known as a "food stamp" or in a new electronic form called Electronic Benefit Transfer (EBT). Go to http://www.fns.usda.gov/fsp/MENU/ADMIN/ebt/faq/faq.htm (or access the site through the text's web site at advanced.swcollege.com) to learn more about EBT. The welfare reform act of 1996 mandates that all states must switch to EBT by October 2002. What type of revenue are food stamps at the state level? How will the switch to EBT from the traditional paper food stamp system change the accounting for the food stamp program at the state level, if at all?

Problem 3-13

Internet case: grants

Bill and Melinda Gates have established a foundation to make grants. One of the programs the Gates Foundation supports is the Library Program to make the Internet accessible in low-income communities at public libraries. The Library Program is attempting to close the "digital divide" between rich and poor in the USA. Go to http://www.fns.usda.gov/fsp/MENU/ADMIN/ebt/faq/faq.htm (or access the site through the text's web site at advanced.swcollege.com) for general information and then to http://www.glf.org/learning/libraries/libraryprogram/usguidelines.htm (or the link at the text's web site) for U.S. Grant Program Guidelines. Several states have qualified for the Library Grant Program in the two-step process. If a state has qualified and then begins to receive funding from the Gates Foundation to distribute to qualified local libraries, what type of revenue is this? How would the grant revenue be accounted for?

Problem 3-14

Internet case: funding formulae

The New York State funding formula for schools intended to fund schools based upon "need" resulted in "rich" schools getting richer and "poor" schools getting poorer. Search the Internet to find a state revenue-sharing or funding formula for local governments or jurisdictions. Explain how the funding formula works and analyze whether the formula is likely to achieve the intended effect.

Problem 3-15

Case: continuous problem

Sea Breeze City is a community on the Gulf Coast with a population of 8,500. The city is governed by an elected six member council who appoint a City Manager to oversee the operations of the city. The main sources of revenue for the city are property taxes, sales taxes, and water billings. The city has established the following funds for accounting purposes:

General Fund – includes general government, public safety, and public works departments.
Debt Service Fund – annual payments of principal and interest on outstanding debt issues of $20 million.
Mosquito Control Fund – City levies an annual tax on all properties for mosquito control purposes.
Water Utility – City operates a desalinization plant and bills customers for water based on usage.
Sea Breeze Marina – City-owned marina and adjacent park offers boatwell rentals to residents with rates set annually to cover the cost of marina operations.
Motor Pool Fund – City owns and maintains a fleet of cars and trucks and charges costs to various city departments based on usage.
Treasurer's Investment Fund – City Treasurer who has a reputation for astute investment ability operates a pooled fund for Sea Breeze City, Sea Breeze Water Utility, Sea Breeze Marina, and neighboring Palm City.

Sea Breeze City has adopted the following budget for the fiscal period January 1, 20X2 – December 31, 20X2 and there are no prior year carry-forwards of prior year appropriations:

Sea Breeze City 20x2 Budget

BE IT RESOLVED: That expenditure authority is hereby appropriated to the following budgetary centers for the fiscal year commencing January 1, 20x2, and ending December 31, 20x2:

General Fund:	
General Government	2,000,000
Public Safety	2,000,000
Public Works	1,000,000
Transfers to Other Funds	1,170,000
Total General Fund	6,170,000
Debt Service Fund	1,100,000
Mosquito Control Fund	50,000
Water Utility Fund	300,000
Sea Breeze Marina Fund	920,000
Motor Pool Fund	70,000
Total Expenditures	8,610,000

AND BE IT FURTHER RESOLVED: That the revenues for the 2002 fiscal year are estimated as follows:

General Fund:

Property tax levy	4,000,000
Sales tax	1,000,000
Grants	300,000
Investment income	1,000,000
Other fees and fines	60,000
Total General Fund	6,360,000

Debt Service

Transfers from Other Funds	1,100,000
Water Utility Fund	425,000
Mosquito Control Fund	55,000
Sea Breeze Marina Fund	1,020,000

Motor Pool Fund

Transfers from Other Funds	100,000
Total Revenues	9,060,000

(Review of Chapter 2)

A. Classify each Seabreeze City fund by category and type.
B. Determine which funds will use budgetary accounts.
C. Record the budget for the funds using budgetary accounts.

(Chapter 3)

D. For each Seabreeze City fund, what type of Revenues, Expenditures or Expenses, Other Financing Sources and Other Financing Uses, and interfund transfers will likely be recorded during the fiscal year?

The Seabreeze City problem will continue in Chapters 4 and 5. In Chapter 4, the transactions for the fiscal year will be recorded in journal entries. In Chapter 5, the financial statements will be prepared.

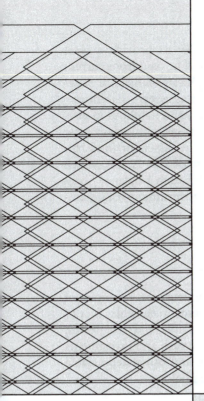

GOVERNMENTAL BALANCE SHEET ACCOUNTS

LEARNING OBJECTIVES

- Demonstrate an understanding of the categories of asset, liability, and equity accounts
- Illustrate the recognition and recording of current and long-term assets
- Explain the methods of accounting for capital assets including infrastructure
- Illustrate the recognition and recording of current and long-term liabilities
- Demonstrate an understanding of the components of fund balance and net assets

GOVERNMENTAL BALANCE SHEET ACCOUNTS

Governments must be accountable for public assets. In order to provide a clear picture of a government's financial health, any liabilities that will be paid from current or future assets must also be reported. The Statement of Net Assets or Balance Sheet shows the entity's financial position at the end of the fiscal year as assets – liabilities = net assets. This chapter explains when and how to record assets and liabilities in governmental, proprietary, and fiduciary funds and typical transactions that impact these accounts. The balance sheet accounts—assets, liabilities, and net assets or fund balance—are the foundation of the government-wide Statement of Net Assets, which will be explained in Chapter 5. The governmental unit produces both a Balance Sheet for governmental funds and a Statement of Net Assets for the government-wide statements at fiscal year-end.

ASSETS

Assets are comprised of two primary categories: current and noncurrent. Examples of **current asset** accounts are cash and cash equivalents, investments, receivables (net of allowance for uncollectible accounts), amounts due from other funds, and inventories. Examples of **noncurrent (long-term) assets** include restricted cash and investments and capital assets. Capital assets include land, infrastructure, and other depreciable long-term assets. Each common type of asset will be described below.

Current assets

Current assets are available to pay for expenditures or liabilities of the current fiscal period. Assets that are likely to be consumed or used up in the current operating period are also classified as current assets.

Cash and cash equivalents.[1] Governments collect taxes and other revenues and must account for a large amount of cash flowing in and out of the governmental unit to pay for expenses or expenditures throughout the fiscal period. The asset account **Cash** includes cash on hand, checks, and funds in checking accounts and other demand deposit accounts with banks and other financial institutions. Cash can also include deposits in investment pools and other accounts that have the same characteristics of demand deposits accounts whereby funds can be deposited and withdrawn at any time without notice or penalty. **Cash equivalents** are defined as short-term, highly liquid investments that can easily be converted to a known amount of cash and that have a maturity of three months or less from the date of purchase. Examples of cash equivalents would be commercial paper, U.S. Treasury bills, certificates of deposit, investment pools, and money market funds. The proprietary fund Statement of Cash Flows, which will be covered in Chapter 5, can incorporate both cash and cash equivalents. Under GASB reporting requirements, governments are given the option of whether they will treat investments that qualify as cash equivalents in the asset category of Cash Equivalents or in the asset category of Investments. The policy for

---

[1]GASB Statement No. 9, *Reporting Cash Flows of Proprietary and Nonexpendable Trust Funds and Governmental Entities That Use Proprietary Fund Accounting*, paragraphs 8–10.

determining which, if any, investments are treated as cash equivalents should be disclosed in the entity's Statement of Significant Accounting Policies that is part of the annual financial report.

To provide additional accountability for assets, financial statement footnote disclosures are required to classify the credit risk associated with deposits.[2] **Credit risk** is the risk that another party to a deposit or an investment transaction (the **counterparty**) will not fulfill its obligation. An example of credit risk would be if a bank failed and was unable to return the amount of a deposit. For purposes of the footnote, **deposits** are considered accounts in banks, savings and loan associations, and credit unions including checking accounts, savings accounts and nonnegotiable certificates of deposit.[3] In order to enhance the safety of deposits, collateral is often required when the amount of deposits exceeds depository insurance limits. **Collateral** (or collateralized) means that the counterparty financial institution has pledged securities to cover the value of the deposit or transaction. The footnote disclosures provide information about whether deposits are insured or collateralized, and if collateralized, the relative safety of how the collateral is held (custodial credit risk). If the collateral is transferred to the entity's safekeeping account at another financial institution, it is classified in the highest category 1 of safety. If the collateral is held by the counterparty's trust department or agent in the entity's name, it is classified as category 2. When collateral is held by the counterparty but not held in the entity's name in the trust department or with an agent, it is considered to be in the lowest category of safety and highest category 3 of risk.

A typical cash transaction would occur if a citizen walked into City Hall with either cash or a check and paid $3,000 in property taxes. The General fund would record this transaction as follows:

Cash	3,000	
Property Taxes Receivable—Current		3,000

As a result of collecting this tax payment, the Cash account is debited and increases and another asset account, Property Taxes Receivable—Current, is credited and decreases.

A common use of cash is to pay for expenses or expenditures. At the time that a check is issued to pay an invoice that was set up as an accounts payable or a vouchers payable of $2,500, a journal entry would be recorded as follows:

Accounts Payable (or Vouchers Payable)	2,500	
Cash		2,500

If the expense or expenditure was not set up as an accounts (or vouchers) payable, the debit entry would go directly to an expense account, such as telephone expense. As a result of the payment of expenses or expenditures illustrated above, an asset account Cash is credited and decreases, and a liability account Accounts Payable is debited and decreases.

---

[2]GASB Statement No. 3, *Deposits with Financial Institutions, Investments, including Repurchase Agreements and Reverse Repurchase Agreements*, paragraph 67.
[3]GASB *Guide to Implementation of Statement No. 3 on Deposits with Financial Institutions, Investments (including Repurchase Agreements), and Reverse Repurchase Agreements*, Question 6.

Investments. When governmental units have cash that is not needed to pay current expenses, they often purchase securities or enter into investment transactions to earn additional revenues through investment income. **Investments** are defined by GASB Statement No. 31 as securities or other assets acquired primarily for the purpose of obtaining income or profit.[4] Typical investments for operating funds might include U.S. Treasury bills or notes, Federal instrumentality securities, commercial paper, money market funds, or repurchase agreements. The types of investments an entity can purchase are generally defined by state statute. Many governments adopt an **investment policy** to further define and restrict the types of permitted investments for their entity. Professional organizations such as the Government Finance Officers Association and the Municipal Treasurers Association recommend that governmental units adopt a written investment policy and have drafted sample documents to guide investment practitioners.[5] In recognition of the importance of investment policies, some states have adopted statutes requiring public entities to adopt investment policies. GASB Statement No. 3 requires that footnote disclosures be made about investment policies and whether the entity has followed the policy throughout the year.

It is a responsibility to invest public monies in a safe and prudent manner. Two major risks associated with investing are credit risk and market risk. The **custodial credit risk** associated with investments is that the party holding the security will fail to return the principal. **Market risk** is the risk that the value of an investment or the value of collateral will decline. Generally the market risk most governmental investments are exposed to relates to shifts in interest rates. Governments should strive to minimize credit risk and the exposure to market risk in the investment of public funds. Footnote disclosures for investments include categorizing the custodial credit risk as well as disclosing the fair value of investments and collateral. The governing body (legislative branch) of a government adopts an investment policy to prevent excessive risks from being taken with public monies that the investment official (executive branch) must follow. The governing body should also provide ongoing oversight of the investment function.

The journal entry to record the purchase of an investment would be a debit to the asset account Investments for the principal cost and if any accrued interest was purchased, there would be a debit to the asset Interest Receivable with a corresponding credit to the asset Cash for the total amount of the transaction. For example, if an entity purchased $1,000,000 par value of a Treasury note with a 5% coupon at a principal cost of $998,000 and $5,000 in accrued interest, the journal entry would be:

Investments—U.S. Treasury	998,000	
Interest Receivable	5,000	
Cash		1,003,000

This journal entry records a decrease of the asset Cash and an increase in the asset accounts Investments and Interest Receivable. The Investments account title can have additional description added to it to further describe the investment. How the valuation of the investment is determined and the methods of recognizing investment income are discussed in the following sections.

---

[4]GASB Statement No. 31, *Accounting and Financial Reporting for Certain Investments and for External Investment Pools*, paragraph 22.

[5]http://www.gfoa.org (Sample Investment Policy), and http://www.mtausc.org (Model Investment Policy).

Orange County Treasurer loses $1.7 billion of $7.4 billion investment portfolio

Mr. Citron, Treasurer of Orange County, had the color and down-home folksiness of many local governmental officials found across the country. He loved W.C. Fields and the USC Trojans (having played clarinet in the marching band), kept all of his own money in savings accounts and certificates of deposit, and dressed colorfully. He could often be seen wearing flamboyant polyester suits to match the holiday—red/white/blue on the Fourth of July, green on Christmas, pastel at Easter, and orange with black on Halloween. He was well liked at the local Elks Club and rarely traveled from home in Santa Ana, California. Taxpayers would have never guessed Mr. Citron would be taking such daring, aggressive, and ultimately foolhardy bets with their tax dollars.

Orange County Treasurer Robert Citron persuaded the Orange County Board of Supervisors to permit him to invest public monies heavily in derivative products. These derivative products were complex financial instruments that bet that interest rates would continue to decline. The derivative products were inverse "floaters" (floating rate obligations) that were chosen to maximize returns if interest rates declined. Mr. Citron leveraged $7.5 billion in public funds into $20 billion of exposure by investing the proceeds of reverse repurchase agreements (covered later in this chapter) in derivatives. These derivative products exposed the county to losses if interest rates began to rise, which is exactly what happened. Just as a gambler hopes his luck will turn at the tables, Mr. Citron continued to hold these positions in the hope of a change in interest rates. The County Board of Supervisors did not monitor or receive interim (monthly or quarterly) mark-to-market reports on these risky investment positions, thus, there was little or no oversight. The losses from these investments actually set a record $1.7 billion before Mr. Citron was removed from his position and the investment positions were closed. No governmental unit in the United States has ever mishandled and lost this amount of public funds. A local CPA had tried to warn the County Board of the high risk in Orange County's investment positions and even unsuccessfully ran against Mr. Citron for the position of Treasurer. After the scandal broke, the local CPA was appointed to the position of Orange County Treasurer. Mr. Citron not only invested Orange County funds but also invested monies belonging to 180 other cities, school districts, sewer agencies, and other entities that participated in an investment pool managed by Orange County. The Orange County Board of Supervisors ultimately settled with governments that participated in this investment pool for 77 cents on the dollar—a loss of 23% in public funds for participating governments.

The SEC issued a report on the Orange County Board of Supervisor's conduct, which is reported at http://www.orrick.com/news/mfp/9604/01.htm and http://www.sec.gov/news/testmony/spch022.txt

Sources: *Derivatives and Bankruptcy in Orange County*, by Phillippe Jorion, University of California at Irvine, Academic Press, September, 1995, *The New York Times* page C1, December 8, 1994, *The Wall Street Journal* page B2, February 8, 1995, page A1 December 7, 1994, *The New York Times* pages 1 and 36, December 11, 1994 and http://www.orrick.com/news/mfp/9604/01.htm)

Valuation of investments and recognition of investment income. The valuation of investments and how to recognize investment income can be a bit confusing because, depending upon the type of investment, the proper method of accounting can be fair value, amortized cost, or historical cost. Adding to the confusion, GASB Statement No. 31 gives governmental units the option of how they will treat certain investments. The valuation and reporting requirements for external investment pools (discussed later in this chapter) has yet another set of rules.

The **fair value method of accounting**[6] should be applied to all investments in debt securities (U.S. Treasury, agency and instrumentality, corporate, and municipal debt securities), equity securities (stock, option contracts, closed-end mutual funds, stock warrants and stock rights), open-end mutual funds, participating interest-earning investment contracts (negotiable certificates of deposit and investment contracts with interest rates tied to a market index) and external investment pools. Under the fair value method of accounting, investments are reported at fair value and the components of investment income are interest income, dividend income, and net increase or decrease in the fair value of investments. **Fair value** is the price a willing buyer would pay a seller in an "arms-length" transaction. For securities that have a quoted market price, the bid price (price at which you can sell) is generally considered the fair value. The **net increase or decrease in the fair value of investments** for a reporting period is the ending fair value less the beginning fair value of the investment(s). The recognition of a net increase in the fair value of investments increases the investment revenue account Net Increase (Decrease) in Fair Value and increases the asset Investments. The recognition of a net decrease in the fair value of investments will decrease the investment revenue account Net Increase (Decrease) in Fair Value and decrease the asset Investments. The important point to remember with the fair value method of accounting is that if the security is held to maturity, the net increase or decrease in the fair value of the investment will equal the difference between the maturity value of the principal and the principal cost of the security. **Interest income** is earned on securities that have a stated interest or coupon rate (which can be fixed or variable) and is calculated as par × interest rate × period of time held. **Dividend income** from equity securities is recognized as of the ex-dividend date.

For example, an entity purchases a $1,000,000 Treasury note with a 5% coupon at a cost of $998,000 on July 1 (no accrued interest) and the security matures on June 30 of the next year. At the end of the fiscal year December 31, the fair value of the Treasury note is $998,500 and a semiannual interest payment was received December 31. The journal entry to record the change in fair value and the income earned through December 31 would be:

Investments—U.S. Treasury	500	
Net Increase in Fair Value of Investments Revenue		500
Cash	25,000	
Interest Income		25,000

When the Treasury note matures on June 30, the entity will receive $1,000,000 in principal and $25,000 in interest. The transaction will be recorded as follows:

Investments—U.S. Treasury	1,500	
Net Increase in Fair Value of Investments Revenue		1,500
Cash	1,025,000	
Investments—U.S. Treasury		1,000,000
Interest Income		25,000

Governmental entities (other than external pools) *may* elect to report certain investments using the **amortized cost method of accounting**.[7] This option applies

---

[6]GASB Statement No. 31.
[7]Ibid, paragraph 9.

to participating interest-earning contracts and certain money market type investments such as commercial paper, banker acceptances and U.S. Treasury, agency and instrumentality securities *that have a remaining maturity at the time of purchase of one year or less.* This option does not apply to asset-backed securities, derivatives, or structured notes such as callable securities. Under the amortized cost method of accounting, investments are reported at amortized cost and the components of investment income are interest income, accretion of discount, amortization of premium, realized gain on sale, and realized loss on sale. **Amortized cost** is calculated as the cost of the security less the amortization of premium (generally calculated on a straight-line basis) or plus the accretion of discount from the date of purchase to the date of the valuation. The recognition of **accretion of discount** increases the Investment Income Revenue—Accretion of Discount and increases the asset Investments. The recognition of **amortization of premium** decreases Investment Income Revenue—Amortization of Premium and decreases the asset Investments. If a security is sold prior to maturity, the difference between the sale price and the amortized cost is charged to investment income as a **Gain on Sale** (increase in revenue) or **Loss on Sale** (decrease in revenue). It is possible that an entity can report some investment assets on the amortized cost method and other investment assets on the fair value method. To record the journal entry for the Treasury note described in the previous example under the amortized cost method of accounting as of December 31, you will need to recognize half of the unamortized discount of the security. The entry would be:

Investments—U.S. Treasury	1,000	
Accretion of Discount Revenue		1,000
Cash	25,000	
Interest Income		25,000

The same amount of accretion of discount and interest income would be recorded for the period January 1–June 30. Note that under the fair value method of accounting, $25,500 in investment income was recognized for the period July 1–December 31 ($500 net increase in fair value and $25,000 in interest income) and $26,500 in investment income was recorded for the period January 1–June 30. Under the amortized cost method of accounting, $26,000 in investment income was recognized for the period July 1–December 31 and for the period January 1–June 30 ($1,000 accretion of discount and $25,000 interest income). Governments that only invest in short-term investments may opt for the amortized cost method because it records a more level stream of income.

Some investments, such as nonparticipating interest-earning investment contracts (nonnegotiable certificates of deposit and repurchase agreement transactions) and 2a7-like external investment pools that maintain a net asset value of $1.00 should be reported at historical cost. A 2a7-like pool is not registered with the SEC, but it operates like a SEC registered mutual fund that follows SEC Rule 2a7 of the Investment Company Act of 1940, which sets forth restrictions on the types of investments and maturity limits held by the fund. Under the **historical cost method of accounting,** investments are reported at historical cost and the components of investment income are interest income and dividends. **Historical cost** is the principal dollars invested in a security, contract, or pool.

Investment positions in open-end mutual funds and 2a7-like pools that *do not* maintain a net asset value of $1.00 should reflect the current share price of the fund or pool. The net increase or decrease in the fair value of the investments should be reported in the financial statements.

Repurchase agreements and reverse repurchase agreements.[8]   Repurchase agreements and reverse repurchase agreements are types of investment transactions. Governments commonly use these transactions to invest excess funds, and billions of dollars are traded in these transactions daily. **Repurchase agreement transactions** (commonly referred to as "repos") are agreements in which a governmental unit (buyer-lender) transfers excess cash to a broker-dealer or other financial institution such as a bank (seller-borrower) in order to earn additional investment income. The broker-dealer provides securities to the entity as collateral (a form of guarantee in case of default on the agreement) and agrees to repay the cash plus interest in exchange for the same securities at some point in the future. In effect, the collateral securities become purchased securities of the government under the terms of a repurchase agreement. The terms of the agreement are detailed in a **master repurchase agreement** between the parties. During the term of the repurchase agreement, interest earned on the collateral securities belongs to the broker-dealer and changes in the fair value of the collateral are recorded by the broker-dealer. Repurchase agreements can have various terms of maturity and interest rates. Overnight repurchase agreements have a fixed interest rate and mature on the next business day. Term repurchase agreements have a fixed maturity date and a fixed interest rate. Open repurchase agreements have no defined maturity date, may be terminated by either party daily, and the interest rate is set each day.

An example transaction would be if a city enters into a $5,000,000 repurchase agreement with a broker-dealer at an interest rate of 5.50% for 14 days. The broker-dealer delivers $5,500,000 par value of a Treasury bill with a market value of $5,150,000 to the city's custodian bank. The city would record the transaction as:

Investments—Repurchase Agreements	5,000,000	
Cash		5,000,000

When the repurchase agreement matures in 14 days, the city would return the collateral security and the transaction would be recorded as follows:

Cash	5,010,694	
Investments—Repurchase Agreements		5,000,000
Interest Income		10,694

The interest income is calculated $5,000,000 \times .0550 \times 14/360$. Most repurchase agreements are considered nonparticipating interest earning investment contracts (because their redemption value is not affected by changes in market rates), and they are recorded at cost.

During the 1980s, many governmental entities suffered losses in repurchase agreements with unscrupulous broker-dealers. E.S.M. Government Securities Inc. and Bevill, Bresler, and Schulman Asset Management Group bilked state and local governments out of millions of dollars of public funds by failing to fulfill repurchase agreements.[9] The entities had not taken care to ensure that the collateral (underlying

---

[8]GASB Statement No. 3, paragraphs 32–62.
[9]http://www.toerien.com/neg_financial_instruments/repurchase_agreement.htm

securities) specified in the repurchase agreement actually existed. Entities trusted the broker-dealers and did not have the collateral securities transferred to their third-party custodian. When the brokerage firms failed to return the cash, the entities found that the collateral securities they had been promised did not exist or that they were pledged to multiple entities. As a result of the large losses many governments experienced by unscrupulous broker-dealers of repurchase agreements, GASB issued Statement No. 3, which requires note disclosures about repurchase agreement transactions and a disclosure of custodial credit risk of the collateral securities (as described earlier in this chapter).

Reverse repurchase agreement transactions are just the opposite of a repurchase agreement. In a **reverse repurchase agreement transaction,** the governmental entity is the seller-borrower who transfers specific securities to the buyer-lender broker-dealer or financial institution in return for cash. The governmental entity promises to return the cash plus interest to the broker-dealer at some point in the future in return for the original securities. Governments may enter into reverse repurchase agreements when they temporarily need cash and do not want to liquidate securities or when they want to use the cash to temporarily invest in other securities in the hopes of earning additional investment income. Reverse repurchase agreement transactions can create risk exposure to entities that use the cash to purchase other securities if interest rates shift and securities must be liquidated at a loss to return the cash to the broker-dealer (as was the case of Orange County). Like repurchase agreements, disclosures about reverse repurchase agreement transactions are made in the notes to financial statements. For accounting purposes, the underlying collateral securities for the reverse repurchase agreement remain as assets in the balance sheet of the governmental entity (seller-borrower), and interest earnings and changes in fair value of the securities are recorded in the government's general ledger. The cash or securities purchased with the cash are also recorded as assets on the balance sheet, and interest earned and changes in the fair value of the additional securities are recognized in the general ledger. This additional asset is offset by a liability, Obligations Under Reverse Repurchase Agreements, for the amount of the cash that must be returned to the broker-dealer (buyer-lender).

An example transaction would be if a city owned a $5,000,000 Treasury note with a 6% coupon and a market value of $5,100,000 and $50,000 in accrued interest and a broker-dealer agreed to enter into a reverse repurchase agreement for $5,000,000 for 14 days at 5.50%. The transaction would be recorded (by the city) as follows:

Cash	5,000,000	
Obligations Under Reverse		
Repurchase Agreement (liability)		5,000,000

The underlying Treasury note would remain as an asset on the balance sheet of the governmental entity. At the end of the reverse repurchase agreement, the entity would return the $5,000,000 plus $10,694 in interest. The interest expense is calculated using the same method as interest income for the repurchase agreement example. The transaction would be recorded as follows:

Obligations Under Reverse		
Repurchase Agreement	5,000,000	
Investment Interest Expenditure	10,694	
Cash		5,010,694

Remember, if additional securities are purchased with the cash, they must also be recorded in the general ledger and as assets on the balance sheet. As you will see in the next section on securities lending, there are similarities in the accounting treatment of the transactions for securities lending and reverse repurchase agreements.

Securities lending.[10]   As a means of earning additional revenues, some governmental units enter into securities lending transactions. Whereas a separate reverse repurchase agreement transaction is recorded each time a specific security is lent, a securities lending arrangement (transaction) may cover all securities or all securities of a particular type that an entity owns for a specific period of time such as a year. Here are the basics of how securities lending works. The government transfers (lends) its securities (investments) to broker-dealers or other financial institutions (borrowers) in return for collateral that can be either cash, other securities, or letters of credit. The government agrees to return the collateral at some time in the future, and the borrower agrees to return the original securities. Generally, the lender can require the borrower to return a specific security whenever the lender wants it back. If the collateral is other securities or a letter of credit, the government receives a loan premium or fee from the borrower as revenue. If the collateral is cash, the borrower may charge the lender a borrower rebate (fee), however, the lender entity is then free to generate additional income by investing the cash in other securities. The lender government generally contracts with a **securities lending agent** to monitor the lending transaction, and the fees to the agent (loan premiums or agent fees) must be recorded as an expense by the lender. GASB reporting standards do not permit netting securities lending fees against revenues. The securities lent remain as assets in the balance sheet of the lender, and interest earnings and changes in fair value of the lent securities are recorded in the general ledger.

Depending upon the terms of the securities lending agreement, the government may also be required to record the collateral (cash or other securities) received as an asset with an offsetting liability account, similar to accounting for reverse repurchase agreements. The collateral securities or cash (or securities purchased with the cash) are recorded as assets on the balance sheet and an offsetting liability account, such as Obligations Under Securities Lending Agreement, is set up for the amount of cash or securities that must be returned to the borrower. The exception to reporting securities lending collateral as assets of the entity is when the collateral is a letter of credit or if the collateral securities cannot be sold or pledged by the lending government unless the borrower defaults. Then no entry is made.

The government has loaned out the securities, which remain as assets on the balance sheet, yet it may now also be required to account for the collateral received as assets. Some would argue this overstates assets and that footnote disclosure alone is more suitable and desirable. Others would argue that the accountability for the collateral requires recording it as an additional asset in the government's care. The "extra" assets represented by the collateral assets are offset by the liability account for the commitment to return this collateral to the broker-dealer. So, the net effect on the overall financial picture of the governmental unit is a "wash." The extra asset account to report the collateral is offset by the liability account. Yet, a casual reader of the financial statements who only glanced at assets would see an incorrect picture because one asset is, in effect, double-counted.

---

[10]GASB Statement No. 28, *Accounting and Financial Reporting for Securities Lending Transactions.*

Several financial statement note disclosures are required for securities lending transactions. The disclosures include a description of the securities lent and collateral received including differences in values and loss indemnification (if any) by the security-lending agent(s). Another important disclosure is the matching of maturities of investments made with cash collateral with the maturities of security loans (essentially checking if investments will mature in time to enable meeting the return of collateral required in the securities lending transaction). The heart of these accounting and reporting requirements for securities lending transactions is to provide a high level of scrutiny and disclosure of information (accountability) about any governmental assets lent to others.

Internal and external investment pools.[11]   Good cash management practices recommend that entities pool the excess cash of various funds for investment purposes. Generally, the income earned on an investment pool is distributed pro rata to the participating funds. How the assets of the investment pool are reported depends upon whether the pool is considered an internal investment pool or an external pool. An **internal investment pool** commingles (pools) assets that belong to the funds or component units of the reporting entity. The internal investment pool will value its assets in the same manner the entity would if the investments were held by any of the individual participating funds. Each participating fund or component unit will report its pro rata share in the investment pool as Equity in Pooled Cash and Investments. So far, the accounting rules are the same.

An **external investment pool** is created when the assets of more than one legally separate entity are commingled for investment purposes. External investment pools can be sponsored by an individual government, jointly by several governments, or by a nongovernmental entity such as a bank. Often, external investment pools are created and managed by a larger governmental unit such as a state or county (the sponsoring government) to put its own excess cash into an investment pool with the excess cash of other smaller governments. The internal portion of the external pool consists of funds belonging to the sponsoring government and its component units and is reported as Equity in Pooled Cash and Investments in each of the participating funds. The external portion of the investment pool consists of the funds belonging to the legally separate entities. The sponsoring government will report the external portion of the pool assets in the fiduciary category of funds as an Investment trust fund. The governmental unit has a fiduciary responsibility over cash entrusted to it by other governmental units. External investment pools have different investment valuation rules than internal pools and other investment assets of governments. If the external investment pool is not considered 2a7-like, all investments of the pool should be reported at fair value except for investments in nonparticipating investment contracts. There is an exception for securities that mature in 90 days or less *from the valuation date*. These securities *may* be reported at amortized cost. The pool can take the fair value of a security 90 days from its maturity date and amortize the difference between the fair value and the maturity value on a straight-line basis over the remaining 90-day life of the security. Remember, the valuation rules for external investment pools pertain to both the internal and external portions of the pool. External investment pools issue separate financial statements including a Statement of Fiduciary Net Assets and a Statement of Changes in Fiduciary Net Assets prepared on the economic resources

---

[11]GASB Statement No. 31, paragraphs 16–19.

measurement focus and accrual basis method of accounting. The financial statements will include the fair value, carrying value (book value) and number of shares or original cost, interest rates, and maturities for each major investment classification.

As an example, a county sponsors an investment pool that includes $10,000,000 that belongs to the county's General fund, $2,000,000 that has been invested by City A and $1,000,000 invested by City B. The county would record the $13,000,000 in investments in the investment pool as follows:

The county General fund would record:

Equity in Pooled Cash and Investments	10,000,000	
Cash		10,000,000

The county would establish an Investment trust fund for the external portion of the investment pool and record:

Cash and Investments	3,000,000	
Deposits in Investment Pool—		
City A (liability account)		2,000,000
Deposits in Investment Pool—City B		1,000,000

Since the Investment trust fund only records the external portion of the assets in the investment pool, the county would maintain a separate ledger that includes both internal and external participants in the pool. The separate ledger would record the investment by the county's General fund as:

Cash and Investments	10,000,000	
Due to General Fund		10,000,000

The use of a separate consolidated ledger for the internal and external portions of an investment pool would assist in the allocation of investment income, since the funds in a pool are comingled.

Individual investment accounts.[12]   Sometimes larger governmental units such as counties or states will manage the investments of other legally separate entities in a separate non-pooled portfolio that the GASB refers to as an **individual investment account.** The governmental unit managing an individual investment account would report the investments in the individual investment account in a separate Investment trust fund and value the securities in the trust fund in the same manner as other investments of the entity (not like an external investment pool). For example, if a county elects to report money market type investments that have a remaining maturity at the time of purchase of one year or less on the amortized cost method, the county would report assets invested for another city in an individual investment account on the same basis. This method of accounting for money market type investments would not be permitted for investment in the county's external investment pool.

Receivables.   Governments set up accounts receivable for funds that are recognizable as due to the entity, but have not been received. Common types of receivables

---

[12]Ibid, paragraph 20.

include taxes receivable, billings for services, and grants receivable. An Accounts Receivable asset account is frequently offset by a contra account, Allowance for Uncollectible Receivables, if the anticipated uncollectible amount is significant. Chapter 3 explained exchange and nonexchange transactions and when to recognize assets in the transactions. In an exchange transaction, a receivable is generally set up when the underlying exchange transaction occurs. For nonexchange transactions, a receivable is recognized as follows: derived tax revenues—when the underlying exchange has occurred; imposed nonexchange revenues—when an enforceable claim has arisen; and government mandated nonexchange transactions and voluntary nonexchange transactions—when all eligibility requirements have been met. A very common receivable account would be Property Taxes Receivable—Current for the amount of the tax levied. Property tax transactions are illustrated in detail in Chapter 3. Governments might also have amounts receivable for a State or Federal grant that would be shown as a State Grant Receivable or Federal Grant Receivable. In most cases, a grant receivable would be recorded at the time the grant is awarded. In governmental funds, the receivable would be recognized only if the grant will be available in the current fiscal period. For example, a city is notified by the Federal government that a $1,000,000 grant for recreation programs has been awarded for use during the current fiscal year. This $1,000,000 grant would be recorded in a Special revenue fund as follows:

Federal Grant Receivable	1,000,000	
Federal Grant Revenue		1,000,000

When the $1,000,000 is paid to the city, the following transaction will be recorded:

Cash	1,000,000	
Federal Grant Receivable		1,000,000

Due from other funds. Amounts due from other funds are a different type of receivable and are recorded as Due from Other Funds. For example, the General fund loans a Capital project fund $500,000 to hire an architect to do the design and blueprints for construction of a fire station. The Capital project fund will repay the General fund when it sells long-term bonds for the building later in the fiscal year. The loan of $500,000 will be recorded in the General fund as follows:

Due from Capital Projects Fund	500,000	
Cash		500,000

The loan of $500,000 will be recorded as a current liability in the Capital projects fund as follows:

Cash	500,000	
Due to General Fund		500,000

Inventories.[13] Governmental funds may record inventory as an expenditure when purchased (**purchase method**) or create an inventory asset account and then charge

---

[13]NCGA Statement No. 1, paragraph 73.

only the items used during the fiscal period to expenditures (**consumption method**). If a government purchases $10,000 in office supplies for operating purposes and charges the supplies directly to expenditures (purchase method), the journal entry would appear as follows:

Office Supplies Expenditure	10,000	
Cash (or Vouchers Payable)		10,000

If a government purchases $10,000 in office supplies but chooses to create an inventory account and charge them to expenditures when they are used and $5,000 worth is used during the fiscal year, the entries would appear as follows:

Office Supplies Inventory	10,000	
Cash (or Vouchers Payable)		10,000
Office Supplies Expenditure	5,000	
Office Supplies Inventory		5,000

Compare the two methods above. In one case, $10,000 is immediately charged to expenditures in the current budget, and in the other case only $5,000 is charged. Clearly, governmental funds have flowed out to purchase $10,000 in supplies, which supports charging $10,000 to expenditures, yet only $5,000 of these supplies have been consumed during the period, which supports charging only $5,000 to expenditures. Which method is correct? Either method may be used by the government. If the purchase method is used and there are significant inventories on hand at the fiscal year-end, GASB requires the remaining inventory to be reported as an asset offset by a reserve in the equity section (Fund Balance—Reserved for Inventories) on the balance sheet. Proprietary funds would report all inventories of consumable materials and supplies as an asset when purchased. As the inventory is used, the asset account would be reduced and an operating expense would be recognized.

Prepaids.   Governments sometimes pay for insurance premiums, lease payments, and other services in advance. For example, a government may pay an annual premium for liability insurance or for a service contract on equipment. Prepaids for governmental funds can be recorded using the purchase method or the consumption method as illustrated above for inventories. Although this is similar to accounting for inventories, if the purchase method is used and significant amounts of prepaids remain unused at the fiscal year-end, they are not required to be reported as assets and will not have a reservation of fund balance established.

Noncurrent assets

Noncurrent is another way of labeling long-term assets unlikely to be consumed or used up within the current operating or fiscal period. A government would account for noncurrent assets that may be available to benefit future periods in this category. Noncurrent assets include capital assets, and restricted cash and investments. Because governmental funds use the modified accrual basis of accounting, noncurrent assets are not recorded within the funds, but are reported in the governmental activities column of the government-wide financial statements.

Restricted assets.[14]   Governmental assets such as cash and investments can be temporarily or permanently restricted. Assets that have restrictions on their use imposed by outside parties or by legal provisions are segregated in the financial statements. This is because the assets are not available to support general operations of the governmental unit. When cash is received for a grant with purpose restrictions that have not been met, the cash would be a temporarily restricted asset. Restrictions are often placed on funds associated with revenue bonds issued by proprietary funds where cash and investments would be restricted to pay debt principal and interest. If the restrictions placed on the assets are self-imposed by the governmental unit, such as setting funds aside for a special purpose, the assets would not be restricted for reporting purposes.

Capital assets.[15]   Assets that have a useful life of more than one fiscal year are generally capitalized rather than charged to an expenditure or expense. If an asset is capitalized, it becomes a long-term or noncurrent asset and the cost of the asset is generally charged to depreciation expense over the useful life of the asset. There are some exceptions to depreciating capital assets that will be covered later in this section. General capital assets associated with governmental fund activities are not reported as assets within the funds, however they are reported in the governmental activities column of the government-wide Statement of Net Assets, which will be explained in Chapter 5. This requires the governmental entity to maintain a subsidiary ledger of general governmental capital assets. Proprietary and fiduciary funds record all capital assets and related depreciation expense within the funds.

For purposes of governmental accounting, capital assets include land and certain improvements and easements associated with the land, infrastructure, buildings and building improvements, works of art and historical treasures, vehicles and equipment, and all other tangible or intangible assets that are used in operations. **Land improvements** include fill, grading and retaining walls, the installation of utilities, the removal or relocation of property on the land, parking lots and fencing constructed on the land, and landscaping.

Infrastructure includes capital assets that are stationary and longer lived than most other capital assets. Common infrastructure assets include roads, street lighting, water and sewer systems, dams, bridges, tunnels, and drainage systems. For purposes of accounting for infrastructure, the GASB further categorizes infrastructure into **networks of assets** and **subsystems of networks.** All of the assets that provide a particular type of service for a government can be categorized as a network of assets. A network of assets can be classified into separate subsystems that include all assets that make up a similar portion or segment of the network. For example, all of the capital assets that comprise a city's water system could be classified as an infrastructure network of assets. Separate subsystems of the water system might include water filtration plants, water mains, and water meters.

GASB Statement No. 34 requires governments to report and capitalize major general infrastructure assets.[16] Major infrastructure assets are based upon the following criteria:

---

[14]GASB Statement No. 34, paragraph 99.
[15]Ibid, paragraphs 18–26 and *IMPLEMENTATIONS GUIDE, Guide to Implementation of GASB Statement 34 on Basic Financial Statements—and Management's Discussion and Analysis—for State and Local Governments, Questions and Answers* numbers 25–80.
[16]GASB Statement No. 34, paragraphs 154–160.

1) Cost or estimated cost of a *subsystem* is at least 5% of the total of all general capital assets; or
2) Cost or estimated cost of a *network* is expected to be at least 10% of the total of all general capital assets

Reporting of any nonmajor networks or subsystems is welcomed and encouraged but not required by GASB Statement No. 34.

Networks and subsystems of infrastructure assets

The terrorist attacks in New York City on September 11, 2001 resulted in the collapse of the twin towers of the World Trade Center. The City of New York suffered considerable damage to the infrastructure surrounding the site of the tragedy including the New York City subway system. The damaged subway tunnels and stations near the disaster site will have to be completely rebuilt. The City of New York subway system would qualify to be recorded as an infrastructure network of assets. The sections of the subway system near the World Trade Center that were significantly damaged would qualify as a subsystem of the network of assets.

Construction-in-progress is also a capital asset. An example of construction-in-progress would be a partially constructed parking garage for an Enterprise fund. The entity would capitalize the partially constructed asset as a capital asset called Construction in Progress. For example, if an Enterprise fund entered into a contract for the construction of a $5,000,000 parking garage, the contractor had billed the fund for $2,500,000 for completed portions of the project, and there is a 10% retainage, the entry would be recorded as follows:

Construction-in-Progress	2,500,000	
Contracts Payable		2,250,000
Contracts Payable—Retainage		250,000

Governmental funds and governmental activities should not capitalize construction period interest,[17] but proprietary funds and business-type activities should capitalize construction period interest related to capital assets in accordance with the provisions of FASB Statement No. 34, *Capitalization of Interest Cost* and FASB Statement No. 62, *Capitalization of Interest Cost in Situations Involving Certain Tax-Exempt Borrowings and Certain Gifts and Grants.*[18] This follows the business-type activity concept of matching the depreciation expense of all related costs of an asset over the period of time the asset will generate revenues. Construction period interest is not capitalized for capital assets used in governmental activities because this would be contradictory to the GASB Statement No. 34 requirement that interest is an indirect expense and should not be allocated to functions or programs.

Capitalizing assets. Is a governmental purchase an expense or expenditure or does it create a capital asset? GASB standards permit governments to set their own limits

---

[17]GASB Statement No. 37, *Basic Financial Statements—and Management's Discussion and Analysis—for State and Local Government's Omnibus,* paragraphs 6–7, 30–35.
[18]GASB *Guide to Implementation of GASB Statement No. 34,* question 31.

for determining what should be capitalized (capitalization threshold). The GFOA recommends that capitalization thresholds should not be less than $5,000.[19]

Example transactions are given below:

A city purchases a $50 copy of the *GASB Codification* for the Chief Financial Officer (CFO). This purchase would be charged to expenditures in the General fund as follows:

Training Materials Expenditure		50
Cash	50	

The city library purchases $10,000 of new books, which are expected to be used for 10 years. The city library would capitalize the new books as a capital asset and depreciate them over a 10-year useful life in the government-wide statements. The purchase would be recorded in the General fund as follows:

Expenditure	10,000	
Cash		10,000

The purchase and annual depreciation expenditure would be reflected in the government-wide statements through reconciling adjustments as follows:

Library Books (Asset)	10,000	
Library Books Expenditure		10,000
Depreciation Expense	1,000	
Accumulated Depreciation—Library Books		1,000

The library books can be depreciated using a composite method due to the small values of each individual book. The Library Books asset account will be reported in the government-wide Statement of Net Assets as $9,000, which is the amount of the asset net of accumulated depreciation ($10,000 Library Books—Accumulated Depreciation —Library Books of $1,000). Why are the library books capitalized? They are a material item that represents a capital asset of the library that is expected to depreciate over time in the primary course of business of the library. Why is the CFO's *GASB Codification* purchase of $50 expensed? It is a de minimus amount and represents a routine expense such as training materials. These simple examples show how general government purchases of books are charged to expenditure in both cases and capitalized in the government-wide statements in only one case that exceeds the capitalization threshold of $5,000.

Let's try another book example: a donor gives the city library a collection of rare books that have a fair market value of $1,000,000. The library accepts the donation of rare books, which has a condition that the books will be permanently retained and protected by the library and cannot be sold. (Refer to Chapter 3, **Donations of works of art or historical treasures**). If the library decides the donated rare books are works of art or historical treasures, it can decide not to capitalize the donation. In that case, the library would record a donation and an equal amount of expenditure in the General fund as follows:

Rare Book Expenditure	1,000,000	
Other Financing Source—Donations		1,000,000

---

[19]GFOA Recommended Practice "Establishing Appropriate Capitalization Thresholds for Capital Assets."

This provides accountability for the donation to show that $1,000,000 in fair market value of rare books was received by the government. Expenditures are recorded as if the books were purchased and the Other Financing Source—Donations account is used to show the source of revenue for the rare books; in this case, a donation. If the library chooses to capitalize the rare book donation instead, it would be reflected in the government-wide financial report as a capital asset:

Rare Book Collection (Asset)	1,000,000	
Miscellaneous Revenue		1,000,000

Governments are encouraged to capitalize such collections, but it is not required. Works of art or historical treasures that are capitalized do not have to be depreciated in most cases. This is because works of art and historical treasures often appreciate in value over time. However, if the works of art and historical treasures are clearly "exhaustible" assets that have a definite useful life, they then should be depreciated.

These simple examples show completely different treatments for the purchase or acquisition of simple assets—books. In the first case where one copy of a reference book, the *GASB Codification* is purchased for the Chief Financial Officer, the book purchase is charged to expenditures. In the second case where the library purchases $10,000 in books with an estimated useful life of 10 years, they are charged to expenditures in the General fund but in the government-wide statements they are capitalized and depreciated. The net asset value at the end of one year would be $9,000. In the third case, the donation of rare books, which are considered works of art or historical treasures, the books can be capitalized or not, but in either case would not be depreciated in the government-wide statements.

Proprietary funds use accrual accounting and capitalize assets and record depreciation within the proprietary funds. Governmental funds do not capitalize assets and do not record depreciation within the governmental funds. However, an adjustment must be made for governmental fund capital assets and related depreciation to create the government-wide statements. Chapter 5 explains these adjustments for capital assets in detail.

Valuation of capital assets. Capital assets are reported at historical cost, the cost at which they were originally acquired plus any ancillary charges such as shipping or installation. Additions to capital assets and improvements that extend the useful life of an asset should be capitalized. Normal repairs and maintenance should be treated as an expense or expenditure. If capital assets are donated, they should be recorded at their fair market value plus any additional ancillary charges at the time of donation. An example of an additional charge would be the cost of transport of a donated capital asset. This transportation charge would be added to the fair market value to obtain the total amount to capitalize for the donated asset. If records about the historical cost are not available, a reasonable estimate of cost should be made.

Depreciation of assets. Governments can use any established depreciation method[20] to depreciate capital assets. Generally, the cost of a capital asset (less any anticipated residual value) is recognized over the estimated useful life of the asset. For example, if an Enterprise fund purchased equipment for $49,000 and the shipping and installation costs were $1,000 the transaction would be recorded as follows:

---

[20]Straight-line, sum-of-the-years-digits, double-declining balance, units-of-productions method, etc.

Equipment	50,000	
Cash (or Accounts Payable)		50,000

If the equipment in the example above had an estimated life of 10 years and no anticipated residual value, the entry to record depreciation for one full year, using the straight-line method, would be as follows:

Depreciation Expense	5,000	
Accumulated Depreciation—Equipment		5,000

Rather than calculate depreciation for each capital asset individually, GASB standards permit governments to utilize composite depreciation and group depreciation methods. **Composite depreciation** establishes an annual depreciation rate for a collection of dissimilar assets, such as all assets in a city's water system. **Group depreciation** establishes an annual depreciation rate for a collection of similar assets, such as all water mains. Capital assets are generally reported net of accumulated depreciation.

Inexhaustible capital assets. **Inexhaustible capital assets** are assets that are expected to have an extraordinarily long life, and they are not depreciated. Land and land improvements such as grading and fill that produce permanent benefits to the land are considered inexhaustible capital assets. Some works of art and historical treasures may also be considered inexhaustible capital assets if their useful lives are exceptionally long or their perpetual preservation is anticipated.

Modified approach for reporting infrastructure.[21] Governments are not required to depreciate infrastructure assets that are part of a network or a subsystem of a network if the entity meets the requirements of the **modified approach** to reporting infrastructure. A government can decide to depreciate one infrastructure network of capital assets and to use the modified approach with another infrastructure network of capital assets. It is not necessary to use the modified approach for all infrastructure networks and subsystems of networks. The modified approach requires the government to maintain the following:

1) An asset management system with the following characteristics:
   a. up-to-date inventory of eligible infrastructure assets
   b. condition assessments of the eligible infrastructure assets and a summary using a measurement scale
   c. annual estimate of the annual amount of funding needed to maintain and preserve infrastructure assets at the condition level established and disclosed by the government
2) Documentation that the eligible infrastructure assets are being preserved at the approximate level or above that the government has established and disclosed. This documentation must:
   a. include a complete condition assessment of eligible infrastructure at least every three years
   b. include results of the three most recent complete condition assessments that show the assets are being maintained at the established condition level.

---

[21]GASB Statement No. 34, paragraphs 23–26.

If the government fails to document the condition assessment, fails to perform the condition assessment, or fails to maintain the infrastructure assets at or above the condition level specified by the government, it may no longer use the modified approach.

The concept behind the modified approach is simple. If a government does not wish to record depreciation on infrastructure, it must then properly assess and maintain the condition of those infrastructure assets at or above an acceptable level established by the governmental unit. This is to prevent postponement of large liabilities for renovation and replacement of infrastructure without adequate disclosure in the financial statement. Another simple way to explain this is that the financial report should warn the public citizenry that infrastructure is not being maintained at or above an acceptable level so that a key bridge uniting the community would not be allowed to deteriorate because of undisclosed deferred maintenance.

Under the modified approach, maintenance and preservation costs are expensed in the period in which they are incurred. However, if the government chooses to depreciate the infrastructure assets, **maintenance costs** will be expensed but **preservation costs** will be capitalized. In either method, any additions and improvements will be capitalized. What is the difference between maintenance and preservation costs? Maintenance costs enable an asset to be utilized during its useful life, but preservation costs extend the useful life of the asset.

If the government capitalizes infrastructure assets, it can choose between recording depreciation expense or utilizing the modified approach for eligible assets that constitute a network or subsystem of infrastructure assets. A government can elect to depreciate one network of infrastructure assets and use the modified approach for another network. If parts of a network or subsystem of infrastructure assets are reported in more than one fund, each part must use the same method.

If a governmental unit changes to the modified approach from recording depreciation expenditure or expense, then this change should be reported as a change in accounting estimate and does not require a restatement of prior periods.[22] During the transition period for implementation of the infrastructure capital asset reporting requirements of GASB 34, governments should disclose in the financial report:

1) Description of the infrastructure assets that are and are not being reported, and
2) Description of eligible infrastructure assets that will be reported on the modified approach.

Governments can begin to report using the modified approach for eligible infrastructure assets as soon as one condition assessment is complete and it documents that the assets are being preserved at or above the condition level established by the governmental unit.

LIABILITIES

Liabilities are comprised of two primary categories: current and noncurrent. The typical **current liabilities** seen on the governmental balance sheet would include accounts payable, vouchers payable, tax anticipation notes payable, and amounts due to other funds. **Noncurrent or long-term liabilities** include long-term bonds, pensions, and capital lease payables. Some liabilities such as compensated absences, claims

---

[22]GASB Statement No. 37, paragraphs 8–9.

and judgments, and bonds, notes, and loans payable can appear as both a current and noncurrent liability.

Current liabilities

Liabilities are classified as current if they are expected to be paid or liquidated with current assets within 12 months. Current liabilities can also be paid by the creation of other current liabilities such as issuing a tax anticipation note.

Accounts payable. An accounts payable is created when a government recognizes an expense or expenditure but has not yet paid the supplier of the goods or services. A typical example of an accounts payable being created and then liquidated when the amount due is paid is shown below:

Expenditures	20,000	
Accounts Payable		20,000
Accounts Payable	20,000	
Cash		20,000

Many governmental units now permit authorized employees to charge operating expenditures to a credit card. This use of credit cards can streamline the purchasing process yet exposes the government to risk of loss if the credit card is used for non-governmental (personal) purchases. Authorized charges on credit cards are a current liability of the government, however, in practice if the charges are paid on or before the due date of the billing, an accounts payable liability is not set up.

Vouchers payable. A voucher is a form that is processed (often electronically) to authorize payment of an invoice from a vendor for goods or services provided to the governmental unit or to reimburse an employee for travel or other expenditures incurred on behalf of the government. When an invoice is received, a vouchers payable is recorded to reflect the current liability to the vendor or employee. For example, a city employee incurs travel expenses while conducting governmental business and submits a $352 travel voucher for those expenditures. The following journal entries illustrate the transaction to record the receipt of the voucher and the subsequent payment after the voucher is processed and approved.

Travel Expenditures	352	
Vouchers Payable		352
Vouchers Payable	352	
Cash		352

Contracts payable. Contracts are generally issued by competitive bid and are common for construction projects or the recurring purchase of goods or services. A contracts payable liability would be set up when the government recognizes the expense or expenditure. In major construction projects, it is common for a government to retain a percentage of payments until the project is completed and passes all inspections. This retained percentage would be recorded in an account called Contracts Payable—Retained Percentage. For example, a city awards a contract for $2,000,000 to construct a neighborhood police station and the contractor submits an invoice for construction completed prior to fiscal year-end in the amount of $1,000,000 (the amount to be retained under contract is 10%). The following journal entries reflect these events:

Encumbrances	2,000,000	
Budgetary Fund Balance Reserved for Encumbrances		2,000,000
Budgetary Fund Balance Reserved for Encumbrances	1,000,000	
Encumbrances		1,000,000
Construction Expenditures	1,000,000	
Contracts Payable		900,000
Contracts Payable—Retained Percentage		100,000

Tax anticipation notes payable.[23]   Tax anticipation notes (TANs) are issued in anticipation of the receipt of tax revenues, and the notes are repaid after the taxes are collected. For example, a governmental unit such as a school district may need to borrow cash short-term to pay current expenditures if revenues are not received until later in the fiscal year. Many school districts incur large expenditures for teacher payrolls and other operating expenditures when school begins in the fall. However, the school district will not receive the property tax payments until January when the annual property tax bills are due. Therefore, the school district must borrow cash to operate in the fall in anticipation of the property taxes it can expect to receive in January when winter tax bills are paid. In fact, many states permit schools to collect property taxes twice a year in the summer and winter to alleviate the need to borrow and incur interest costs. A tax anticipation note is a current liability because the tax note will be repaid within the current fiscal period when the taxes are received. The journal entry to record the school district borrowing $5,000,000 for 4 months would be recorded as follows:

Cash	5,000,000	
Tax Anticipation Note Payable		5,000,000

When the tax anticipation note is repaid, there will be an interest expenditure due as well to pay the lender for the use of the funds for this period.

Revenue anticipation notes payable.[24]   Occasionally, governmental units issue short-term notes in anticipation of the receipt of revenues other than taxes. Like tax anticipation notes, the revenue anticipation notes (RANs) are repaid during the fiscal year when the revenue is received. Like a TAN, a current liability would be recorded when the revenue anticipation notes are issued.

City of New York issues $1 billion revenue anticipation notes

The City of New York will issue $1 billion in short-term notes to provide cash to pay clean-up costs from the terrorist attacks that destroyed the World Trade Center twin towers. The $1 billion in notes is being issued in anticipation of federal aid. If the City does not receive the federal aid within a year, it will have to refinance the notes with long-term bonds.

Source: *"City to Sell Debt as It Waits for Promised Federal Billions," The New York Times,* September 29, 2001, page B9.

---

[23]NCGA Interpretation 9, *Certain Fund Classifications and Balance Sheet Accounts.*
[24]*Ibid.*

Matured bonds and interest payable.   Governmental type funds, which include Debt service funds, generally recognize an expenditure and a liability for principal and interest payments on bonds when the payment becomes due. A governmental entity will contract with a fiscal agent to keep track of the bondholders and to distribute the principal and interest payments. The entry to record the transfer of cash to the fiscal agent for $2,000,000 of principal payments and $500,000 of interest payments due would be:

Cash with Fiscal Agent	2,500,000	
Cash		2,500,000
Debt Service Principal Expenditure	2,000,000	
Debt Service Interest Expenditure	500,000	
Matured Bonds Payable		2,000,000
Matured Interest Payable		500,000

When the paying agent makes payments to the bondholders, the entry would be:

Matured Bonds Payable	2,000,000	
Matured Interest Payable	500,000	
Cash with Fiscal Agent		2,500,000

If the same transaction was recorded in an Enterprise fund, a nonoperating interest expense account would be debited for the amount of the interest due and the long-term liability account Bonds Payable would be debited (reduced) by the amount of the principal payment. Otherwise, the entries would be the same.

Accrued interest payable.   An accrued interest payable liability is recorded at fiscal year-end in the proprietary funds to recognize the amount of interest expense accrued on outstanding bonds. This represents an accrual of a portion of the next interest payment and is recorded because proprietary funds use the accrual method of accounting. An accrual is not set up for principal payments on bonds.

Deferred revenue and unearned revenue.   A liability, deferred revenue, is set up to record revenue that has been received but does not meet the criteria for revenue recognition. Deferred revenue can include both unearned revenue and unavailable revenue. **Unearned revenue** is generally associated with nonexchange transactions where either a time or purpose restriction has not been met. **Unavailable revenue** is associated with the modified accrual basis of accounting where a revenue may have been earned, but is not available to finance expenditures of the current fiscal period.

Amounts due to other funds.   Funds can borrow money from each other. An example of an interfund borrowing is illustrated in the Due from Other Funds section earlier in this chapter where the Capital projects fund borrows cash from the General fund. The Capital projects fund would have an account Due to General Fund as a current liability account until it pays the General fund.

   A governmental entity that collects property taxes on behalf of its own General fund and for other governmental units would use an Agency fund to record the levy, collection, and distribution of taxes. The Agency fund would record the amounts due to other funds and due to other governmental units. For example, a county would record the levy, collection, and distribution of taxes as follows:

Property Taxes Receivable	5,000,000	
Due to General Fund (of county)		3,000,000
Due to School District		1,000,000
Due to City		1,000,000
Cash	5,000,000	
Property Taxes Receivable		5,000,000
Due to General Fund	3,000,000	
Due to School District	1,000,000	
Due to City	1,000,000	
Cash		5,000,000

As you will learn in Chapter 5, if the Agency fund had a balance at fiscal year-end, the amounts due internally to the General fund would have to be eliminated (netted) and only the amounts reflecting the fiduciary responsibility for assets of others would be included in the financial report.

Noncurrent liabilities

Noncurrent liabilities are long-term liabilities that are not expected to be paid or liquidated within the current fiscal year. Examples of these liabilities would include the remaining principal outstanding on long-term debt, net pension obligations, and the noncurrent portion of liabilities for compensated absences, claims and judgments, and landfill closure and post-closure costs. Governmental funds do not record liabilities that are not expected to be paid with current financial resources. Long-term liabilities associated with governmental funds would, however, be reported on the government-wide Statement of Net Assets.

Bonds payable.   Long-term bonds are often issued by governmental units to pay for capital projects or assets. Bonds enable the government to pay for the cost of a large capital improvement or asset over a longer period of time. The cost of capital (borrowing) is generally low due to the federal tax-exempt status of long-term bonds issued by state or local governmental units. In addition, most states that have income taxes also exempt from tax the interest bondholders receive from that state's bonds or bonds issued by a municipality or other governmental entity located within that state. Basically, governmental units often pay 2% or more less for interest on long-term capital than a similar corporate entity would pay to borrow such funds. If a corporation is paying 8% to borrow, a governmental unit may be able to borrow tax-exempt at 6%.

Bonds are generally "priced" near the time of issuance in the competitive market for municipal bonds. The pricing results in a range of interest rates (or yields to the bondholders) depending upon the maturity of the individual bond within the bond offering. For example, the short bonds that will have the principal amount paid off within the first 5–10 years will usually have a different interest rate (or yield to the bondholder) than the long bonds that extend to 20–30 years maturity .

The journal entry to record issuance of general obligation bonds payable by the governmental funds follows:

Cash	50,000,000	
Other Financing Source—Bond Proceeds		50,000,000

The amount of bonds payable from governmental funds is maintained on a subsidiary ledger and will be reported only in the government-wide financial statements.

A long-term liability Bonds Payable is used to record proprietary fund debt. In order to be classified as proprietary fund debt, the debt must be directly related to the fund and the debt must be repaid from the proprietary fund resources. Proprietary funds often issue revenue bonds that pledge future revenue streams for the repayment of debt to finance capital projects. The journal entry to record the issuance of $10 million of Enterprise fund debt with $100,000 of issuance cost would be:

Cash	9,900,000	
Bond Issuance Cost	100,000	
Bonds Payable		10,000,000

Term bonds are a type of bond that has the entire principal of the issue due at the end of a certain period of time. They are uncommon in practice. It would be similar to a 15-year home mortgage that only required annual interest to be paid and then demanded the entire principal amount at the end of the 15 years. Governmental units usually seek to smooth debt service to an equal and level amount across years and often may have legal restrictions that prevent them from issuing term bonds. Term bonds would be a noncurrent liability as the principal is not due until the completion of the specified term.

Serial bonds have equal amounts of bond principal due each year. For example, a $30,000,000 30-year long-term serial bond issue would have $1,000,000 of principal due each year. The interesting aspect of this is that it would not result in level debt service (that is, the combined interest and principal due each year would not be equal because the amount of interest due each year would change as the outstanding principal is paid down). In practice, governments generally "size" the bond issue. Sizing means the underwriter (investment banker or financial institution hired by the governmental entity to market the bonds) will adjust the amounts of bond principal and interest due for each year of the issue to achieve a level debt service (equal amount of principal and interest due each year) and to meet market demand for the bonds. In fact, a governmental unit may size a new bond issue to achieve and maintain a level (or equal) amount of debt service each year for all of its outstanding long-term debt portfolio. This is simply prudent fiscal and budgetary management.

Conduit debt obligations[25] exist when a governmental unit issues debt for a third party that is not part of the issuer's financial reporting entity. The governmental unit does not have to account for this conduit debt as its repayment is the obligation of a third party. However, it must provide footnote disclosure of the nature and amount of the conduit debt obligation. An example would be where a Downtown Development Authority wants to issue bonds for a new convention center. The city is authorized to issue the debt on behalf of the Downtown Development Authority but is not obligated in any manner to repay the bonds. The project (which has a public purpose) has a lower cost-of-capital as a tax-exempt bond issue. The city, however, must disclose the bonds issued but is not required to account for them as a liability. The city is just a conduit to issue the debt for another entity.

Debt refundings.[26]   Sometimes it is advantageous for governments to refund existing long-term debt by issuing new debt. In a **refunding,** the new debt proceeds are

---

[25]GASB Interpretation No. 1, *Disclosure of Conduit Debt Obligations.*
[26]GASB Statement No. 7, *Advance Refundings Resulting in Defeasance of Debt.*

used to repay the old debt. If the proceeds are used to immediately repay or refund the bondholders' principal in advance of the maturity date, it is considered a **current refunding.** The ability to refund long-term debt prior to maturity requires a "call" provision in the bond. Purchasers of municipal bonds with a call feature generally demand additional interest (or basis points) for a government to have the right to recall or refund the debt obligation. As a result, many governments do not issue debt with the ability to call it in and refund it.

In an **advance refunding** of long-term debt, the new debt proceeds are irrevocably set aside (often with an escrow agent) to repay the old bond issue principal and interest as it comes due. The most common reason for an advance refunding would be to lower the interest rate (and interest cost) on the outstanding debt because interest rates have fallen. The savings can be substantial on a large long-term bond issue. Another reason to advance refund might be to get rid of legal restrictions (covenants) of a bond issue or to change the maturity structure of the debt. **Defeasance** is a term that means repayment of debt. **In-substance defeasance** means that the governmental unit has not repaid the long-term debt but has legally satisfied this obligation by irrevocably setting aside monies in trust to repay principal and interest obligations as they come due under the old debt covenants (legal agreements).

If the government has arranged an in-substance defeasance of long-term debt in an advance refunding, the old debt should be removed from noncurrent liabilities. The new debt issued should be reported as a noncurrent liability. The journal entry to report the issuance of the new debt for a governmental fund is reported in the fund receiving the money as follows:

Cash	50,000,000	
Other Financing Source—		
Proceeds of Refundings Bonds		50,000,000

The portion of the new debt used for removal of the old debt that has met the criteria for an in-substance defeasance would then be recorded as follows:

Other Financing Use—Payments to		
Refunded Bond Escrow Agent	20,000,000	
Cash		20,000,000

Footnote disclosure of the in-substance defeasance is required as well as the **economic gain or loss** on the advance refunding. The computation of economic gain or loss is intended to determine that the future stream of principal and interest payments on the new debt does not exceed the stream of principal and interest payments required to satisfy the old debt. In other words, a present value savings was achieved by this advance refunding that saves the citizens money on debt service.

Special assessment debt.[27] **Capital improvement-type special assessments** assess property holders for capital improvements to their property. The government issues long-term debt to finance the project, completes the capital project, and services the long-term debt with annual assessments collected from the benefiting property owners. The annual levy of the special assessment and the debt service payment would be

---

[27]GASB Statement No. 6, *Accounting and Financial Reporting for Special Assessments.*

recorded for in the Debt service fund. The long-term debt should be reported as a noncurrent liability of the governmental unit on the government-wide financial statements if the entity is **obligated in some manner,** as follows:

1) Obligated to pay deficiencies if lien foreclosure is not sufficient
2) Required to establish a reserve, sinking fund, or guarantee
3) Required to cover delinquencies until foreclosure proceeds are received
4) Government must purchase properties sold for nonpayment of assessments
5) Government is authorized, but not required, to establish a reserve, sinking fund, or guarantee and does so
6) Government may establish separate fund to redeem special assessment debt and it does so
7) Government states it may cover delinquencies even though not obligated legally
8) Legal decisions make it probable the government would be held responsible

Service-type special assessments assess recipients of specific services such as snow plowing and garbage collection and should be recorded in the fund that would normally provide that service (often the General fund). Service-type special assessments generally do not incur related special assessment debt, and they are not recorded as a liability.

Pensions.[28] There are two common types of pension plans: defined benefit and defined contribution plans. A **defined benefit plan** specifies the benefit that will be paid to the retiree based upon years of service and salary. Defined benefit plans may also provide other types of postemployment benefits such as disability benefits, life insurance, and healthcare. Annual contributions are made to fund defined benefit plans based upon actuarial assumptions as to the amount needed to fund the future benefit. A defined benefit plan will create a current liability for the current required contribution and a noncurrent liability Net Pension Obligation (NPO) for the amount required and not yet funded to meet future obligations. A **defined contribution** plan specifies the amount that the employer must annually contribute to the pension plan for each employee. A defined contribution plan could create a current liability for a required contribution that will be paid in the current fiscal year. For many years, defined benefit plans were the most common form of pensions, however, governmental units are beginning to shift to defined contribution plans to limit their financial responsibility for future pensions and help ensure current funding meets the appropriate level. Extensive disclosures about pension plans are required in the annual financial report.

Postemployment healthcare benefits[29] include medical, dental, vision and other health-related benefits. They can be provided as part of a defined benefit plan or through a separate plan. Like a pension plan, a current liability is created for the required current year contribution and a noncurrent liability is created for the amount required and not yet funded to meet future obligations. Separate reporting and note disclosure is required for postemployment healthcare benefits that are provided through a defined benefit plan so that plan assets can be attributed to the portion of the plan providing the specific type of benefit.

---

[28]GASB Statement No. 27, *Accounting for Pensions by State and Local Governmental Employers.*
[29]GASB Statement No. 26, *Financial Reporting for Postemployment Healthcare Plan Administered by a Defined Benefit Pension Plan.*

Capital lease payable[30] is the long-term capital lease obligation due for capital assets acquired under a capital lease agreement. There are two types of leases: capital and operating leases. In Chapter 1, the hierarchy of GAAP was explained. The GASB has adopted the criteria of FASB Statement No. 13 on leases to determine if the lease is an operating or a capital lease and to provide guidance on the valuation of the lease. **Operating leases** are short-term arrangements to use the equipment or asset. They are charged to expenditures and do not create a capital asset. If a current amount is due on an operating lease, it would be shown as a current liability. **Capital leases** provide ownership of or the option to purchase the asset at the end of the term of the lease and do create a capital asset and a noncurrent liability for the long-term capital lease payable. For accounting purposes, a capital lease is treated the same as if debt were issued to purchase the asset.

Capital leases are popular among governments for two reasons: 1) a capital lease can provide current technology that is frequently replaced rather than purchasing a capital asset, and 2) it increases spending authority in the current budget. A purchase of a capital asset will be fully charged to the current budget as an expenditure. A capital lease will only charge a fraction of the total cost to the current budget as an expenditure. The difference between the total cost of purchasing the capital asset and the capital asset lease payment is *available* to be spent in the current period.

For example, a city enters into an $80,000 capital lease for equipment that requires a $20,000 down payment. The capital lease would be recorded in the General fund as follows:

Equipment Expenditure	80,000	
Other Financing Source—Capital Lease		80,000
Debt Service Principal Expenditure	20,000	
Cash		20,000

The same lease would be recorded in an Enterprise fund as follows:

Equipment (Asset)	80,000	
Capital Lease Payable		60,000
Cash		20,000

Note that the lease should be valued at the net present value of future minimum lease payments when it is recorded in a proprietary fund.

● **INTERPRETIVE EXERCISE**

A governmental unit has a choice of purchasing a fleet of police cars for $300,000 or leasing them (with an option to purchase at lease-end) for $60,000 per year over a 5-year lease. How would purchase of the police cars through a capital lease increase spending authority in the current budget?

---

[30]NCGA Statement No. 5, *Accounting and Financial Reporting Principles for Lease Agreements of State and Local Governments.*

If in a rare circumstance, a government should be the lessor (the lessor is the party providing the capital asset to and being leased by the lessee) this will create a noncurrent asset or lease receivable for the government. This would be a highly unusual occurrence.

Current and noncurrent liabilities

Some liabilities can appear as both a current and a noncurrent liability. The amount due within the current fiscal period is reported as a current liability and the remainder due in future periods is reported as a noncurrent liability.

Bond anticipation notes.[31]   **A bond anticipation note** (BAN) is a short-term note issued by a government that anticipates issuing long-term bonds in the near future, generally to fund a construction project. The bond anticipation note is repaid from the proceeds of the long-term debt when it is issued. The note is intended as a short-term, temporary financing of the amount necessary (usually not the full cost) to start a project until long-term financing can be obtained. Bond anticipation notes can be either current or noncurrent liabilities depending upon whether they have a maturity that extends beyond the current fiscal period. Generally, a BAN is set up as a short-term liability like a TAN. If, however, longer-term financing to repay the BAN is in place by the time the financial statement is issued, the BAN proceeds would be reflected as an Other Financing Source rather than a fund liability.

In practice, bond anticipation notes are uncommon. A government would generally not take the risk of undertaking a major capital project by borrowing monies short-term with bond anticipation notes. If the bonds were not issued due to adverse market conditions, unfavorable bond rating, or other factors, the government would have to find funds in the current budget to repay the bond anticipation notes.

The issuance of long-term bonds requires time for due diligence (a process that ensures that all important financial and nonfinancial matters are fully disclosed to the prospective bond purchaser), a prospectus to be prepared, and meetings with rating agencies to secure a bond rating. Investment bankers and bond attorneys have to spend many hours preparing the legal documents and marketing the long-term bonds at the optimum market point to minimize interest cost. Yet, few governmental financial managers would take the risk to proceed with a major construction project by signing bond anticipation notes for short-term financing. A conservative approach is more common where the governmental financial manager will actually take the longer time period to make sure all of the funding, including long-term bonds, is in place before moving forward on the construction project. The journal entry to record the issuance of $10,000,000 in bond anticipation notes that will be repaid during the current fiscal year would appear as follows:

Cash	10,000,000	
Bond Anticipation Notes Payable		10,000,000

Demand bonds.[32]   Demand bonds simply mean that a governmental unit has issued a long-term bond with a demand ("put") feature, which permits the purchaser or

---

[31]FASB Statement No. 6, *Classification of Short-Term Obligations Expected to Be Refinanced.*
[32]GASB Interpretation No. 2, *Demand Bonds Issued by State and Local Governmental Entities.*

bondholder to require the issuer to redeem the principal plus accrued interest on the bond upon demand, usually with 1 to 30 days notice. Demand bonds are not very common because governmental units generally want certainty in planning their future debt service.

Because the bondholder has the right to demand the principal amount on a short-term basis, demand bonds should be reported as current liabilities unless *all of the following conditions are met:*

1) A take-out agreement exists with another financial institution to provide funds in the event of a put and the take-out funds will then convert to a long-term obligation of some type;
2) The take-out agreement does not expire within 1 year from fiscal year-end;
3) The take-out agreement or any obligations incurred under the agreement are not cancelable by the lender within 1 year from fiscal year-end; and
4) The lender is financially capable of honoring the take-out agreement.

If all of the conditions above are met, the demand bond proceeds would be reported as an Other financing source and recorded like other long-term debt. The journal entry to record the issuance of $10,000,000 in demand bonds and current liability for the bonds that *do not* meet the take-out agreement provisions would be as follows:

Cash	10,000,000	
Demand Bonds Payable		10,000,000

There are special provisions for recording the current debt service payment of demand bonds that are reflected as a current liability in a governmental fund. The debt service principal and interest payments would be offset by an Other financing source. The entry to record the principal payment of $1,000,000 and interest payment of $500,000 on the $10,000,000 demand bond would be:

Demand Bonds Payable	1,000,000	
Debt Service Principal Expenditure	1,000,000	
Debt Service Interest Expenditure	500,000	
Cash		1,500,000
Other Financing Source— Principal on Demand Bonds		1,000,000

Compensated absences[33] are those absences for which employees will be paid, such as vacation and sick leave. Compensated absences should be accrued as a liability when the benefits are earned if both of the following conditions are met:

1) The employees' rights to receive compensation are attributable to services already earned; and
2) It is probable the employer will compensate the employees for the benefits through paid time off or cash payments at termination or retirement.

Benefits that are earned but are expected to lapse, such as sick time that is lost if not used, should not be accrued. A current liability would be set up for the portion of the compensated absences (vacation and sick leave) that will be expected to be paid to

---

[33]GASB Statement No. 16, *Accounting for Compensated Absences.*

governmental employees during the current fiscal budget period. A noncurrent liability that is adjusted annually will be set up for the remaining compensated absence liability that is expected to be paid to governmental employees in future fiscal periods. Governmental funds recognize a liability and an expenditure for the noncurrent liability only when the benefits are paid or expected to be paid within the fiscal year. Proprietary funds will recognize a noncurrent liability at the time that the noncurrent liability is determined as they utilize the accrual method of accounting. Governmental units will show a noncurrent liability in the government-wide Statement of Net Assets at the end of the fiscal year for the governmental funds' noncurrent liability for compensated absences.

Governments are very labor-intensive and have a high percentage of their budget devoted to paying for labor. Governmental employees often have very generous fringe benefit packages particularly in the area of vacation or sick leave; that is, compensated absences. In fact, it is common for all of the accrued vacation leave of a police officer or other governmental employee to be fully paid at the departing hourly rate upon retirement, and the sick leave is often paid at retirement at a sliding scale up to 50% based upon years of service at the current base salary rate. There are two main reasons why liberal fringe benefits are granted: 1) governmental employees often have a base salary that is lower than they could competitively obtain in the private sector; they sacrifice current earnings to serve the public, and 2) it increases spending authority to give governmental employees generous vacation and sick leave rather than increasing base annual pay, which would come from the current, rather than future, fiscal years.

Claims and judgments.[34]   A government can be responsible for and risk losses as a result of a claim due to the following events or actions:

1) Torts (claims against the government for personal injury)
2) Theft of, damage to, or destruction of assets
3) Business interruption
4) Errors or omissions
5) Job-related illnesses or injuries to employees
6) Acts of God (natural disaster such as a tornado or an earthquake)

To the extent the risk of loss from a claim has not been transferred to an unrelated outside party through insurance or participation in insurance pools, governmental entities must recognize the loss or expected claim as an expense or expenditure. If it is probable that a claim will be paid and the amount of the claim can be estimated, the amount of the claim should be expensed and offset with a liability account Claims and Judgments. A governmental unit can incur both a current and noncurrent liability as a result of claims and judgments. The current liability will be the amount of claims and judgments expected to be paid within the current budgetary fiscal period. The noncurrent liability represents the remainder of the outstanding claims and judgments against the governmental unit. Noncurrent liabilities for claims and judgments are not set up in the governmental funds. Proprietary funds will recognize a noncurrent liability at the time that the noncurrent liability is determined. Governmental units will show a noncurrent liability in the government-wide Statement of Net Assets at the

---

[34]NCGA Statement No. 4, *Accounting and Financial Reporting Principles for Claims and Judgments and Compensated Absences.*

end of the fiscal year for any governmental fund noncurrent liability for claims and judgments.

Risk management by governmental units can result in the creation of insurance pools. Governments may decide that they do not wish to incur the cost of external insurance, yet wish to share risk with other governmental units. Governments can join together to form an insurance pool to share risk for potential claims and judgments in the future. These insurance pools are called public entity risk pools. The accounting for public entity risk pools depends upon whether the government transfers risk to the pool or simply shares risk with the pool.

● INTERPRETIVE EXERCISE

Governmental immunity occurs when citizens vote to limit their right to sue the government for certain events. Remember that governments are formed by citizens, and those citizens can choose to limit their own rights by adopting governmental immunity. What impact could a broad policy of governmental immunity have upon the liability for claims and judgments?

Landfill closure and postclosure costs.[35] Municipal solid waste landfills (MSWLF), commonly referred to as "dumps," are organized into cells, and once a cell is full, proper capping and closure must occur to be in compliance with federal, state and local environmental laws. These capping and closure costs as well as the postclosure care and monitoring, which is required by law, can be substantial. If a government operates an MSWLF, it will have a current and noncurrent liability for closure and postclosure care. The estimate for these costs must include:

1) Cost of equipment and facilities to be constructed near or at closure such as gas monitoring, and groundwater monitoring systems,
2) Cost of final capping, and
3) Cost of monitoring during postclosure such as maintaining the cap or cover, or monitoring emissions.

This estimate of total closure and postclosure cost is critical as it will be amortized across the fill period of the MSWLF according to the following formula for calculating the amount to expense in the current period:

$$\frac{\text{Estimated total cost} \times \text{cumulative capacity used}}{\text{Total estimated capacity}} \quad \text{less} \quad \text{Amount previously recognized}$$

In essence, this formula allocates the estimated closure and postclosure costs across the period of use of the landfill on the basis of capacity used during the fiscal period. This is prudent financial management because it takes large future costs and allocates them across the current period of benefit or use and, therefore, ensures they are properly funded. The amount determined as the current portion of closure and postclosure costs will be charged to expenditures during the current period.

Governmental funds will not recognize an accrued liability for postclosure costs on the balance sheet. However, the amount of accrued liability for anticipated

---

[35]GASB Statement No. 18, *Accounting for Municipal Solid Waste Landfill Closure and Postclosure Care Costs.*

postclosure cost will be reported as a liability on the government-wide financial statements. The GFOA recommends that landfill closure and postclosure costs be recorded in a proprietary fund. A proprietary fund will set up a short-term liability that will be expensed for the amount of liability incurred in the current period and a long-term liability for the remainder of the accrued liability to be paid in future years. The journal entry to record $85,000 of closure and postclosure costs in a proprietary fund for the county landfill during the current period would be:

Landfill Expenses	85,000	
Landfill Closure and Postclosure Care Liability		85,000

When landfill closure and postclosure expenses are actually paid, the amount of the liability will be reduced. For example, $8,000 in closure costs are paid:

Landfill Closure and Postclosure Care Liability	8,000	
Cash		8,000

● **INTERPRETIVE EXERCISE**

If 20% of the total capacity of the landfill is "used" or filled in one fiscal year, how much of the total closure and postclosure costs will be charged to the current year's expenditures? Why are these future costs being charged to the current budget?

FUND BALANCE (OR EQUITY)

The fund balance of a governmental fund is the difference between assets and liabilities. The fund balance of a governmental fund generally has two components: **reserved and unreserved.** The unreserved portion is available for the governing body to appropriate. A government can further classify the unreserved portion of fund balance as **designated and undesignated.** The designated portion would indicate funds that the governing body has self-imposed a limitation on the use of fund balance that it intends to use for a future specific project. The reserved portion represents resources not available for spending such as inventories or prepaids, or resources that have legal restrictions involving outside parties, such as contracts payable. Common examples of a portion Fund Balance being reserved would be Reserved for Inventories or Reserved for Encumbrances. The unreserved portion can be designated to indicate funds set aside to fund some specific purpose.

The fund balance of a proprietary fund is that of a business within the governmental unit. The proprietary fund equity will reflect the total net assets, which is Assets – Liabilities = Net Assets. Net Assets of proprietary funds are further classified into one of the following categories: **Invested in Capital Assets Net of Related Debt, Restricted, or Unrestricted.** Only assets that have external restrictions imposed by creditors, grantors, contributors, or laws are classified as restricted net assets. For example, an Enterprise fund would report the funds accumulated to pay the debt service on a revenue bond as Restricted for Debt Service.

Fiduciary funds report net assets as the difference between assets and liabilities. The net assets of fiduciary funds are not further classified.

SUMMARY

Chapter 4 had the following learning objectives:

- Demonstrate an understanding of the categories of asset, liability, and equity accounts
- Illustrate the recognition and recording of current and long-term assets
- Explain the methods of accounting for capital assets including infrastructure
- Illustrate the recognition and recording of current and long-term liabilities
- Demonstrate an understanding of the components of fund balance and net assets

A government creates and uses accounting systems to record transactions and economic events that occur throughout the budgetary fiscal year. Balance sheet accounts are used to record the assets or resources as well as liabilities or claims against the resources. The GASB has issued numerous statements that provide guidelines for recording specific types of assets and liabilities that are common to governmental entities. Fund balance or net asset accounts reflect the difference between total assets and total liabilities of the fund.

As Chapter 3 illustrated, the operating and budgetary accounts are closed to zero at the end of the fiscal year. However, the asset, liability, and equity or fund balance accounts are not closed. The asset, liability and equity or fund balance accounts will have balances at the end of the fiscal year and are reported in a financial statement called the Balance Sheet. The **basic accounting equation** is: **Assets – Liabilities = Net Assets or Fund Balance.** Asset accounts normally have debit balances, and liabilities and fund balance or equity accounts normally have credit balances. This chapter illustrated accounting for assets, liabilities, and fund balances or equity accounts. In Chapter 5, governmental financial statements will be illustrated using the operating accounts shown in Chapter 3 and the Balance Sheet accounts shown in Chapter 4.

QUESTIONS

1. Explain the difference between current and noncurrent assets and liabilities.
2. What is credit risk and what is market risk?
3. Why is an investment policy important?
4. What is the fair value method of accounting for investments?
5. What is a repurchase agreement and why is collateral important?
6. Explain how a securities lending agreement works.
7. What type of receivables might be found on a governmental balance sheet?
8. What is the method of accounting for inventory?
9. What is infrastructure and how do governments account for it?
10. Explain the modified approach to accounting for infrastructure.
11. If a capital asset is being constructed, will the fund capitalize interest on the capital asset?
12. Explain why a government would issue tax anticipation notes.
13. What is the difference between a demand bond and a regular bond payable?
14. What is a conduit debt obligation?
15. What is the economic gain or loss that is required to be disclosed on an advance refunding of long-term debt?
16. When would a government record a capital lease payable?
17. What are compensated absences and are they a current or noncurrent liability?
18. Provide an example of a claim or judgment that should be recorded as a governmental liability.

19. How is the annual expense or expenditure for landfill closure and postclosure cost measured and calculated?
20. What is the difference between reserved and unreserved fund balance?

EXERCISES

Exercise 4-1

Multiple Choice—Select the best answer for each of the following:

1. A current asset would be:
   a. city checking account
   b. deposit in investment pool
   c. receivable from state government
   d. all of the above
2. A noncurrent asset would be:
   a. city hiking trail
   b. outdated procedures manual
   c. taxes receivable
   d. none of the above
3. The fair value method of accounting:
   a. requires the city sell all assets at the fair market value
   b. requires all governmental assets be reported at fair market value
   c. results in an increase in the investments account if fair market value rises
   d. results in a decrease in the investments account if fair market value rises
4. The amortized cost method of accounting requires that:
   a. premium be amortized across the life of the investment
   b. accretion of discount reflects the amortization of premium
   c. the investment be sold at a gain
   d. the investment be sold at a loss
5. In a repurchase agreement, the government:
   a. agrees to repurchase the collateral
   b. contracts with a broker-dealer who agrees to repurchase the collateral
   c. agrees to repurchase the Treasury bonds
   d. uses a third-party custodian to collect the interest earnings
6. In a securities lending agreement, the government:
   a. borrows securities from the federal government
   b. must always record assets for both collateral and the securities lent
   c. loans securities to a broker-dealer as an investment transaction
   d. lends security to homeowners for mortgage lending transactions in their city
7. A governmental unit can create a receivable account for:
   a. property taxes
   b. federal grants
   c. billings for service
   d. all of the above
8. Capital assets include:
   a. current assets
   b. operating leases
   c. noncurrent or long-term assets
   d. inventory assets
9. The modified approach for reporting infrastructure requires:
   a. an asset management system
   b. a condition assessment
   c. annual estimate of amount of funding needed to maintain assets as condition level specified by the government
   d. all of the above

10. When a government capitalizes infrastructure assets, it can:
    a. choose to record depreciation expense on all infrastructure assets
    b. choose to only record depreciation expense on infrastructure assets of the proprietary funds
    c. choose to only record depreciation expense on infrastructure assets of the fiduciary funds
    d. do only a and b

Exercise 4-2

Multiple Choice—Select the best answer for each of the following:

1. A school district needs to pay teacher salaries in the fall but does not expect property tax revenues to be received from payment by residents until late fall or early winter. The school district could:
   a. issue Bonds
   b. issue Bond Anticipation Notes
   c. issue Accounts Payable vouchers
   d. issue Tax Anticipation Notes

2. A serial bond:
   a. is issued by the City of Battle Creek, which is the cereal capital of the world
   b. is issued to keep bond issuers coming back for future installments
   c. is issued with equal amounts of principal coming due in future periods
   d. is the normal method of issuing long-term debt

3. A term bond:
   a. requires a minimum term before it earns interest
   b. has interest due at certain periods
   c. requires that the principal be repaid in full at the end of a specified term
   d. has none of the above

4. An advance refunding of long-term debt with negative present value savings might be undertaken due to the pressing need to:
   a. remove legal impairments to future actions
   b. obtain funds to support the current budget
   c. pay off the old debt to issue more new debt
   d. obtain funds to purchase capital assets

5. A defined benefit pension plan:
   a. defines the amount employees contribute
   b. defines the amount employers contribute
   c. defines the future pension based upon past service
   d. does both b and c

6. Vacation and sick leave are large liabilities in governmental units. The amount of compensated absences liability (vacation and sick leave) that is accrued is:
   a. the long-term liability to be paid in future periods
   b. the short-term liability to be paid from future period trust funds
   c. an important yet de minimus sum of money in a fiscal year
   d. an equal annual amount

7. The "dump" or MSWLF (Municipal Solid Waste Landfill) has to record an estimate of closure and postclosure liability. This will be recorded as:
   a. an allocation of closure and postclosure costs
   b. a net amount that does not include final capping costs
   c. a net amount of refuse sent to the "dump" during the fiscal year
   d. an allocation of free money from the government

8. Fund balance is partitioned into:
   a. reserved
   b. unreserved
   c. reserve for encumbrances
   d. both a and b

9. A defined contribution plan:
   a. defines the contributions by employees
   b. defines the contributions by employers
   c. makes it easier for the governmental unit to budget pension costs
   d. does both b and c
10. The balance sheet of a government unit would include:
    a. current assets only
    b. depreciation expense
    c. noncurrent assets only
    d. cash and cash equivalents

Exercise 4-3

Multiple Choice—Select the best answer for each of the following:

1. The "in-substance"defeasance of debt would require that:
   a. all bondholders turn their bonds in
   b. a "call" feature exists on the bonds
   c. monies are irrevocably set aside to pay off the bonds
   d. all of the above happen
2. External investment pools can record:
   a. an asset for the securities
   b. a liability for the funds invested for other governments
   c. a net increase or decrease in the fair value of the investments
   d. all of the above
3. Claims and judgments are:
   a. a liability for all settled claims and judgments against the governmental unit
   b. an estimated liability for current amounts to be paid for claims and judgments
   c. an estimated liability for future amounts to be paid for claims and judgments
   d. both b and c
4. Public entity risk pools are created when governmental units choose to:
   a. establish governmental immunity to prevent claims
   b. invest in private insurance companies
   c. share risk for potential claims and judgments
   d. sell insurance to private citizens
5. A demand bond must be reported as a current liability if:
   a. the "take-out" agreement expires in 1 year
   b. the take-out agreement is cancelable
   c. the take-out agreement is with a lender who lacks the ability to pay off the bonds currently
   d. any of the above occurs
6. Land improvements at a state park do not include:
   a. parking lots
   b. fencing
   c. rustic cabins for camping
   d. perennial flower gardens
7. An inexhaustible capital asset would be:
   a. a building built on bedrock
   b. a Monet painting in the city museum
   c. an oil reserve
   d. none of the above
8. The purchase of office supplies on the purchases method would result in:
   a. a debit to office supplies inventory
   b. a credit to office supplies expenditure
   c. both a and b
   d. a debit to office supplies expenditure

9. The purchase of office supplies on the consumption method would result in a:
   a. debit to office supplies inventory
   b. credit to office supplies inventory
   c. debit to expenditures
   d. credit to expenditures
10. An agency fund is not likely to have a fund balance because:
   a. fund assets should equal fund liabilities
   b. it does not sell services
   c. it records agency transactions
   d. all of the above occurs

Exercise 4-4

Investment policy

The Securities and Exchange Commission is investigating allegations that a Salomon Smith Barney broker may have recommended investments unsuitable for San Bernadino County, which had losses of $6 million and bribed county officials with expensive dinners and trips to Paris and Greece (*The Wall Street Journal*, pages C1–C2, September 26, 2000). Ironically, San Bernadino county borders Orange County. What could have prevented these losses and this investigation?

Exercise 4-5

Investments

What accounts are typically debited and credited when:
   a. a government purchases an investment
   b. a government investment matures
   c. a government enters into a repurchase agreement
   d. a government enters into a securities lending agreement

Exercise 4-6

Investment pools

The county manages an investment pool that several local governments participate in.
   a. How will the county record the internal portion of the investment pool?
   b. How will the county record the external portion of the investment pool?

Exercise 4-7

Inventory

Seaside City maintains a significant inventory of office supplies for use by governmental and proprietary funds. The governmental funds account for their portion of the supplies inventory on the purchases method and the proprietary funds account for their portion of the supplies inventory on the consumption method. What is the difference in accounting for the two methods? Why does the consumption method require a corresponding reservation of fund balance for inventories in the governmental funds?

Exercise 4-8

Issuance of debt

Rapid City plans to issue long-term debt to finance several capital outlay building projects in the amount of $30,000,000 and repay these bonds over 30 years. Rapid City would like to have level debt service over the life of the debt. Should Rapid City issue demand bonds, term bonds with a balloon payment of $6,000,000 due every 5 years, or serial bonds?

Exercise 4-9   **Debt refundings**

Rapid City was advised by the investment banker they hired to issue the $30,000,000 of new debt (see Exercise 4-8) that they should also consider advance refunding an additional $20,000,000 of old debt outstanding that has a 6.8% interest rate as current rates are expected to be about 5.2% at time of issuance. The old debt is "callable," but the administrative costs of "calling" the old bonds is much greater than just irrevocably setting aside sufficient monies from the refunding to repay the old debt across its remaining life. Should Rapid City accept the investment banker's advice and do the advance refunding and will it qualify as an "in-substance defeasance"?

Exercise 4-10   **Infrastructure**

Rustbelt City has neglected to maintain its roads and bridges and has serious damage to this infrastructure that is estimated to require $30,000,000 of expenditures to repair to acceptable minimum standards. Rustbelt City is also preparing to implement accounting for capital assets including infrastructure. Which method would you recommend to account for the roads and bridges of Rustbelt City: a) capitalize and depreciate, or b) the modified approach? Given the deteriorated state of the roads and bridges, what will be the impact of each method upon the financial report?

Exercise 4-11   **Pensions**

Arson City has an extremely generous pension plan for its fire department employees because of the dangerous work they do and the high workload. The Arson City Manager is considering switching from a defined benefit plan to a defined contribution plan to control costs. How will the switch in plans control costs and enable the Arson City Manager to better plan for the future?

Exercise 4-12   **Claims and judgments**

How will adopting a policy of governmental immunity, which prevents tort actions against the governmental unit by citizens (such as sidewalk fall injuries), limit the current and long-term liabilities for claims and judgments?

PROBLEMS

Problem 4-1   **Accounting for investments**

The City of Tupelo has a variety of investments and requests advice on when it should use the fair value method of accounting or the amortized cost method of accounting. The City has a significant amount of commercial paper that will mature this year as well as U.S. Treasury securities that mature in the next two to three fiscal years. The commercial paper has declined in value, and the U.S. Treasuries have increased in value due to market forces. The City also invests in a 2a7-like pool (that maintains a net asset value of $1.00). Which accounting method should the City of Tupelo use for each type of investment?

Problem 4-2   **Repurchase and reverse repurchase agreements**

Cash City engages in the following investment transactions:
  a. executes a repurchase agreement in the amount of $10,000,000
  b. executes a reverse repurchase agreement in the amount of $2,000,000
  c. the repurchase agreement matures and income of $22,106 is received
  d. the reverse repurchase agreement matures and an expense of $6,102 is paid
Record these transactions in journal entries.

Problem 4-3	**Receivables**

Gold City General fund:
  a. receives a $1,000,000 State grant, which must be passed through to eligible recipients for job training programs
  b. is notified that they will receive $3,200,000 for this fiscal year's state revenue-sharing program for general governmental purposes
  c. levies property taxes in the amount of $6,000,000, and 2% are estimated to be uncollectible
  d. loans the Capital projects fund $400,000

Record these transactions in journal entries.

Problem 4-4	**Employee benefits**

The City of Coldwater has the following employee benefit programs: vacation and sick leave with 100% payable at termination and no maximum on the number of hours that can be accumulated during an employee's career, defined benefit pension plan that has a 6 months of service vesting requirement and pays 3% a year of service, and minimum retirement age is 45. The City Finance Officer has lunch with the City Manager and tries to explain that these employee benefits are too costly. Explain the accounting issues related to these benefit programs.

Problem 4-5	**Fund Balance**

The City of Clueville has the following totals extracted from the Statement of Net Assets (or Balance Sheet):

Total Assets		18,000,000
Total Liabilities		12,000,000
Reservations of Fund Balance:		
Encumbrances	280,000	
Inventory	200,000	

What is the amount of Unreserved Fund Balance?

Problem 4-6	**Receivable for grant**

The State of Arkansas grants $1,000,000 to a city to create a visitor's center for tourists. How would the city record this grant (show journal entries):
  a. upon notification of the grant
  b. upon receipt of the grant

Problem 4-7	**Inventory method**

The City of Seneca Falls had $8,000 of office supplies on hand at the beginning of the fiscal year and $10,000 in inventory at fiscal year-end. During the fiscal year, the City of Seneca Falls purchased $33,800 in office supplies.
  a. What is the amount of office supplies used by the City during the fiscal year?
  b. Record the journal entries for office supplies under the consumption method.
  c. Record the journal entries for office supplies under the purchases method.

Problem 4-8	**Capital assets**

The City of Grand Gulch has the following capital assets:
   a. historic town hall, no records on original cost, $800,000 on capital renovations, $100,000 on maintenance
   b. equipment, original cost $1,000,000, varying useful life of assets, many need repair or replacement
   c. infrastructure, streets and sidewalks and street-lighting and one public park that has capital improvements for play structures of $100,000 erected 2 years ago with a useful life of 10 years

How should the City of Grand Gulch proceed to implement GASB Statement No. 34 and record capital assets?

Problem 4-9	**In-substance defeasance**

The City of Idlewild has $20,000,000 in long-term debt outstanding at a 6.2% interest rate, which was issued when it had a BBB-rating due to some fiscal mismanagement. The new management team notices that the market rate for tax-exempt issues with a BBB-rating is now at 5.2%, and they believe that they can persuade Fitch or Moody's to improve their rating due to their strong financial management and forecast for the future. They decide to do an advance refunding of the long-term debt with an in-substance defeasance. What will the City of Idlewild have to record for:
   a. the in-substance defeasance
   b. the new debt issued

Problem 4-10	**Claims and judgments**

Identical twins Sue and Sally saunter into a city park. They see a sign that warns them not to lean over to look at the natural waterfall because of "danger." The sisters are having so much fun that they forget about the sign and lean over to see the waterfall in the sunlight. Sue falls to her death and the city pays $500,000 to the family. Sally is caught upon the restraining chain and experiences significant injury to her arm from trying to hold Sue from falling to her death. How would the city account for Sally's lawsuit for damages in the amount of $5,000,000 and the payment for Sue's death of $500,000?

Problem 4-11	**Agency fund**

Record the following journal entries
   a. The county levies property taxes for the city ($2,000,000) and local schools ($3,000,000) and $1,000,000 for the county itself
   b. The county collects the property taxes
   c. The county distributes the property taxes collected

Problem 4-12	**Putting it all together—review chapters 3–4**

Record the following journal entries for a Capital projects fund:
   a. The City Council authorizes construction of a fire station to be financed by issuing bonds in the amount of $5,000,000. The Capital projects fund records appropriations as a memorandum entry only (does not record the budget in accounts).
   b. The General fund loans the Capital projects fund $100,000 for initial expenses.
   c. The Capital projects fund issues bonds in the amount of $5,000,000.
   d. The Capital projects fund issues a construction contract for $5,000,000 that has specified 5% will be retained until the building is complete and passes inspections.
   e. The contractor bills the city $2,000,000 for construction so far.
   f. The Capital projects fund repays the General fund for the loan.
   g. The Capital projects fund pays the contractor's bill.

Problem 4-13

Internet research: investment policy

Go to http://www.gfoa.org/, the home web site for the Government Finance Officers Association (GFOA). Select *Special Reports/Samples* and under *Samples* select *Sample Investment Policy*. The Sample Investment Policy covers issues such as yield, risk, parameters for investments, and many other topics. If a city council were to adopt the Sample Investment Policy recommended by GFOA, what types of requirements would be imposed upon the finance officer's or treasurer's investment practices?

Problem 4-14

Internet research: investment policy

Go to http://www.gfoa.org/, the home web site for the Government Finance Officers Association (GFOA). Select *Special Reports/Samples* and under *Samples* select *Sample Investment Policy*. What mistakes were made by the Orange County Board of Supervisors in overseeing the investment of public funds? Mr. Citron was actually issuing reverse repurchase agreements to obtain more cash to invest in derivative products that were essentially "betting" that interest rates would fall, exposing Orange County to a large amount of market risk. If the Orange County Board of Supervisors had adopted the GFOA Recommended Sample Investment Policy (see problem above), would it have prevented the $1.7 billion in losses Mr. Citron incurred? Go to http://www.oc.ca.gov/treas/mrsep99/fitch999.htm and read Fitch's report on Orange County's compliance with its current investment policy.

Problem 4-15

Internet research

Go to http://home-news.excite.com/news/ap/000921/02/lease-back-school and read "Niagra High: Snazzy Public School." This Associated Press news report on September 21, 2000, tells about a revolutionary new high school that was built with private financing and is leased to the school district. Read the article and explain how the Niagra Falls School District should account for the lease transaction and whether they should account for the high school as a capital asset. Do you think governmental entities should be permitted to lease large facilities like this high school?

Problem 4-16

Case—Sea Breeze City continuous problem

The trial balance for the funds at the beginning of the year was:

General fund

Cash	500,000	
Investments in Pooled Cash	20,000,000	
Fund Balance—Unreserved		20,500,000

Sea Breeze City has the following General Government capital assets:

Buildings (including City Hall)	20,000,000	
Accumulated Depreciation—Buildings		5,000,000
Land (including park)	20,000,000	
Equipment	5,000,000	
Accumulated Depreciation—Equipment		3,000,000
Infrastructure (the modified approach has been adopted)		
Road System	10,000,000	
Water System	10,000,000	

Sea Breeze City has the following General Government long-term debt:

General Obligation Bonds	20,000,000

The Debt Service fund has no account balances at the beginning of the year. All of the monies received last year were paid in debt service.

Mosquito Control fund

Cash	20,000	
Fund Balance—Unreserved		20,000

Water Utility fund

Cash	50,000	
Investments in Pooled Cash	500,000	
Accounts Receivable	20,000	
Capital Assets:		
Land	2,000,000	
Buildings	4,000,000	
Accumulated Depreciation—Buildings		2,000,000
Equipment	3,000,000	
Accumulated Depreciation—Equipment		2,000,000
Net Assets Invested in Capital Assets		5,000,000
Net Assets Unrestricted		570,000

Sea Breeze Marina fund

Cash	100,000	
Investments in Pooled Cash	500,000	
Capital Assets—Docks and Boatwells	5,000,000	
Accumulated Depreciation—Docks and Boatwells		3,000,000
Net Assets Invested in Capital Assets		2,000,000
Net Assets Unrestricted		600,000

Motor Pool fund

Capital Assets—Motor Vehicles and Equipment	120,000	
Accumulated Depreciation—Motor Vehicles and Equipment		60,000
Net Assets Invested in Capital Assets		60,000

1. Record the following transactions in each fund.

General fund
   a. Property taxes of $4,000,000 were levied with a 2% estimate of uncollectible taxes.
   b. Local sales taxes of $1,100,000 were remitted within legal due dates.
   c. Property taxes of $3,800,000 were collected; the remainder became delinquent with a 2% estimate of uncollectible delinquent taxes, and penalties and interest of $10,000 were assessed.
   d. A transfer of $1,100,000 for payment of $1,000,000 principal and $100,000 interest was made to the Debt service fund.
   e. Supplies of $200,000 were ordered. The City uses the purchases method.
   f. Public Safety is awarded a $300,000 grant from the State to upgrade its communications and information systems within two years so the systems will integrate with the State network and receives the cash.
   g. The City collects licenses and fees of $22,000.
   h. The invoice for supplies was received at $205,000 and processed for payment (General Government $110,000, Public Safety $40,000, and Public Works $55,000).
   i. The invoice for supplies was paid.
   j. The city collects parking and traffic fines of $39,000.
   k. Salary and fringe benefit expenditures totaled $4,000,000 during the fiscal year and were paid (General Government $1,430,000, Public Safety $1,700,000 and Public Works $870,000).
   l. Public Safety enters into a $300,000 contract with ABC Systems to upgrade the communications and information systems.

m. Other expenditures totaled $500,000 during the fiscal year and were paid (General Government $400,000, Public Safety $50,000, and Public Works $50,000).

n. A citizen slipped on the sidewalk outside City Hall entering to pay her property tax bill. A lawsuit for $500,000 has been filed and will not go to trial for at least one year. The City Attorney deems it probable, based upon current case law, that payment of $20,000 could be paid for this claim.

o. A partial billing for communications equipment installed of $200,000 from ABC Systems is received and paid.

p. A citizen donated $2,000,000 to maintain a park near the Marina for sunset parties to toast the sunset and required that one party per year for local residents of Sea Breeze City be funded from the investment earnings of this gift. The donor stipulated that for five years only investment income can be used for the party and thereafter the principal and interest can be used for any public purpose. The City establishes a new fund for this gift.

q. Billings of $50,000 from the Water Utility fund are received and paid (General Government $50,000).

r. A citizen donated a historical "cigarette boat" to the City to help create interest in the "sunset party" by giving free rides in the boat. The boat's original cost was $50,000 and current market value is at least $100,000. The City accepts the boat and classifies it as a historical treasure and decides not to capitalize it.

s. Billings of $50,000 from the Motor Pool fund are received and paid (General Government $5,000, Public Safety $30,000, and Public Works $15,000).

t. Income distribution was received from the Treasurer's Investment fund (see Treasurer's Investment fund item b).

Debt Service fund

a. The debt service fund receives the transfer from the General Fund. The funds are forwarded to the City's fiscal agent.

b. The fiscal agent pays $1,000,000 principal and $100,000 interest due on long-term debt relating to the governmental funds to the bondholders.

Mosquito Control fund

a. Mosquito control tax of $55,000 was levied and billed and 100% is estimated to be collected.

b. The Mosquito Control fund receives $52,250 from tax collections; the remainder became delinquent. The delinquent balance is expected to be collected within 60 days after fiscal year-end.

c. The Mosquito Control fund contracts with Ace Pest Control to conduct a mosquito control spraying program during the year for $50,000.

d. Ace Pest Control conducts the mosquito control program and submits a bill for services rendered.

e. The Ace Pest Control bill is paid.

Water Utility fund

a. The water utility bills the General fund $50,000 for water usage and citizens and businesses of Sea Breeze $350,000 for water usage.

b. $395,000 is collected; $50,000 from the General fund and $345,000 from citizens.

c. Operating expenses of $255,000 ($225,000 salaries and fringe benefits and $30,000 in supplies) are recorded and paid.

d. Equipment was purchased at a cost of $$20,000.

e. Billings of $50,000 for motor vehicle usage from the Motor Pool fund is paid.

f. Annual depreciation expense of $80,000 is recorded ($40,000 on the desalinization plant building and $40,000 on all equipment).

g. Income distribution was received from the Treasurer's Investment fund (see Treasurer's Investment fund item b).

Sea Breeze Marina fund
  a. Billings for boatwell leases to lessees are sent totaling $1,000,000.
  b. Payments of $990,000 are received.
  c. Revenue bonds of $5,000,000 are issued to pay for construction of additional docks and boatwells.
  d. A contract for $5,000,000 is awarded to Westwind Construction company for design and construction of additional docks and boatwells. The contract specifies a 5% retention on all billings until the project is satisfactorily completed. (Reminder: encumbrances are not recorded in proprietary funds).
  e. Westwind Construction submits a bill for $5,000,000 for work completed.
  f. Operating expenses of $825,000 ($270,000 salaries and fringe benefits, $400,000 routine repairs and replacement on docks and boatwells, $155,000 other expenses).
  g. Annual depreciation expense of $125,000 is recorded on docks and boatwells.
  h. The dock and boatwell project passes inspection, and Westwind Construction is paid in full.
  i. The accrued interest on the revenue bonds is $25,000 at fiscal year-end.
  j. Income distribution was received from the Treasurer's Investment fund (see Treasurer's Investment fund item b).

Motor Pool fund
  a. Billings of $50,000 to the General fund and $50,000 to the Water Utility fund are sent.
  b. Billings sent (a.) are paid by the General fund and Water Utility fund.
  c. Operating expenses (salaries and fringe benefits of $50,000, $24,000 repairs and maintenance, and gasoline of $10,000) are paid.
  d. Annual depreciation expense of $14,000 on motor vehicles and equipment is recorded.

Treasurer's Investment fund
  a. At the beginning of the fiscal year, investments have a fair market value of $26,000,000. Participation in the fund is as follows:

Sea Breeze General fund	20,000,000
Sea Breeze Water Utility fund	500,000
Sea Breeze Marina fund	500,000
Palm City	5,000,000
	26,000,000

  b. Interest income of $1,000,000 is received from investments. A cash distribution of the $1,000,000 income is made pro rata to the participants in the fund. Record the transaction in each of the participant funds. (Round to the nearest dollar).
  c. At fiscal year-end, the fair market value of securities is $26,300,000. Record the transaction in each of the participant funds.
2. Prepare the appropriate closing entries and the trial balance for all funds at the end of the fiscal year.

CHAPTER 5

GOVERNMENTAL FINANCIAL REPORTING

LEARNING OBJECTIVES

- Demonstrate an understanding of the governmental financial reporting entity
- Demonstrate an understanding of the financial reporting model
- Illustrate the components of fund financial statements
- Illustrate the components of government-wide statements
- Explain the reconciliation of fund financial statements to government-wide statements

GOVERNMENTAL FINANCIAL REPORTING ENTITY[1]

The concept of financial accountability of elected officials is reflected in the standards adopted by the Governmental Accounting Standards Board for annual financial reporting. Citizens want a clear picture of the financial health of their government. They also want to know how their tax dollars were spent and how much it costs to provide major services such as public safety or public works. To provide a complete picture of the accountability of the elected officials, the annual financial report needs to cover all of the activities the elected officials are responsible and accountable for, which may include the activities of other closely related agencies. Many governmental activities are intertwined with other legally separate agencies, commissions, and boards established to deliver specific services. For example, a public bus system that provides transportation services throughout a city might be governed by a legally separate authority whose board members are appointed by the mayor of the city. Should the bus authority, which provides bus transportation within the city (a public purpose), be included or excluded from the city's financial report? This section explains how the primary government's relationships with other governmental units and authorities must be examined to determine if other entities, like the bus authority, should be included as component units in the annual financial report.

The GASB has established criteria for defining the **financial reporting entity** that determine what related governmental units should be included in the annual financial report. The financial reporting entity should include:[2]

1) the **primary government,**
2) organizations for which the primary government is **financially accountable,** and
3) other organizations for which the nature and significance of their relationship with the primary government are such that exclusion would cause the reporting entity's financial statements to be misleading or incomplete.

A **primary government**[3] is defined as a state, or a general purpose local government (city, county, etc.), or a special-purpose government (school district, special district, etc.). A special-purpose government qualifies as a primary government *only* if the following conditions are met:

1) it has a separately elected governing body,
2) it is **legally separate,** and
3) it is **fiscally independent** of other governments.

A government has a **legally separate** status if it has the corporate powers of the right to sue and be sued, and it can buy and sell or lease property in its own name. Any special-purpose government that is not legally separate will be reported as part of the primary government that holds its corporate powers. A special-purpose government is **fiscally independent** if it has the authority to do *all* of the following without any other government's approval: 1) establish a budget, 2) levy taxes or set rates and charges, and 3) issue long-term debt or bonds. If a special-purpose government needs approval from another government that is only ministerial or compliance-oriented, it would not impact fiscal independence.

---

[1]GASB Statement No. 14, *Defining the Financial Reporting Entity.*
[2]Ibid, paragraph 12.
[3]Ibid, paragraphs 13–18.

The financial reporting entity must include all component units.[4] **Component units** are any other legally separate organizations that the primary government is financially accountable for or that should be included to prevent the financial statements from being misleading or incomplete. **Financial accountability** exists if:

1) the primary government appoints a majority of the governing body *and*
2) the primary government can **impose its will** on the organization, or there is a potential that the organization could create a **financial benefit or burden** to the primary government.

In addition, financial accountability *may* exist if an organization is fiscally dependent on the primary government even though it has a separately elected governing board. The primary government can **impose its will** on an organization if it has the power to do *any* of the following actions:

1) Remove appointed members of the governing board at will.
   Example: The mayor can remove any member of the local bus authority for any reason at any time.
2) Modify or approve the budget.
   Example: The city council can change the budget of the local bus authority.
3) Modify or approve rate or fee changes.
   Example: The city council can increase or decrease rates or veto rate changes.
4) Overrule or modify decisions of the governing board.
   Example: The city council can change decisions made by the local bus authority's governing board.
5) Appoint, hire, fire, or reassign management of the governmental unit.
   Example: The mayor or city council can fire the executive director of the local bus authority.

The primary government has a **potential financial benefit or burden** if *any* of the following conditions exist:

1) The primary government can use or access the organization's resources.
   Example: The city council can use excess profits from the local bus authority for government purposes.
2) The primary government is obligated or has assumed an obligation to finance or pay any deficits of the organization.
   Example: The city must fund deficits of the local bus authority.
3) The primary government is obligated in some manner to repay debt of the organization.
   Example: The city has some legal obligation to repay debt of the local bus authority.

The primary government is **obligated in some manner** if it is: legally obligated to repay the debt; required to cover shortfalls in debt service until the governmental unit can obtain resources; required to or authorized to and does set aside reserves to repay the debt; authorized to and does establish a fund for debt redemption; may cover deficiencies in event of default; or legal decisions make it likely that the primary government will be responsible for the debt in the event of a default. In other words, the

---

[4]Ibid, paragraphs 20–37.

primary government must step up to the plate in some way to pay the component unit's liabilities if the component unit is unable to do so.

When defining the financial reporting entity, the GASB recognized that there might be instances where there is a relationship between the primary government and another entity that does not nicely fit into the description of financially accountable. That is why the GASB added the category of other organizations whose exclusion from the annual financial report would be misleading to the definition of a component unit.

All of the organizations that are legally separate for which the primary government is financially accountable are considered component units. Component units are further classified as either **blended** or **discretely presented.**[5] If the activities of a component unit are so intertwined with the primary government that it, in substance, operates as part of the primary government, the component unit's data should be combined with the primary government's data and blended. A component unit should be blended in either of the following circumstances:

1) The governing bodies of the component unit and the primary government are substantively the same, or
2) The component unit provides services primarily to the primary government, operating much like an internal service fund.

For example, a building authority might be established for the sole purpose of overseeing the construction and financing of a convention center owned by the primary government. With the exception of the General fund, each fund of the blended component unit would be reported as if it were a fund of the primary government. Because there can be only one General fund, the blended unit's General fund would be reported as a Special revenue fund.

The vast majority of component units will not be blended, however, and their data will be discretely presented in a separate column(s) in the government-wide financial statements of the primary government. Discrete presentation means that the component unit's data is presented together with but separate from the primary government's data. GAAP also require that additional information about major discretely presented units be presented in the financial statements. This can be accomplished in one of three ways: 1) separate columns for major discretely presented units on the government-wide financial statements; or 2) including a combining statement of discretely presented component units; or 3) presenting condensed financial statements on major discretely presented units in the notes to the financial statements. The sample government-wide financial statements illustrated later in this chapter demonstrate the reporting of discretely presented component units.

The following is an analysis of how a primary government would evaluate whether another entity should be reported as a component unit. A city establishes a downtown development authority (DDA) for the public purpose of financing and constructing a convention center to stimulate business activity in the downtown community. The DDA has the power to set its own budget, issue long-term debt, levy taxes in the downtown development district, and the city is not responsible for the debt of the DDA. The DDA board is appointed by the mayor of the city for three-year staggered terms, and members cannot be removed without cause. Should the DDA be included as a component unit of the city (primary government)? Is there financial

---

[5]Ibid, paragraphs 42–54.

accountability? The city does appoint a majority of the governing board, but can the city impose its will upon the DDA? The appointed board cannot be removed without cause, budget and taxes are set by the DDA, debt is issued by the DDA and is not an obligation of the city in any way, and the DDA board cannot be overruled by the city council nor can the city remove the management of the DDA. Clearly, the city cannot impose its will upon the DDA, so the DDA would not be included as a component unit in the city's financial report. The DDA will issue an annual financial report as a primary government in its own right. The definition of the financial reporting entity is an important first step in determining the scope of the financial report to be prepared at fiscal year-end.

● **INTERPRETIVE EXERCISE**

> The city bus system is a separate authority with a governing board appointed by the mayor. The bus system is financially independent of the city. The city is not responsible for the bus system authority's debt or deficits, but it does provide a significant operating subsidy to support the bus authority's operations. Based upon this limited information, can the city impose its will upon the bus system authority? Should the city include the bus system authority in the city's annual financial report?

FINANCIAL REPORTING MODEL

The **financial reporting model** defines what information must be included in a governmental unit's external annual financial report. GASB Statement No. 34 prescribed a new financial reporting model that is designed to provide information in a more business-like format. This was the first major change in the governmental reporting model in over 20 years. The minimum requirements for general purpose external financial statements include:[6]

1) Management's Discussion and Analysis (MD&A);
2) Basic Financial Statements that include fund financial statements, government-wide financial statements, and notes to the financial statements; and
3) Required Supplementary Information (RSI) other than MD&A.

Each of the components of the financial reporting model will be covered in this chapter. The Required Supplementary Information includes the Management's Discussion and Analysis, budgetary comparison schedules for governmental funds, and information about infrastructure condition and maintenance if the modified approach to reporting infrastructure is used. RSI information is differentiated from the financial statements because the information is not included in the scope of an audit of a government's financial statements. In other words, an auditor will not render an opinion on whether the RSI information is "fairly presented" or not.

Two different measures of accountability—fiscal accountability and operational accountability—are incorporated in the financial reporting model.[7] **Fiscal accountability** demonstrates that the governmental activities of the entity have complied with

---

[6]GASB Statement No. 34, paragraph 6.
[7]Ibid, paragraphs 203–223.

public decisions (generally through the budgetary process) regarding raising and spending public funds. **Operational accountability** demonstrates how efficiently the business-type activities of the entity have met their operating objectives. The focus on accountability through financial reporting is demonstrated in the government-wide Statement of Net Assets that provides information about the entity's overall fiscal health, the Statement of Activities that demonstrates the cost of providing services, and Management's Discussion and Analysis that provides a narrative explanation of financial information.

Many governmental entities go beyond the basic requirements of the financial reporting model and provide a more detailed level of accountability through the publication of a **Comprehensive Annual Financial Report** (CAFR). The CAFR is an external annual financial report of a governmental unit that incorporates the minimum external reporting requirements as well as additional important information about the reporting entity. The GASB outlines the minimum requirements for the CAFR that include Basic Financial Statements and Required Supplementary Information to be presented in the following order:

Comprehensive Annual Financial Report (CAFR)[8]

1. Introductory Section
   - Table of contents, letter(s) of transmittal, and other material deemed appropriate by management
2. Financial Section
   - Auditor's Report
   - Management's Discussion and Analysis (MD&A)
   - Basic Financial Statements
     Government-wide statements
        Statement of Net Assets
        Statement of Activities
     Fund financial statements
        Governmental funds:
           Balance Sheet
           Statement of Revenues, Expenditures, and Changes in Fund Balance
              including Reconciliation to government-wide statements
        Proprietary funds:
           Statement of Net Assets or Balance Sheet
           Statement of Revenues, Expenses, and Changes in Fund Net Assets
           Statement of Cash Flows
        Fiduciary funds (and component units that are fiduciary in nature):
           Statement of Fiduciary Net Assets
           Statement of Changes in Fiduciary Net Assets
     Notes to the financial statements
   - Required Supplementary Information other then MD&A
   - Combining statements and individual fund statements and schedules
        Combining statements
        By fund type—when there is more than one nonmajor fund

---

[8]GASB *Codification of Governmental Accounting and Financial Reporting Standards as of June 30, 2000,* Section 2200. 105.

> For discretely presented component units—when the reporting entity has more than one nonmajor component unit
> Individual fund statements—when the primary government has only one nonmajor fund of a given fund type
> Schedules
> Schedules necessary to demonstrate compliance with legal and contractual provisions
> Schedules to present information spread throughout the statements that can be brought together and shown in greater detail
> Schedules to present greater detail for information reported in the statements

3. Statistical Section

Management's discussion and analysis

The MD&A should include an introduction and analytical discussion of the financial statements. The MD&A is a major revolution in governmental financial reporting because it requires governmental managers to explain the financial information to the user of the report in a detailed and informational manner. This should enable the casual reader or citizen to understand and interpret the financial information in the financial report. At a minimum, the MD&A must include:[9]

1) Brief discussion of the financial statements
2) Condensed financial information from the government-wide financial statements comparing current year to prior year including:
   a. Total assets, distinguishing between capital and other assets
   b. Total liabilities, distinguishing between long-term and other liabilities
   c. Total net assets, distinguishing between amounts invested in capital assets, net of related debt; restricted amounts; and unrestricted amounts
   d. Program revenues by major source
   e. General revenues by major source
   f. Total revenues
   g. Program expenses, at a minimum by function
   h. Total expenses
   i. Excess (deficiency) before contributions to term and permanent endowments or permanent fund principal, special and extraordinary items, and transfers
   j. Contributions
   k. Special and extraordinary items
   l. Transfers
   m. Change in net assets
   n. Ending net assets
3) Analysis of the government's overall financial position and results of operations—address both governmental and business-type activities and discuss reasons for significant changes from the prior year not just report amounts of change between years. Report major economic factors such as change in employment base that significantly affected operating results.
4) Analysis of balances and transactions of individual funds including reasons for significant changes in fund balances.

---

[9]GASB Statement No. 34, paragraphs 8–11.

5) Analysis of significant variations between original and final budget amounts and between final and actual budget results. Explain any currently known reasons for the variations that could affect future services or liquidity.
6) Description of significant capital asset and long-term debt activity during the year, commitments for capital expenditures, credit rating changes, and debt limitations that affect the financing of planned facilities or services.
7) Discussion by governments that use the modified approach to report some or all of their infrastructure assets including:
   a. Significant changes in the assessed condition of eligible infrastructure from previous condition assessments
   b. How the current assessed condition compares with the condition level the government has established
   c. Any significant differences from the estimated annual amount to maintain and preserve eligible infrastructure assets compared with the actual amounts spent during the current period
8) Description of currently known facts, decisions, or conditions that are expected to have a significant effect on financial position (net assets) or results of operations (revenues, expenses, and other changes in net assets).

The MD&A is a great opportunity for the financial managers of governmental units to "lift the veil" on governmental financial performance through a comprehensive and clear explanation of the current year operating results and performance. For example, item 8 above gives the financial manager an opportunity to discuss matters such as a major manufacturing plant closing that could negatively impact tax revenues in future periods. A government is required to disclose currently known facts, which means events that have happened after the close of the fiscal year, but before the CAFR is published, which could impact the future operations of the government. The MD&A provides management an opportunity to explain and analyze the financial information contained within the financial report for the user; to tell a story about the government's financial results and any other information known that could affect future results.

Fund financial statements

Specific fund financial statements are required for each of the three categories of funds. The required fund financial statements defined in the financial reporting model are:

Governmental funds:
  Balance Sheet
  Statement of Revenues, Expenditures, and Changes in Fund Balances
  Reconciliation to government-wide statements
Proprietary funds:
  Statement of Net Assets or Balance Sheet
  Statement of Revenues, Expenses, and Changes in Fund Net Assets or Fund Equity
  Statement of Cash Flows
Fiduciary funds:
  Statement of Fiduciary Net Assets
  Statement of Changes in Fiduciary Net Assets

Governmental fund financial statements:[10]

Governmental fund financial statements are prepared using the current financial resources measurement focus and modified accrual basis of accounting. Because the current financial resources measurement focus is used, nonfinancial assets such as general capital assets of the entity as well as noncurrent long-term liabilities are not reported in the fund financial statements. There are two required governmental fund financial statements: the Balance Sheet and the Statement of Revenues, Expenditures, and Changes in Fund Balances. A separate column is used in each statement for the General fund, each major fund, and the aggregated nonmajor funds. The reporting entity must classify each governmental fund and each enterprise fund as a **major** or a **nonmajor fund.** The General fund is always a major fund. Other funds should be classified as major funds if the total assets, liabilities, revenues, or expenditures/expenses of the individual fund are:[11] 1) 10% or more of the corresponding element total (assets, liabilities, etc.) excluding extraordinary items for all funds of that type (total governmental or total enterprise), **and** 2) at least 5% of the corresponding element total for all governmental and enterprise funds combined. The nonmajor funds are combined in one column as "other funds" in the financial statements. A nonmajor fund can be classified as a major fund and presented in a separate column if the government officials believe that the fund is of interest or important to financial statement users.

The **Governmental Funds Balance Sheet** has two major sections: 1) Assets, and 2) Liabilities and Fund Balances. Assets and liabilities are listed in order of relative liquidity, meaning how quickly they can be converted to cash. Typical asset and liability accounts were covered in Chapter 4 under current assets and current liabilities. Fund balances are classified as reserved and unreserved. The reserved fund balance should be classified to disclose the specific purposes for the reserves such as reserved for inventories or reserved for encumbrances. **Reserved** indicates that portion of fund balance is not available to be appropriated. Unreserved fund balances should be displayed by fund type such as General fund and Special revenue funds. The unreserved fund balances *may* be further classified as designated and undesignated. **Designated** indicates that the governing body has self-imposed a limitation on the use of fund balance that it intends to use in the future for a specific purpose. The designation is self-imposed and can be removed by the governing body if they wish to appropriate these funds for other purposes.

The governmental fund financial statements must include a summary reconciliation to the government-wide financial statements either at the bottom of the financial statements or in an accompanying schedule. This summary reconciles total governmental fund balances to net assets of governmental activities in the government-wide statement of net assets to include effects of (but not limited to):[12]

1) Reporting capital assets (and depreciation) instead of expenditures for capital outlays
2) Adding general long-term liabilities
3) Reducing deferred revenue for amounts not "available" under modified accrual

---

[10]Ibid, paragraphs 78–90.
[11]Ibid, paragraphs 75–76 and GASB Statement No. 37, *Basic Financial Statements and Management's Discussion and Analysis—for State and Local Government: Omnibus,* paragraph 15.
[12]GASB Statement No. 34 paragraph 85.

Sample City[13]
Balance Sheet
Governmental Funds
December 31, 2002

	General	HUD Programs	Community Redevelopment	Route 7 Construction	Other Governmental Funds	Total Governmental Funds
ASSETS						
Cash and cash equivalents	$3,418,485	$1,236,523	$ —	$ —	$ 5,606,792	$ 10,261,800
Investments	—	—	13,262,695	10,467,037	3,485,252	27,214,984
Receivables, net	3,644,561	2,953,438	353,340	11,000	10,221	6,972,560
Due from other funds	1,370,757	—	—	—	—	1,370,757
Receivables from other governments	—	119,059	—	—	1,596,038	1,715,097
Liens receivable	791,926	3,195,745	—	—	—	3,987,671
Inventories	182,821	—	—	—	—	182,821
Total assets	$9,408,550	$7,504,765	$13,616,035	$10,478,037	$10,698,303	$ 51,705,690
LIABILITIES AND FUND BALANCES						
Liabilities:						
Accounts payable	$3,408,680	$ 129,975	$ 190,548	$ 1,104,632	$ 1,074,831	$ 5,908,666
Due to other funds	—	25,369	—	—	—	25,369
Payable to other governments	94,074	—	—	—	—	94,074
Deferred revenue	4,250,430	6,273,045	250,000	11,000	—	10,784,475
Total liabilities	7,753,184	6,428,389	440,548	1,115,632	1,074,831	16,812,584
Fund balances:						
Reserved for:						
Inventories	182,821	—	—	—	—	182,821
Liens receivable	791,926	—	—	—	—	791,926
Encumbrances	40,292	41,034	119,314	5,792,587	1,814,122	7,807,349
Debt service	—	—	—	—	3,832,062	3,832,062
Other purposes	—	—	—	—	1,405,300	1,405,300
Unreserved, reported in:						
General fund	640,327	—	—	—	—	640,327
Special revenue funds	—	1,035,342	—	—	1,330,718	2,366,060
Capital projects funds	—	—	13,056,173	3,569,818	1,241,270	17,867,261
Total fund balances	1,655,366	1,076,376	13,175,487	9,362,405	9,623,472	34,893,106
Total liabilities and fund balances	$9,408,550	$7,504,765	$13,616,035	$10,478,037	$10,698,303	

Amounts reported for *governmental activities* in the statement of net assets are different because:

Capital assets used in governmental activities are not financial resources and therefore are not reported in the funds.	161,082,708
Other long-term assets are not available to pay for current-period expenditures and therefore are deferred in the funds.	9,348,876
Internal service funds are used by management to charge the costs of certain activities, such as insurance and telecommunications, to individual funds. The assets and liabilities of the internal service funds are included in governmental activities in the statement of net assets.	2,994,691
Long-term liabilities, including bonds payable, are not due and payable in the current period and therefore are not reported in the funds.	(84,760,507)
Net assets of governmental activities	$123,558,874

Explanations of the reconciling amounts need not to be as detailed as the ones illustrated here. In some cases, detailed explanations on the face of the statements may eliminate the need for further descriptions in the notes. On the other hand, long, complicated explanations on the statement may distract the users' attention from the other information presented. Preparers should weigh the advantages of eliminating the need for users to refer to the notes against the possible disadvantage of overloading the statement with information. The reconciliation could be presented on an accompanying page, rather than on the face of the statement.

---

[13]Ibid, Illustration C-1.

4) Adding internal service fund net asset balances
(Internal service fund asset and liability balances that are not eliminated as an intercompany elimination in the statement of net assets should normally be reported in the governmental activities column).[14]

Remember that governmental funds utilize the modified accrual basis of accounting (see Chapter 2), however, the government-wide statements are prepared on the accrual basis of accounting. This is why only the governmental funds prepare such a reconciliation to **convert and consolidate** their fund financial statements to government-wide financial statements. Under the modified accrual basis of accounting, governmental funds do not record 1) capital assets or depreciation, or 2) long-term (noncurrent) liabilities, so these items must be "reconciled" to create the governmental activities column in the government-wide statement. The modified accrual basis for revenue recognition of 3) "available" has to be adjusted to the government-wide revenue recognition when "earned" on the accrual basis. Internal service funds are an intergovernmental service unit that should essentially be eliminated when the government-wide statements are prepared. This reconciliation of 4) Internal service fund is essentially eliminating the effects of self-dealing within the governmental unit doing business with itself before the government-wide statements are prepared. If any residual balance of the internal service fund remains after adjustments are made, it will appear in the governmental activities column.

The **Governmental Funds Statement of Revenues, Expenditures, and Changes in Fund Balance** is presented in the following format:[15]

Revenues (detailed)
Expenditures (detailed)
　　　Excess (deficiency) of revenues over expenditures
Other financing sources and uses, including transfers (detailed)
Special and extraordinary items (detailed)
　　　Net change in fund balances
Fund balances—beginning of period
Fund balances—end of period

Revenues should be classified and reported by major revenue sources such as property taxes or sales taxes. Expenditures should be classified by functions such as general government and public safety. Debt service and capital outlay expenditures are listed separately. Other financing sources and uses include the proceeds of long-term debt and transfers in or out of the funds. **Special and extraordinary items** are transactions that are not within the control of the government such as losses due to natural disasters or that are infrequent or unusual such as the sale of public lands.

Reconciliations to the government-wide statements required for the Statement of Revenues, Expenditures, and Changes in Fund Balances include the following:[16]

1) Reporting revenues on the accrual basis
2) Reporting depreciation expense versus capital outlay expenditures

---

[14]Ibid, paragraph 62.
[15]Ibid, paragraph 86.
[16]Ibid, paragraph 90.

3) Reporting long-term debt proceeds as liabilities versus other financing sources, and reporting debt service payments as a reduction of liabilities versus an expenditure
4) Reporting other expenditures on the accrual basis
5) Adding net revenues or (expense) of Internal service funds

Sample City[17]
Statement of Revenues, Expenditures, and Changes in Fund Balances
Governmental Funds
For the Year Ended December 31, 2002

	General	HUD Programs	Community Redevelopment	Route 7 Construction	Other Governmental Funds	Total Governmental Funds
REVENUES						
Property taxes	$51,173,436	$ —	$ —	$ —	$ 4,680,192	$ 55,853,628
Franchise taxes	4,055,505	—	—	—	—	4,055,505
Public service taxes	8,969,887	—	—	—	—	8,969,887
Fees and fines	606,946	—	—	—	—	606,946
Licenses and permits	2,287,794	—	—	—	—	2,287,794
Intergovernmental	6,119,938	2,578,191	—	—	2,830,916	11,529,045
Charges for services	11,374,460	—	—	—	30,708	11,405,168
Investment earnings	552,325	87,106	549,489	270,161	364,330	1,823,411
Miscellaneous	881,874	66,176	—	2,939	94	951,083
Total revenues	86,022,165	2,731,473	549,489	273,100	7,906,240	97,482,467
EXPENDITURES						
Current:						
General government	8,630,835	—	417,814	16,700	121,052	9,186,401
Public safety	33,729,623	—	—	—	—	33,729,623
Public works	4,975,775	—	—	—	3,721,542	8,697,317
Engineering services	1,299,645	—	—	—	—	1,299,645
Health and sanitation	6,070,032	—	—	—	—	6,070,032
Cemetery	706,305	—	—	—	—	706,305
Culture and recreation	11,411,685	—	—	—	—	11,411,685
Community development	—	2,954,389	—	—	—	2,954,389
Education—payment to school district	21,893,273	—	—	—	—	21,893,273
Debt service:						
Principal	—	—	—	—	3,450,000	3,450,000
Interest and other charges	—	—	—	—	5,215,151	5,215,151
Capital outlay	—	—	2,246,671	11,281,769	3,190,209	16,718,649
Total expenditures	88,717,173	2,954,389	2,664,485	11,298,469	15,697,954	121,332,470
Excess (deficiency) of revenues over expenditures	(2,695,008)	(222,916)	(2,114,996)	(11,025,369)	(7,791,714)	(23,850,003)
OTHER FINANCING SOURCES (USES)						
Proceeds of refunding bonds	—	—	—	—	38,045,000	38,045,000
Proceeds of long-term capital-related debt	—	—	17,529,560	—	1,300,000	18,829,560
Payment to bond refunding escrow agent	—	—	—	—	(37,284,144)	(37,284,144)
Transfers in	129,323	—	—	—	5,551,187	5,680,510
Transfers out	(2,163,759)	(348,046)	(2,273,187)	—	(219,076)	(5,004,068)
Total other financing sources and uses	(2,034,436)	(348,046)	15,256,373	—	7,392,967	20,266,858
SPECIAL ITEM						
Proceeds from sale of park land	3,476,488	—	—	—	—	3,476,488
Net change in fund balances	(1,252,956)	(570,962)	13,141,377	(11,025,369)	(398,747)	(106,657)
Fund balances—beginning	2,908,322	1,647,338	34,110	20,387,774	10,022,219	34,999,763
Fund balances—ending	$ 1,655,366	$1,076,376	$13,175,487	$9,362,405	$ 9,623,472	$ 34,893,106

[17]Ibid, Illustration C-2.

Sample City[18]
Reconciliation of the Statement of Revenues, Expenditures,
and Changes in Fund Balances of Governmental Funds
to the Statement of Activities
For the Year Ended December 31, 2002

Net change in fund balances—total governmental funds	$ (106,657)
Amounts reported for *governmental activities* in the statement of activities are different because:	
Governmental funds report capital outlays as expenditures. However, in the statement of activities, the cost of those assets is allocated over their estimated useful lives as depreciation expense. This is the amount by which capital outlays exceeded depreciation in the current period.	14,039,717
In the statement of activities, only the gain on the sale of the park land is reported, whereas in the governmental funds, the proceeds from the sale increase financial resources. Thus, the change in net assets differs from the change in fund balance by the cost of the land sold.	(823,000)
Revenues in the statement of activities that do not provide current financial resources are not reported as revenues in the funds.	1,920,630
Bond proceeds provide current financial resources to governmental funds, but issuing debt increases long-term liabilities in the statement of net assets. Repayment of bond principal is an expenditure in the governmental funds, but the repayment reduces long-term liabilities in the statement of net assets. This is the amount by which proceeds exceeded repayments.	(16,140,416)
Some expenses reported in the statement of activities do not require the use of current financial resources and therefore are not reported as expenditures in governmental funds.	(1,245,752)
Internal service funds are used by management to charge the costs of certain activities, such as insurance and telecommunications, to individual funds. The net revenue (expense) of the internal service funds is reported with governmental activities.	(758,808)
Change in net assets of governmental activities	$ (3,114,286)

The adjustments that need to be made to convert the fiscal year-end governmental fund accounts to consolidated government-wide financial statements can be grouped into the six steps explained below. It is important to remember that the adjusting entries should only be made on a conversion spreadsheet and *not* posted to the general ledger.

1) **Establish the governmental fund capital assets.** Establish the capital asset account and any contra-asset account for accumulated depreciation and a corresponding entry to fund balance for the net assets invested in capital assets. GFOA recommends that a capitalization threshold of $5,000 be established, and assets acquired for less than $5,000 should be expensed rather than capitalized.

    a.   Start with existing capital assets and accumulated depreciation from prior fiscal year-end.

Capital Asset (by type—Building, Equipment, etc.)	Debit
Accumulated Depreciation (by type)	Credit
Fund Balance	Credit

    (By type means that instead of Capital Asset, the asset type should be recorded as what it is: Building, Equipment, Land, Furniture, etc.)

    b.   Establish capital assets acquired or created during this fiscal year.

       1.   Capital outlay

Capital Asset (by type)	Debit
Expenditure—Capital Outlay	Credit

---

[18]Ibid, Illustration C-3.

2. Construction-in-progress

Construction-in-Progress	Debit	
Expenditure—Capital Outlay		Credit

3. Capital leases

Capital Asset (by type)	Debit	
Expenditure—Capital Lease		Credit

4. Donated capital assets

Capital Asset (by type)	Debit	
Miscellaneous Revenues		Credit

(Record capitalized asset at fair market value at time of donation.)

c. Adjust for disposal of capital assets during the year and record gains and losses.

1. Sale of capital asset

Other Financing Source—Sale of Capital Asset	Debit	
Accumulated Depreciation (by type)	Debit	

(This eliminates the amount previously recorded.)

Loss-Sale of Capital Asset (if a loss occurs)	Debit	
Gain-Sale of Capital Asset (if a gain occurs)		Credit
Capital Asset—(by type)		Credit

(Record either the gain or the loss; but **not both.**)

2. Trade-in of capital asset

Capital Asset (by type—new asset acquired)	Debit	
Accumulated Depreciation (asset traded)	Debit	
Loss-Sale of Capital Asset (if a loss occurs)	Debit	
Gain-Sale of Capital Asset (if a gain occurs)		Credit
Capital Asset (by type—asset traded)		Credit

(Record either the gain or the loss; but **not both.**)

3. Scrap of capital asset

Accumulated Depreciation (asset scrapped)	Debit	
Loss-Scrap of Capital Asset (if a loss occurs)	Debit	
Gain-Scrap of Capital Asset (if a gain occurs)		Credit
Capital Asset (by type asset scrapped)		Credit

(Record either the gain or the loss; but **not both.** If the asset scrapped was fully depreciated, then there will be no gain or loss recorded.)

2) **Determine the long-term, noncurrent governmental fund debt outstanding.**

a. Start with long-term governmental fund debt established at prior fiscal year-end.

Fund balance	Debit	
Bonds Payable		Credit

(Record Bonds Payable net of unamortized premium or discount.)

b. Establish long-term debt issued by governmental funds during the current fiscal year.

1. Record long-term debt issued during the year by governmental funds.

Other Financing Source—Bond Proceeds	Debit
Deferred Charge—Issuance Costs	Debit
Discount—Bonds Payable	Debit
Premium—Bonds Payable	Credit
Expenditure—Issuance Costs	Credit
Bonds Payable	Credit

(If issuance costs are to be amortized, they will be established as a Deferred Charge and debited; if a Discount, it will similarly be established as a debit and amortized; if a Premium, it will be established as a credit and amortized; there can only be a discount OR a premium—both **cannot** be recorded.)

2. Record capital leases entered into during fiscal year by governmental funds.

Other Financing Sources—Capital Lease	Debit

(This eliminates the amount previously recorded.)

Capital Lease Payable	Credit

3. Record in substance-defeasance advance refunding of governmental fund debt.

Other Financing Sources—Bond Proceeds	Debit
Deferred Charge—Issuance Costs (new)	Debit
Deferred Charge—Refunding	Debit
General Obligation Debt—Bonds Payable(old)	Debit
General Obligation Debt—Bonds Payable (new)	Credit
Expenditure—Issuance Costs	Credit

(removal of old debt and establish new debt and costs to amortize)

c. Adjust for payment of debt principal and capital lease payments.

1. Payment of debt principal.

Bonds Payable	Debit
Expenditure—Debt Service Principal	Credit

2. Payment of capital lease principal.

Capital Lease Payable	Debit
Expenditure—Capital Lease Principal	Credit

3) **Restate governmental fund revenues to accrual**—record adjusting entries to translate modified accrual to accrual.

a. Remove revenues "available" this year in governmental funds that were "earned" in prior year.

Revenue (insert type, property tax, income tax, etc.)	Debit
Deferred Revenue (insert type)	Debit
Unreserved Fund Balance	Credit

(Adjust government-wide net assets because revenue was previously recognized when earned.)

b. Record revenues "earned" this year that were not "available."

Deferred Revenue (insert type)	Debit
Revenue (Insert type, interest, property tax, etc.)	Credit

(Evaluate deferred revenues to determine the source and period it was earned.)

c. Amortize premium on long-term bonds issued by governmental funds.

Premium—Bonds Payable	Debit	
Revenue—Premium Amortization		Credit

(Any systematic, rational method may be used to amortize the premium.)

4) **Restate governmental fund expenses to accrual**—record adjusting entries to translate modified accrual expenditures to accrual expenses. <u>Relabel all expenditures as expenses</u>.

a. Remove expenditures that are related to a prior year.

Compensated Absences Payable	Debit	
Expenditures (by program, public safety, etc.)		Credit
Claims and Judgments Payable	Debit	
Expenditures (by program, public safety, etc.)		Credit

(Amounts charged to expenditures and recorded as a liability in current year are reversed.)

Accrued Interest Payable	Debit	
Debt Service—Interest Expense		Credit

(Governmental funds recognize interest on long-term debt when the payment is made rather than when it accrues, therefore, the amount related to a prior period is removed from expense and the prior period accrued interest payable is reduced.)

b. Establish expenses that should be accrued as a liability even though they will not be paid with "available" governmental fund resources.

Expenditures (by program)	Debit	
Accrued Interest Payable		Credit
Compensated Absences Payable		Credit
Claims and Judgments Payable		Credit
Landfill Closure and Postclosure Costs Payable		Credit
Net Pension Obligation		Credit

c. Record depreciation expense on all capital assets by functional program

Expenditures depreciation (by program)	Debit	
Accumulated Depreciation (by type)		Credit

d. Amortize any deferred charges like bond issuance costs, bond discount, etc. Any reasonable, systematic allocation method is acceptable.

Expenditures (by program)	Debit	
Debt Service—Interest Expense	Debit	
Deferred Charges—Bond Issuance Costs		Credit
Discount on Bonds Payable		Credit

5) **Consolidate and eliminate the internal service funds.** The Internal service funds should operate at "break-even" and, therefore, any profit or loss should be allocated prorata to the funds it did business with. Profit or loss generated internally (doing business with the government itself) is allocated back by functional program. Profit or loss generated externally (from outside the primary government) and interest earned from investments or interest expense on debt go into the government-wide statements. Internal service funds may service both governmental and business-type activities. Remember that these adjusting entries are **not** recorded in the general ledger but in a conversion worksheet to create the government-wide statements. The conversion worksheet starts with governmental fund accounts, so Internal service fund accounts will be allocated to create the

consolidated government-wide statements (in which the Internal service funds do not appear). For example, the first entry below is an adjusting entry that "moves" these balance sheet accounts from the Internal service fund to the governmental activities totals in the government-wide statements. After closing entries at fiscal year-end in the Internal service fund, the following adjusting entries would be required:

a. Allocate the balance sheet accounts of the Internal service funds.

Asset (accounts by title)	Debit	
Liabilities (accounts by title)		Credit
Fund Balance		Credit

(This "moves" these accounts from the Internal service fund to the governmental activities column in the consolidated government-wide statements.)

b. Allocate the revenues and expenses related to external activities of the Internal service fund as these should appear in the government-wide statements.

Expenses (accounts by title)	Debit	
Fund Balance	Debit or Credit	

(can be either debit or credit depending on expenses and revenues amounts)

Revenues (accounts by title)		Credit

(This "moves" the revenues and expenses to the governmental activities column for the government-wide statements.)

c. "Look-back" allocation of net income for internal activities of the Internal service fund to the governmental and proprietary funds (if loss, the fund balance would be credited and expenditures by functional program would be increased rather than reduced as shown below).

Fund Balance	Debit	
Expenditures (by functional program—governmental activities)		Credit
Due to Other Funds (proprietary fund share of profit		Credit

6) Make other consolidation adjustments.

a. Remove the operating transfers in and out between governmental funds. Total up and net them out; they should be equal!

Transfers in	Debit	
Transfers out		Credit

b. Remove the interfund borrowings between governmental funds. Total up and net them out; they should be equal!

Due to Other Funds	Debit	
Due from Other Funds		Credit

c. Net any internal balances between governmental and proprietary funds.

Advances from Other Funds	Debit	
Due to Other Funds	Debit	
Internal Balances	Debit or Credit	
Advances to Other Funds		Credit
Due from Other Funds		Credit

d. Eliminate transfers of capital assets from governmental funds to the Internal service fund. This entry removes the transfer out from governmental funds to the Internal service fund.

Fund Balance	Debit	
Accumulated Depreciation (by type)	Debit	
Transfers Out		Credit
Capital Asset (by type)		Credit

The **consolidation**[19] process requires that most interfund activity be eliminated to prepare the government-wide financial statements. Just as General Motors would consolidate activity between the parent company and subsidiaries, the governmental unit must consolidate interfund activity. Interfund loans and interfund reimbursements should be eliminated. Interfund services used and provided that generate revenues and expenses that are allocated between functions should **not** be eliminated in order to arrive at a true net cost of each government function in the Statement of Activities. Interfund transfers are consolidated by removal from the appropriate column and then by elimination from the consolidated total column for the primary government in the government-wide statement of activities.

The 2001 GAAFR,[20] uses a conversion worksheet to take the governmental fund trial balance at fiscal year-end, prepare the reconciling adjustments such as depreciation expenditures and accrued interest, and go from fund-type statements to the government-wide statements required by GASB Statement No. 34. It is important to remember that the conversion is a worksheet event solely to prepare the year-end financial report and that the adjusting entries made on the worksheet are **not** posted to the general ledger. Another method of preparing the government-wide statements would be to maintain a separate fund or ledger throughout the fiscal year to track the adjusting items for the government-wide statements.

Proprietary fund financial statements[21]

Proprietary fund financial statements are prepared using the economic resources measurement focus and the accrual basis of accounting. Three financial statements are required for proprietary funds: Statement of Net Assets or Balance Sheet; Statement of Revenues, Expenses, and Changes in Fund Net Assets or Fund Equity; and Statement of Cash Flows. Like governmental funds, Enterprise funds have a separate column for each major fund and aggregate nonmajor Enterprise funds. All Internal service funds are combined and shown in a separate column after the total of all Enterprise funds.

Governments are given the option of providing a **Statement of Net Assets** in the format where Assets – Liabilities = Net Assets or providing a **Balance Sheet** in the format of Assets = Liabilities + Net Assets (Equity) for Proprietary funds. The format used for the fund statements should also be used for the corresponding government-wide statement. Both assets and liabilities are presented in a classified format that distinguishes between current and long-term. Like the governmental funds, assets and liabilities are listed in order of liquidity. Net assets are presented as three components: **invested in capital assets, net of related debt; restricted** (distinguishing between restrictions imposed by law and restrictions imposed by external parties); and **unrestricted net assets.** The net assets invested in capital assets is netted as capital assets

---

[19]Ibid, pages 126–130.
[20]*Governmental Accounting, Auditing, and Financial Reporting*, by Steven J. Gauthier, Government Finance Officers Association, 2001.
[21]GASB Statement No. 34, paragraphs 91–105.

less accumulated depreciation less outstanding related debt. For example, if a building that cost $20,000,000 has accumulated depreciation of $3,000,000 and the outstanding long-term bonds issued to purchase the building are $12,000,000, the net

Sample City[22]
Statement of Net Assets
Proprietary Funds
December 31, 2002

	Business-type Activities— Enterprise Funds			Governmental Activities— Internal Service Funds
	Water and Sewer	Parking Facilities	Totals	
ASSETS				
Current assets:				
Cash and cash equivalents	$ 8,416,653	$ 369,168	$ 8,785,821	$ 3,336,099
Investments	—	—	—	150,237
Receivables, net	3,564,586	3,535	3,568,121	157,804
Due from other governments	41,494	—	41,494	—
Inventories	126,674	—	126,674	139,328
Total current assets	12,149,407	372,703	12,522,110	3,783,468
Noncurrent assets:				
Restricted cash and cash equivalents	—	1,493,322	1,493,322	—
Capital assets:				
Land	813,513	3,021,637	3,835,150	—
Distribution and collection systems	39,504,183	—	39,504,183	—
Buildings and equipment	106,135,666	23,029,166	129,164,832	14,721,786
Less accumulated depreciation	(15,328,911)	(5,786,503)	(21,115,414)	(5,781,734)
Total noncurrent assets	131,124,451	21,757,622	152,882,073	8,940,052
Total assets	143,273,858	22,130,325	165,404,183	12,723,520
LIABILITIES				
Current liabilities:				
Accounts payable	447,427	304,003	751,430	780,570
Due to other funds	175,000	—	175,000	1,170,388
Compensated absences	112,850	8,827	121,677	237,690
Claims and judgments	—	—	—	1,687,975
Bonds, notes, and loans payable	3,944,609	360,000	4,304,609	249,306
Total current liabilities	4,679,886	672,830	5,352,716	4,125,929
Noncurrent liabilities:				
Compensated absences	451,399	35,306	486,705	—
Claims and judgments	—	—	—	5,602,900
Bonds, notes, and loans payable	54,451,549	19,544,019	73,995,568	—
Total noncurrent liabilities	54,902,948	19,579,325	74,482,273	5,602,900
Total liabilities	59,582,834	20,252,155	79,834,989	9,728,829
NET ASSETS				
Invested in capital assets, net of related debt	72,728,293	360,281	73,088,574	8,690,746
Restricted for debt service	—	1,451,996	1,451,996	—
Unrestricted	10,962,731	65,893	11,028,624	(5,696,055)
Total net assets	$ 83,691,024	$ 1,878,170	$ 85,569,194	$ 2,994,691
			↑	↓

Even though internal service funds are classified as proprietary funds, the nature of the activity accounted for in them is generally *governmental*. By reporting internal service funds separately from the proprietary funds that account for business-type activities, the information in the "Totals" column on this statement flows directly to the "Business-type Activities" column on the statement of net assets, and the need for a reconciliation on this statement is avoided.

[22]Ibid, Illustration D-1.

asset invested in capital assets would be $5,000,000. Restricted net assets are further classified into expendable and nonexpendable restricted net assets when permanent endowments are included. Unrestricted net assets reflect the remaining net assets not in the other categories.

The proprietary funds **Statement of Revenues, Expenses, and Changes in Fund Net Assets (or Fund Equity)** is presented in the following format (see page 144):[23]

> Operating revenues (detailed)
> > Total operating revenues
> Operating expenses (detailed)
> > Total operating expenses
> > > Operating income (loss)
> Nonoperating revenues and expenses (detailed)
> > Income before other revenues, expenses, gains, losses, and transfers
> Capital contributions (grant, developer, and other), additions to permanent and term endowments, special and extraordinary items (detailed) and transfers
> > Increase (decrease) in net assets
> Net assets—beginning of period
> Net assets—end of period

The statement distinguishes between operating and nonoperating revenues and expenses. **Operating revenues and expenses** are directly related to the services provided or goods produced by the Enterprise fund. **Nonoperating revenues** would include most nonexchange transactions and investment income. **Nonoperating expenses** would include interest expense. Revenues are reported by major source. Expenses can be presented either by function such as cost of sewer service or by object such as salaries and wages. (Functions, programs, activities, and objects were covered in Chapter 2.)

The proprietary funds **Statement of Cash Flows**[24] can focus on changes in either cash or cash and cash equivalents (as defined in Chapter 4). In practice, most governmental units use the cash method. This statement is presented using the direct method of presenting cash flows from operating activities. The main categories of the statement are cash flows from operating activities; cash flows from noncapital financing activities; cash flows from capital and related financing activities; and cash flows from investing activities. There is also a required reconciliation of operating income (or loss) to net cash provided by operating activities. Operating activities result from providing goods and services and include all transactions that are not capital and related financing, noncapital financing, or investing activities. Noncapital financing activities include all borrowings and repayments that do not result in the acquisition, construction, or improvement of capital assets, whereas capital financing activities do result in the acquisition, construction, or improvement of capital assets. Investing activities include buying and the disposition of debt, equity, or other investment instruments.

Reconciliation of internal service funds.   When converting to the government-wide financial statements, the activities of the Internal service funds are consolidated and allocated back to the funds that used Internal fund services. This consolidation eliminates the effects of self-dealing within the governmental unit. In effect, any profit or

---

[23]Ibid, paragraph 101.
[24]GASB Statement No. 9.

Sample City[25]
Statement of Revenues, Expenses, and Changes in Fund Net Assets
Proprietary Funds
For the Year Ended December 31, 2002

	Business-type Activities—Enterprise Funds			Governmental Activities—Internal Service Funds
	Water and Sewer	Parking Facilities	Totals	
Operating revenues:				
Charges for services	$11,329,883	$ 1,340,261	$12,670,144	$15,256,164
Miscellaneous	—	3,826	3,826	1,066,761
Total operating revenues	11,329,883	1,344,087	12,673,970	16,322,925
Operating expenses:				
Personal services	3,400,559	762,348	4,162,907	4,157,156
Contractual services	344,422	96,032	440,454	584,396
Utilities	754,107	100,726	854,833	214,812
Repairs and maintenance	747,315	64,617	811,932	1,960,490
Other supplies and expenses	498,213	17,119	515,332	234,445
Insurance claims and expenses	—	—	—	8,004,286
Depreciation	1,163,140	542,049	1,705,189	1,707,872
Total operating expenses	6,907,756	1,582,891	8,490,647	16,863,457
Operating income (loss)	4,422,127	(238,804)	4,183,323	(540,532)
Nonoperating revenues (expenses):				
Interest and investment revenue	454,793	146,556	601,349	134,733
Miscellaneous revenue	—	104,925	104,925	20,855
Interest expense	(1,600,830)	(1,166,546)	(2,767,376)	(41,616)
Miscellaneous expense	—	(46,846)	(46,846)	(176,003)
Total nonoperating revenue (expenses)	(1,146,037)	(961,911)	(2,107,948)	(62,031)
Income (loss) before contributions and transfers	3,276,090	(1,200,715)	2,075,375	(602,563)
Capital contributions	1,645,919	—	1,645,919	18,788
Transfers out	(290,000)	(211,409)	(501,409)	(175,033)
Change in net assets	4,632,009	(1,412,124)	3,219,885	(758,808)
Total net assets—beginning	79,059,015	3,290,294	82,349,309	3,753,499
Total net assets—ending	$83,691,024	$ 1,878,170	$85,569,194	$ 2,994,691
			↑	↓

Even though internal service funds are classified as proprietary funds, the nature of the activity accounted for in them is generally *governmental*. By reporting Internal service funds separately from the proprietary funds that account for business-type activities, the information in the "Totals" column on this statement flows directly to the "Business-type Activities" column on the statement of net assets, and the need for a reconciliation on this statement is avoided.

loss of the Internal service funds are allocated back pro rata to the funds that used the internal service. This allocation process is called a "look-back" approach; in effect, profit or loss is allocated based upon a look-back at the activities in the past fiscal year. If there is a profit, the expense by function charged to the funds will be reduced, and if there is a loss, the expenses will be increased. If any residual balance of the Internal service fund remains after adjustments are made (generally resulting from the incidental provision of services to entities other than the reporting government), the pro rata share of operating revenues, expenses and net profit (loss) will appear in the governmental activities column of the government-wide statements. Because of these eliminations to consolidate interfund activity, Internal service funds are not included on the government-wide financial statements.

---

[25]GASB Statement No. 34, Illustration D-3.

Sample City[26]
Statement of Cash Flows
Proprietary Funds
For the Year Ended December 31, 2002

	Business-type Activities—Enterprise Funds			Governmental Activities—Internal Service Funds
	Water and Sewer	Parking Facilities	Totals	
CASH FLOWS FROM OPERATING ACTIVITIES				
Receipts from customers	$11,400,200	$1,345,292	$12,745,492	$15,326,343
Payments to suppliers	(2,725,349)	(365,137)	(3,090,486)	(2,812,238)
Payments to employees	(3,360,055)	(750,828)	(4,110,883)	(4,209,688)
Internal activity—payments to other funds	(1,296,768)	—	(1,296,768)	—
Claims paid	—	—	—	(8,482,451)
Other receipts (payments)	(2,325,483)	—	(2,325,483)	1,061,118
Net cash provided by operating activities	1,692,545	229,327	1,921,872	883,084
CASH FLOWS FROM NONCAPITAL FINANCING ACTIVITIES				
Operating subsidies and transfers to other funds	(290,000)	(211,409)	(501,409)	(175,033)
CASH FLOWS FROM CAPITAL AND RELATED FINANCING ACTIVITIES				
Proceeds from capital debt	4,041,322	8,660,778	12,702,100	—
Capital contributions	1,645,919	—	1,645,919	—
Purchases of capital assets	(4,194,035)	(144,716)	(4,338,751)	(400,086)
Principal paid on capital debt	(2,178,491)	(8,895,000)	(11,073,491)	(954,137)
Interest paid on capital debt	(1,479,708)	(1,166,546)	(2,646,254)	41,616
Other receipts (payments)	—	19,174	19,174	131,416
Net cash (used) by capital and related financing activities	(2,164,993)	(1,526,310)	(3,691,303)	(1,264,423)
CASH FLOWS FROM INVESTING ACTIVITIES				
Proceeds from sales and maturities of investments	—	—	—	15,684
Interest and dividends	454,793	143,747	598,540	129,550
Net cash provided by investing activities	454,793	143,747	598,540	145,234
Net (decrease) in cash and cash equivalents	(307,655)	(1,364,645)	(1,672,300)	(411,138)
Balances—beginning of the year	8,724,308	3,227,135	11,951,443	3,747,237
Balances—end of the year	$ 8,416,653	$ 1,862,490	$10,279,143	$ 3,336,099
Reconciliation of operating income (loss) to net cash provided (used) by operating activities:				
Operating income (loss)	$ 4,422,127	$ (238,804)	$ 4,183,323	$ (540,532)
Adjustments to reconcile operating income to net cash provided (used) by operating activities:				
Depreciation expense	1,163,140	542,049	1,705,189	1,707,872
Change in assets and liabilities:				
Receivables, net	653,264	1,205	654,469	31,941
Inventories	2,829	—	2,829	39,790
Accounts and other payables	(297,446)	(86,643)	(384,089)	475,212
Accrued expenses	(4,251,369)	11,520	(4,239,849)	(831,199)
Net cash provided by operating activities	$ 1,692,545	$ 229,327	$ 1,921,872	$ 883,084

Note: The required information about noncash investing, capital, and financing activities is not illustrated.

---

[26]Ibid, Illustration D-4.

Fiduciary fund financial statements[27]

The fiduciary fund financial statements are prepared using the economic resources measurement focus and accrual basis of accounting. Two financial statements are required for fiduciary funds: the Statement of Fiduciary Net Assets and the Statement of Changes in Fiduciary Net Assets.

The **Statement of Fiduciary Net Assets** uses the net asset format of Assets – Liabilities = Net Assets. A separate column should be used for each Fiduciary fund type included in the statement. If there is more than one Pension (and other employee benefit) trust fund, financial statements for each fund should be included in the notes to the financial statements if separate financial statements are not issued by each of the funds. When Agency funds are included in the Statement of Fiduciary Net Assets, the Agency fund assets should be equal to the Agency fund liabilities since the funds are only held in an agency capacity for others. If an Agency fund is used as a clearing account to collect and distribute funds, such as taxes, any portion of the assets due to another fund of the reporting entity should be reported in the appropriate fund rather than the Agency fund.

Sample City[28]
Statement of Fiduciary Net Assets
Fiduciary Funds
December 31, 2002

	Employee Retirement Plan	Private Purpose Trusts	Agency Funds
ASSETS			
Cash and cash equivalents	$ 1,973	$ 1,250	$ 44,889
Receivables:			
Interest and dividends	508,475	760	—
Other receivables	6,826	—	183,161
Total receivables	515,301	760	183,161
Investments, at fair value:			
U.S. government obligations	13,056,037	80,000	—
Municipal bonds	6,528,019	—	—
Corporate bonds	16,320,047	—	—
Corporate stocks	26,112,075	—	—
Other investments	3,264,009	—	—
Total investments	65,280,187	80,000	—
Total assets	65,797,461	82,010	$228,050
LIABILITIES			
Accounts payable	—	1,234	$ —
Refunds payable and others	1,358	—	228,050
Total liabilities	1,358	1,234	$228,050
NET ASSETS			
Held in trust for pension benefits and other purposes	$65,796,103	$80,776	

> Statements of individual pension plans and external investment pools are required to be presented in the notes to the financial statements if separate GAAP statements for those individual plans or pools are not available.

---

[27]Ibid, paragraphs 106–110.
[28]Ibid, Illustration E-1.

The **Statement of Changes in Fiduciary Net Assets** includes information about additions to, deductions from, and the net increase (decrease) in net assets for each fiduciary fund type. Agency funds are not included in the statement because Agency funds do not have net assets.

Sample City[29]
Statement of Changes in Fiduciary Net Assets
Fiduciary Funds
For the Year Ended December 31, 2002

	Employee Retirement Plan	Private Purpose Trusts
ADDITIONS		
Contributions:		
Employer	$ 2,721,341	$ —
Plan members	1,421,233	—
Total contributions	4,142,574	—
Investment earnings:		
Net (decrease) in fair value of investments	(272,522)	—
Interest	2,460,871	4,560
Dividends	1,445,273	—
Total investment earnings	3,633,622	4,560
Less investment expense	216,428	—
Net investment earnings	3,417,194	4,560
Total additions	7,559,768	4,560
DEDUCTIONS		
Benefits	2,453,047	3,800
Refunds of contributions	464,691	—
Administrative expenses	87,532	678
Total deductions	3,005,270	4,478
Change in net assets	4,554,498	82
Net assets—beginning of the year	61,241,605	80,694
Net assets—end of the year	$65,796,103	$80,776

> Statements of individual pension plans and external investment pools are required to be presented in the notes to the financial statements if separate GAAP statements for those individual plans or pools are not available.

Government-wide financial statements[30]

The cornerstone of governmental financial reporting is accountability. The government-wide statements are designed to foster accountability by displaying the operating activity and financial position of the primary government as a whole as well as its component units. There are two government-wide financial statements: 1) the Statement of Net Assets, and 2) the Statement of Activities. The government-wide Statement of Net Assets strives to inform the user about the current and noncurrent assets and liabilities of the government including capital assets and infrastructure. The Statement of Activities displays the net cost of providing governmental services such as public safety. Governmental and business-type activities of the primary government are presented in separate columns followed by a total column. Discretely presented component units are displayed in one or more columns to the right of the primary

[29]Ibid, Illustration E-2.
[30]Ibid, paragraph 6 and paragraphs 12–16.

government total. As explained earlier in this chapter, GAAP require additional information about major discretely presented component units in the financial statements. Fiduciary activities are not included in these statements.

The government-wide financial statements are prepared using the economic resources measurement focus and accrual basis of accounting. Because the fund financial statements for the governmental funds are prepared on the modified accrual basis of accounting, the data must be converted to the accrual basis. Steps to assist in the conversion of the data were presented earlier in this chapter.

The preparation of the government-wide financial statements requires **consolidation** of information through the elimination or reclassification of interfund activities, which could overstate assets and liabilities of the primary government.[31] Funds within a reporting entity may have receivables or payables due to other funds. These due to and due from other funds are netted and eliminated when preparing the government-wide statements. If there are net amounts due or payable between governmental activity funds and business-type funds, the amount is presented as an internal balance. Because Internal service funds provide services to and generate revenues from other funds of the government, there is, in effect, a double reporting of revenues and expenses. To eliminate the double reporting, the cost of providing the internal services is allocated back to each of the funds receiving the services. This process is explained with the proprietary fund financial statements.

The **Statement of Net Assets**[32] has three major sections: Assets, Liabilities, and Net Assets. Assets and Liabilities are presented in order of their relative liquidity. Liquidity means how quickly the item can be converted to cash. The assets and liabilities are classified as either current or noncurrent as explained in Chapter 4. Because the statement is prepared using the accrual basis of accounting, capital assets and long-term debt are included. GASB Statement No. 34 recommends that the Statement of Net Assets be presented in the **net assets format** of Assets – Liabilities = Net Assets, although the balance sheet format of Assets = Liabilities + Net Assets can be used. Therefore, the Statement of Net Assets is essentially a Balance Sheet that is reformatted slightly. The Statement of Net Assets presents net assets in three categories:

1) **Invested in capital assets, net of related debt.** The net assets in this category consist of capital assets net of accumulated depreciation, less any outstanding debt related to the acquisition, construction, or improvement of the asset.

    Example: If the new City Hall cost $20,000,000 to build, $500,000 in depreciation has been recognized, and $12,000,000 of the bonds issued to finance the construction are still outstanding, the value of the building would be reported as $7,500,000, net of related debt.

2) **Restricted.** Net assets that have restrictions on their use are displayed by purpose of restriction, with nonexpendable assets of endowments and permanent funds reported separately. Only restrictions that arise from the following sources should be reported as restricted assets:

    a. External restrictions placed by creditors, grantors, contributors, or laws of other governments

        Example: If a citizen donates cash that is restricted for use to maintain a park, its value would be reported as a restricted asset because the donor has restricted the use of the asset.

---

[31]Ibid, paragraphs 51–62.
[32]Ibid, paragraphs 30–37.

   b. Imposed by constitutional or enabling legislation

      Example: If a State law restricts oil and gas tax revenues to be used for environmental protection or for acquisition of State lands, any unspent funds would be recorded as a restricted asset.

3) **Unrestricted.**   Unrestricted net assets are those assets that are not in either capital assets or restricted assets.

      Example: A city has unrestricted cash available to be appropriated or expended. This is also the amount of net assets not reported in the two categories above.

Note the three categories of restrictions and the distinction between governmental and business-type activities and the separate column for component units in the Statement of Net Assets that follows on page 150.

    The **Statement of Activities**[33] presents the net expense or revenue of each function of governmental activities and each different identifiable activity[34] of business-type activities. Governments are required to present governmental activities, at a minimum, by function. Examples of **functions** are public safety (police and fire protection services), sanitation (garbage removal), and parks and recreation. The format of the statement presents the expenses associated with each function (direct expenses) of the government, followed by the revenues attributable to the function (program revenues) and then a net of the expenses and revenues. The concept is to "report the relative financial burden of each of the reporting government's functions on its taxpayers."[35] Taxpayers pay taxes to fund governmental functions. The Statement of Activities will display clearly to the taxpayer the net cost or revenue for each governmental function. This provision enables users of the Statements to see the net cost of governmental services such as public safety and public works and then compare that cost per capita with other governmental units in the same region. The user can then conclude whether that function is being provided at a comparable cost to that provided by other similar governmental units (this is a form of benchmarking). Obviously, a government is not a profit-seeking entity, so the Statement of Activities will generally show net costs/outflow of financial resources for each primary governmental function. For example, a public safety will generally show a net cost, or negative number, in the Statement of Activities as the government will spend more to run the public safety department than it generates in revenue.

    The allocation of direct expenses by **function** is required. Direct expenses are those that are clearly identifiable to a specific function or activity. General governmental and administrative activities are considered indirect expenses of other functional units and are permitted to be allocated to functional units but are not required to be allocated. Only direct expenses are required to be allocated. Depreciation expense for assets that are associated with a function should be charged directly to that function. Depreciation expense for general infrastructure assets should not be allocated to functional units. Interest expense on long-term debt that is "essential to the creation or continuing existence of a program and it would be misleading to exclude the interest from direct expenses"[36] should be charged to that function. Interest expense on general long-term liabilities is an indirect expense and is not required to be

---

[33]Ibid, paragraphs 38–56.
[34]GASB Statement No. 37, paragraph 10.
[35]GASB Statement No. 34
[36]Ibid, paragraph 46.

Sample City[37]
Statement of Net Assets
December 31, 2002

	Primary Government			
	Governmental Activities	Business-type Activities	Total	Component Units
ASSETS				
Current assets:				
Cash and cash equivalents	$ 13,597,899	$ 8,785,821	$ 22,383,720	$ 303,935
Investments	27,365,221	—	27,365,221	7,428,952
Receivables (net)	12,833,132	3,609,615	16,442,747	4,042,290
Internal balances	175,000	(175,000)	—	—
Inventories	322,149	126,674	448,823	83,697
Total Current Assets	54,293,401	12,347,110	66,640,511	11,858,874
Noncurrent assets:				
Restricted cash and cash equivalents	—	1,493,322	1,493,322	—
Capital assets:				
Land and infrastructure	118,620,361	34,788,333	153,408,694	751,239
Depreciable buildings, property, and equipment, net	51,402,399	116,600,418	168,002,817	36,993,547
Total noncurrent assets	170,022,760	152,882,073	322,904,833	37,744,786
Total Assets	224,316,161	165,229,183	389,545,344	49,603,660
LIABILITIES				
Current liabilities:				
Accounts payable	6,783,310	751,430	7,534,740	1,803,332
Deferred revenue	1,435,599	—	1,435,599	38,911
Current portion of long-term obligations	9,236,000	4,426,286	13,662,286	1,426,639
Total current liabilities	17,454,909	5,177,716	22,632,625	3,268,882
Noncurrent liabilities:				
Noncurrent portion of long-term obligations	83,302,378	74,482,273	157,784,651	27,106,151
Total liabilities	100,757,287	79,659,989	180,417,276	30,375,033
NET ASSETS				
Invested in capital assets, net of related debt	103,711,386	73,088,574	176,799,960	15,906,392
Restricted for:				
Capital projects	11,705,864	—	11,705,864	492,445
Debt service	3,020,708	1,451,996	4,472,704	—
Community development projects	4,811,043	—	4,811,043	—
Other purposes	3,214,302	—	3,214,302	—
Unrestricted (deficit)	(2,904,429)	11,028,624	8,124,195	2,829,790
Total net assets	$123,558,874	$ 85,569,194	$209,128,068	$19,228,627

allocated. If a governmental unit decides to use a full-cost approach, then direct and indirect expenses should be presented in separate columns to enhance comparability with other governments that only allocate direct costs.

Capital assets should be reported net of accumulated depreciation in the Statement of Net Assets. The total of accumulated depreciation can be reported within the statement or in the notes. Depreciation expenditure or expense should be reported in the Statement of Activities.

Governmental entities are also required to identify (or categorize) revenues as either general revenues or program revenues. **General revenues** support general governmental activities and services. **Program revenues** are restricted for use in spe-

---

[37]Ibid, Illustration A-1 and A-2.

cific programs. Program revenues are derived directly from the program or other parties external to the government. As Sample City's Statement of Activities shows, the program revenues are displayed by source and function or functional program such as Public Safety or Health and Sanitation so that the net cost or revenue of each functional program can be shown. The three categories of program revenues are:

1) **Charges for services** that are derived from exchange and exchange-like transactions such as fees for services.
2) **Program-specific operating grants and contributions** that are derived from mandatory and voluntary nonexchange transactions that are restricted for a specific program.
3) **Program specific capital grants and contributions** that are restricted to purchase, construct, or renovate capital assets related to a specific program.

Revenues must be identified as either **program revenues** or **general revenues** for the Statement of Activities. The *source* of revenue is the primary criteria to determine if it is a program or general revenue:[38]

1) Revenue from purchasers, users, or those who benefit from the goods or services of the program are always a **program revenue.**
   Example: A citizen purchases electric power from the city, so this is program revenue for the utility.
2) Revenue from parties who are not citizens (other governments, nongovernmental entities, and individuals) is a **program revenue** if restricted to a program(s) or a **general revenue** if not restricted.
   Example: The Federal government gives the State government funds to build a highway, so this will be a program revenue for the program that accounts for highway construction.
   Example: An elderly citizen donates cash to the government with no restrictions on use of the cash, so this will be a general revenue that the government may utilize in whatever way it sees fit.
3) Revenue from taxpayers of the government is always a **general revenue** even if restricted to a specific program.
   Example: Income or property taxes paid by taxpayers are general revenues for governmental use.
4) Revenue from the government itself is a **general revenue** unless required to be reported as **program revenue.**
   Example: Income from investment of excess cash would be general revenue available for governmental use.
   Example: Income from investments held in an endowment received from a donor, which restricted earnings for use for environmental protection will be accounted for as a program revenue in the account for the environmental protection program.

General revenues are summarized and displayed at the bottom of the Statement of Activities. Unless required by law or contract, general revenues are never allocated to the functional programs. The following sources of revenues are reported separately below general revenues: contributions to term and permanent endowments, contributions to permanent fund principal, special and extraordinary items, and transfers.

---

[38]Ibid, paragraph 47.

Special items are significant transactions that are either unusual or infrequent in nature that are under the control of the entity, such as the sale of a government-owned office building. **Extraordinary items** are both unusual in nature and infrequent in occurrence and generally not under the control of the entity, such as the receipt of Federal funds to rebuild infrastructure after an earthquake.

Sample City[39]
Statement of Activities
For the Year Ended December 31, 2002

| Functions/Programs | Expenses | Program Revenues | | | Net (Expense) Revenue and Changes in Net Assets | | | |
| | | Charges for Services | Operating Grants and Contributions | Capital Grants and Contributions | Primary Government | | | Component Units |
					Governmental Activities	Business-type Activities	Total	
Primary government:								
Governmental activities:								
General government	$ 9,571,410	$ 3,146,915	$ 843,617	$ —	$ (5,580,878)	$ —	$ (5,580,878)	$ —
Public safety	34,844,749	1,198,855	1,307,693	62,300	(32,275,901)	—	(32,275,901)	—
Public works	10,128,538	850,000	—	2,252,615	(7,025,923)	—	(7,025,923)	—
Engineering services	1,299,645	704,793	—	—	(594,852)	—	(594,852)	—
Health and sanitation	6,738,672	5,612,267	575,000	—	(551,405)	—	(551,405)	—
Cemetery	735,866	212,496	—	—	(523,370)	—	(523,370)	—
Culture and recreation	11,532,350	3,995,199	2,450,000	—	(5,087,151)	—	(5,087,151)	—
Community development	2,994,389	—	—	2,580,000	(414,389)	—	(414,389)	—
Education (payment to school district)	21,893,273	—	—	—	(21,893,273)	—	(21,893,273)	—
Interest on long-term debt	6,068,121	—	—	—	(6,068,121)	—	(6,068,121)	—
Total governmental activities	105,807,013	15,720,525	5,176,310	4,894,915	(80,015,263)	—	(80,015,263)	—
Business-type activities:								
Water	3,595,733	4,159,350	—	1,159,909	—	1,723,526	1,723,526	—
Sewer	4,912,853	7,170,533	—	486,010	—	2,743,690	2,743,690	—
Parking facilities	2,796,283	1,344,087	—	—	—	(1,452,196)	(1,452,196)	—
Total business-type activities	11,304,869	12,673,970	—	1,645,919	—	3,015,020	3,015,020	—
Total primary government	$117,111,882	$28,394,495	$5,176,310	$6,540,834	(80,015,263)	3,015,020	(77,000,243)	—
Component units:								
Landfill	$ 3,382,157	$ 3,857,858	$ —	$ 11,397	—	—	—	487,098
Public school system	31,186,498	705,765	3,937,083	—	—	—	—	(26,543,650)
Total component units	$ 34,568,655	$ 4,563,623	$3,937,083	$ 11,397	—	—	—	(26,056,552)
		General revenues:						
		Taxes:						
		Property taxes, levied for general purposes			51,693,573	—	51,693,573	—
		Property taxes, levied for debt service			4,726,244	—	4,726,244	—
		Franchise taxes			4,055,505	—	4,055,505	—
		Public service taxes			8,969,887	—	8,969,887	—
		Payment from Sample City			—	—	—	21,893,273
		Grants and contributions not restricted to specific programs			1,457,820	—	1,457,820	6,461,708
		Investment earnings			1,958,144	601,349	2,559,493	881,763
		Miscellaneous			884,907	104,925	989,832	22,464
		Special item—Gain on sale of park land			2,653,488	—	2,653,488	—
		Transfers			501,409	(501,409)	—	—
		Total general revenues, special items, and transfers			76,900,977	204,865	77,105,842	29,259,208
		Change in net assets			(3,114,286)	3,219,885	105,599	3,202,656
		Net assets—beginning			126,673,160	82,349,309	209,022,469	16,025,971
		Net Assets—ending			$123,558,874	$85,569,194	$209,128,068	$19,228,627

---

[39]Ibid, Illustration B-1.

Note the beauty of the Statement of Activities in clearly displaying to a citizen or taxpayer the amount of program revenues and expenses for each governmental function. The Statement of Activities clearly creates accountability for individual programs by displaying the **net revenue** or **net cost** of each functional program. The public safety function had a net cost of $32,275,901 as a governmental activity as compared to the water program, which produced a net revenue of $1,723,526 as a business-type activity. This amount could be divided by the number of citizens and compared to the net cost per capita for the public safety function of similar size cities.

● **INTERPRETIVE EXERCISE**

The city has the following revenues during the fiscal year: property tax revenues, water and utility fees from users, investment income from pension trust funds, investment income from General fund repurchase agreements, and dog license fees. Which revenues will be program revenues and which revenues will be general revenues?

The government-wide financial statements display to the uninformed user the net cost or net revenue of governmental programs and the net assets by governmental or business-type activity. The MD&A precedes both government-wide statements to provide the user with an explanation and analysis of the government's financial report and performance during the past fiscal year.

Required Supplementary Information[40]

The financial reporting model defines certain Required Supplementary Information (RSI), which must be included in a primary government's external annual financial report. In addition to the Management's Discussion and Analysis, RSI includes Budgetary Comparison Schedules, and, if applicable, information about infrastructure condition and maintenance if the modified approach to reporting infrastructure is used, defined benefit pension plan funding, and public-entity risk pool trend data.

Budgetary Comparison Schedules should be presented at a minimum for the General fund and each major Special revenue fund that legally adopts a budget. The budget information can be presented either in the format it was adopted or in the format of the Statement of Revenues, Expenditures, and Changes in Fund Balance. In either case, if the budget was not adopted in conformance with GAAP, a reconciliation to GAAP must be presented. The Budgetary Comparison Schedule should present the following information:

1) The original budget that was adopted before the beginning of the fiscal period;
2) The final budget that includes any legally authorized changes to the original budget; and
3) The actual revenues, expenditures, and other inflows and outflows reported on the same basis as the budgetary information.

Although not required, the reporting entity can include a column for the variance between the final budget and actual amounts. Note disclosures for the Budgetary Comparison Schedule are required for any expenditure in individual funds that exceed the appropriated amounts.[41]

---

[40]Ibid, paragraphs 129–133.
[41]GASB Statement No. 37, paragraph 19.

Sample City[42]
Budgetary Comparison Schedule
General Fund
For the Year Ended December 31, 2002

> The variance column is optional.

	Budgeted Amounts		Actual Amounts (Budgetary Basis)	Variances with Final Budget Positive (Negative)
	Original	Final		
Budgetary fund balance, January 1	$ 3,528,750	$ 2,742,799	$ 2,742,799	$ —
Resources (inflows):				
Property taxes	52,017,833	51,853,018	51,173,436	(679,582)
Franchise taxes	4,546,209	4,528,750	4,055,505	(473,245)
Public service taxes	8,295,000	8,307,274	8,969,887	662,613
Licenses and permits	2,126,600	2,126,600	2,287,794	161,194
Fines and forfeitures	718,800	718,800	606,946	(111,854)
Charges for services	12,392,972	11,202,150	11,374,460	172,310
Grants	6,905,898	6,571,360	6,119,938	(451,422)
Sale of land	1,355,250	3,500,000	3,476,488	(23,512)
Miscellaneous	3,024,292	1,220,991	881,874	(339,117)
Interest received	1,015,945	550,000	552,325	2,325
Transfers from other funds	939,525	130,000	129,323	(677)
Amounts available for appropriation	96,867,074	93,451,742	92,370,775	(1,080,967)
Charges to appropriations (outflows)				
General government:				
Legal	665,275	663,677	632,719	30,958
Mayor, legislative, city manager	3,058,750	3,192,910	2,658,264	534,646
Finance and accounting	1,932,500	1,912,702	1,852,687	60,015
City clerk and elections	345,860	354,237	341,206	13,031
Employee relations	1,315,500	1,300,498	1,234,232	66,266
Planning and economic development	1,975,600	1,784,314	1,642,575	141,739
Public safety:				
Police	19,576,820	20,367,917	20,246,496	121,421
Fire department	9,565,280	9,559,967	9,559,967	—
Emergency medical services	2,323,171	2,470,127	2,459,866	10,261
Inspections	1,585,695	1,585,695	1,533,380	52,315
Public works:				
Public works administration	388,500	385,013	383,397	1,616
Street maintenance	2,152,750	2,233,362	2,233,362	—
Street lighting	762,750	759,832	759,832	—
Traffic operations	385,945	374,945	360,509	14,436
Mechanical maintenance	1,525,685	1,272,696	1,256,087	16,609
Engineering services:				
Engineering administration	1,170,650	1,158,023	1,158,023	—
Geographical information system	125,625	138,967	138,967	—
Health and sanitation:				
Garbage pickup	5,756,250	6,174,653	6,174,653	—
Cemetery:				
Personal services	425,000	425,000	422,562	2,438
Purchase of goods and services	299,500	299,500	283,743	15,757
Culture and recreation:				
Library	985,230	1,023,465	1,022,167	1,298
Parks and recreation	9,521,560	9,786,397	9,756,618	29,779
Community communications	552,350	588,208	510,361	47,847
Nondepartmental:				
Miscellaneous	—	259,817	259,817	—
Contingency	2,544,049	—	—	—
Transfers to other funds	2,970,256	2,163,759	2,163,759	—
Funding for school district	22,000,000	22,000,000	21,893,273	106,727
Total charges to appropriations	93,910,551	92,205,681	90,938,522	1,267,159
Budgetary fund balance, December 31	$ 2,956,523	$ 1,246,061	$ 1,432,253	$ 186,192

---

[42]GASB Statement No. 34, Illustration G-1.

If the modified approach to reporting infrastructure is used, schedules should be presented to provide the following information about infrastructure condition and maintenance:

1) The assessed condition of eligible infrastructure assets for the current period and three most recent assessments, including the date of the assessment; and
2) The estimated annual cost for the current year to maintain and preserve the eligible infrastructure assets and the actual amount spent for each of the last five years.

In addition, information should be provided about the basis used for condition assessments, the level of condition that should be maintained, and any other important factors that may impact the condition of the infrastructure.

If the reporting entity sponsors a defined benefit pension plan, a schedule that compares actuarially calculated funding requirements with actual pension contributions must be prepared. A schedule that compares the trend of actuarially calculated accrued liability for future pension benefits with assets in the pension plan is also required.

If the reporting entity participates in a public-entity risk pool for risk financing and insurance-related activities, additional information about the trend in revenues and estimated and actual claims for the pool must be provided as RSI.

Notes to the financial statements

Information that is essential to understanding the financial statements is required to be included in footnote disclosure. The notes to governmental financial reports can be quite extensive because of the number of footnote disclosures prescribed by GAAP.

Some of the more common footnote disclosures are:

Summary of significant accounting policies

Cash and cash equivalents—policy of definition

How much will it cost to implement GASB Statement No. 34?

GASB considered implementation costs in developing the GASB Statement No. 34 financial reporting model. The GASB's desire to minimize implementation costs influenced the decision to retain Governmental Fund-type statements so that governments would not have to substantially modify their current accounting information system. GASB was mindful that governments had recently incurred systems costs due to Y2K conversions and did not want to develop a model that would require another major information systems modification and related costs. Standard & Poor's did a survey of 100 governments, and 40 State and local governments responded to estimate GASB 34 implementation costs. The Standard & Poor's survey reported that implementation costs could range from $35,000 to $500,000 for cities, $35,000 to $2 million for counties, and $2 to 4 million for states. Governments expected to implement GASB Statement No. 34 early (prior to required implementation) are higher-rated credits with databases and staff already in place, which are adequate to prepare the new statements.

(Source: "In S&P Survey, Governments Project the Costs of GASB 34," by Lynn Hume in *The Bond Buyer*, pages 1 and 33, November 10, 2000.

Cash deposits with financial institutions
Investment disclosures
Policy for capitalizing and depreciating capital assets
Debt service requirements
Lease obligations
Interfund balances and transfers
Encumbrances outstanding
Subsequent events

Additional guidance for footnote disclosures can be found in GASB Statement No. 38, *Certain Financial Note Disclosures.*

PUTTING IT ALL TOGETHER

The following example illustrates: 1) basic transactions in Governmental Funds: general and capital projects and in Proprietary Funds: internal service and enterprise; 2) preparing fund financial statements for Governmental and Proprietary Funds; 3) preparing a consolidated trial balance at fiscal year-end and adjustments to reconcile to the government-wide statements; and 4) preparing government-wide financial statements.

Governmental fund activity

The General fund had the following trial balance at the beginning of the fiscal year:

Cash	500,000	
Investments	5,000,000	
Accounts Receivable	100,000	
Accounts Payable		50,000
Fund Balance Unreserved		5,550,000

The following transactions were recorded during the year:

Estimated Revenues	10,000,000	
Appropriations		9,500,000
Budgetary Fund Balance		500,000
(Record the budget)		

Taxes Receivable—Current	9,500,000	
Allowance for Uncollectible Taxes—Current		100,000
Property Tax Revenue		9,400,000
(Record the property tax levy)		

Cash	100,000	
Accounts Receivable		100,000
(Record various payments received)		

Accounts Payable	50,000	
Cash		50,000
(Record payment of outstanding invoices)		

Expenditures	8,000	
Due to Internal Service Fund		8,000
(Record purchase of supplies from Internal service fund)		

Cash	9,300,000	
Taxes Receivable—Current		9,300,000
(Record receipt of property taxes)		

Expenditures	9,000,000	
Cash		9,000,000
(Record payment of general government salaries & benefits)		

Expenditures	16,000	
Due to Enterprise Fund		16,000
(Record purchase of power from Enterprise fund)		

Due from Capital Projects Fund	500,000	
Cash		500,000
(Record loan of $500,000 to Capital projects fund)		

Encumbrances	420,000	
Fund Balance Reserved for Encumbrances		420,000
(Record supplies purchase order with estimate of amount due)		

Fund Balance Reserved for Encumbrances	420,000	
Encumbrances		420,000
(Reverse estimate of amount due now that actual invoice of $400,000 is received)		

Supplies Expenditures	400,000	
Accounts Payable		400,000
(Record invoice for supplies received but not yet paid)		

Due to Enterprise Fund	16,000	
Due to Internal Service Fund	8,000	
Cash		24,000
(Pay amounts due to other funds)		

Cash	20,000	
Other Financing Source—Sale of Equipment		20,000
(Record sale of fully depreciated equipment)		

Accounts Payable	400,000	
Cash		400,000
(Record payment of outstanding invoice)		

Cash	1,500,000	
Investments		1,000,000
Investment Income		500,000
(Record maturity of an investment and investment income)		

Property Tax Revenue	9,400,000	
Investment Income	500,000	
Other Financing Source—Sale of Equipment	20,000	
Budgetary Fund Balance	80,000	
Estimated Revenues		10,000,000

(Closing entry to close actual revenues against the estimated amount. Note that the actual revenues received were less than the estimate, so Budgetary Fund Balance must be decreased/debited.)

Appropriations	9,500,000	
Budgetary Fund Balance		76,000
Expenditures		9,424,000

(Closing entry to close approved spending against actual spending. In this case, the actual spending is less than the approved level, so Budgetary Fund Balance must be increased/credited.)

Budgetary Fund Balance	496,000	
Unreserved Fund Balance		496,000

(Closing entry for Budgetary Fund Balance)

The General Fund Balance Sheet at fiscal year-end would appear as follows:

General Fund
Balance Sheet
(date)

ASSETS

Cash	$1,446,000
Investments	4,000,000
Taxes Receivable—net	100,000
Due from Capital Projects Fund	500,000
Total assets	$6,046,000

LIABILITIES AND FUND BALANCE

Total liabilities	$ -0-

Fund Balance:	
Unreserved	6,046,000
Total liabilities and fund balances	$6,046,000

The General Fund Statement of Revenues, Expenditures, and Changes in Fund Balances would appear as follows:

General Fund
Statement of Revenues, Expenditures, and Changes in Fund Balances
For the Year Ended (date)

REVENUES

Property Taxes	$9,400,000
Investment Income	500,000
Total revenues	$9,900,000

EXPENDITURES:

Current:	
General Government	$9,424,000
Excess of revenues over expenditures	$ 476,000

OTHER FINANCING SOURCES (USES)

Sale of Equipment	20,000
Net change in fund balance	496,000
Fund balance—beginning	5,550,000
Fund balance—ending	$ 6,046,000

The Capital projects fund is established as a newly created governmental fund during the fiscal year, so there is no beginning trial balance. Remember that capital assets and long-term bonds are not recorded in the governmental funds but must be recorded in the government-wide statements. The governmental fund-type statements must be adjusted with a reconciliation to create the capital asset and long-term debt accounts in the government-wide statements. The following transactions were recorded during the year:

Cash	500,000	
Due to General Fund		500,000
(Record loan from General fund)		

Expenditures	400,000	
Cash		400,000
(Payment of architect to draw up plans for building; no encumbrance was previously recorded)		

Cash	10,000,000	
Other Financing Source—Bond Proceeds		10,000,000
(Record issuance of long-term debt to construct a building to house general government offices)		

Encumbrances	9,400,000	
Fund Balance Reserved for Encumbrances		9,400,000
(Record construction contract)		

Fund Balance Reserved for Encumbrances	3,000,000	
Encumbrances		3,000,000
(Record receipt of progress billing of $3,000,000 on construction contract)		

Expenditures—Capital Outlay	3,000,000	
Contracts Payable		2,700,000
Contracts Payable—Retained Percentage		300,000
(Record expenditure for progress billing with 10% retention until completion of contract)		

Contracts Payable	2,700,000	
Cash		2,700,000
(Record payment of contract billing less 10% retained until satisfactory completion)		

Other Financing Sources—Bond Proceeds	$10,000,000	
Unreserved Fund Balance		200,000
Expenditures—Capital Outlay		3,400,000
Encumbrances		6,400,000
(Closing entry at fiscal year-end)		

The Capital Projects Fund Balance Sheet would appear as follows:

Capital Projects Fund
Balance Sheet
(date)

ASSETS

Cash	$7,400,000
Total assets	$7,400,000

LIABILITIES AND FUND BALANCE

Liabilities:

Contracts Payable—Retained percentage	$ 300,000
Due to General Fund	500,000
Total liabilities	800,000

Fund Balances:

Reserved for Encumbrances	6,400,000
Unreserved	200,000
Total fund balances	6,600,000
Total liabilities and fund balances	$7,400,000

The Capital Projects Fund Statement of Revenues, Expenditures, and Changes in Fund Balance would appear as follows:

Capital Projects Fund
Statement of Revenues, Expenditures, and Changes in Fund Balance
For the year ended (date)

REVENUES	$ -0-
EXPENDITURES	
Capital Outlay	3,400,000
Deficiency of revenues over expenditures	(3,400,000)
OTHER FINANCING SOURCES (USES)	
Proceeds of bonds	10,000,000
Net change in fund balances	6,600,00
Fund Balance—beginning	-0-
Fund Balance—ending	$ 6,600,000

The basic transactions in the General fund and Capital projects fund have been recorded for the fiscal year's activity. The next step is to prepare the combined Governmental Funds Balance Sheet and Statement of Revenues, Expenditures, and Changes in Fund Balances. This is when the reporting entity would need to determine whether funds are major or nonmajor. The General fund is always a major fund. As you will see when the Proprietary fund example is complete, the total assets of the Capital projects fund is more than 10% of all governmental fund assets and more that 5% of the corresponding total for all governmental funds and proprietary funds combined, therefore, the Capital projects fund is a major fund. A reconciliation of amounts reported for governmental activities in the government-wide Statement of Net Assets to the combined Balance Sheet is presented at the bottom of the statement.

Combined Balance Sheet
Governmental Funds
(date)

	General Fund	Capital Projects Fund	Total Governmental Funds
ASSETS			
Cash	$1,446,000	$7,400,000	$ 8,846,000
Investments	4,000,000	—	4,000,000
Receivables, net	100,000	—	100,000
Due from Other Funds	500,000	—	500,000
Total assets	$6,046,000	$7,400,000	$13,446,000
LIABILITIES AND FUND BALANCES			
Liabilities:			
Contracts Payable—			
Retained Percentage	—	$ 300,000	$ 300,000
Due to Other Funds	—	500,000	500,000
Total liabilities	-0-	800,000	800,000
Fund Balances:			
Reserved for Encumbrances	—	6,400,000	6,400,000
Unreserved, reported in:			
General fund	6,046,000	—	6,046,000
Capital Projects Fund	—	200,000	200,000
Total fund balances	6,046,000	6,600,000	12,646,000
Total liabilities and fund balances	$6,046,000	$7,400,000	

Amounts reported for governmental activities in the Statement of Net Assets are different because:

Capital assets used in governmental activities are not financial resources and therefore are not reported in the funds. 17,700,000

Internal service funds are used by management to charge the costs of certain activities such as supplies to individual funds. The assets and liabilities of the internal service funds are included in governmental activities in the statement of net assets. 30,667

Long-term liabilities, including bonds payable, are not due and payable in the current period and therefore are not reported in the funds. (10,000,000)

Net assets of governmental activities $20,376,667

The components of the changes in the net assets of governmental activities are as follows:

The following governmental funds capital assets will be included in the government-wide Statement of Net Assets:

Land and Infrastructure	10,000,000
Buildings	5,000,000
Accumulated Depreciation—Buildings	(1,000,000)
Equipment	600,000
Accumulated Depreciation—Equipment	(300,000)
	14,300,000

In addition, the Capital Outlay in the Capital Projects Fund will be converted to a capital asset. 3,400,000

  17,700,000

The Internal service fund will end the fiscal year with net assets that will be displayed in the governmental funds. 31,000

The operating income of $1,000 will be allocated $667 to the General Fund and $333 to the Enterprise utility fund, which is reported as a business-type activity. (333)

  30,667

The Other Financing Source for the issuance of bonds in the Capital Projects Fund is converted to a long-term liability. (10,000,000)

The Governmental Funds Adjustment Spreadsheet using the six steps shown later in this exercise will further demonstrate the conversion from the governmental fund statements to the government-wide Statement of Net Assets.

Combined Statement of Revenues, Expenditures, and Changes in Fund Balances
Governmental Funds
For period ending (date)

	General Fund	Capital Projects Fund	Total Governmental Funds
REVENUES			
Property Taxes	$9,400,000	$ —	$ 9,400,000
Investment Income	500,000	—	500,000
Total revenues	9,900,000	—	9,900,000
EXPENDITURES			
Current:			
General Government	9,424,000	—	9,424,000
Capital Outlay	—	3,400,000	3,400,000
Total expenditures	9,424,000	3,400,000	12,824,000
Excess (deficiency) of Revenues Over Expenditures	476,000	(3,400,000)	(2,924,000)
OTHER FINANCING SOURCES (USES)			
Sale of Equipment	20,000	—	20,000
Proceeds of Bonds	—	10,000,000	10,000,000
Total Other Financing Sources (uses)	20,000	10,000,000	10,020,000
Net Change in Fund Balances	496,000	6,600,000	7,096,000
Fund Balances—beginning	5,550,000	—	5,550,000
Fund Balances—ending	$6,046,000	$ 6,600,000	$12,646,000

Reconciliation of the Statement of Revenues, Expenditures,
and Changes in Fund Balances of Governmental Funds
to the Statement of Activities
For the Year Ended (date)

Net change in fund balances—total governmental funds	$ 7,096,000
Amounts reported for governmental activities in the Statement of Activities are different because:	
Governmental funds report capital outlays as expenditures. However, in the Statement of Activities, the cost of those assets is allocated over their estimated useful lives as depreciation expense. This is the amount by which capital outlays exceeded depreciation in the current period.	3,400,000
In the statement of activities, only the gain on the sale of the equipment is reported, whereas in the governmental funds, the proceeds from the sale increase financial resources. Thus, the change in net assets differs from the change in fund balance by the cost of the equipment sold less accumulated depreciation.	-0-
Revenues in the statement of activities that do not provide current financial resources are not reported as revenues in the funds.	-0-
Bond proceeds provide current financial resources to governmental funds, but issuing debt increases long-term liabilities in the Statement of Net Assets. Repayment of bond principal is an expenditure in the governmental funds, but the repayment reduces long-term liabilities in the Statement of Net Assets. This is the amount by which proceeds exceeded repayments.	(10,000,000)
Some expenses reported in the Statement of Activities do not require the use of current financial resources and therefore are not reported as expenditures in governmental funds.	-0-
Internal service funds are used by management to charge the costs of certain activities, such as supplies to individual funds. The net revenue (expense) of Internal service funds is reported in governmental activities.	667
Change in net assets of governmental activities	$ 496,667

Proprietary fund activity

The Internal service supplies fund started the fiscal year with $30,000 in Supplies Inventory and $30,000 in Unrestricted Net Assets. The following transactions were recorded during the year:

Due from General Fund	8,000	
Due from Enterprise Fund	4,000	
Operating Revenues		12,000
(Billings to departments)		
Supplies Expense	11,000	
Supplies Inventory		11,000
(Physical inventory conducted)		
Cash	12,000	
Due from General Fund		8,000
Due from Enterprise Fund		4,000
(Received payments from departments)		
Operating Revenues	12,000	
Supplies Expense		11,000
Unrestricted Net Assets		1,000
(Close operating accounts at fiscal year-end)		

The Internal Service Supplies Fund Statement of Net Assets would appear as follows:

Internal Service Supplies Fund
Statement of Net Assets
(date)

ASSETS	
Current assets:	
Cash	$12,000
Supplies Inventory	19,000
Total current assets	31,000
LIABILITIES	-0-
NET ASSETS	
Unrestricted	31,000
Total net assets	$31,000

The following statement illustrates the Statement of Revenues, Expenses, and Changes in Fund Net Assets for the Internal Service Supplies Fund.

Internal Service Supplies Fund
Statement of Revenues, Expenses, and Changes in Fund Net Assets
For the year ended (date)

Operating revenues:	
Sale of supplies	$12,000
Operating expenses:	
Supplies expense	11,000
Operating income	1,000
Change in net assets	1,000
Total net assets—beginning	30,000
Total net assets—ending	$31,000

The Internal service fund did not have any nonoperating revenues or expenses and only served other funds within the governmental unit. The Internal service fund will be eliminated in the reconciliation of governmental funds to create the government-wide statements. The operating income of $1,000 will be allocated ratably to the two funds that did business with the Internal service fund. The General fund had $8,000 of the $12,000 total sales, so it will receive $667 of the $1,000 operating income as a reduction of the expenditure. The Enterprise fund had $4,000 of the $12,000 total sales, so it will receive $333 of the $1,000 operating income.

Internal Service Supplies Fund
Statement of Cash Flows
(date)

CASH FLOWS FROM OPERATING ACTIVITIES

Receipts from customers—interfund services provided	$12,000
Net cash provided by operating activities	12,000

CASH FLOWS FROM NONCAPITAL FINANCING ACTIVITIES

	=

CASH FLOWS FROM CAPITAL AND RELATED FINANCING ACTIVITIES

	=

CASH FLOWS FROM INVESTING ACTIVITIES

	=
Net increase (decrease) in cash and cash equivalents	12,000
Balances—beginning of year	—
Balances—end of year	$12,000

Reconciliation of operating income to net cash provided (used) by operating activities:

Operating income	$ 1,000
Adjustments to reconcile operating income to net cash (provided) by operating activities:	
Change in assets and liabilities:	
Inventories	11,000
Net cash provided by operating activities	$12,000

The Enterprise utility fund started the year with the following trial balance:

Cash	100,000	
Capital Assets—Buildings	2,000,000	
Accumulated Depreciation	(100,000)	
Net Assets—Invested in Capital Assets		1,900,000
Net Assets—Unrestricted		100,000

The following transactions occurred during the year.

Operating Expenses—Supplies	4,000	
Due to Internal Service Fund		4,000
(Purchase of supplies from Internal Service Fund)		

Due from General Fund	16,000	
Accounts Receivable	364,000	
Operating Revenues		380,000
(Record billings to customers)		
Cash	150,000	
Accounts Receivable		150,000
(Record receipt of billings)		
Operating Expenses—Salaries	200,000	
Cash		200,000
(Payment of salaries)		
Operating Expenses—Depreciation	100,000	
Accumulated Depreciation—Capital Assets		100,000
(Record depreciation expense on capital assets)		
Cash	2,000,000	
Revenue Bonds Payable		2,000,000
(Issued revenue bonds to construct building addition)		
Construction in Progress	1,000,000	
Contracts Payable		900,000
Contracts Payable—Retained Percentage		100,000
(Billing by contractor for building construction; 10% retention)		
Cash	16,000	
Due from General Fund		16,000
(General Fund pays billing)		
Due to Internal Service Fund	4,000	
Cash		4,000
(Pay billing from Internal Service Fund)		
Operating Revenue	380,000	
Operating Expenses—Supplies		4,000
Operating Expenses—Salaries		200,000
Operating Expenses—Depreciation		100,000
Unrestricted Net Assets		76,000
(Closing entry fiscal year-end)		

The Enterprise Utility Fund Statement of Net Assets would appear as follows:

Enterprise Utility Fund
Statement of Net Assets
(date)

ASSETS

Current assets:

Cash	$2,062,000
Accounts Receivable	214,000
Total current assets	2,276,000

Noncurrent assets:

Capital Assets

Buildings	2,000,000
Construction in Progress	1,000,000
Accumulated Depreciation	(200,000)
Total noncurrent assets	2,800,000
Total assets	5,076,000

LIABILITIES

Current liabilities:

Contracts Payable	900,000
Contracts Payable— Retained Percentage	100,000
Total current liabilities	1,000,000

Noncurrent liabilities:

Revenue Bonds Payable	2,000,000
Total liabilities	3,000,000

NET ASSETS

Invested in capital assets, net of related debt	800,000
Restricted for construction	1,000,000
Unrestricted	276,000
Total net assets	$2,076,000

The following statement illustrates the Statement of Revenues, Expenses, and Changes in Fund Net Assets for the Enterprise Utility Fund.

Enterprise Utility Fund
Statement of Revenues, Expenses, and Changes in Fund Net Assets
For the year ended (date)

Operating revenues:

Charges for services	$ 380,000
Total operating revenues	380,000

Operating expenses:

Salaries	200,000
Supplies	4,000
Depreciation	100,000
Total operating expenses	304,000
Operating income	76,000

Nonoperating revenues (expenses):   —

Change in net assets	76,000
Total net assets—beginning	2,000,000
Total net assets—ending	$2,076,000

A Statement of Cash Flows for the Enterprise Utility Fund would be prepared as follows:

Enterprise Utility Fund
Statement of Cash Flows
(date)

CASH FLOWS FROM OPERATING ACTIVITIES	
Receipts from customers	$ 150,000
Receipts from customers—interfund services provided	16,000
Payments to employees	(200,000)
Payments for interfund services used	(4,000)
Net cash used by operating activities	(38,000)
CASH FLOWS FROM NONCAPITAL FINANCING ACTIVITIES	—
CASH FLOWS FROM CAPITAL AND RELATED FINANCING ACTIVITIES	
Proceeds from capital debt	2,000,000
CASH FLOWS FROM INVESTING ACTIVITIES	—
Net increase (decrease) in cash and cash equivalents	1,962,000
Balances—beginning of year	100,000
Balances—end of year	$2,062,000
Reconciliation of operating income to net cash provided (used) by operating activities:	
Operating income	$ 76,000
Adjustments to reconcile operating income to net cash (used) by operating activities:	
Depreciation expense	100,000
Change in assets and liabilities:	
Increase in accounts receivable, net	(214,000)
Net cash used by operating activities	$ (38,000)

The basic transactions in the Internal service supplies fund and the Enterprise utility fund have been recorded for the fiscal year's activity. Preparation of the combined Statement of Net Assets for Proprietary Funds; combined Statement of Revenues, Expenses, and Changes in Fund Net Assets for Proprietary Funds; and the combined Statement of Cash Flows for Proprietary Funds is the next step in the process of preparing the required fund financial statements. This is when the reporting entity would determine whether each enterprise fund is a major or nonmajor fund. Since the total assets of the Enterprise utility fund are more than 10% of all Enterprise fund assets and more than 5% of the corresponding elements of total assets for all governmental funds and proprietary funds combined, it would be a major fund. Note that Internal service fund activity is reported in a separate column in each of the statements. If there had been more than one Internal service fund, the totals would have been combined into one column for the statements.

Combined Statement of Net Assets
Proprietary Funds
(date)

	Business-type Activities Enterprise Funds		Governmental Activities—Internal
	Utility Fund	Totals	Service Funds
ASSETS			
Current assets:			
Cash	$2,062,000	$2,062,000	$12,000
Receivables, net	214,000	214,000	—
Inventories	—	—	19,000
Total current assets	2,276,000	2,276,000	31,000
Noncurrent assets:			
Capital Assets:			
Buildings	2,000,000	2,000,000	—
Construction in Progress	1,000,000	1,000,000	—
Less Accumulated Depreciation	(200,000)	(200,000)	—
Total noncurrent assets	2,800,000	2,800,000	—
Total assets	5,076,000	5,076,000	31,000
LIABILITIES			
Current liabilities:			
Contracts Payable	900,000	900,000	—
Contracts Payable—Retained Percentage	100,000	100,000	—
Total current liabilities	1,000,000	1,000,000	—
Noncurrent liabilities:			
Bonds payable	2,000,000	2,000,000	—
Total liabilities	3,000,000	3,000,000	—
NET ASSETS			
Invested in capital assets, net of related debt	800,000	800,000	—
Restricted for construction	1,000,000	1,000,000	—
Unrestricted	276,000	276,000	31,000
Total net assets	$2,076,000	$2,076,000	$31,000
Adjustment to reflect the consolidation of Internal service fund activities to related Enterprise funds		333	
Total net assets of business-type activities		$2,076,333	

Combined Statement of Revenues, Expenditures, and Changes in Fund Net Assets
Proprietary Funds
For period ending (date)

	Business-type Activities Enterprise Funds		Governmental Activities—Internal
	Utility Fund	Totals	Service Funds
Operating revenues:			
Charges for services	$ 380,000	$ 380,000	$ —
Miscellaneous	—	—	12,000
Total operating revenues	380,000	380,000	12,000
Operating expenses:			
Personal services	200,000	200,000	—
Other supplies and expenses	4,000	4,000	11,000
Depreciation	100,000	100,000	—
Total operating expenses	304,000	304,000	11,000
Operating income (loss)	76,000	76,000	1,000
Nonoperating revenues (expenses):	—	—	—
Change in net assets	76,000	76,000	1,000
Net assets—beginning	2,000,000	2,000,000	30,000
Net assets—ending	$2,076,000	2,076,000	$31,000
Adjustment to reflect the consolidation of Internal service fund activities to related Enterprise funds		333	
Change in net assets of business-type activities		$2,076,333	

Combined Statement of Cash Flows
Proprietary Funds
For period ending (date)

	Business-type Activities Enterprise Funds		Governmental Activities—Internal
	Utility Fund	**Totals**	**Service Funds**
CASH FLOW FROM OPERATING ACTIVITIES			
Receipts from customers	$ 150,000	$ 150,000	$ —
Receipts from customers—internal	16,000	16,000	12,000
Payments to employees	(200,000)	(200,000)	—
Internal activity—payments to other funds	(4,000)	(4,000)	—
Net cash provided by operating activities	(38,000)	(38,000)	12,000
CASH FLOWS FROM NONCAPITAL FINANCING ACTIVITIES	—	—	—
CASH FLOWS FROM CAPITAL AND RELATED FINANCING ACTIVITIES			
Proceeds from capital debt	2,000,000	2,000,000	—
CASH FLOWS FROM INVESTING ACTIVITIES	—	—	—
Net increase (decrease) in cash and equivalents	1,962,000	1,962,000	12,000
Balances—beginning of the year	100,000	100,000	—
Balances—end of the year	$2,062,000	$2,062,000	$12,000
Reconciliation of operating income (loss) to net cash provided (used) by operating activities:			
Operating income (loss)	$ 76,000	$ 76,000	$ 1,000
Adjustments to reconcile operating income to net cash provided (used) by operating activities:			
Depreciation expense	100,000	100,000	—
Change in assets and liabilities:			
Receivables, net	(214,000)	(214,000)	—
Inventories	—	—	11,000
Net cash provided by operating activities	$ (38,000)	$ (38,000)	$12,000

Preparing the government-wide statements

The government-wide statements are prepared using the economic resources measurement focus and the accrual basis of accounting, so adjustments must be made to convert the governmental fund statements to the government-wide statements. Since the adjustments are not posted to the general ledger, a separate spreadsheet can be used to track the six-step conversion process. Begin the spreadsheet with a trial balance format by entering the amounts in the total governmental funds column for each category of Assets and Liabilities listed on the Combined Balance Sheet. Next, add the amounts in the total governmental funds column for each category of Revenue and Expenditure listed on the Combined Statement of Revenues, Expenditures, and Changes in Fund Balances. The *beginning* fund balance for total governmental funds is used to complete the initial trial balance for the spreadsheet.

Follow the six-step adjustment process described earlier in this chapter to complete the conversion to the government-wide financial statements.

1) Establish the governmental fund capital assets.
   Add the following beginning capital assets and accumulated depreciation to the trial balance on the spreadsheet:

Land and Infrastructure	10,000,000
Buildings	5,000,000
Accumulated Depreciation	(1,000,000)
Equipment	600,000
Accumulated Depreciation	(300,000)
Addition to Fund Balance	14,300,000

Convert the capital outlay expenditure ($3,400,000) to create the asset Construction-in-Progress as an adjustment.

Adjust for the sale of fully depreciated equipment ($20,000).

2) Determine the outstanding governmental fund long-term debt.

Any long-term governmental debt outstanding at the beginning of the fiscal year would be added to the trial balance on the spreadsheet. In this case, there was none.

Establish long-term debt issued during the year ($10,000,000) to create the liability as an adjustment.

3) Restate governmental fund revenues to accrual.

No adjustments needed in this case.

4) Restate governmental fund expenditures to accrual.

No adjustments needed in this case. There was no accrued interest on the new bond issue at the end of the fiscal year.

5) Consolidate and eliminate Internal service funds.

Allocate the assets, liabilities and fund balance listed in the Internal service funds column on the Proprietary Statement of Net Assets.

Allocate the income ($1,000) listed in the Internal service funds column on the Proprietary Funds Combined Statement of Revenues, Expenditures, and Changes in Net Fund assets ratably to the funds that did business with the Internal service fund (total revenue $12,000 – General fund $8,000 and Enterprise fund $4,000).The General fund will receive $667 ($8,000/$12,000 × $1,000), and the Enterprise fund will receive $333 ($4,000/$12,000 × $1,000). The General fund and the Enterprise fund will reflect the income as a reduction of expenditures by program.

6) Other consolidation adjustments.

Remove interfund borrowings between governmental funds ($500,000 loan from General fund to Capital projects fund).

Net any internal balances between governmental and proprietary funds. ($333 allocation of internal service fund income to proprietary Enterprise fund is converted from a Due to and shown instead as an internal balance).

Once the adjustments are completed, the beginning trial balance amounts are adjusted and the ending trial balance column is completed. Totals from the ending trial balance will be used in the appropriate governmental activities column on the government-wide Statement of Net Assets and Statement of Activities financial reports. Note on the government-wide Statement of Activities the total expenses of the Utility fund have been reduced by the $333 allocation of income from the Internal service fund.

Governmental Funds Adjustment Spreadsheet

Accounts	Beginning Trial Balance		Adjustments				Ending Trial Balance	
Assets:								
Cash	8,846,000		5)	12,000			8,858,000	
Investments	4,000,000						4,000,000	
Taxes Receivable—net	100,000						100,000	
Due from Capital Projects Fund	500,000				6)	500,000		
Internal Balances					6)	333		333
Supplies Inventory			5)	19,000			19,000	
Land and Infrastructure	1) 10,000,000						10,000,000	
Buildings	1) 5,000,000						5,000,000	
Accumulated Depreciation Buildings		1) 1,000,000						1,000,000
Equipment	1) 600,000				1)	20,000	580,000	
Accumulated Depreciation Equipment		1) 300,000	1)	20,000				280,000
Construction in Progress			1)	3,400,000			3,400,000	
Liabilities:								
Due to General Fund		500,000	6)	500,000				
Due to Utility Fund			6)	333	5)	333		
Contracts Payable—Retained Percentage		300,000						300,000
Bonds payable					2)	10,000,000		10,000,000
Fund Balance:		5,550,000	5)	1,000	5)	31,000		5,580,000
Net Assets Added		1) 14,300,000						14,300,000
Revenues:								
Property tax revenues		9,400,000						9,400,000
Investment income		500,000						500,000
Gain on Sale of Capital Asset					1)	20,000		20,000
Expenditures:								
General government	9,424,000				5)	667	9,423,333	
Capital outlay	3,400,000				1)	3,400,000		
Other financing sources/uses:								
Sale of Equipment		20,000	1)	20,000				
Issuance of bonds		10,000,000	2)	10,000,000				
Total	41,870,000	41,870,000		13,972,333		13,972,333	41,380,333	41,380,333

Six adjustments were made to consolidate interfund borrowings, convert capital outlay to create the asset for construction in progress, convert bonds issued from other financing source to liability for bonds payable, sale of fully depreciated equipment, allocate assets, liabilities, and fund balance of internal service fund, allocate profit of internal service fund (note utility fund allocation of $333), and consolidate the net due to or due from accounts between governmental and business-type activities. The balances for assets, liabilities, and net assets or fund balance and revenues and expenditures were then distributed into the appropriate column for the Statement of Activities or Statement of Net Assets (after adjusting entries for conversion from governmental fund to government-wide statements). Also note that capital assets of the governmental funds were added to the trial balance with a corresponding net asset invested in capital assets.

The numbers in parentheses refer to the six steps explained on pages 136–141 and illustrated on pages 169–170.

Government-wide Statement of Net Assets
(date)

	Primary Government			
	Governmental Activities	Business-type Activities	Total	Component Units
ASSETS				
Current assets:				
Cash and Cash Equivalents	$ 8,858,000	$2,062,000	$10,920,000	—
Investments	4,000,000	—	4,000,000	—
Receivables (net)	100,000	214,000	314,000	—
Internal Balances	(333)	333	—	—
Inventories	19,000	—	19,000	—
Total current assets	12,976,667	2,276,333	15,253,000	—
Noncurrent Assets:				
Capital Assets:				
Land and Infrastructure	10,000,000	—	10,000,000	—
Depreciable Buildings, Property, and Equipment, net	4,300,000	1,800,000	6,100,000	—
Construction in Progress	3,400,000	1,000,000	4,400,000	—
Total noncurrent assets	17,700,000	2,800,000	20,500,000	—
Total Assets	30,676,667	5,076,333	35,753,000	—
LIABILITIES				
Current liabilities:				
Accounts Payable	300,000	1,000,000	1,300,000	—
Total current liabilities	300,000	1,000,000	1,300,000	—
Noncurrent liabilities:				
Noncurrent Portion of Long-Term Obligations	10,000,000	2,000,000	12,000,000	—
Total liabilities	10,300,000	3,000,000	13,300,000	—
NET ASSETS				
Invested in capital assets, net of related debt	7,700,000	800,000	8,500,000	—
Restricted for:				
Capital projects	6,400,000	1,000,000	7,400,000	—
Unrestricted	6,276,667	276,333	6,553,000	—
Total net assets	$20,376,667	$2,076,333	$22,453,000	—

Government-wide Statement of Activities
(date)

		Program Revenues			Net (Expense) Revenue and Changes in Net Assets			
					Primary Government			
Functions/Programs	Expenses	Charges for Services	Operating Grants and Contributions	Capital Grants and Contributions	Governmental Activities	Business-type Activities	Total	Component Units
Primary government:								
Governmental activities:								
General government	$9,423,333	$ —	$—	$—	$(9,423,333)	$ —	$(9,423,333)	—
Business-type activities:								
Utility	303,667	380,000	—	—	—	76,333	76,333	—
Total primary government	$9,727,000	$380,000	$—	$—	(9,423,333)	76,333	(9,347,000)	—
Component units:								
Total component units	$ —	$ —	$—	$—	—	—	—	—
			General revenues:					
			Taxes:					
			Property taxes, levied for general purposes		9,400,000	—	9,400,000	—
			Investment earnings		500,000	—	500,000	—
			Miscellaneous		20,000	—	20,000	—
			Total general revenues, special items, and transfers		9,920,000	—	9,920,000	—
			Change in net assets		496,667	76,333	573,000	—
			Net assets—beginning		19,880,000	2,000,000	21,880,000	—
			Net Assets—ending		$20,376,667	$2,076,333	$22,453,000	—

SUMMARY

Chapter 5 had the following learning objectives:

- Demonstrate an understanding of the governmental financial reporting entity
- Demonstrate an understanding of the financial reporting model
- Illustrate the components of fund financial statements
- Illustrate the components of government-wide statements
- Explain the reconciliation of fund financial statements to government-wide statements.

In previous chapters, the concepts of budgetary accounting, modified accrual, fund accounting, governmental, and business-type activities have been illustrated. In addition, the revenues, expenditures or expenses, assets, liabilities, and equity accounts have been explained. Now, the accounts and transactions combine at the end of the fiscal year to produce a financial report of the fiscal year's activities. First, the governmental entity must define the governmental reporting entity to determine the scope of the audit and financial report. The financial reporting model defined by GASB Statement No. 34 includes a government-wide Statement of Net Assets and a government-wide Statement of Activities. In addition, the financial reporting model includes fund financial statements and a reconciliation of government fund statements prepared on the modified accrual basis to the government-wide statements that are prepared on the accrual basis of accounting. The financial reporting model also includes Management's Discussion and Analysis, other Required Supplementary Information, and notes to the financial statements.

A P P E N D I X   1 # Financial Reports Prior to GASB 34 Implementation

The financial reporting requirements that are in effect until governments are required to implement GASB Statement No. 34 under the phase-in schedule do not have functional or government-wide statements. Fund-type statements were combined for each type of fund to get a total for Capital project funds, for example, and then a combining statement added the combined totals to present an aggregated view of all of the funds.

**NCGA Statement No. 1 Annual Financial Reports
superseded by GASB Statement No. 34**

Balance Sheets
    Combined and combining level for all fund types and account groups
Operating Statements
    Governmental funds:
        Combined and combining Statements of Revenues, Expenditures,
            and Changes in Fund Balance
        Combined Statement of Revenues, Expenditures, and Changes in Fund Balances
            Budget and Actual—General and Special Revenue Fund Types for
            which budgets have been enacted
    Proprietary funds:
        Combined and combining Statement of Revenues, Expenses, and
            Changes in Retained Earnings
        Combined and combining Statement of Cash Flows

Fiduciary funds:

Accrual basis fiduciary funds prepared statements like Proprietary funds

Modified accrual basis fiduciary funds prepared statements like
Governmental funds

Account Groups

Statement of Changes in General Fixed Assets

Statement of Changes in General Long-Term Debt

Some elements of the superseded statements have been retained within the fund-type statements required by GASB Statement No. 34. The Governmental funds are required to produce a Balance Sheet and Statement of Revenues, Expenditures, and Changes in Fund Balance under both the old and the new models. However, the Governmental funds must now prepare a reconciliation to the government-wide statements. The Proprietary funds are required to produce a Balance Sheet; Statement of Net Assets; Statement of Revenues, Expenses, and Changes in Retained Earnings (Net Assets); and Statement of Cash Flows under both the old and new models. However, the Internal service funds will generally not appear in the new government-wide statements.

Implementation of GASB Statement No. 34

The requirements of GASB Statement No. 34 are effective as follows:

Phase 1: Governments with annual revenues of $100 million or more must implement for periods beginning after June 15, 2001.

Phase 2: Governments with annual revenues of $10 million or more but less than $100 million must implement for periods beginning after June 15, 2002.

Phase 3: Governments with total annual revenues less than $10 million must implement for periods beginning after June 15, 2003.

The implementation of the capital asset reporting provisions for general infrastructure assets as prescribed in GASB Statement 34 is slightly different from the above dates. Prospective reporting of infrastructure assets is required at the effective implementation date for Phase 1, 2, and 3 governments. Phase 1 and Phase 2 governments are required to go back and retroactively capitalize and report all major general infrastructure assets that have been acquired or had major capital improvements since July 1, 1980, in fiscal years beginning after June 15, 2005, for Phase 1 and after June 15, 2006 for Phase 2. Phase 3 governments may retroactively capitalize and report all major general infrastructure assets but are not required to do so.

QUESTIONS

1. What is the difference between the primary government and component unit?
2. What are the criteria to determine if a primary government can impose its will upon a component unit?
3. What is the difference between discrete and blended presentation of component units in the financial report?
4. What are the three categories of net assets in the Statement of Net Assets?
5. Will the salary expenditure to pay the chief financial officer's salary be required to be allocated across programs in the Statement of Activities?
6. Is depreciation expenditure or expense required to be allocated across programs in the Statement of Activities?

7. Is a general property tax revenue a program revenue or a general revenue?
8. What financial statements are required for Fiduciary funds? Are these statements consolidated into the government-wide financial statements?
9. What is the difference between *consolidated* rather than *combined* financial statements?
10. What is the difference between major and nonmajor funds?
11. Why are Internal service funds eliminated in the process of preparing consolidated government-wide statements?
12. Do revenues appear before or after expenses in the government-wide Statement of Activities?
13. Why are governmental fund interfund transfers and loans eliminated to prepare the consolidated government-wide statements?
14. The budgetary comparison schedule includes the original and final budget. The actual expenses are compared with the final budget to compute a variance. Why aren't the actual expenses compared to the original budget?
15. Why are gains or losses recorded on sale or disposal of governmental fund capital assets in the process of consolidating and converting to the government-wide statements?

EXERCISES

Exercise 5-1

Multiple Choice—Select the best answer for each of the following:

1. A city is **financially accountable** for another governmental unit if it:
   a. appoints the governing board or imposes its will
   b. appoints the governing board
   c. imposes its will
   d. does both b and c
2. A city can **impose its will** on another governmental unit if it:
   a. suggests changes in the budget
   b. recommends when rates or fees should be increased
   c. overrules a decision of the governing board
   d. has a moral but not legal obligation to repay its debt
3. A city is **obligated in some manner** to repay debt of another government if it:
   a. sets aside a reserve to repay the debt
   b. is required to set aside a reserve to repay the debt
   c. collects and remits payments for debt service
   d. notifies bondholders in the event of default
4. The basic financial statements include:
   a. the required supplementary information
   b. the government-wide statements
   c. the fund-type statements
   d. both b and c
5. The required governmental fund statements include a:
   a. Statement of Financial Position
   b. Statement of Activities
   c. Statement of Cash Flows
   d. Statement of Revenues, Expenditures, and Changes in Fund Balance
6. The government-wide statements include a:
   a. Statement of Activities
   b. Statement of Cash Flows
   c. Statement of Financial Position
   d. Balance Sheet

7. The proprietary fund statements include:
    a. a Statement of Activities
    b. a Statement of Net Assets
    c. a Statement of Cash Flows
    d. both b and c
8. The required supplementary information in a governmental financial report includes a:
    a. Statement of Activities
    b. Management Discussion and Analysis
    c. Statement of Net Assets
    d. Statement of Cash Flows
9. The Management Discussion and Analysis is:
    a. audited
    b. prepared by the auditor
    c. prepared by management
    d. prepared by the auditor and management
10. The Management Discussion and Analysis includes:
    a. condensed financial information comparing the current to prior year
    b. discussion of the government's overall financial position
    c. discussion of significant capital asset and debt activity
    d. all of the above

Exercise 5-2

Multiple Choice—Select the best answer for each of the following:

1. The minimum requirements for general-purpose financial statements include:
    a. Required Supplementary Information
    b. Basic Financial Statements
    c. Management Discussion and Analysis
    d. all of the above
2. The Management Discussion and Analysis section of the financial report includes:
    a. a forecast of operating results for the next fiscal period
    b. known facts, decisions, or conditions that could affect the future financial position
    c. a historical review of trends in operating results for the past 20 years
    d. none of the above
3. The governmental fund balance sheet lists assets and liabilities:
    a. in alphabetical order
    b. in functional program order
    c. in order of relative liquidity
    d. in appropriated and unappropriated order
4. The consolidation process converts governmental fund statements to:
    a. accrual basis of accounting
    b. eliminate internal service funds
    c. add capital assets and long-term liabilities
    d. all of the above
5. The process to convert governmental fund statements to government-wide will:
    a. add governmental fund inventories on hand
    b. eliminate borrowings between governmental funds
    c. record capital assets and related depreciation
    d. do both a and c
6. The consolidation process to convert governmental fund statements to government-wide will:
    a. remove gains and losses on sale of capital assets
    b. reduce deferred revenue for amount already "earned"
    c. adjust revenues to reflect the amount "available"
    d. record long-term liabilities issued during the year as other financing sources

7. The process to convert governmental fund statements to government-wide will:
   a. add revenues "earned" this fiscal year that were not "available"
   b. remove revenues "available" this fiscal year that were not "earned"
   c. remove interfund borrowings between governmental funds
   d. do all of the above
8. The Proprietary funds Statement of Cash Flows category for noncapital financing activities includes:
   a. repaying tax anticipation notes issued to provide cash to pay current operating expenses
   b. repaying revenue bonds payable issued to construct a building
   c. repaying tax anticipation notes issued to provide cash to pay for capital improvements
   d. investing in long-term bonds
9. The "look-back" approach:
   a. allocates profit or loss of Fiduciary funds
   b. allocates profit or loss of Internal service funds
   c. allocates cash flow based upon operating activity in the General fund
   d. allocates fund balance of the Capital projects fund after construction is complete
10. Depreciation expense is recorded:
    a. in the Governmental funds
    b. in the Capital projects funds
    c. in the Proprietary funds
    d. in all of the above

Exercise 5-3

Multiple Choice—Select the best answer for each of the following:

1. In the Statement of Activities, the governor's salary and household allowance will:
   a. be required to be allocated across all State governmental functions
   b. be required to be charged to indirect expenses
   c. be charged against the largest State programs
   d. not be required to be allocated or directly charged to any State program
2. In the Statement of Activities, depreciation expense on the State Capitol will:
   a. be allocated across all State governmental functions
   b. be allocated directly to administration
   c. not be allocated to any functional units
   d. be allocated to the largest functional unit
3. Property taxes of the governmental unit are:
   a. a general revenue
   b. a program revenue
   c. a special program revenue allocated across units
   d. none of the above
4. Government-wide financial statements use:
   a. the modified accrual method of accounting
   b. the economic resources measurement focus
   c. the accrual method of accounting
   d. both b and c
5. The net cost or net revenue of a governmental program or functional unit can be found in the:
   a. Balance Sheet
   b. Statement of Revenues, Expenditures, and Changes in Fund Balance
   c. Statement of Activities
   d. Statement of Net Assets
6. Interest expense on long-term debt for an asset that is essential to a program should:
   a. be allocated across programs as an indirect expense
   b. be charged to the General Fund as a direct expense
   c. not be allocated as interest expense is always an indirect expense
   d. be allocated directly to the program

7. The required governmental fund financial statements do *not* include a:
   a. Balance Sheet
   b. Statement of Activities
   c. Statement of Revenues, Expenditures, and Changes in Fund Balance
   d. Reconciliation to government-wide statements
8. The reconciliation from governmental funds to government-wide statements would include amounts for:
   a. payments on long-term debt
   b. accrued interest
   c. payments to acquire capital assets
   d. all of the above
9. If a governmental fund trades in a capital asset, it will appear as:
   a. a credit to other financing source in the governmental fund
   b. a credit to fixed assets in the governmental fund
   c. a gain or loss in the government-wide statement of activities
   d. both a and c
10. If a governmental fund issues long-term debt, it will appear as:
   a. a credit to other financing source in the governmental fund
   b. a long-term liability in the governmental fund
   c. a nonoperating revenue in the government-wide statement of activities
   d. none of the above

Exercise 5-4   Definition of the entity

The Big State University receives operating revenues from tuition and fees and a State appropriation. The State legislature is not responsible for Big State University debt and does not approve their budget but does provide 50% of Big State's revenues. Big State University's governing Board of Control is appointed by the governor. Board members are appointed for a four-year term and can only be removed for cause. Should Big State University be included in the State financial report? If yes, should the presentation in the report be discrete or blended?

Exercise 5-5   Governmental vs. business-type activity

Root City provides weekly garbage collection and recycling pickup at no charge to residents and pays for the sanitation service with property tax revenue. Park City provides garbage collection to residents, but the residents must purchase the colored trash bags and pay an additional fee if they want a monthly recycling pickup. Is Root City's garbage collection and recycling a governmental or business-type activity? Is Park City's garbage collection and recycling service a governmental-type or business-type activity?

Exercise 5-6   Statement of Net Assets

Carville City has the following accounts: Cash $800,000, Accounts Payable $200,000, Bonds Payable $5,000,000, Property Taxes Receivable $300,000, Capital Assets $6,000,000 net of accumulated depreciation, Unreserved Fund Balance $2,100,000, and Supplies Inventory $200,000. What order will these assets appear in the Statement of Net Assets? Why?

Exercise 5-7   Donation of capital assets

River City has received donations during the fiscal year of land to be used for a nature trail, a small warehouse building that they intend to use for storage, and $1,000,000 to beautify parks. What category of net assets will each donation be classified as: invested in capital assets, net of related debt; restricted net assets; or unrestricted net assets?

Exercise 5-8   **Capital asset and bonds**

The City of Carsonville constructs a new fire station for $5,000,000 and pays for the expenditure by issuing bonds of $4,000,000 and spending general tax revenue of $1,000,000 of fund balance.

    a. Show the journal entries to record these transactions.

    b. How will these transactions be reported or reflected in the Statement of Activities and Statement of Net Assets?

Exercise 5-9   **Statement of activities**

The City of Saline spent $8,000,000 on its public safety department, which provides police and fire protection to residents for free. The City provided tax revenues of $1,000,000 to support the Enterprise fund, which sells electric power to residents. The public safety department is supported by an appropriation of $8,200,000 of general tax revenues and generated $100,000 from tickets and fines. The enterprise fund is supported by fees for the electric power charged to and paid by users of $3,700,000 and spent $3,800,000 on operating expenses this year. The Enterprise fund received a $100,000 grant for pollution control equipment. How will the net cost or net revenue of these activities be displayed in the Statement of Activities?

Exercise 5-10   **Reconciliation**

The Village of Jeddo plans to implement GASB Statement No. 34 during the next fiscal year. The chief financial officer understands how to prepare the governmental fund statements but does not understand what items will be required to prepare the reconciliation to the government-wide statements. The Village has no long-term debt outstanding, but the General fund does have some capital assets and infrastructure. What would you tell the chief financial officer (CFO) to explain what the reconciliation between the fund-type and government-wide statements is intended to accomplish? What will be reconciling items in the Village of Jeddo reconciliation of governmental fund-type to government-wide statements?

Exercise 5-11   **Footnote disclosure**

The number of required footnote disclosures under GAAP is quite extensive. Does the extensive footnote disclosure indicate the financial reporting model is inadequate to provide information that users need?

Exercise 5-12   **Implementation of GASB Statement No. 34**

The City of Middleville has a June 30 fiscal year-end and total annual revenues of $30 million. The CFO asks when the city will be required to implement GASB Statement No. 34 for financial reporting and for infrastructure. The CFO heard someone say that only prospective reporting for infrastructure was required for smaller governments and wonders if that will apply to Middleville. For what fiscal year does Middleville have to implement GASB Statement 34 financial reporting? When does Middleville have to implement infrastructure reporting, and will they be able to only report prospectively as the CFO hopes?

PROBLEMS

Problem 5-1

Conceptual—Implementation GASB 34

The estimated implementation costs are quite high from Standard & Poor's survey responses from 40 State and local governments. What are some of the factors in a government's current records and accounting system that could indicate implementation costs will or will not be high to implement GASB Statement No. 34? What are some of the requirements for financial reporting in GASB Statement No. 34 that will require major modifications in current financial databases or accounting systems and will increase implementation costs? Do you believe the cost of implementation of GASB 34 will be worth the benefit?

Problem 5-2

Major vs. nonmajor funds

The City of Aeron had total assets of $45,000,000. The governmental funds had the following total assets: General $7,000,000, Special Revenue $2,000,000, Capital Projects $400,000 and Debt Service 600,000. The Capital projects fund is constructing a new convention center which is a very important project for the City. The City's Water Enterprise fund had total assets of $35 million.

    a. Which funds are major funds?
    b. Can nonmajor funds be reported as major funds anyway?

Problem 5-3

Analyze adjustment spreadsheet

Go to the "Governmental Funds Adjustment Spreadsheet" presented on page 171. For each listed:

    a. Compare the adjustments column to the six step process on pages 136–141 and
        169–170. Explain each entry.
    b. Will these adjustments be posted to the General Ledger?

Problem 5-4

Inventories

The City of Coleville had an inventory of office supplies for general governmental use on hand at the beginning of the fiscal year of $35,000. Additional supplies in the amount of $50,000 were ordered. The supplies arrived with an invoice of $48,000 due to discounts on some items, and the invoice was submitted for approval to pay. The supplies were paid for three weeks after delivery. At fiscal year-end, the physical inventory of office supplies showed that $42,000 was on hand.

    a. Record the journal entries for these transactions using the consumption method.
    b. Record the journal entries for these transactions using the purchases method.
    c. Explain what reconciling item from governmental fund to government-wide statements will be needed if 1) the consumption method was used, or 2) the purchases method was used.

Problem 5-5

Capital assets

The City of Decker acquired the following capital assets during the fiscal year:
1. Two police cars for $20,000 each with a trade-in allowance of $6,000 for two police cars traded in. (The police cars traded in were held beyond their useful life and original cost of $9000 each was fully depreciated under accrual accounting.)
2. Capital projects fund partially constructed a building, spending $20,000,000 to date.
    a. Prepare the governmental fund journal entries for these transactions.
    b. Prepare the reconciling adjusting entries that would be necessary to adjust governmental fund fiscal year-end accounts to government-wide accrual financial statements.

| Problem 5-6 | **Deferred revenues** |

The City of Hudson has a fiscal year-end of June 30. The City of Hudson loaned several full-time firefighters to the National Park Service during May to aid in fighting forest fires in the Western United States. The firefighters stayed on the City's payroll, and the National Park Service signed a contract in May agreeing to reimburse the City for $200,000 in services rendered on September 30.

    a. Prepare the journal entry to record in the General fund the contract signed by the National Park Service.

    b. Prepare the reconciling adjustment, if any, that would be required to prepare the government-wide financial statements.

| Problem 5-7 | **Donated capital assets** |

Eastpointe City received a donation of an office building valued at $8,000,000.

    a. What journal entry would have been recorded in the governmental funds?

    b. Prepare the reconciling adjustment, if any, that would be required to prepare the government-wide financial statements.

| Problem 5-8 | **Capital assets** |

The town of Northview sold some forest land to a timber company for $10,000,000. The forest land was originally donated to Northview when it was worth $3,000,000. Northview purchased park land for $8,000,000.

    a. What journal entries would have been recorded in the governmental funds?

    b. Prepare the reconciling adjustments, if any, that would be required to prepare the government-wide financial statements.

| Problem 5-9 | **Long-term liabilities** |

The City of Tecumseh issued $50,000,000 in long-term bonds with total issuance costs of $300,000 and a discount of $2,000,000.

    a. What journal entry would have been recorded in the governmental funds?

    b. Prepare the reconciling adjustments, if any, that would be required to prepare the government-wide financial statements. Issuance costs and bond discount are being amortized evenly over the 30-year term of the bonds.

| Problem 5-10 | **Long-term liabilities** |

West Village had interest accrued of $50,000 on debt of the General fund and $250,000 on investments of the Fiduciary funds at fiscal year-end. In addition, the governmental fund long-term portion of compensated absences and claims and judgments was $1,000,000 and $400,000, respectively.

    a. What journal entry would have been recorded in the governmental funds?

    b. Prepare the reconciling adjustments, if any, that would be required to prepare the government-wide financial statements.

| Problem 5-11 | **Interfund transactions** |

Cherry Creek City had the following interfund transactions during the fiscal year:
1) Enterprise fund bills General fund $300,000 for power, 2) General fund loans Capital projects fund $300,000 to start construction project, 3) General fund transfers $250,000 to Debt service fund to pay debt service, 4) General fund pays enterprise fund $200,000 for partial payment of power billing, 5) General fund contributes capital of $100,000 to start up Internal service fund.

    a. What journal entries would have been recorded in the governmental funds?

    b. Prepare the reconciling adjustments, if any, that would be required to prepare the government-wide financial statements.

Problem 5-12

Journal entries and consolidation

The General fund entered into the following transactions during the fiscal year:
1. Levied property taxes of $10,000,000 with 5% estimated uncollectible and collected 98%.
2. Paid salaries and wages of $6,000,000
3. Compensated absences related to salaries and wages of $200,000 current; $800,000 non-current
4. Transferred $300,000 to Debt service fund for bond repayment
5. Purchased office equipment for $700,000 with 7-year useful life (city uses straight-line depreciation)
6. Purchased water and sewer services from the Enterprise fund for $200,000
7. Contributed $200,000 to start up a new Internal service fund
8. Sold fully depreciated computer equipment for $1,000 for scrap; original cost $20,000
9. Paid expenditures for utility bills of $1,000,000
10. Received judgment for lawsuit of police brutality for $200,000 to be paid during next fiscal year
    a. What journal entry would have been recorded for each of these transactions in the General fund?
    b. Prepare closing entries and a preliminary trial balance.
    c. Set up a conversion worksheet using the preliminary trial balance, prepare and post the reconciling adjustments, if any, and carry amounts across into the government-wide financial statement columns.

Problem 5-13

Look-back approach

The Internal service fund had sales of $200,000 to the General fund, $100,000 to the Capital projects fund, and $200,000 to the Enterprise fund during the fiscal year. The net profit generated in the Internal service fund for the fiscal year was $25,000. The Capital projects fund was the only fund that had not paid the Internal service fund by fiscal year-end. To convert to consolidated government-wide statements:
   a. What adjustment, if any, is required for the amount the Capital projects fund owes the Internal service fund at fiscal year-end?
   b. What allocation will be required of the Internal service fund's net profit using the look-back approach?

Problem 5-14

Internet research

Select a governmental unit and go to the Internet to obtain their most recent annual financial report (many governments have their annual financial report available on the government's web site). Review the financial statements and determine what obvious changes will be required and what conversion adjustments likely need to be made to convert the financial statements to a GASB Statement No. 34 model. If the government has already implemented GASB Statement No. 34, determine what conversion adjustments were made to governmental fund statements to produce the consolidated government-wide statements.

Problem 5-15

Internet research

The City of Orlando has early-implemented GASB Statement 34 in their most recent financial report for fiscal year-end September 30. This is a useful reference to see the new financial reporting requirements come to life (located at http://www.ci.orlando.fl.us/departments/finance/documents.htm under CAFR). Go to the Statement of Activities and determine what the net cost or net revenue of the primary programs of the City of Orlando are. Go to the Statement of Net Assets and determine if the capital assets reported include infrastructure or not.

Problem 5-16   **Case—Sea Breeze City continuous problem**

Sea Breeze City. Start with the fiscal year-end trial balance prepared in Chapter 4—Sea Breeze City. Sea Breeze City has decided to begin to early implement GASB 34 to the extent possible so that it can be ready for the required implementation for fiscal year-end beginning after June 15, 2003. General government buildings have an estimated life of 40 years and general government equipment have an estimated life of 15 years. General obligation bonds have accrued interest of $20,000 at fiscal year end. Prepare the following CAFR financial statements from this trial balance.

a. Fund financial statements including reconciliation to government-wide statements.
b. Conversion adjustments (Use Excel spreadsheet to display conversion adjustments from trial balance and governmental fund financial statements to the government-wide financial statements.)
c. Government-wide financial statements

NOT-FOR-PROFIT ACCOUNTING AND FINANCIAL REPORTING

- Describe the types of not-for-profit organizations
- Describe the funds for not-for-profit organizations
- Explain accounting for contributions
- Explain accounting for investments
- Illustrate the basic financial statements

INTRODUCTION

What is a **not-for-profit organization?** As stated in Chapter 1, a not-for-profit organization is one that has "predominantly nonbusiness characteristics that heavily influence the operations of the organization."[1] Not-for-profit organizations are different from business enterprises and similar to governmental units because they possess the following characteristics:

- No direct relationship between resources provided and goods or services received from the organization
- Operating goals and purposes that are not profit-based
- Absence of defined ownership interests

Not-for-profit organizations include human service organizations, churches, foundations, private nonprofit hospitals and schools, and other organizations. Not-for-profit organizations represent an important and growing sector of the economy. There were 819,008 charitable not-for-profit organizations in 2000[2] as compared to 692,524 in 1997.

The GAAP Hierarchy Summary in Chapter 1 (Exhibit 1-1 on page 7) illustrates that not-for-profit organizations (including all nongovernmental not-for-profits) follow FASB accounting and financial reporting standards, while governmental organizations (including all governmental not-for-profits) follow GASB accounting and financial reporting standards. Chapter 6 explains and illustrates FASB accounting and financial reporting standards for not-for-profit organizations.

The AICPA issues two Audit and Accounting Guides that relate to not-for-profit organizations: *Health Care Organizations* and *Not-for-Profit Organizations*. The AICPA previously had separate Audit and Accounting Guides for *Colleges and Universities* and *Voluntary Health and Welfare Organizations*, but those were consolidated into the current Audit and Accounting Guide for *Not-for-Profit Organizations* to reflect the 1993 financial reporting model for all not-for-profit organizations established by FASB Statement No. 117, *Financial Statements of Not-for-Profit Organizations*. Therefore, the AICPA Audit and Accounting Guide for *Not-for-Profit Organizations* applies to all not-for-profit organizations. Specific guidance for both governmental and not-for-profit health care organizations is found in a separate AICPA Audit and Accounting Guide for *Health Care Organizations*. Governmental health care organizations and governmental colleges and universities are special purpose governments and follow GASB reporting requirements in a format similar to an Enterprise fund. These unique requirements are illustrated in Chapter 7.

TYPES OF NOT-FOR-PROFIT ORGANIZATIONS

The AICPA Audit and Accounting Guide for Not-for-Profit Organizations applies to the following *nongovernmental* not-for-profit organizations:[3]

---

[1]FASB Concepts Statement No. 4, December 1980.
[2]*Internal Revenue Service Data Book 2000*, Publication 55B.
[3]AICPA Audit and Accounting Guide, *Not-for-Profit Organizations, with Conforming Changes as of May 1, 2001*, paragraph 1.02.

- Cemetery organizations
- Civic and community organizations
- Colleges and universities
- Elementary and secondary schools
- Federated fund-raising organizations
- Fraternal organizations
- Labor unions
- Libraries
- Museums
- Other cultural organizations
- Performing arts organizations
- Political parties
- Political action committees
- Private and community foundations
- Professional associations
- Public broadcasting stations
- Religious organizations
- Research and scientific organizations
- Social and country clubs
- Trade associations
- Voluntary health and welfare associations
- Zoological and botanical societies

FUNDS AND FUND ACCOUNTING[4]

Nongovernmental, not-for-profit organizations may utilize fund accounting in their internal accounting systems. Not-for-profit and health care organizations use a net asset approach to financial reporting and are not required to display funds in their external financial reports. FASB Statement No. 117 created a financial reporting model that classifies net assets as: unrestricted, temporarily restricted, and permanently restricted. Statement No. 117 permits individual fund reporting in the external financial report so long as the three net asset classes also display the required information. The internal use of funds is permitted under GAAP, and funds do remain in use by many not-for-profit organizations in internal accounting and reporting.

A not-for-profit fund is a fiscal entity with a self-balancing set of accounts with asset, liability and fund balance, equity or net asset accounts just like a government's funds. Again, a subtle underlying purpose of fund accounting is to provide accountability for public or donated funds and internal control over the monies. The not-for-profit organization is accountable to the donors or providers of other sources of funds who want to ensure that monies are utilized for the intended purposes. Fund accounting can assist in segregating and tracking the use of donated or restricted monies for the intended purpose.

---

[4]*Financial Accounting and Reporting Manual for Higher Education*, paragraph 302, Fund Groups Used by Colleges and Universities, National Association of College and University Business Officers (NACUBO) and AICPA Audit and Accounting Guide, *Not-for-Profit Organizations, with Conforming Changes as of May 1, 2001.* Chapter 16, paragraphs 16.01–16.19.

The categories and types of fund names vary between not-for-profit and government organizations simply because different organizations came up with different categories and names for funds. The college and university organization of finance officers is called the National Association of College and University Business Officers (NACUBO). NACUBO developed a *Financial Accounting and Reporting Manual,* which has accounting and reporting guidelines for college and universities. The Government Finance Officers Association (GFOA) developed the *Governmental Accounting, Auditing and Financial Reporting* "blue book" that reflects the use of the General and Special Revenue funds to account for general governmental operations. In contrast, NACUBO's manual reflects the use of a Current fund composed of two parts, Restricted and Unrestricted, to account for general operations of a college or university. The Current fund and General and Special Revenue Funds both account for general operating activities but simply were given different names long ago.

The following exhibit shows the fund categories and types for not-for-profit organizations and governmental organizations.

EXHIBIT 6-1   Comparison of Similar Funds between Not-for-Profit and Governmental Organizations

Not-for-profit organizations	Governmental organizations
Unrestricted current, Unrestricted operating, or General	General
Restricted current, Restricted operating, or Specific-purpose	Special revenue
Plant fund: investment in plant	Capital projects
Plant fund: retirement of indebtedness	Debt service
Endowment	Permanent
Unrestricted current, Unrestricted operating, or General account for auxiliary enterprises	Enterprise
Endowment	Private-purpose trust
Agency or Custodian	Agency
Internal Service, Pension and Employee Benefit Trust, and Investment Trust funds have no similar counterpart fund in not-for-profit organizations. Plant fund: Renewal and replacement; Plant fund: unexpended; Land, building, and equipment; and Annuity and Life-income funds have no similar counterpart funds in governmental organizations.	

Exhibit 6-1 shows a comparison of the governmental funds discussed in Chapter 2 and the not-for-profit funds explained in this chapter. Funds of governmental and not-for-profit organizations account for similar activities but have different names.

The concept underlying funds and fund accounting systems is that once the specific purpose or legal restriction (or absence thereof) associated with resources is identified, then it is recorded in the appropriate fund. For example, the governmental proprietary funds account for business-type activities within a governmental unit and use accrual accounting. Not-for-profit organizations have three different categories of endowments: permanent, term and quasi- to account for monies with different levels of external or internal restrictions. The use of separate funds segregates resources by the purpose or activity intended. The funds and fund accounting system were created to be accountable for public monies and donated resources to citizens or donors. The funds and fund accounting system for governmental and not-for-profit organizations bear little similarity to accounting for a publicly traded corporation except in accounting for business-type activities in proprietary funds. Business-type activities are often called auxiliary enterprises in not-for-profit organizations.

NOT–FOR–PROFIT FUND CATEGORIES AND TYPES

Not-for-profit organizations have fund categories and types that can vary among not-for-profit. For example, general operating activity is recorded in the Unrestricted current fund for a college and university and in the General fund for a health care organization. Voluntary health and welfare and other not-for-profit organizations might use Unrestricted operating or the General fund.

Not-for-profit organizations fund categories and types[5]

Current fund category:

(1) Unrestricted current (or Unrestricted operating, or General)
(2) Restricted current (or Restricted operating, or Specific-purpose)

Plant (or Land, building, and equipment) fund category:

(1) Unexpended plant funds
(2) Funds for renewal and replacement
(3) Funds for retirement of indebtedness
(4) Investment (or net investment) in plant

Other individual fund types:

(1) Loan funds
(2) Endowment funds
(3) Annuity and life-income (Split-interest) funds
(4) Agency (or Custodian) funds

Current fund category

The **Current fund** consists of two parts: **Unrestricted and Restricted.** The Unrestricted portion of the Current fund records general operating activities that have no external restrictions. The Restricted portion accounts for monies that have an external restriction placed upon their use (law, grant, donor, contract, etc). Both the Restricted and Unrestricted parts of the Current fund account for general operating activity and resources. Colleges and universities, voluntary and health and welfare organizations, and other not-for-profits use the Current fund. Colleges and universities record the sales and services of auxiliary enterprises such as the bookstore and food services in the Current fund.

If the governing board designates some assets (board-designated), that is not a restriction upon the use of those assets. The board can always change its mind, so no

---

[5]AICPA Audit and Accounting Guide, *Not-for-Profit Organizations, with Conforming Changes as of May 1, 2001*, paragraphs 16.01–16.19.

external restriction exists on board-designated assets. Therefore, board-designated assets are considered unrestricted net assets.

Some not-for-profit organizations use either the **Unrestricted operating** fund or **General fund** to record general operating activities instead of the Unrestricted current fund. Health care institutions use the General fund. If the Unrestricted operating or General fund is used, they are *not* partitioned into two parts like the Current fund.

The restricted part of Current funds can also be called **Restricted operating** or **Specific purpose** funds. Organizations such as health care organizations that use the General fund might use a Specific purpose fund to record restricted resources. In all cases, the fund accounts for resources that are to be used for current operating purposes, but the external provider of the resources has placed a restriction on the use of the monies. This is similar to the Special Revenue fund of governmental units.

A college would record faculty and staff salaries and tuition and fees in the Unrestricted current funds. A college would record federal research grants in the Restricted current funds. Health care organizations use the General fund to account for operating activities. Health care organizations would record Federal research grants in the Specific purpose fund. Health care organizations bill most of their expenses to third-party payors (such as insurance companies) for patient services. Therefore, health care organizations record most of their expenses in the General fund to ensure costs are captured and billed out to third-party payors. These Unrestricted current or General funds are similar to the General fund of governmental units.

Plant fund category

The Plant fund category consists of four self-balancing subgroups: **Unexpended, Renewal and replacement, Retirement of indebtedness,** and **Investment in plant.** Colleges and universities use the Plant fund with four parts to account for capital assets and related indebtedness. Health care organizations record capital assets in the General fund so that depreciation expense can be included in billings to third-party payors (insurance companies) for health care services. Voluntary health and welfare or other not-for-profit organizations may use a Land, building and equipment fund instead of the Plant fund.

Unexpended plant funds record resources that are available to acquire fixed assets such as buildings and equipment. Construction in progress may be recorded here or in the Investment in plant subgroup. Debt related to assets that have not yet been capitalized in the Investment in plant subgroup would be reported here. Examples of items that would increase this fund would be donations, grants, gains and investment earnings on Unexpended plant funds, or bond proceeds issued to acquire capital assets. Examples of items that would decrease this fund would be expenses to acquire capital assets and investment activity.

Renewal and replacement plant funds record resources used for renewal and replacement of Plant fund assets. It is often difficult to distinguish additions and improvements to plant[6] from renewal and replacement, and some capital projects may be partitioned into two parts: an improvement portion to be capitalized and a renewal and replacement portion to be expensed. An improvement improves performance of or extends the useful life of an asset and would not be accounted for in

---

[6]*Financial Accounting and Reporting Manual for Higher Education,* NACUBO, paragraph 302.52.

Renewal and Replacement. Improvements generally involve removal and replacement of a significant part or component of the asset with a part that has improved or superior operating capability.[7] Renewal and replacements do not extend the asset's useful life and are not capitalized. Renewal and replacement would remove and replace a component or part with a part with similar operating capability and performance. Improvements are capitalized and would be transferred to the Investment in plant subgroup as they are completed. Renewal and replacement are expensed.

Retirement of indebtedness plant funds record resources set aside to pay the principal and interest (debt service) expenses on long-term debt issued to acquire Plant fund capital assets.

Investment in plant funds record the net assets invested in capital assets. Capital assets are recorded here as well as any liabilities associated with those assets. For example, the university dormitories would be recorded here as a fixed asset, and any debt issued to build those dormitories would also be recorded here until it was paid in full. For example, a copying machine purchased under a capital lease would be recorded here as a capital asset and depreciated along with the corresponding capital lease payable. Capital assets from land to library books are also recorded in this subgroup. The net investment in plant fund balance reflects the excess of plant capital assets over related liabilities. The net investment in plant fund balance will be permanently or temporarily restricted if the donor has imposed a permanent or temporary restriction upon the asset.

● **INTERPRETIVE EXERCISE**

A college receives tuition and fee revenue, endowment donations, and starts construction of additional dormitories. A hospital receives patient service revenues and a federal grant for cancer research. What funds will record these activities?

Other not-for-profit fund types

Loan funds.   Loan funds record resources set aside for loans to people: students, faculty, staff, or other constituents. These resources may be donated or provided by the governing board of the institution. Loan funds are generally associated with colleges and universities. Health care, voluntary health and welfare, and other not-for-profit organizations generally do not have Loan funds.

Loan funds typically operate on a "revolving" fund basis. In other words, monies within the fund are loaned out and "revolve" back in as the loan is repaid to be loaned out again. The monies within the Loan fund continually revolve out in a loan, back in as repaid, and out again in a new loan. Interest, if any, will add to the monies available in the Loan fund. Administrative expenses for the Loan fund may be charged directly to it.

Loan funds can also establish a reasonable estimate of uncollectible accounts. The composite method allocates a charge for the provision for loan losses to each loan balance when establishing the allowance for doubtful accounts. The direct method deducts the total provision for loan losses from the loan fund at the end of the fiscal

---

[7]Ibid.

period and then reverses the provision at the beginning of the next fiscal year. This is to establish a reasonable estimate in the financial report, yet actual losses are not charged to the specific loan until incurred.

One example of a Loan fund transaction would be where a college wants to encourage faculty to adopt technology and purchase computers for work at home. The college provides loans to faculty to purchase computers with a payroll deduction repayment plan that charges no interest on the loan.

Endowment funds. There are three types of endowment funds: **Permanent endowment, Term endowment,** and **Quasi-endowment.** "A true endowment fund may be established only by a donor and can never be expended."[8]

The **Permanent endowment** fund records resources that are required by an external donor or source to be kept permanently restricted (in perpetuity; forever). The donor may also have specified how the investment earnings from this permanent endowment are to be expended. An endowment would occur when a dot.com millionaire donates funds to his alma mater for scholarships. The dot.com millionaire specifies that the donated principal cannot be spent, but the investment earnings will be spent on scholarships. The donated principal would be a permanently restricted endowment. The investment earnings would be temporarily restricted until expended on scholarships.

The **Term endowment** fund has an externally-imposed restriction that requires the monies to be kept in trust until a specific point in time or the occurrence of an event specified by the donor. A term endowment would be used when a donor specifies that the monies donated are available for use at a specific point in time or when a certain restriction is satisfied. A donor might specify a date or condition that must be met for the donation to be expended. Until this date or condition is met, the principal donated cannot be spent. The investment income may be spent depending upon whether the donor has placed any time or purpose restriction on those earnings.

For example, an elderly professor who is a Master Gardener donates $200,000 to be held in trust for ten years with earnings to be used to beautify the campus with perennial gardens. At the end of ten years, the Master Gardener professor specifies that $100,000 should be used to purchase and plant unique horticultural trees, bushes, and gardens throughout the campus, and the other $100,000 may be used in any manner the university desires. The investment earnings will be used for ten years to create perennial gardens with the temporarily restricted $200,000 retained in a Term endowment fund. At the end of ten years, the $200,000 will be removed from the Term endowment fund: $100,000 will be temporarily restricted net assets for use to purchase and plant unique horticultural trees, bushes, and gardens throughout the campus, and $100,000 will be unrestricted net assets available for the university to spend as it wishes.

The **Quasi-endowment** fund accounts for resources that have been set aside or restricted by the organization itself. The Quasi-endowment can be construed as a restriction that can be removed by the organization itself, so it is *not* a true endowment with external legal restrictions. A Quasi-endowment fund would be used when the governing board sets aside monies for a certain intended purpose. Of course, the governing board could always change its mind and vote in the future to use the money for a different purpose. A Quasi-endowment is not a "true" endowment because it is

---

[8]Ibid, paragraph 302.31.

a *designation* of funds *within* the organization that can be changed in the future. A quasi endowment represents unrestricted board-designated net assets.

Endowment funds can be found in any type of not-for-profit organization. Not-for-profit organizations seek donations to increase their endowments so they will generate investment earnings to fund future activities and projects. Endowment funds provide a safety net for not-for-profit organizations because the investment earnings from large endowments can provide protection from a downturn in normal donations and other revenues in the future. A large endowment assures the not-for-profit organization that it will have sufficient monies from investment earnings on the endowment to fund its programs in the future.

Annuity and Life-income (Split interest) funds. Annuity and Life-income funds record resources that have a split interest. For example, resources are donated by an individual who will receive an annuity or life-income in return. Therefore, the resources do not completely belong to the not-for-profit organization until it has fulfilled the terms of the annuity or life-income agreement, which generally provides benefits to the donor. There is a split interest: part of the resources will be returned to the donor per the annuity or life-income agreement, and the remainder will become the property of the not-for-profit organization when the agreement is fulfilled. Annuity agreements provide for payments to donors for a fixed period of time. Life-income agreements provide for payments to donors for the remainder of their life.

In a common "split-interest" agreement, a donor may want to ensure an asset is donated to a favorite charity yet retain the use and enjoyment of it for the remainder of his/her life or a fixed term of a capital asset (such as a principal residence or tract of land). At the death of the donor or end of the fixed term, the capital asset will become the property of the not-for-profit organization. If the agreement is irrevocable, the donation will be recognized as temporarily restricted revenue until the donor's death or fixed term occurs. Other split-interest agreements could include charitable lead trusts, perpetual trusts held by third parties, charitable remainder trusts, charitable gift annuities, and pooled (life) income funds.

Agency (or Custodian) funds. Agency funds record resources that do not belong to the not-for-profit organization. In most cases, these resources are being held by the not-for-profit organization before being transferred to a third party according to some criteria or legal restrictions. For example, dormitory damage deposits would be held in an Agency fund. The deposits will be returned to the students upon departure from the dormitory. Student organization funds may also be held in Agency funds on behalf of the organization.

In summary, Unrestricted Current and Restricted Current funds are used by colleges and universities, voluntary health and welfare, and other not-for-profit organizations to account for operating activity. Health care organizations use the General fund to account for operating activity, capital assets, and long-term debt. Health care organizations use the Specific purpose fund to account for restricted resources. Colleges and universities use the Plant fund's four subgroups to account for capital assets and related liabilities. Voluntary health and welfare and other not-for-profit organizations use the Land, building, and equipment fund to account for capital assets. Loan funds are generally found at colleges and universities, whereas Endowments can be found at any not-for-profit organization. Annuity or Life-income funds can be found at any not-for-profit organization that markets these opportunities for income to donors who wish to receive income for a specified period or for life and donate the remainder to the organization. Endowment funds are used by all not-for-profit organizations. Agency funds can be found at any not-for-profit organization that is handling monies on behalf of another organization or recipient.

REVENUES

Health care organizations derive their primary revenues from providing health care services, while colleges and universities derive their primary revenues from providing higher education. Voluntary health and welfare organizations derive their primary revenue from voluntary contributions. All not-for-profit organizations may obtain revenues from exchange transactions, grants, contributions, and other sources. FASB Statement No. 116, *Accounting for Contributions Received and Contributions Made* provides guidance for accounting for contributions that are used in *all* not-for-profit organizations.

Contributions

Contributions are the lifeblood of many not-for-profit organizations. The accounting for contributions is central to recording the activities of not-for-profit organizations. Many not-for-profit organizations obtain the majority of their revenues from donors through contributions. The recognition of these contributions is an important topic in not-for-profit accounting and reporting. Revenues are recognized on the accrual basis of accounting. Specific guidance for the recognition of contribution revenue is given below.

A **contribution** is defined in FASB Statement No. 116 as an "unconditional transfer of cash or other assets to an entity or a settlement or cancellation of its liabilities in a voluntary nonreciprocal transfer by another entity acting other than as an owner."[9] A contribution must be 1) a nonreciprocal transfer, 2) made or received voluntarily, 3) a transfer to or from nonowners, and 4) unconditional. A nonreciprocal transfer means that the donor expects and receives nothing in return for the contribution. The contribution must be made or received voluntarily; no coercion or requirement to donate such as settlement of a lawsuit can exist. The contribution must be a transfer to or from nonowners, which means that the donors cannot have an ownership interest. Contributions are often labeled as Support or Public Support revenues in voluntary health and welfare and other not-for-profit organizations.

Promises to give.[10]   The first step in accounting for contributions is to determine if there is a valid **promise to give.** Many not-for-profit organizations conduct fundraising campaigns by mail or telephone and solicit pledges or promises to give from donors. An important issue in accounting for contributions is to determine whether the **promise to give** is legally enforceable and if there is evidence of the donor's intent. FASB Statement No. 116 requires that documentation exists to confirm the donor's intent such as a pledge card, correspondence, or records of telephone conversations or logs of promises made orally, which can verify a legally enforceable intent

---

[9]FASB Statement No. 116, *Accounting for Contributions Received and Contributions Made*, paragraph 5.
[10]AICPA Audit and Accounting Guide, *Not-for-Profit Organizations, with Conforming Changes as of May 1, 2001*, paragraphs 5.35–5.39.

or promise to give. If the donor is free to change his/her mind about the donation, it is a statement of intent but not a promise to give.

Example 1: A donor says that he/she is going to change a life insurance policy to name the not-for-profit organization as beneficiary. This is a statement of intent but not a promise to give, which would require an irrevocable change of beneficiary on the life insurance policy.

Example 2: A donor specifies in his/her will that the museum will receive $50,000 upon the donor's death. The will is clear intent to give, but unless it is irrevocable, the donor can change his/her mind, so there is not a clear promise to give. The will is unconditional in that it is certain the donor will eventually die, but because there is no promise to give, the museum will not recognize a contribution.

Example 3: A phonathon may produce many pledges or promises to give that are documented by a phone log indicating the amount and each donor's name and address and possibly a history of past giving as well. These pledges are recognized as contribution revenue at the time of the pledge unless the donor specifies some condition (future or uncertain event or barrier to overcome).

The practical impact of recognizing revenue from pledges (valid promises to give) not yet collected is that not-for-profit organizations may show substantial revenue that is not yet available to spend. The pledges will be recorded as temporarily restricted revenue until paid because the donor is paying in the future and, therefore, there is a time restriction on the contribution.

Does recognizing a promise to give as revenue overstate income?

The Museum of Contemporary Art in Chicago sued a married couple for failing to honor their promise to give $5 million documented in a 1990 letter of intent. The letter of intent also made it clear that the promise would be binding upon their estate if the donors died. The museum asserts that it used this first pledge toward construction of a new $46 million museum in soliciting funds from other contributors and recorded the $5 million promise as revenue as required by FASB. The couple changed their mind and refused to pay the $5 million after one of them resigned from the museum's board in 1991. The museum will have to write off this $5 million promise as a bad debt because the donors have publicly refused to pay and the museum previously recognized the revenue as required by FASB 116.[11] If the museum collects any payment from the couple as a result of the lawsuit, it will no longer be recognized as a contribution because it is not a voluntary transfer.

Conditional versus unconditional. The second step in accounting for contributions is to determine if the contribution is **conditional or unconditional.** An unconditional contribution will be recognized as revenue. A conditional contribution cannot be recognized until the condition is met, although disclosure is permitted of the conditional contribution. A contribution is conditional if a donor specifies a condition that is a future and uncertain event before the contribution may be recognized.

Remote events that would prevent the contribution from occurring that are unlikely to happen are *not* considered conditions. For example, a donor specifies that she will donate $50,000 unless America adds Puerto Rico as a state within three months. It is unlikely that statehood for Puerto Rico will occur in three months, so this is a

---

[11]"Chicago art museum sues donor deadbeats." *Grand Rapids Press,* January 25, 1998.

remote event unlikely to happen and does not prevent the $50,000 from being recognized as a temporarily restricted contribution.

Death and the passage of time are *not* considered conditions. Death is not a condition because even though it is a future event, it is not uncertain that the donor will eventually die.

In a conditional contribution, the donor will have the right of return of the donated assets if these future and uncertain conditions are not met. Therefore, it makes sense that the conditional contribution would *not* be recognized. Conditions are distinctly different from donor restrictions. The donor-imposed restriction can be satisfied by the passage of time or by actions of the organization. A restricted contribution will be recorded. A conditional contribution may be disclosed but will not be recorded as revenue until the condition is met.

Restrictions.   The third step in accounting for contributions is to determine the level of restriction on the contribution to properly classify the net assets received. All contributions must be classified in one of three categories: 1) **Unrestricted**—no donor-imposed restrictions—available for use at discretion of the not-for-profit organization, 2) **Temporarily restricted**—donor-imposed restriction that can be satisfied by the passage of time or actions of the organization, 3) **Permanently restricted**—donor-imposed restriction that cannot be removed by the organization. A **temporary restriction** is satisfied by the passage of time or actions of the organization. A **permanent restriction** cannot be removed by the organization. A donation to an endowment is a permanent restriction where the donor has specified that the donation itself can never be expended. The financial report will classify net assets into these three categories: unrestricted, temporarily restricted, and permanently restricted to clearly display the availability and donor's intent. Common donor restrictions are for time or purpose and create a fiduciary responsibility for the not-for-profit organization to satisfy the donor's restriction. The contribution will be classified as temporarily restricted until the time or purpose restriction is met.

Time restriction.   A time restriction can occur if 1) the donor has not yet paid the contribution so it is temporarily restricted until the donor pays, or 2) the donor specifies a time period when the contribution may be used so it is temporarily restricted until that time period occurs, and 3) the donor specifies that the contribution must remain intact for all time (in perpetuity) and may never be used so it is permanently restricted. A restricted donation is recognized at the time of pledge by the donor.

If the donation is going to be paid within a year, the net realizable fair market value is recorded. The net realizable fair market value is the amount that is net of any estimate for uncollectible pledges. If the donation is going to be paid over time, the organization will recognize the net present value of the future stream of payments. In either case, the donation will be classified as temporarily restricted until paid.

Purpose restriction.   A purpose restriction may be placed by the donor on the contribution to specify a use for the monies. A contribution that has a purpose restriction will be temporarily restricted until the monies are spent for the restricted purpose. At the time the monies are spent for the restricted purpose, the temporarily restricted net assets will be reclassified as unrestricted. The expense will be paid from the unrestricted funds that have just been reclassified.

A purpose restriction by the donor can be implicit without being expressly stated. For example, a donor responds to a mailing from a not-for-profit organization seeking donations for construction of a new building. Although the donor does not specify the purpose restriction for use for the building on the check or in writing, it is implicitly understood that the donation returned in the Building fund envelope is in response to the solicitation for the building and is restricted for that purpose. If the donation is restricted as to purpose, the donation will be classified as temporarily restricted until used for that specified purpose.

To summarize, there are three basic steps in accounting for contributions:

1) Determine if there is a valid promise to give.
   If yes, go to step 2. If no, stop.
2) Determine if the contribution is unconditional.
   If yes, go to step 3. If no (conditional), stop and footnote disclosure is optional.
3) Determine the level of restriction on the contribution to properly classify it as unrestricted, temporarily restricted, or permanently restricted.

All contributions must be classified into one of three categories: **unrestricted,** which are immediately available for any use the organization wishes, **temporarily restricted,** which have a time or purpose restriction that has not yet been met, and **permanently restricted,** which must remain intact forever.

● **INTERPRETIVE EXERCISE**

Sally and Sue are alumni of Boulder University. Sally promises to give $1,000 to Boulder University for scholarships in six months. Sue tells Boulder University that she will give Boulder University $50,000 if the novel she is in the process of writing makes it on *The New York Times* Best Seller List. Evaluate the two donations to determine if: a) a promise to give exists, b) the donation is conditional or unconditional, and c) what type of restriction, if any, was placed on the donation.

Type of Contribution	Accounting Recognition
1. Unconditional, unrestricted	recognize at time of donation
2. Unconditional, restricted	recognize at time of donation
3. Conditional, unrestricted	recognize when condition is met
4. Conditional, restricted	recognize when condition is met

Unconditional, unrestricted.   The donor makes no conditions or restrictions on an unconditional, unrestricted contribution and gives the not-for-profit organization full discretion over use of the funds. The unconditional, unrestricted contribution is recognized as unrestricted support when the donation is received.

Example 1. An unrestricted donation of cash to a not-for-profit organization. The journal entry to record an unrestricted donation of $100 cash would be recorded as follows:

Cash	100	
Contribution Revenue—Unrestricted		100
(record receipt of donation)		

Unconditional, restricted.   The contribution is recognized at the time of donation but may need to be classified as temporarily or permanently restricted depending on what the donor specified. The donor might agree to pay the donation over time, which will temporarily restrict the contribution. The donor might specify the donation can only be used over certain time periods, which would also temporarily restrict the contribution. The donor could also specify a purpose for the donation, which would temporarily restrict the donation. If the donor specifies that only the earnings from investment of the contribution can be expended and the contribution itself must be kept in an endowment, the contribution would be permanently restricted. When a temporary restriction of time or purpose for donated funds is met, the net assets are reclassified as unrestricted.

Example 1. An unrestricted pledge to donate $100 made over the phone was documented by a phone log. The donor pays the pledge two months later. The phone log documents a valid promise to give. This is an unconditional, unrestricted contribution.

Contributions Receivable	100	
Contribution Revenue—Temporarily Restricted		100
(record pledge)		
Cash	100	
Contributions Receivable		100
(record receipt of pledge donation)		
Temporarily Restricted Net Assets—		
Reclassifications Out	100	
Unrestricted Net Assets—		
Reclassifications In		100
(reclassification of amounts received)		

Example 2. An unrestricted pledge to donate $1,000 over the next four years is received in writing. The fair value of a promise to give over a future period of time is the present value of the future cash flows discounted at a risk-free rate of return. The pledge received in writing documents a valid promise to give. This is an unconditional, unrestricted contribution. The journal entry to record a pledge of $1,000 estimated to be fully collectible that is payable over four years with a present value of future cash flows of $760 would be recorded as follows:

Contributions Receivable	1,000	
Contribution Revenue—Temporarily Restricted		760
Discount on Contributions Receivable		240
(record contribution to be paid over four years)		

The likelihood of collection can also be considered and result in a lesser amount of Contributions Receivable and Contribution Revenue being recorded. In this case, the pledge is estimated to be fully collectible.

Example 3. A pledge of $2,000 is made to a women's shelter to purchase cell phones for battered women to use. The cell phones are purchased and the pledge is collected. The journal entries to record these transactions are shown below:

Contributions Receivable	2,000	
Contribution Revenue—Temporarily Restricted		2,000
(record pledge)		

Cash	2,000	
Contributions Receivable		2,000
(record collection of pledge donation)		
Program Expense—Cell phones	2,000	
Cash		2,000
(purchase of cell phones)		
Temporarily Restricted Net Assets—		
Reclassifications Out	2,000	
Unrestricted Net Assets—		
Reclassifications In		2,000
(reclassification of amounts received)		

The cell phones were expensed rather than capitalized due to their low individual cost (less than $100 each) and because they are given away and are not required to be returned.

Conditional, unrestricted. A donor can make a contribution conditional upon overcoming a certain barrier or a future or uncertain event. This is a conditional contribution, but it is not restricted in any way by the donor as to time or purpose.

Example 1. Donnie Daredevil decides to walk across the Grand Canyon on a tightrope. Donnie pledges $100,000 to his favorite charity if he survives the walk and is paid the $500,000 fee from the television network paying to broadcast the event. Is this a restricted or conditional donation? This is a conditional donation because the $100,000 will not be contributed unless Donnie survives the walk, which is a future and uncertain event. However, it is not restricted because Donnie is permitting his favorite charity to decide when and how to use the contribution. It will not be recognized until Donnie survives the walk across the Grand Canyon and is paid the $500,000 fee but the pledge may be disclosed.

Example 2. Elderly Emma tells the zoo that she intends to change her will to bequest $200,000 to them upon her death. There is an intent to give but no promise to give, so no contribution would be recorded. If Emma does irrevocably change her will, then an unrestricted contribution would be recorded because Emma's death is a future but not an uncertain event that would be considered a condition.

Conditional, restricted. A conditional, restricted contribution requires that a barrier be overcome or a future and uncertain event occur *and* the donor also makes some type of time or purpose restriction. A conditional, restricted contribution would not be recognized as revenue but may be disclosed.

Example 1. A donor notifies his alma mater, a public university, that he will donate $10,000,000 to create an endowment to generate income for scholarships to be awarded to African American students. However, the donor also specifies that the university must achieve a goal of at least 10% African Americans enrolled out of the total student enrollment (currently at 2%) before the contribution will be made. The contribution depends on the university achieving a goal. This enrollment goal is a barrier to overcome and a future and uncertain event. The donor has placed a permanent restriction on the $10,000,000 and a temporary purpose restriction on the investment earnings. The conditional, restricted contribution will be recorded if and when the condition is met. The $10,000,000 contribution will not be recognized until the condition or goal of 10% enrollment is achieved.

Should not-for-profit organization web sites be able to link to profit sites on the web?

The IRS has been soliciting comments during the period of October 2000 through February 2001 on what type of "linking" and online Internet fund-raising activities should be permitted tax-free for not-for-profit organizations.[12] The IRS is concerned about not-for-profit organization web sites providing links to political web sites and to web sites where merchandise is sold. Not-for-profit organizations are not permitted to endorse political campaigns and retain tax-exempt status. Limited lobbying is permitted. Not-for-profit organizations that engage in business activities such as selling goods are subject to an Unrelated Business Income Tax (UBIT). Several not-for-profit organizations complained that the IRS is seeking to overregulate not-for-profit activity and that they should not interfere with Internet links by not-for-profits. For example, it makes sense that the League of Women Voters would have links to political candidates and campaign web sites because one of the goals of the organization is to provide access to voter information. The IRS should not regulate to prohibit such activity. It also can make sense for not-for-profits to provide links to web sites that sell goods their members may find of interest. It does not necessarily follow that a Greenpeace web link on its site to a bookstore web site that sells environmental books results in any profit at all for Greenpeace. The link may just be a service for members to find information they may be interested in that relates to the goals of the not-for-profit organization. Others say that the IRS is correct to provide some guidance on Internet links by not-for-profits because it would not be appropriate to overlook the possibilities for abuse and a tax haven for business income to result.

Gifts-in-kind. Noncash contributions, "gifts-in-kind," should be reported as contributions according to the criteria above and recorded at their fair market value at time of donation if the item can be used or sold.[13] No contribution should be recognized if the donated items have no value and cannot be used or sold. If the property to be donated declines in value after the contribution is initially recognized but before collection, either an expense or a loss must be recognized with a corresponding amount of decline in contribution revenue (previously recognized). If the property to be donated increases in value, no recognition is required of the gain unless the property is equity or debt securities with readily determinable market values as defined in FASB Statement No. 124. If a pledge to donate becomes uncollectible, a bad debt expense should be recognized.

Donations of utilities such as electrical, telephone, or the use of facilities are recognized at their fair rental value (or normal cost) and expensed when used.[14]

Not-for-profit organizations can act as agents transferring resources between a provider and recipient. In that case, the resources would be accounted for as an asset and a corresponding amount of liability while the organization has custody of the asset. The subsequent transfer of these assets would reduce the asset and liability accounts accordingly.[15]

---

[12] *"Charities Find a Gray Area on the Net,"* The New York Times, February 12, 2001, page C4.

[13] AICPA Audit and Accounting Guide, *Not-for-Profit Organizations, with Conforming Changes as of May 1, 2001,* paragraphs 5.07–5.09.

[14] Ibid, paragraphs 5.42–5.43.

[15] Ibid, paragraph 5.06.

Split-Interest Agreements.[16] Split-interest agreements commonly used by not-for-profit organizations to solicit contributions include charitable lead trusts, perpetual trusts held by third parties, charitable remainder trusts, charitable gift annuities, and pooled life income funds. These agreements all have a donor making an initial gift (or intent to give) with distributions specified to certain beneficiaries during the term of the split-interest agreement and the remaining assets specified to be transferred to or retained by other specified beneficiaries. A common example would be that the donor signs a legal agreement to transfer title to an investment asset at death but retains all investment income from the asset while still living. The "split interest" is one interest of the donor for investment income and the other interest of the not-for-profit organization for the asset. The asset will be contributed upon death, so it is an unconditional restricted contribution, but the investment income will flow to the donor until death. The beneficiaries can be the donor or other parties specified by the donor and the not-for-profit organization. Revocable split-interest agreements are recorded as intents to give. Irrevocable split-interest agreements are recorded as charitable contributions. The contribution revenues will be recorded as unrestricted, temporarily restricted, or permanently restricted, according to the terms of the split-interest agreement.

Contributed Services.   Contributed services are only recognized as contributions if they "create or enhance a nonfinancial asset"[17] such as contributed labor for construction of a building, or if they meet the following criteria:

1) The organization would have to otherwise purchase the service
2) The service is a specialized skill
3) The individual providing the service has the specialized skill

Examples of specialized skills include accounting, financial, legal, electrical, plumbing, etc. If the contributed services meet the criteria to be recognized as contribution revenue, they are to be valued at the fair market value and an equal corresponding amount of expense would be recorded as if the organization had purchased the needed service. A lawyer contributes $2,000 of services to draft legal agreements for the not-for-profit organization. This contributed service is a specialized skill that would have to be purchased otherwise. The contribution is unconditional, and unrestricted and would be recorded as follows:

Legal Expenses	2,000	
Contribution Revenue—Unrestricted		2,000
(to record donated specialized legal services)		

Not-for-profit organizations often have many volunteers, but few of those volunteers' services will qualify as contributions to be recognized as they do not require specialized skills that would otherwise have been purchased by the organization. The recognition of those specialized skills donated with a corresponding amount of expense recognized provides accountability and also shows the "true" level of expense the organization would have incurred if the services had not been donated.

---

[16]Ibid, paragraphs 6.01–6.14.
[17]Ibid, paragraphs 5.40–5.41.

● **INTERPRETIVE EXERCISE**

A plumber repairs a broken water line at a homeless shelter. The plumber also helps the shelter staff clean up the water in the basement and shovels some snow off the sidewalk on the way back to his truck. What services, if any, of the plumber should be recognized as a contribution by the homeless shelter?

Accounting for collections.[18]   A not-for-profit organization may maintain a collection of works of art, historical treasures, or other assets. These would commonly be found in a museum. A collection of works of art or historical treasures, or similar assets should be recorded at historical cost or estimated fair value at the time of donation. All of the following conditions must be met for items to be considered part of or a collection:

   a. Held for public exhibition, education, or research in furtherance of public service, rather than financial gain.
   b. Protected, kept unencumbered, cared for, and preserved.
   c. Subject to an organizational policy that requires the proceeds from sales of collection items to be used to acquire other items for collection.

These criteria were established by the FASB in Statement No. 116 and also adopted by GASB as discussed in Chapter 3. *All* items in a collection must be capitalized or not capitalized. Selective capitalization of items is *not* permitted. There is no journal entry to record a donation of a work of art that the donor specifies should be kept in perpetuity worth $15,000 to a collection that is not capitalized. However, if the collection was capitalized, the journal entry for this contribution would be as follows:

Art Collection (asset)	15,000	
Contribution Revenue—Permanently Restricted		15,000
(to record donation of a work of art that is capitalized)		

Exchange transactions[19]

Not-for-profit organizations engage in many common exchange transactions such as paying employee salaries in return for the employees' services or selling goods. Many fund-raising activities also have an exchange component in the contribution transaction. For example, in exchange for an unrestricted donation of $50, an organization might send a coffee mug, calendar, or similar small acknowledgment to the donor. The cost of this coffee mug or calendar should be charged to fund-raising expense so long as the value of the item exchanged is nominal in relation to the contribution received. The journal entry would be recorded as follows:

Cash	50	
Contribution Revenue—Unrestricted		50
(record contribution of $50)		
Fund-raising Expense	1	
Inventory—Fund-raising Materials		1
(record expense of contribution acknowledgment)		

---

[18]Ibid, paragraphs 7.06–7.10.
[19]Ibid, paragraphs 5.1–5.19.

However, if a fund-raising black-tie dinner is held at an expensive restaurant and donors receive a dinner worth $100 in return for a donation of $200, the dinner fee of $100 would be recorded as cost of direct benefits to donors, rather than as a fund-raising expense.

Cash	200	
Special Events Revenue		200
(record revenue from special event)		
Cost of direct benefits to donors	100	
Cash		100
(record payment of dinner expense for donor at special event)		

In the coffee mug example, the entire contribution of $50 is recorded as contribution revenue and the $1 mug is a fund-raising expense. In the dinner example, the $200 donation is special event revenue, and the cost of this direct benefit to the donor will be shown as an expense of $100.

EXPENSES, GAINS, AND LOSSES

FASB standards define expenses for not-for-profit organizations as the outflow or using up of assets or incurring liabilities related to carrying out the entities' ongoing major or central operations. Expenses are differentiated from losses, which are decreases in net assets resulting from incidental transactions or other events not related to the entities, ongoing major or central operations. Examples of losses would include losing a lawsuit, sale of equipment at a loss, or a loss in the fair value of investments. Likewise, a gain is differentiated from revenues.[20]

Expenses are recognized on the accrual basis of accounting. Typical expenses would include salaries and fringe benefits, supplies, utilities, and depreciation. Even though certain fund-raising costs may benefit future periods, they should be expensed as they are incurred. Advertising is expensed as incurred except for direct-response advertising that is likely to result in future benefits, which would be capitalized. Start-up costs of a new facility or a new service are expensed as incurred.

FASB Statement No. 117 requires expenses (not losses) to be reported by the **Program service** or **Supporting service** functional classification[21] in the financial statements or in note disclosure. Program services appear after Operating Revenues and Gains and before the Supporting services functional classifications in the Statement of Activities. This enables donors to quickly see how much of the Public Support revenues (monies obtained from external donors and sources) is spent on program services as compared to supporting services. For example, if Public Support was $100,000, Program Services were $90,000 and Supporting Services were $10,000, a donor could conclude that 90% of the Public Support is spent on the Program Services. The functional reporting classification is required for voluntary health and welfare organizations and is optional for not-for-profit organizations including colleges and universities.

---

[20]Ibid, paragraphs 13.02 and 13.17–13.18.
[21]Ibid, paragraphs 13.30–13.37.

Program services are "the activities that result in goods or services being distributed for beneficiaries, customers, or members that fulfill the purposes or mission for which the organization exists. Those services are the major purpose for and the major output of the organization and often relate to several major programs."[22] All program-related sale of goods or services and other program-related activity revenues may include the costs of sale and other associated costs. Each not-for-profit should report program expenses by major function. In some cases, one category will do. In others, several program functions may be required. For example, the American Red Cross groups its vast array of international services into six program functions: Armed Forces Emergency Services, Disaster Services, Biomedical Services, Health and Safety Services, Community Services, and International Services.

Supporting services include functional classifications of 1) Management and general, 2) Fund-raising activities, and 3) Membership-development activities. **Management and general** expenses include normal management and administrative functions such as accounting, management of contracts, budgeting and salaries for the chief executive officer, and support staff and expenses of the governing board. Soliciting external funds, exchange transactions, and public informational activities are all charged to Management and general. Program services and fund-raising for contributions should *not* be charged to Management and general. Interest costs that cannot be directly allocated should be charged to Management and general. **Fund-raising activities** include expenses of fund-raising campaigns, donor mailings, special events, and other activities related to soliciting contributions from external donors. **Membership-development activities** include expenses to obtain new members and costs associated with relations with current members. If members receive benefits, it is an exchange transaction. If members do not receive any significant benefits or have any duties, then the costs of soliciting members may be charged to Fund-raising activities instead. In some cases, it may be appropriate to allocate part of the expenses associated with members between Fund-raising and Membership-development activities.

Expenses should be directly allocated to the Program services or Supporting services function. However, if direct allocation is not feasible or practical, a reasonable allocation method based on financial or nonfinancial data may be utilized to allocate costs. For example, rent for a building could be allocated based upon square footage utilized.

Fund-raising activities sometimes include components that would generally be considered program activities or supporting services. For example, a fund-raising brochure might include membership information. For such joint activities, specific costs should be charged to each activity (fund-raising and membership development) and joint costs should be allocated between the two.

If a not-for-profit organization reduces the amount charged for goods or services, the amount of reduction should be reflected as an expense. For example, if a university reduces tuition and fees for graduate teaching assistants: 1) the full amount of tuition should be recorded as revenue, and 2) the full amount of reduction in the tuition and fees should be recorded as an expense.

Sale of goods and services. Not-for-profit organizations may have expenses related to sale of goods or services. The accounting for such costs depends upon the nature of the activity and how it relates to the not-for-profit organization's programs. If a

---

[22]FASB Statement No. 117 *Financial Statements for Not-for-Profit Organizations*, paragraph 27.

botanical garden has a garden store that is a major activity, the garden store's sales and cost of sales should be reported and displayed separately. Because the garden store is directly related to the botanical garden's primary program, the store would be a program service and the cost of sales will be a program expense. If the botanical garden has a small cafe that is a major activity but is not related to the garden's primary program, the cafe's cost of sales will be reported as a supporting service. If the botanical garden has a volunteer group of Master Gardeners who produce and sell a vegetarian cookbook that is not likely to recur again and produces $200 of profit, it will be considered an incidental activity and the net gain (or loss) is reported. The net gain (or loss) from an incidental activity such as the cookbook is not reported in the functional classification but as a gain or loss.

Special events and fund-raising activities.[23]   Not-for-profit organizations may hold special events or fund-raising activities (gala dinners, parties, theatrical performances, etc.) that provide a direct benefit to those attending. If the special event or fund-raising activity is a major event that is central to the organization, such as their Annual Spring Ball, the gross amount of revenues and related expenses will each be reported. However, if the event is a minor, incidental event that is not central to the organization, it is permissible to net the revenues and expenses.

The not-for-profit organization may choose how to report the expenses associated with direct benefits to donors at special events in the Statement of Activities. These direct benefits may be shown in the Statement of Activities as 1) a separate line item deducted from the Special Event Revenues, or 2) as an Expense in the Statement of Activities. The accounting for the contributions from a special event was illustrated in Exchange Transactions earlier in this chapter and showed the amount of special event revenue related to a black-tie fund-raising dinner was $200. The dinner (direct benefit) received by the donor was recorded as Costs of Direct Benefits to Donors of $100. This special event could be displayed in the Statement of Activities Revenues section as follows:

Special event revenue	$200
Cost of direct benefits to donors	(100)
Net revenues from special events	$100

This special event could also be displayed as Special event revenue of $200 in the Revenue section of the Statement of Activities and as a separate line in the expense section as Costs of direct benefits to donors of $100. If the fair market value of the dinner was $125, the special event could also be displayed as follows:

Contributions		$ 75
Dinner sales	$125	
Less: costs of direct benefits to donors	(100)	
Gross profit on special events		25
Contributions and net revenues from special events		$100

The not-for-profit organization can choose any of these three presentations in the Statement of Activities to report revenues and expenses from Special Events.

---

[23]AICPA Audit and Accounting Guide, *Not-for-Profit Organizations with Conforming Changes as of May 1, 2001*, paragraphs 13.22–13.27.

ASSET, LIABILITY, AND NET ASSET ACCOUNTS

Not-for-profit organizations record assets, liabilities, and net assets on the accrual basis of accounting. There are many similarities between the accounts used for governmental entities and not-for-profit organizations. Some of the accounts that are covered by FASB Statements or that have specific importance in not-for-profit accounting are covered in this chapter. Collections assets are discussed earlier in the chapter in the Contributions section because these assets are often donated.

Cash and Cash Equivalents.[24] Not-for-profit organizations have definitions of cash and cash equivalents that are very similar to the definitions for governmental entities that are described in Chapter 4. Cash and cash equivalents that have restrictions on their use are reported separately from those available for current use on the financial statements.

Inventory. Inventory should be recorded at cost, or if the inventory items are donated, they should be valued at estimated cost.

Property and Equipment.[25] Not-for-profit organizations use property and equipment accounts instead of capital asset accounts. Typical assets found in property and equipment accounts would include land that is not depreciated and the following assets that are depreciated: land improvements, buildings, equipment, furniture, motor vehicles, and similar type assets. Leased property and equipment and improvements to leased property are also recorded. Construction in process is also recorded as an asset. A unique not-for profit asset is the value of contributed use of facilities and equipment.

Property and equipment assets that are purchased are recorded at cost, and contributed items are recorded at estimated fair value at the time of the contribution. Depreciation is recognized over the estimated life of all purchased and contributed property and equipment except for land. Collections are reported separately and are not depreciated if the items are considered inexhaustible. If property or equipment is sold or disposed of, a gain or loss may be recognized on the transaction.

Other assets. Some of the other asset accounts that may be recorded by not-for-profit organizations include prepaid expenses and deferred charges.

Debt obligations. Like governmental entities, some not-for-profit organizations issue tax-exempt debt. This is often done through conduit debt of a state financing authority, such as a Hospital Finance Authority. The debt is issued by the state, however the not-for-profit organization is responsible for the repayment of the bonds. The amount of outstanding debt is recorded in a liability account and reported on the financial statements.

Other liabilities. Not-for-profit organizations record other liabilities such as accounts payable and deferred revenues on the accrual basis of accounting. If an

[24]Ibid, paragraphs 4.01–4.05.
[25]Ibid, paragraphs 9.01–9.15.

organization receives a contribution that requires periodic payments to others (such as a split-interest agreement), a liability would be set up for the annuity obligations.

Net assets.[26]   FASB Statement No. 117 created a financial reporting model that classifies net assets as: Unrestricted, Temporarily restricted, and Permanently restricted. **Permanently restricted net assets** have a donor-imposed restriction that cannot be removed by the organization or the passage of time. The restrictions will remain in perpetuity. **Temporarily restricted net assets** have a donor-imposed restriction that can be satisfied by the passage of time or actions of the organization, such as using funds for a specified purpose. Temporarily restricted net assets are reclassified as Unrestricted when the conditions of the temporary restriction have been met. **Unrestricted net assets** include all other assets that do not have a donor restriction on their use.

INVESTMENTS[27]

Not-for-profit organizations may purchase investments or receive investment assets as contributions. Investment revenues may be reported net of related investment expenses if footnote disclosure is made. Numerous disclosures about investments are required in the financial report.

Investments that are purchased will be recorded at their original cost. Investments that are contributed will be recorded at fair market value at the date of contribution.

Example 1. The Symphony Society purchases $200,000 in Treasury bonds. In this case, the fair market value and cost are the same at the time of acquisition, and the purchase is recorded as follows.

Investments	200,000	
Cash		200,000

Example 2. The Symphony Society receives an unrestricted donation of 1,750 shares in xyz.com that is currently trading at $200 a share at the date of donation. The donor's cost basis in the shares is $10 a share. The Symphony Society will recognize a contribution at the fair market value of $350,000 (1,750 shares × $200 per share) rather than the donor's basis of $17,500. Gifts of substantially appreciated stock such as xyz.com enable the donor to avoid capital gains tax on the appreciation of $332,500 in this example. The donation will be recorded as follows:

Investments	350,000	
Contributions Revenue—Unrestricted		350,000

Investment income (such as interest and dividends) is recognized when earned. Investment income will increase unrestricted net assets unless the donor has stipulated a time or purpose restriction on the income. If the donor stipulated a temporary or permanent restriction on the investment income from the donated investment, the income will increase temporarily restricted or permanently restricted net assets. In the

---

[26]Ibid, paragraphs 11.01–11.11.
[27]Ibid, paragraphs 8.01–8.29.

absence of any donor guidance on how investment income should be used, investment income will increase unrestricted net assets.

FASB Statement No. 124, *Accounting for Certain Investments Held by Not-for-Profit Organizations*, requires not-for-profit organizations to report investments in equity and debt securities with readily determinable market values at their fair market value and report all unrealized gains and losses in the Statement of Activities in the Net Appreciation in Investments account. Realized and unrealized gains and losses on investments are reported in the Statement of Activities as increases or decreases in unrestricted net assets *unless* the use of investment gains and losses was temporarily or permanently restricted by the donor of those assets. If the donor stipulated a temporary or permanent restriction on the investment gains and losses from the donated asset, the gains or losses will increase or decrease temporarily restricted or permanently restricted net assets. Gains and investment income limited to specific uses by donor-imposed restrictions will only increase unrestricted net assets if the donor's restrictions are met in the same reporting period as the gains and losses occur.

Example 1.[28] A library invests excess unrestricted cash in 200 shares of Books.com stock purchased at fair market value of $20,000 on 7/22/X2. At fiscal year-end 12/31/X2, the fair market value of the Books.com investment is $60,000. During the next fiscal year on 3/22/X3, the library sells 100 shares of the Books.com investment for $35,000. At fiscal year-end 12/31/X3, the fair market value of the Books.com remaining investment is $5,000.

7/22/X2	Investments—Unrestricted	20,000	
	Cash—Unrestricted		20,000
	(record purchase of 200 shares of Books.com)		
12/31/X2	Investments—Unrestricted	40,000	
	Net Appreciation on Investments— Unrestricted		40,000
	(recognize appreciation gain on Books.com)		
3/22/X3	Cash—Unrestricted	35,000	
	Investments—Unrestricted		30,000
	Gain on Sale of Investments—Unrestricted		5,000
	(recognize gain on sale of investments—35,000 less original cost $10,000 + $20,000 appreciation)		
12/31/X3	Net Appreciation on Investments— Unrestricted	25,000	
	Investments—Unrestricted		25,000
	(recognize decrease in value of investments)		

The unrestricted net asset value of the Investments account is $5,000 at 12/31/X3. FASB Statement No. 124 requires that the net appreciation (change in fair market value) of the Books.com investment be recognized at each fiscal year-end, which resulted in a $40,000 gain and a $25,000 loss being recognized each year. In addition, half of the Books.com investment was sold for a $5,000 gain. The net gains to date since original purchase of the investment is $20,000 ($40,000 + $5,000 − $25,000).

---

[28]Ibid, paragraph 8.1, Table 8.1.

Endowment returns rise and fall with the markets

A survey of 20 of the richest universities in the country found an astonishing change in returns from 1999 to 2000 on endowments. The University of Notre Dame had the largest change with return on investments in endowments of 58% in 1999 and only 3% in 2000. In 2001, 6 of the 25 largest university endowment funds in the country lost market value. FASB 124 requires that investments be marked to market values, so many endowments that showed large gains in 1999 will be posting small gains or even losses in 2000 and 2001. Other university officers are more concerned about the effect on future contributions to endowment funds of the stock market decline, fearing a bear market will chill donations. The comparisons of investment gains and losses from 1999 to 2001 will show large changes due to the requirement of FASB 124 to book these market value changes and reflect the change in net assets. The decline in market value in September 2001, following the terrorist attacks, could produce large losses. The decline in endowment wealth among universities will probably rank as the worst year ever in 2001. A survey of 50 colleges revealed that 37 posted negative rates of return in 2001. In 2000 large endowments over $1 billion had rates of return averaging 29%, and in 2001 many may face negative returns, a huge about-face in endowment earnings. Yale went from 41% in 2000 to 9.2% in 2001, and Harvard went from 32.2% in 2000 to –2.7% in 2001.

Sources: "No Gain, Slight Pain—The wealthiest universities maintain confidence despite sagging returns on endowments." *The Chronicle of Higher Education*, March 16, 2001, pages A29–A30, "Wealthiest Colleges Lost Billions in Endowment Value in Last Year," *The Chronicle of Higher Education*, October 19, 2001, pages A24–A26.

Donor-restricted endowment fund investments. Donor restrictions may require that a contribution be permanently or temporarily restricted. The net appreciation or investment income generated from donated assets should be reported as a change in unrestricted net assets unless the donor (or related law) specifies that it be temporarily or permanently restricted. If the donor (or law) does specify that the investment income be temporarily or permanently restricted, that restriction will apply to any net appreciation on those investments as well.

FASB Statement No. 124[29] provides that any losses on investments of a donor-restricted endowment fund should first reduce temporarily restricted net assets to the extent that any donor restrictions on net appreciation have not been met, and second, reduce unrestricted net assets. If a donor-restricted endowment fund falls below the level required by the donor or law, then subsequent gains should be used first to restore the fair value of the assets to the required level, (increase unrestricted net assets) and second to increase restricted net assets if there is a donor restriction.

BASIC FINANCIAL STATEMENTS

A complete set of financial statements for a not-for-profit organization will include a Statement of Financial Position (balance sheet), Statement of Activities (operating statement), and Statement of Cash Flows with accompanying note disclosure as

---

[29]FASB Statement No. 124 *Accounting for Certain Investments Held by Not-for-Profit Organizations*, paragraphs 12 and 13.

appropriate for all three statements. A Statement of Functional Expenses is required only for voluntary health and welfare organizations.

Basic Financial Statements	
Not-for-profit organizations	**Governmental organizations**
Statement of Financial Position	Statement of Net Assets
Statement of Activities (or Statement of Changes in Net Assets)	Statement of Activities
Statement of Cash Flows	Statement of Cash Flows (Proprietary funds only)
Statement of Functional Expenses (Voluntary Health and Welfare organizations only)	

The **Statement of Financial Position** reflects the not-for-profit organization's balance sheet and orders assets and liabilities based on liquidity. Two years of data may be shown to promote comparisons.

Not-for-Profit Organization
Statement of Financial Position
For fiscal period ended on June 30, 20X1

	20X1	20X0
Assets:		
Cash	$20,000	$15,000
Land buildings, and equipment	60,000	50,000
Total Assets	$80,000	$65,000
Liabilities and net assets:		
Accounts payable	$10,000	$15,000
Notes payable	20,000	10,000
Total Liabilities	30,000	25,000
Net assets:		
Unrestricted	$25,000	$15,000
Temporarily restricted	10,000	20,000
Permanently restricted	15,000	5,000
Total net assets	$50,000	$40,000
Total liabilities and net assets	$80,000	$65,000

The **Statement of Activities** reports revenues, gains, expenses, losses, and changes in the three categories of net assets. The Statement of Activities can present expenses and losses by program or functional classifications or natural classifications such as salaries and depreciation.

Not-for-Profit Organization
Statement of Activities
For fiscal period ended on June 30, 20X1

Change in unrestricted net assets:	
Revenues and gains:	
Contributions	$55,000
Total unrestricted revenues and gains	55,000
Net assets released from restrictions	
Satisfaction of program restrictions	13,000
Expiration of time restrictions	12,000
Total net assets released from restrictions	25,000
Total unrestricted revenues, gains, and other support	80,000
Expenses and losses:	
Program X	40,000
Program Y	10,000
Management and general	10,000
Fund-raising	10,000
Total expenses and losses	70,000
Increase in unrestricted net assets	10,000
Change in temporarily restricted net assets:	
Contributions	15,000
Net assets released from restrictions	(25,000)
Decrease in temporarily restricted net assets	(10,000)
Change in permanently restricted net assets:	
Contributions	8,000
Income on long-term investments	2,000
Increase in permanently restricted net assets	10,000
Increase in net assets:	10,000
Net assets at beginning of year	40,000
Net assets at end of year	$50,000

The Statement of Activities summarizes the reclassifications in assets from one class of net assets to another. For example, when donor-imposed restrictions expire or are satisfied, the asset will move from temporarily restricted to unrestricted. If a $100 contribution is received that is temporarily restricted as to time or purpose by the donor, it will be a temporarily restricted net asset. When the time or purpose restriction is met, the temporarily restricted net asset will be reclassified as an unrestricted net asset. The journal entries to reflect this are as follows:

Cash	100	
Contributions Revenue—Temporarily Restricted		100
(donor-imposed restriction is met during same fiscal year as contribution)		
Contributions Revenue—Temporarily Restricted	100	
Contributions Revenue—Unrestricted		100

The **Statement of Cash Flows** provides information about cash receipts and cash payments by the not-for-profit organization during the fiscal period. The Statement of Cash Flows helps users assess the organizations' ability to generate future cash flow, pay their liabilities and expenses, and illustrates why the change in net assets shown on the Statement of Activities does not normally equal the change in cash during the fiscal period.

Not-for-Profit Organization
Statement of Cash Flows (direct method)
For fiscal period ended on June 30, 20X1

Cash flows from operating activities:	
Cash received from contributors	$70,000
Cash paid to employees and suppliers	75,000
Net cash used by operating activities	(5,000)
Cash flows from investing activities:	
Purchase of equipment	(10,000)
Net cash used by investing activities	(10,000)
Cash flows from financing activities:	
Proceeds from contributions restricted for:	
Investment in endowment	8,000
Other financing activities:	
Borrowing from notes payable	10,000
Interest and dividends restricted for reinvestment	2,000
Net cash used by financing activities	20,000
Net increase in cash and cash equivalents	5,000
Cash and cash equivalents at beginning of year	15,000
Cash and cash equivalents at end of year	$20,000
Reconciliation of change in net assets to net cash used by operating activities:	
Change in net assets	$10,000
Adjustments to reconcile change in net assets to net cash used by	
operating activities:	
Increase in equipment	(10,000)
Decrease in accounts payable	(5,000)
Increase in notes payable	10,000
Contributions restricted for long-term investment	(8,000)
Interest and dividends restricted for long-term investment	(2,000)
Net cash used by operating activities:	$ (5,000)

Cash flows from operating activities includes all cash flows related to operations that are not included in investing or financing activities.[30] Investing activities include all investment transactions. Financing activities include cash contributions that are specified for purchase of capital assets. If a donor provides cash but restricts its use to long-term, it may not qualify as a cash equivalent for the Statement of Cash Flows.

---

[30]FASB Statement 95 *Statement of Cash Flows*, paragraph 21.

Not-for-profit organizations may use the direct or indirect method to prepare the Statement of Cash Flows. The direct method reports cash received and used in operating activities to determine net cash provided by operating activities. The direct method (example on previous page) also has a reconciliation of the change in net assets to net cash flow from operating activities. The indirect method (American Red Cross, page 215) starts with the change in net assets and reconciles that to the net cash flow from operating activities. In a sense, the direct method starts with cash inflows and outflows from operations and reconciles it to the changes in net assets, whereas the indirect method starts "backwards" with the change in net assets and reconciles that to the net cash flow from operating activities.

Statement of Cash Flows—Cash Flow Categories

Not-for-profit organizations	Governmental organizations
Operating activities	Operating activities
Investing activities	Investing activities
Financing activities	1. Noncapital financing activities
	2. Capital and related financial activities

● **INTERPRETIVE EXERCISE**

On September 11, 2001,[31] terrorist attacks with passenger airplanes resulted in the twin towers of the World Trade Center in New York City crumbling to the ground and the Pentagon also severely damaged. The damage, loss of life, and injured and relief effort required in the wake of this tragic event is unparalleled in United States history. Fundraising campaigns began immediately for the American Red Cross across the nation. The American Red Cross raised over $547 million dollars in the days after the attack,[32] the most contributions it has ever received for any disaster in history. Review the American Red Cross financial statements as of June 30, 1999, shown on the following pages. Go to the web site for the American Red Cross at http://www.redcross.org/ and evaluate what impact this disaster has had upon revenues and expenses in the Statement of Activities and Statement of Functional Expenses, and upon the Unrestricted, Temporarily Restricted, and Restricted net asset positions in the Statement of Financial Position as compared to the position at June 30, 1999.

The **Statement of Functional Expenses** is only required for voluntary health and welfare organizations. The Statement provides information about expenses by natural classifications (such as salaries and benefits for each of the functional classifications). American Red Cross's Statement appears on page 216.

The American Red Cross is an international voluntary health and welfare organization. The financial statements for fiscal year ending June 30, 1999 appear on page 213.[33]

---

[31]"U.S. Attacked, Hijacked Jets Destroy Twin Towers and Hit Pentagon in Day of Terror", *The New York Times*, Page A1, September 12, 2001.

[32]"Nation's Generosity Is Almost Overwhelming," *USA Today*, page 8a, September 27, 2001, "Red Cross ends pleas for Sept. 11 relief fund," *USA Today*, October 31, 2001.

[33]http://www.redcross.org

American Red Cross Financial Statements
Consolidated Statement of Financial Position
June 30, 1999

(With summarized information as of June 30, 1998)
(In thousands)

Assets	Unrestricted	Temporarily Restricted	Permanently Restricted	Totals 1999	1998
Current assets:					
Cash and cash equivalents	$ 100, 481	41,281	897	142,659	151,688
Investments	354,436	16,833	15,518	386,787	267,491
Receivables, net of allowance for doubtful accounts of $21,901 in 1999 and $24,471 in 1998:					
Trade	212,284	8,219	—	220,503	202,080
Contributions, current portion	18,580	114,653	811	134,044	172,272
Other	—	—	6,459	6,459	6,338
Inventories, net of allowance for obsolescence of $8,528 in 1999 and $6,631 in 1998	146,752	741	—	147,493	120,759
Other assets	10,764	5,260	55	16,079	14,794
Total current assets	843,297	186,987	23,740	1,054,024	935,422
Investments	657,681	95,507	263,699	1,016,887	954,982
Contributions receivable	4,242	29,239	2,309	35,790	22,490
Prepaid pension costs	16,256	—	—	16,256	29,953
Land, buildings, and other property, net	671,065	—	—	671,065	636,982
Other assets	28,897	892	5,630	35,419	41,218
Total assets	$2,221,438	312,625	295,378	2,829,441	2,621,047
Liabilities and Net Assets					
Current liabilities:					
Accounts payable and accrued expenses	$ 235,760	7,897	—	243,657	222,086
Current portion of debt	82,165	—	—	82,165	82,779
Postretirement benefits	12,631	—	—	12,631	12,068
Other current liabilities	30,753	841	3,642	35,236	22,010
Total current liabilities	361,309	8,738	3,642	373,689	338,943
Debt	156,021	—	—	156,021	180,105
Postretirement benefits	95,733	—	—	95,733	90,095
Other liabilities	67,211	601	30	67,842	67,875
Total liabilities	680,274	9,339	3,672	693,285	677,018
Net assets	1,541,164	303,286	291,706	2,136,156	1,944,029
Commitments and contingencies					
Total liabilities and net assets	$2,221,438	312,625	295,378	2,829,441	2,621,047

American Red Cross
Consolidated Statement of Activities

Year Ended June 30, 1999
(With summarized information for the year ended June 30, 1998)
(In thousands)

Assets	Unrestricted	Temporarily Restricted	Permanently Restricted	Totals 1999	Totals 1998
Operating revenues and gains:					
Public support:					
United Way and other federated	$ 60,139	132,647	—	192,786	215,638
Disaster relief	—	172,231	—	172,231	71,707
Legacies and bequests	46,030	10,851	9,557	66,438	90,877
Service and materials	14,725	38,814	—	53,539	29,398
Grants	12,288	114,330	—	126,618	88,534
Other contributions	165,805	38,102	1,879	205,786	159,001
Products and services:					
Biomedical	1,320,150	—	—	1,320,150	1,144,693
Program materials	111,736	1,250	—	112,986	105,322
Contracts	40,899	—	—	40,899	38,288
Investment income	80,546	1,181	757	82,484	90,364
Other revenues	45,883	1,699	—	47,582	46,531
Net assets released from restrictions	432,695	(432,695)	—	—	—
Total operating revenues and gains	2,330,896	78,410	12,193	2,421,499	2,080,353
Operating expenses:					
Program services:					
Armed Forces Emergency Services	62,921	—	—	62,921	62,679
Disaster Services	321,539	—	—	321,539	192,623
Biomedical Services	1,362,896	—	—	1,362,896	1,257,883
Health and Safety Services	170,235	—	—	170,235	160,062
Community Services	108,072	—	—	108,072	98,447
International Services	37,059	—	—	37,059	19,216
Total program services	2,062,722	—	—	2,062,722	1,790,910
Supporting services:					
Fund raising	88,925	—	—	88,925	73,424
Management and general	131,423	—	—	131,423	100,130
Total supporting services	220,348	—	—	220,348	173,554
Total operating expenses	2,283,070	—	—	2,283,070	1,964,464
Change in net assets from operations	47,826	78,410	12,193	138,429	115,889
Nonoperating activities—investment income in excess of amounts designated for current operations	51,314	466	1,918	53,698	77,705
Change in net assets	99,140	78,876	14,111	192,127	193,594
Net assets, beginning of year	1,442,024	224,410	277,595	1,944,029	1,750,435
Net assets, end of year	$1,541,164	303,286	291,706	2,136,156	1,944,029

American Red Cross
Consolidated Statement of Cash Flows

Year Ended June 30, 1999
(With summarized information for the year ended June 30, 1998)
(In thousands)

	1998	1999
Cash flows from operating activities:		
Change in net assets	$192,127	193,594
Adjustments to reconcile change in net assets to net cash provided by operating activities:		
Depreciation and amortization	73,006	68,187
Provision for doubtful accounts receivable	15,008	12,178
Provision for obsolete inventory	11,800	3,203
Net gain on sales of fixed assets	(6,581)	(14,166)
Net gains on investments	(77,249)	(111,186)
Contributions and income restricted for long-term investment	(12,193)	(16,260)
Changes in operating assets and liabilities:		
Increases in receivables	(8,624)	(33,943)
Increases in inventories	(38,534)	(28,818)
(Increases) decreases in prepaid expenses and other assets	4,514	(27,760)
Decreases in prepaid pension cost	13,697	4,024
Increases in accounts payable and accrued expenses	21,571	43,765
Increases in other liabilities	13,193	14,316
Increases to postretirement benefits	6,201	5,024
Net cash provided by operating activities	207,936	112,158
Cash flows from investing activities:		
Purchases of fixed assets	(110,992)	(99,779)
Proceeds from sales of fixed assets	10,484	18,014
Purchases of investments	(238,003)	(274,483)
Proceeds from sales of investments	134,051	213,681
Net cash used in investing activities	(204,460)	(142,567)
Cash flows from financing activities:		
Permanently restricted contributions and income	12,193	16,260
Proceeds from borrowings	35,233	64,369
Repayment of debt	(59,931)	(41,549)
Net cash provided by (used in) financing activities	(12,505)	39,080
Net increase (decrease) in cash and cash equivalents	(9,029)	8,671
Cash and cash equivalents, beginning of year	151,688	143,017
Cash and cash equivalents, end of year	$142,659	151,688
Supplemental disclosures of cash flow information—Cash paid during the year for interest	$ 18,307	17,873

American Red Cross
Consolidated Statement of Functional Expenses

Year Ended June 30, 1999
(With summarized information for the year ended June 30, 1998)
(In thousands)

Program Services	Armed Forces Emergency Services	Disaster Services	Biomedical Services	Health and Safety Services	Community Services	International Services	Total Program Services
Salaries and wages	$35,517	61,245	551,856	82,314	49,160	4,070	784,162
Employee benefits	7,518	12,981	118,412	16,733	10,338	838	166,820
Subtotal	43,035	74,226	670,268	99,047	59,498	4,908	950,982
Travel and maintenance	1,882	27,648	28,003	4,500	3,675	465	66,173
Equipment maintenance and rental	1,731	15,170	45,242	4,595	5,082	260	72,080
Supplies and materials	3,246	20,233	275,343	30,343	11,580	2,419	343,003
Contractual services	9,251	31,449	282,421	23,745	16,485	1,247	364,598
Financial and material assistance	1,606	145,955	17,087	1,534	7,214	27,649	201,045
Depreciation and amortization	2,170	6,858	44,693	6,471	4,538	111	64,841
Total expenses	$62,921	321,539	1,362,896	170,235	108,072	37,059	2,062,722

Supporting Services	Fund Raising	Management and General	Total Supporting Services	Totals 1999	Totals 1998
Salaries and wages	$31,332	51,008	82,340	866,502	811,158
Employee benefits	6,440	11,137	17,577	184,397	168,962
Subtotal	37,772	62,145	99,917	1,050,899	980,120
Travel and maintenance	3,909	5,830	9,739	75,912	57,912
Equipment maintenance and rental	1,602	3,844	5,446	77,526	66,453
Supplies and materials	12,959	8,592	21,551	364,554	321,334
Contractual services	30,085	43,296	73,381	437,979	369,092
Financial and material assistance	580	1,569	2,149	203,194	101,366
Depreciation and amortization	2,018	6,147	8,165	73,006	68,187
Total expenses	$88,925	131,423	220,348	2,283,070	1,964,464

PUTTING IT ALL TOGETHER

The following example illustrates sample transactions for a not-for-profit Art Museum and then puts together the end-of-the-year financial statements. The Art Museum is a not-for-profit organization that is not required to prepare a functional expense statement. The Art Museum Board of Directors has decided not to capitalize their art collection. The trial balance at the beginning of the fiscal year appears as follows:

Art Museum
Trial Balance
July 1, 20X0

	Unrestricted	Temporarily Restricted	Permanently Restricted	Total
Assets:				
Cash	$ 11,000	$ 3,000	$ 4,000	$ 18,000
Contributions				
Receivable	—	11,000	—	11,000
Investments	45,000	55,000	1,000,000	1,100,000
Gift shop inventory	20,000	—	—	20,000
Furniture & fixtures	100,000	—	—	100,000
Accumulated				
Depreciation—furniture				
& fixtures	(5,000)	—	—	(5,000)
Museum Building	1,500,000	—	—	1,500,000
Accumulated				
Depreciation—Museum	(900,000)	—	—	(900,000)
Land	100,000	—	—	100,000
Total Assets	$871,000	$ 69,000	$1,004,000	$1,944,000
Liabilities and Net Assets:				
Accounts Payable	$ 5,000	—	—	$ 5,000
Mortgage Payable	400,000	—	—	400,000
Capital Lease Payable	20,000	—	—	20,000
Total Liabilities	$425,000	—	—	$425,000
Net Assets:	$446,000	$ 69,000	$1,004,000	$1,519,000

The following transactions summarize activities that occurred at the Art Museum during the fiscal year:

Cash	900,000	
Admission Fees		900,000

(record admission receipts for the year)

Salaries & Wages Expense	500,000	
Employee Benefits Expense	100,000	
Cash		600,000

(record payments to employees for the year; 20% relates to management and general administration of the museum)

Utilities Expense	30,000	
Cash		30,000

(record payment for utilities)

Capital Lease Payable	4,000	
Mortgage Payable	22,000	
Cash		26,000

(record payments on long-term liabilities)

Temporarily Restricted Net Assets—Reclassifications Out	5,000	
Unrestricted Net Assets—Reclassifications In		5,000

(reclassify temporarily restricted net assets—program restriction satisfied; donor specified donation be used to pay mortgage on building)

Cash	60,000	
Gift Shop—Sales Revenue		60,000
Gift shop inventory	55,000	
Accounts Payable		55,000
(record receipt of gift shop inventory)		

Accounts Payable	60,000	
Cash		60,000
(record payment of accounts payable)		

Cost of Goods Sold	45,000	
Gift Shop Inventory		45,000
(adjust inventory to reflect physical inventory at fiscal year-end)		

Contributions Receivable	400,000	
Contributions Revenue—Temporarily Restricted		400,000
(record pledges to Art Museum as a result of phonathon)		

Legal and Accounting Expense	3,000	
Contributions Revenue—Unrestricted		3,000
(record contribution of specialized legal and accounting services)		

Cash	206,000	
Contributions Receivable		206,000
(receipt of payment for pledges)		

Temporarily Restricted Net Assets — Reclassifications Out	206,000	
Unrestricted Net Assets — Reclassifications In		206,000
(reclassify temporarily restricted net assets due to payment of pledges—time restriction satisfied)		

(Painting donated to collection—collection not capitalized so no entry required)

Cash	50,000	
Special Events Revenue		50,000
(record receipts from annual spring reception at museum for donors)		

Cost of Direct Benefit to Donors	10,000	
Accounts Payable		10,000
(record catering bill for spring reception for donors)		

Depreciation Expense	55,000	
Accumulated Depreciation—Museum Building		50,000
Accumulated Depreciation—Furniture & Fixtures		5,000
(record annual depreciation on capital assets)		

Cash	110,000	
Investment Revenue—Temporarily Restricted		6,000
Investment Revenue—Unrestricted		104,000
(record interest and dividends; no change in fair market value of investments occurred)		

Closing entries at fiscal year-end:

Contributions Revenue—Unrestricted	3,000	
Admission Fees	900,000	
Gift Shop Sales Revenue	60,000	

Special Event Revenue	50,000	
Investment Revenue	104,000	
Unrestricted Net Assets—Reclassifications In	211,000	
Cost of Goods Sold		45,000
Cost of Direct Benefits to Donors		10,000
Salaries and Wages Expense		500,000
Fringe Benefits Expense		100,000
Utilities Expense		30,000
Legal and Accounting Expense		3,000
Depreciation Expense		55,000
Unrestricted Net Assets		585,000

(closing of unrestricted accounts)

Contributions Revenue—Temporarily Restricted	400,000	
Investment Revenue	6,000	
Temporarily Restricted Net Assets—		
Reclassifications Out		211,000
Temporarily Restricted Net Assets		195,000

(closing of temporarily restricted accounts)

(no permanently restricted activity during fiscal year to close)

Art Museum
Statement of Activities
for fiscal year-end June 30 20X1

	Unrestricted	Temporarily Restricted	Permanently Restricted	Total
Revenues, Gains, & Other Support				
Contributions	$ 3,000	$ 400,000	—	$ 403,000
Admission Fees	900,000			900,000
Gift Shop Sales	$60,000			
Less: Cost of Goods Sold	45,000			
Gift Shop Net Income	15,000			15,000
Special Event Revenue	$50,000			
Cost Direct Benefit to Donors	10,000			
Net revenue from special event	40,000			40,000
Investment revenue	104,000	6,000		110,000
Net Assets released from restrictions:				
Satisfaction of program restriction	5,000	(5,000)	—	—
Satisfaction of time restriction	206,000	(206,000)	—	—
Total revenues, gains, other support	1,273,000	195,000	-0-	1,468,000
Expenses:				
Salaries and Wages	$ 500,000	—	—	$500,000
Fringe Benefits	100,000	—	—	100,000
Utilities	30,000	—	—	30,000
Legal and Accounting	3,000	—	—	3,000
Depreciation	55,000	—	—	55,000
Total expenses	688,000	—	—	$688,000
Change in net assets	585,000	195,000	-0-	780,000
Net assets beginning of fiscal year	446,000	69,000	1,004,000	1,519,000
Net assets end of fiscal year	$1,031,000	$264,000	$1,004,000	$2,299,000

Art Museum
Statement of Financial Position
(at June 30, 20X0 and 20X1)

	20X0	20X1
Assets:		
Cash	$ 18,000	$ 628,000
Contributions Receivable	11,000	205,000
Investments	1,100,000	1,100,000
Gift Shop Inventory	20,000	30,000
Furniture & Fixtures	100,000	100,000
Accumulated Depreciation—Furniture & Fixtures	(5,000)	(10,000)
Museum	1,500,000	1,500,000
Accumulated Depreciation—Museum	(900,000)	(950,000)
Land	100,000	100,000
Total Assets	$1,944,000	$2,703,000
Liabilities and Net Assets:		
Accounts Payable	$ 5,000	$ 10,000
Capital Lease Payable	20,000	16,000
Mortgage Payable	400,000	378,000
Total Liabilities	$ 425,000	$ 404,000
Net Assets	$1,519,000	$2,299,000
Total Liabilities and Net Assets	$1,944,000	$2,703.000

Art Museum
Statement of Cash Flows
For fiscal year ended June 30, 20X1

Cash Flows from Operating Activities:	
Admission Fees	$900,000
Gift Shop Sales	60,000
Contributions	206,000
Special Events	50,000
Employee Salaries & Wages	(500,000)
Employee Fringe Benefits	(100,000)
Utilities	(30,000)
Payment on accounts payable to vendors	(60,000)
Interest and dividends on investments	110,000
Net cash provided by operating activities	$636,000
Cash Flows from Investing Activities:	
Net cash provided by investing activities	0
Cash Flows from Financing Activities:	
Payment of capital lease	$ (4,000)
Payment of mortgage	(22,000)
Net cash used by financing activities	$ (26,000)
Net increase in cash and cash equivalents	$610,000
Cash and cash equivalents July 1, 20X0	18,000
Cash and cash equivalents June 30, 20X1	$628,000
Reconciliation of change in net assets to net cash provided by operating activities:	
Change in net assets	$780,000
Adjustments to reconcile change in net assets to net cash provided by operating activities	
Depreciation	55,000
Increase in contributions receivable	(194,000)
Increase in gift shop inventory	(10,000)
Increase in accounts payable	5,000
Net cash provided by operating activities	$636,000

Art Museum
Statement of Functional Expenses
For fiscal year end, June 30, 20X1
(in thousands)

| | Total | Program Services | | Supporting Services | |
		Museum	Gift Shop	Management	Fund-Raising
Salaries & Wages	$500	$400	—	$100	—
Fringe Benefits	100	80	—	20	—
Utilities	30	30	—	—	—
Legal and Accounting	3	—	—	3	—
Depreciation	55	50	—	5	—
Cost of Goods Sold	45	—	45	—	—
Direct Cost of Special Events	10	—	—	—	10
Total	$743	$560	$ 45	$128	$10

Although a Statement of Functional Expenses would not be required, it shows the amount spent on the main museum program is $560 or 75% of the total expenses and that management and general administration takes 17% of total expenses. This example illustrates basic activities, transactions, journal entries, and financial statements for a not-for-profit organization.

SUMMARY

Chapter 6 had the following learning objectives:

- Describe the types of not-for-profit organizations
- Describe the funds for not-for-profit organizations
- Explain accounting for contributions
- Explain accounting for investments
- Illustrate the basic financial statements

In Chapter 1, the basic differences between governmental organizations, not-for-profit organizations and for-profit organizations was outlined and the hierarchy of GAAP (Exhibit 1-1, page 7) set forth the sources of GAAP for each type of organization. Chapter 6 begins with a basic review of the concepts presented in Chapter 1 and then lists the types of not-for-profit organizations. Funds that may be used within not-for-profit accounting systems are listed and discussed. Chapter 6 illustrates and explains the accounting and financial reporting established by FASB for nongovernmental not-for-profit organizations. FASB Statement No. 116 established common methods of accounting for contributions. FASB Statement No. 117 established a common financial reporting model for all not-for-profit organizations. FASB Statement No. 124 established common methods of reporting on investments for all not-for-profit organizations. The FASB standards common to all types of not-for-profit organizations are set forth and illustrated. Chapter 7 covers some of the unique characteristics of health care organizations and colleges and universities as well as *Government Auditing Standards* and the single audit.

QUESTIONS

1. What are some of the unique characteristics of not-for-profit organizations?
2. What are the major categories of not-for-profit organizations?
3. Who sets accounting standards for not-for-profit organizations?
4. Is fund accounting required for not-for-profit organizations?
5. What are the four categories of Plant funds?
6. How does the Current fund compare to the General fund?
7. What is the difference between an improvement to plant and renewal and replacement?
8. Which part of Plant fund accounts for construction in progress?
9. What are the three types of endowment funds? Explain the differences among them.
10. What is the difference between an intent to give and a promise to give?
11. What is the difference between a condition and a restriction on a contribution?
12. What is a "split-interest" donation?
13. What type of special event would be partly accounted for as an exchange transaction?
14. What are the three classifications of net assets that appear in the Statement of Financial Position?
15. What type of organization prepares a Statement of Functional Expenses? What are the functional classifications for expenses?

EXERCISES

Exercise 6-1   **Multiple Choice—Select the best answer for each of the following:**

1. The public university collects tuition and fees from students. These revenues will be recorded in the:
   a. General fund
   b. Restricted current fund
   c. Tuition revenue fund
   d. Unrestricted current fund
2. The hospital bills patients for care provided. These revenues will be recorded in the:
   a. Unrestricted current fund
   b. Patient care fund
   c. General fund
   d. Specific-purpose fund
3. The university sets aside funds to build a new classroom building in the future. These monies will be recorded in the:
   a. Unrestricted current fund
   b. Plant fund: Renewal and replacement
   c. Plant fund: Investment in plant
   d. Plant fund: Unexpended funds
4. The university starts construction of a classroom building. The construction-in-progress will be recorded in:
   a. Plant fund: Renewal and replacement
   b. Plant fund: Unexpended funds
   c. Plant fund: Investment in plant
   d. either b or c
5. The university issues bonds to pay for construction of a new building. The bonds payable will be recorded in the:
   a. Plant fund: Retirement of indebtedness
   b. Plant fund: Investment in plant
   c. Plant fund: Renewal and replacement
   d. Plant fund: Unexpended funds

6. The university pays principal and interest on the bonds issued to pay for construction of a new building. The payment of principal and interest can affect accounts in:
   a. Plant fund: Investment in plant
   b. Unrestricted current fund
   c. Plant fund: Retirement of indebtedness
   d. all of the above

7. The Loan fund records:
   a. long-term bonds issued to finance a new building
   b. short-term notes issued to meet payroll
   c. loans to students
   d. none of the above

8. A Quasi-endowment fund records:
   a. an endowment that the donor has not decided a final purpose restriction for
   b. an endowment that results from a split-interest agreement
   c. a term endowment expiring within the current period
   d. resources the institution itself has set aside

9. A hospice collects donations that will be used to pay for care for patients dying of AIDS. These monies will be recorded in the:
   a. Endowment fund
   b. Permanent fund
   c. Specific-purpose fund
   d. Agency fund

10. Annie Alumni donates $200,000 to Big University and specifies that the monies must be held in trust until she dies and then can be used to beautify the campus with flower gardens. These monies will be recorded in the:
    a. Permanent trust fund
    b. Agency fund
    c. General fund
    d. Term endowment fund

Exercise 6-2

Multiple Choice—Select the best answer for each of the following:

1. A hospice constructs a patient care center and issues long-term bonds to finance construction. The capital asset for the care center and the long-term bonds will be recorded in the:
   a. Plant fund: Investment in plant
   b. General fund
   c. Specific purpose fund
   d. Plant fund: Renewal and replacement

2. A split-interest donation will be recorded in:
   a. the General fund
   b. the Endowment fund
   c. the Annuity and life-income fund
   d. none of the above

3. Movie mogul tells his alma mater that he may decide to donate a substantial amount of cash to Media University if they will award him an honorary doctorate degree and rename their theater in his honor. This would be considered:
   a. a nonreciprocal transfer
   b. an exchange transaction
   c. a promise to give
   d. none of the above

4. Sally Snowflake tells the Handicapped Ski Foundation that she might leave her home and surrounding 10-acre ranch in Vail, Colorado, to the foundation when she gets around to writing a will. Sally's intent to give her ranch in Colorado to the Handicapped Ski Foundation should be recorded by them as:
   a. a promise to give
   b. a contribution revenue
   c. an optional footnote disclosure
   d. a deferred contribution revenue

5. Bob Baseball makes a pledge of $100 over the phone to support the Coopersville Hall of Fame. Bob promises to pay the pledge within 90 days, and the pledge is documented by a phone log. The Coopersville Hall of Fame should record:
   a. an unconditional promise to give
   b. a conditional promise to give
   c. a conditional intent to give
   d. none of the above

6. Fred gets a call from the Chicago Symphony and pledges $500 to be paid within 60 days. The Chicago Symphony should record:
   a. a $500 unrestricted contribution
   b. a $500 intent to give in the footnotes
   c. a $500 temporarily restricted contribution
   d. none of the above

7. Jane likes to go jogging and decides to pledge $1,000 to her favorite charity, Paws-with-a-Cause, which trains dog guides, and will be payable *if* she can complete the Boston Marathon. Jane has never even run a 5K marathon but is very optimistic that she can complete the Boston Marathon with some serious training. Paws-with-a-Cause should record:
   a. an unrestricted contribution of $1,000
   b. a temporarily restricted contribution of $1,000
   c. a footnote disclosure of conditional contribution of $1,000
   d. none of the above

8. Pacifist Peg pledges $100,000 to Promote Peace Foundation with the condition that she will pay the pledge within 60 days *unless* world peace is achieved. The Promote Peace Foundation should record:
   a. nothing as this is a conditional contribution
   b. a footnote disclosure of the pledge
   c. an unrestricted contribution of $100,000
   d. a temporarily restricted contribution of $100,000 as the achievement of world peace is a remote event

9. Nervous Nellie pledges $10,000 to the Human Rights Organization with the condition that she will pay the pledge within 60 days *unless* the Federal Reserve Board increases interest rates at its next meeting in 30 days. The Human Rights Organization should record:
   a. nothing as this is a conditional contribution
   b. a permanently restricted contribution
   c. an unrestricted contribution of $10,000
   d. a temporarily restricted contribution of $10,000 as the lowering of interest rates is a remote event

10. Fearless Fran decides to donate $500,000 to Save the Earth foundation if her small Internet company can successfully launch its web site and stock offering for $50,000,000 of investor capital in an IPO. The web site sells hemp clothing and other clothing made from natural products. Sales to date have totaled $100,000 in the past six months but hits are increasing on the web site. Save the Earth foundation should record:
    a. nothing as this is a conditional contribution
    b. a permanently restricted contribution
    c. an unrestricted contribution of $500,000
    d. a temporarily restricted contribution of $500,000 as the failure of the IPO to raise $50,000,000 is a remote event

Exercise 6-3   **Multiple Choice—Select the best answer for each of the following:**

1. Alcoholics Anonymous (AA) receives meeting space from a local business in a conference room. The space is provided to AA free of charge, and the business has no other use for the space at the weekend time that AA meets and could not otherwise rent the space. The fair market value of the space for the meeting period is $200 per month. AA should record:
   a. $200 temporarily restricted revenue
   b. $200 unrestricted revenue
   c. $200 permanently restricted revenue
   d. $0 as the donated space has no market value to the business contributing it

2. AT&T donates long-distance services to a phonathon for a local charity. The cost of the long-distance services provided the evening of the phonathon is $1,200. The charity should record:
   a. $0 as AT&T paid nothing for the service
   b. $1,200 temporarily restricted revenue
   c. $1,200 unrestricted revenue
   d. $1,200 permanently restricted revenue

3. Mildred notifies her local church that she has signed a revocable agreement to donate her palatial home in the country to the church for a meditation retreat center. The church should record:
   a. a capital asset for the fair market value of the home
   b. an unrestricted contribution
   c. a temporarily restricted contribution
   d. nothing as the agreement is revocable

4. A CPA firm donates audit and accounting services that would normally be billed at $5,000 to the local homeless shelter. In addition, several employees of the CPA firm donate 200 hours (billing rate normally $50/hour) to clean and paint the shelter and landscape the grounds. The homeless shelter should record:
   a. $10,000 unrestricted revenue
   b. $15,000 unrestricted revenue
   c. $5,000 unrestricted revenue
   d. none of the above

5. An art collector donates a famous painting to the local art museum valued at $200,000. The art museum immediately sells the painting to pay current operating expenses. The art museum does not capitalize its collection. The art museum should record:
   a. $200,000 capital asset
   b. $200,000 unrestricted contribution revenue
   c. $200,000 permanently restricted revenue
   d. $0 because it is a collectible asset

6. An art collector donates a famous painting to the local art museum valued at $200,000. The art museum exhibits the painting as part of its collection. The art museum does not capitalize its collection. The art museum should record:
   a. $200,000 capital asset
   b. $200,000 unrestricted contribution revenue
   c. $200,000 permanently restricted revenue
   d. $0 because it is a part of a collection

7. Sandra donates $75 to public television, which sends Sandra a T-shirt to wear with their logo imprinted on it. The T-shirt cost public television $3. The public television station should record:
   a. $72 unrestricted contribution revenue
   b. $72 unrestricted and $3 temporarily restricted revenue
   c. $75 unrestricted revenue
   d. $72 permanently restricted revenue

8. Lydia attends a gala charity ball and pays $500 for the ticket to attend. The charity expends $100 for each person in catering and entertainment. The charity should record:
   a. $500 unrestricted contribution revenue
   b. $500 special events revenue
   c. $100 cost of direct benefits to donors
   d. both b and c
9. Dan donates to his favorite charity 100 shares of substantially appreciated stock valued at $100 per share that cost Dan $10 a share. The charity should record:
   a. an unrestricted donation of $1,000
   b. an unrestricted donation of $9,000
   c. an unrestricted donation of $10,000
   d. none of the above
10. The Global Charity had investments in public-traded securities of $100,000. At the end of the fiscal year, the market value of these securities was $104,000. Global Charity should record:
    a. unrestricted net appreciation on investments of $104,000
    b. unrestricted net appreciation on investments of $4,000
    c. temporarily restricted net appreciation on investments of $4,000
    d. none of the above

Exercise 6-4

Matching-funds

Match the transaction with the appropriate fund to account for it:

Transaction	Fund
a. college pays faculty salaries	General
b. city pays police salaries	Special revenue
c. county collects taxes	Unrestricted current
d. hospital pays nurses	Restricted current
e. student gets loan from university	Enterprise
f. city puts pension funds in trust	Internal service
g. college pays debt service on bonds	Debt service
h. city receives payment for water/sewer bills	Loan
i. state pays debt service on bonds	Pension trust
j. city collects green fees at city golf course	Plant: Retirement of indebtedness

Exercise 6-5

Matching-funds

Match the transaction with the appropriate fund to account for it:

Transaction	Fund
a. city receives donation to buy land for park	Plant: Renewal and replacement
b. college receives donation of land for campus	General
c. student pays tuition and fees	Restricted current
d. student drops class and gets refund	Unrestricted current
e. donor makes pledge to Habitat for Humanity	Special revenue
f. city starts major renovation of city hall	Debt service
g. college starts building dormitory	Capital project
h. citizen pays parking ticket	Plant: Investment in plant
i. state escheats unclaimed property	Permanent fund
j. university receives federal research grant	Private-purpose trust fund

Exercise 6-6	### Funds

Name the not-for-profit fund that is most similar to the governmental fund listed below:

   a. Private-purpose trust
   b. Special revenue
   c. Internal service
   d. Agency
   e. General
   f. Investment trust
   g. Capital projects
   h. Enterprise
   i. Debt service
   j. Permanent

Exercise 6-7	### Promise to give

The Chicago Museum of Contemporary Art sued a married couple for collection of a $5 million promise to give that was never paid despite a letter of intent that was binding on the couple's estate. Would the promise be recognized as revenue and, if so, when would it have been recognized as revenue? Will the museum have to record the lawsuit in the financial accounting system and, if so, how?

Exercise 6-8	### Contributions

The Global-Warming Organization receives free use of a conference room for meetings from Jones Corporation. Jones Corporation does specify that the Global-Warming Organization must reserve the space 60 days in advance and it will only be available if not otherwise reserved for Jones Corporation business activity. The conference room space is 100 square feet and Jones pays $300 a month to their landlord for rental of this room. Which one of the four types of contributions is this? What would Global-Warming have to record for this contribution?

Exercise 6-9	### Funds

The Canyon University governing board decides that growing enrollment requires more classroom space. Canyon University does not have enough funds left over in the current budget to spend $40 million for a new classroom building, so the board decides to issue long-term bonds to borrow the money. Construction starts on the new classroom building. Where will Canyon University account for the debt issued to fund the construction? Where will Canyon University account for the construction of the new classroom building? Where will Canyon University account for the repayment of principal and interest on the long-term bonds issued to construct the new classroom building?

Exercise 6-10	### Funds

The Healthy Hospital and Creative University apply together and receive a federal research grant for a joint research project to study how to prevent the accumulation of brain plaque that leads to Alzheimer's disease. Where will the Healthy Hospital account for its portion of the grant? In what fund will the Creative University account for its portion of the grant?

Exercise 6-11

Contribution of services

The Helping Hands organization asks a local CPA firm to contribute audit services to audit their annual financial report. The CPA firm contributes the audit services to the organization and normally would have billed $1,500 for this audit. The CPA firm also solicits volunteers from among its employees to plant flowers in the landscaping in front of the Helping Hands building one Saturday. The flowers donated cost $300 and the employees worked for 12 hours (their average pay rate would normally be $30/hour at the CPA firm). What type of contributions are these? What should Helping Hands record to account for these contributions?

Exercise 6-12

Contribution of services

Thousands of volunteers assisted with the tasks associated with cleanup, demolition, and removal of the remains of the World Trade Center twin towers in New York in the wake of the terrorist attacks on September 11. Many volunteers provided simple comforts such as donating new socks for firefighters and demolition crews and cooking hot meals on site, while others provided specialized skills such as ironworkers removing beams and debris. Would these contributions be recorded as revenue by the City of New York?

PROBLEMS

Problem 6-1

Funds

A private college has the following transactions. What fund will account for these transactions?
a. payment of faculty salaries
b. interest on endowment
c. construction of dormitories
d. issuance of bonds to build dormitories
e. restricted grant to conduct research
f. loans to students
g. annuity payments to donors
h. investment income on unrestricted contributions

Problem 6-2

Funds

A not-for-profit hospital has the following transactions. What fund will account for these transactions?
a. payment of nurses' salaries
b. interest on endowment
c. construction of hospital wing
d. issuance of bonds to build hospital wing
e. restricted grant to conduct research
f. loans to interns
g. annuity payments to donors
h. investment income on unrestricted contributions

Problem 6-3

Contributions

Which of the following will result in contribution revenue being recognized? If so, how much?
  a. Donor intends to give $10,000 upon death.
  b. Donor signs will to give $10,000 upon death
  c. Donor irrevocably signs pledge to give $10,000 upon death.
  d. Donor enters into life-income agreement to donate $1,000,000 upon death with investment income flowing to donor while alive
  e. Donor goes to annual grand charity ball and pays $1,000 for admission, receiving dinner/dance valued at $100

Problem 6-4

Contributions

Which of the following will result in contribution revenue being recognized by a qualified charity? If so, how much?
  a. Tom the Tightrope artist pledges to donate $1,000,000 if he walks across Niagara Falls on a tightrope and is paid $2,000,000 for the stunt.
  b. Wally the Weatherman pledges to donate $1,000 if he correctly predicts the weather for one week.
  c. Dan Detective provides specialized background checks worth $5,000 on employees to a charity that solicits contributions from high-income individuals.
  d. Sam donates his time (valued at $10/hour) to clean the grounds and sidewalks for a local museum.
  e. Larry the Lawyer donates his time (valued at $100/hour) to handle contracts and other legal matters for a local museum.

Problem 6-5

Contributions

Which of the following will result in contribution revenue being recognized by a qualified charity? If so, how much?
  a. Phil Philately donates a valuable stamp worth $500 to a local homeless shelter that immediately sells it for $1,000.
  b. Phil Philately donates a valuable stamp worth $500 to a local stamp society that adds it to its collection, which it does capitalize.
  c. Phil Philately donates a valuable stamp worth $500 to the Smithsonian Museum that adds it to its collection, which it does not capitalize.

Problem 6-6

Contributions

Record the following transactions for the charity in journal entries:
  a. Melissa donates $1,000 cash to the Humane Society
  b. Melissa donates 100 hours of her time to clean cages at the Humane Society. The Humane Society only uses volunteers for this work.
  c. Melissa pledges $500 to United Way and signs up to pay the pledge over the next 12 months through payroll deduction.
  d. Melissa cleans out her attic and donates old clothing that has no resale value to her local Goodwill society.
  e. Melissa pledges $1,000 to her local church to be paid over the next year.
  f. Melissa pledges $100 to replace the organ at her church and agrees to pay this pledge in the next month.

Problem 6-7   **Contributions**

Record the following transactions for the charity in journal entries:

    a. Dan danced all night at the charity ball. Dan's corporation paid $10,000 for a table at this gala event and five employees and their five spouses attended and received dinner/dancing valued at $100 each.

    b. Dan donated 200 hours as a baseball coach for an inner-city baseball team. The teams are only staffed by volunteers. Dan normally earns $32 an hour at his workplace.

    c. Dan responds to a mailing and pledges $200 to the local Boy Scout troop. He receives a mug, which cost the troop $1.

    d. Dan inherits a remote parcel of forest land valued at $75,000. Dan donates the land to the local Boy Scout troop. The troop immediately sells the land for $75,000.

    e. Dan inherits a remote parcel of forest land valued at $75,000. Dan donates the land to the local Boy Scout troop. The troop turns the land into a Boy Scout campsite.

Problem 6-8   **Investments**

Record the journal entries to reflect the following transactions investing permanently restricted funds. The donor has not specified that the earnings or gains/losses be restricted in any way:

    a. Charity purchases investment valued at $100,000.

    b. At fiscal year-end, investment is valued at $105,000.

    c. Dividends of $3,000 are received.

    d. At next fiscal year-end, the investment is valued at $103,000.

    e. Dividends of $3,000 are received.

Problem 6-9   **Functional classification**

Determine whether the following items should be classified as **program** or **supporting service** expenses for the Leukemia/Lymphoma Society:

    a. research on leukemia/lymphoma

    b. dinner for donors

    c. management salaries

    d. disaster relief expenses

    e. mugs and key chains given to donors

    f. cost of maintaining donor mailing lists

    g. interest costs on mortgage for administrative headquarters

    h. cost of audit and printing of annual report

    i. public advertisements

Problem 6-10   **Special events**

The Art Institute hosted its annual black-tie dinner/dance. Record attendance generated donations of $100,000, and the cost of hosting the event was $20,000.

    a. Record the special event in journal entries.

    b. Show the two acceptable presentations of this information in the Statement of Activities.

Problem 6-11

Journal entries

The Botanical Garden had the following transactions occur during its fiscal year. Record these events in journal entries.

    a. Pledges of $100,000 were made for the new perennial garden.

    b. Unrestricted donations of $900,000 were received in cash.

    c. Expenses of $10,000 were incurred to purchase plants for the new perennial garden.

    d. A special butterfly exhibit was held to generate additional donations for general operations. $100,000 in admission fees was received, and attendees received a special butterfly pin that cost the garden $750.

    e. Employees were paid $400,000 during the year (including fringe benefits).

    f. Volunteers donated 10,000 hours of service valued at $8/hour. However, the garden would not have hired employees to do this work.

    g. A violent storm broke several windows, and local firms donated repairs and materials valued at $8,000.

Problem 6-12

Journal entries

Start with the Art Museum Statement of Financial Position Assets, Liabilities, and Net Assets balances at fiscal year-end June 30, 20X1, shown in the Putting It All Together example in the chapter.

    a. Record the following transactions for fiscal year July 1, 20X1, to June 30, 20X2, in journal entries.

    1. Admission fees of $850,000 were received.

    2. Salaries and wages of $500,000 and $100,000 in fringe benefits were paid.

    3. The capital lease payable of $4,000 and mortgage payable of $22,000 payments were made.

    4. Utility charges of $28,000 were paid.

    5. The Gift Shop ordered and received inventory of $45,000 and had sales of $65,000. Inventory at fiscal year-end was $18,000.

    6. The phonathon yielded pledges of $300,000; 50% were paid before fiscal year-end.

    7. A donor made a donation of $500,000 to be permanently invested with earnings to be used to support general operating activity ($5,000 in interest was received during this fiscal year).

    8. Accounts payable were paid in full before fiscal year-end.

    9. The annual spring reception generated $70,000 in revenue and cost $15,000.

    10. Depreciation expense of $50,000 on the museum, and $5,000 on furniture & fixtures was recorded.

    11. Investment income of $108,000 temporarily restricted and $6,000 unrestricted was received (in addition to the $5,000 mentioned above in item 7).

    12. Closing entries were recorded.

    b. Prepare the basic financial statements for the Art Museum at fiscal year-end June 30, 20X2.

Problem 6-13

Internet case: Conceptual

    a. Go to the National Center for Charitable Statistics http://nccs.urban.org/ and find the charitable contributions for the most recent year for your state. Do you think the tax law permitting deduction of charitable contributions stimulates contributions?

    b. Go to http://www.guidestar.org/ and select a not-for-profit organization. Take a look at the information provided on the web site and see if you can determine what percentage of total contributions goes toward primary programs and what percentage goes toward management, administrative, and fund-raising expenses.

Problem 6-14 **Internet Research: Not-for-profit funds**

Go to the Harvard University Budget Fact Book for Fiscal Year 1999–2000 http://vpf-web.harvard.edu/Budget/factbook/99-00/. What funds would Harvard University need to use to account for the 1999–2000 budget?

Problem 6-15 **Internet Research: Contributions**

Fred Philanthropist decides he would like to make a gift to the Mayo Clinic. He looks at the Mayo Clinic web site for information on how to make this gift. Go to http://www.mayo.edu/develop/develop.html. Fred decides to make a $1,000,000 gift with 50% to be designated for medical education and 50% designated for medical research. How would the Mayo Clinic account for this gift?

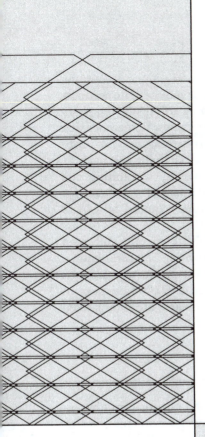

CHAPTER 7

HEALTH CARE ORGANIZATIONS, COLLEGES AND UNIVERSITIES, AND AUDITING

LEARNING OBJECTIVES

- Demonstrate an understanding of accounting and reporting for health care organizations
- Demonstrate an understanding of accounting and reporting for colleges and universities
- Explain basic *Government Auditing Standards* auditing principles
- Explain basic requirements of the single audit

INTRODUCTION

Health care organizations and colleges and universities have some unique accounting and reporting requirements due to the nature of their operating activity. The accounting and reporting requirements explained in Chapter 6 apply to all not-for-profit health care organizations and not-for-profit colleges and universities. Remember that governmental organizations follow GASB and nongovernmental not-for-profit organizations follow FASB according to the hierarchy of GAAP (Exhibit 1-1, page 7). There are several unique health care and college and university accounting and reporting requirements that are explained in this chapter. The financial statements for a hospital and also for governmental colleges and universities required by GASB Statements No. 34 and 35 are illustrated in this chapter.

The Federal single audit must be done in accordance with Generally Accepted Government Auditing Standards (GAGAS) in *Government Auditing Standards* known as "the yellow book." State and local governments and not-for-profit organizations are required to have a single audit if they receive and expend $300,000 or more in Federal funds annually. The GAGAS yellow book auditing standards are summarized at the end of the chapter.

HEALTH CARE ORGANIZATIONS

Health care organizations are classified as either investor-owned not-for-profit enterprises (private), not-for-profit business oriented organizations, governmental health care organizations, or voluntary health and welfare organizations. All health care organizations use the accrual method of accounting. This chapter will cover the special accounting and reporting requirements for not-for-profit health care organizations and governmental health care organizations. Voluntary health and welfare organizations are covered under the AICPA Audit and Accounting Guide for *Not-for-Profit Organizations* as covered in Chapter 6, and for-profit organizations are not covered in this book.

The AICPA Audit and Accounting Guide for *Health Care Organizations* applies to the following organizations:[1]

- Clinics, emergency care facilities and similar facilities
- Continuing care retirement communities
- Health maintenance organizations (HMOs) and similar plans
- Home health agencies
- Hospitals
- Nursing homes
- Drug and alcohol and other rehabilitation facilities

All nongovernmental not-for-profit health care organizations will follow the guidance in this AICPA Audit and Accounting Guide. In general, most of the not-for-profit accounting concepts discussed in Chapter 6 also apply to not-for-profit health care organizations. Governmental health care organizations are generally considered proprietary governmental activities that should apply FASB standards issued before

---

[1]AICPA Audit and Accounting Guide for *Health Care Organizations with Conforming Changes as of May 1, 2001*, preface vii.

November 30, 1989 and *may* apply FASB standards developed for business enterprises issued after that date *that are not in conflict with GASB statements.*[2] Since FASB statements No. 116, 117, and 124 have provisions for not-for-profit organizations, rather than business enterprises, they would not be applicable to governmental health care organizations.[3]

Tax exempt status

Most not-for-profit health care organizations are exempt from federal income tax under Section 501(c)(3) of the Internal Revenue Code. They will be subject to an unrelated business income tax (UBIT), like other not-for-profit organizations, if they regularly engage in a trade or business that is not substantially related to their primary purpose. Health care activities that could generate a UBIT liability are the sale of pharmaceuticals to the general public, laboratory services to private patients of physicians housed in hospital-owned offices, or property rental. Auxiliary activities that would not generate UBIT are normally ancillary activities provided for the convenience of customers or employees, such as a gift shop, cafeteria, or parking structure.[4] These activities are recorded in the General fund as part of operating activity.

In recent years, the Internal Revenue Service has launched several investigations of hospitals and health care organizations for violations of tax-exempt status ranging from arbitrage issues (investing tax-exempt bond proceeds at a higher interest rate) on tax-exempt bonds to the adequacy of community benefits provided.

● **INTERPRETIVE EXERCISE**

> A hospital cafeteria has excellent cuisine and competes directly with a local restaurant across the street, but the net income is not subject to UBIT. The hospital pharmacy competes directly with Rite-Aid located across the street, and the net income is subject to UBIT. Will the hospital cafeteria or pharmacy activities be subject to UBIT?

Health care environment

Health care expenditures exceeded $1 trillion a year in the United States[5] representing 13.5% of the gross domestic product[6] in 1999. There is a very fragmented system of health care providers and health care payors resulting in a strong competitive environment and complicated pricing and payment systems. Payors include federal Medicare and Medicaid, managed care, capitation contracts, preferred providers, employer contracts, and self-pay. All of these payors seek to limit risk and control health care expenditures, so that contracts with health care organizations often set

---

[2]GASB Statement No. 20, *Accounting and Financial Reporting for Proprietary Funds and Other Governmental Entities That Use Proprietary Fund Accounting*, paragraphs 6–7, and GASB Statement No. 29, *The Use of Not-for-Profit Accounting and Financial Reporting Principles by Governmental Entities.*

[3]AICPA Audit and Accounting Guide for *Health Care Organizations*, paragraph 1.37.

[4]Ibid, paragraph 7.10.

[5]National Center for Health Statistics, Health, United States, 1999, Hyattsville, Md., Table 119, page 287, http://www.cdc.gov/nchs.

[6]Ibid, Table 116, page 284.

caps or limits upon reimbursement, hence, shifting financial risk to the health care organization. Health care expenditures have been rising sharply, averaging a 10.6% annual increase from 1960 to 1997.[7] Therefore, the risk of spiraling expenditures that could create deficits if not fully reimbursed under existing payor contracts is a constant pressure in health care management.

Limits on reimbursement in Medicaid and Medicare payment systems have placed increased pressure upon the net profits of health care organizations as a result of the 1997 Balanced Budget Amendment that reduced available funding. This had a direct impact upon many hospitals' bottom line, pushing many into a net operating deficit position. The 1999 Balanced Budget Relief Act restored $16 billion in funding, but some of this "funding" was just a postponement of additional cuts scheduled to take effect in 2000–2002.

The Health Insurance Portability and Accountability Act (HIPPA) of 1996 focuses upon administrative simplification to prevent fraud and abuse in federal health care reimbursement. HIPPA establishes a standardized coding system for covered patient information to be stored electronically at all points in the chain of health care service. Although HIPPA may ultimately result in operating efficiencies due to standardized national coding, the implementation of HIPPA places additional demands and stress upon health care organizations.[8]

The accounting and financial reporting standards for health care organizations are designed to clearly reflect the total costs of providing health care services. Most not-for-profit and governmental health care organizations are intended to be self supporting from the fees charged for the services they provide.

Health care reimbursement and contracts

The majority of health care goods and services are paid for by third-party payors or insurance companies. This reimbursement system drives the accounting for health care organizations that record most of their operating activity in the General fund to ensure that all costs are included in costs billed to third-party payors. Capital assets are included in the General fund to ensure that depreciation expense is captured and included in costs billed. Long-term liabilities are also included in the General fund to ensure that interest expense is fully captured and included in costs billed.

There are a wide variety of pricing issues in health care due to the large number of third-party payors ranging from private insurance companies, health maintenance organizations (HMOs), employer contracts, and preferred provider contracts to payment directly by the patient. Each of these payors may be charged a different "price" for the same service. Hospitals have chargemaster files with thousands of prices for goods and services ranging from a surgical procedure to an aspirin tablet dispensed for pain. A chargemaster file is a master list of the price of each good (medication, prosthesis, surgical screw, etc.) or service (surgical service, inpatient bed/day, physical therapy, etc.) the health care provider places on the billings to patients. The price of each of these goods and services may vary depending upon who the payor is. These pricing issues can lead to adjustments in expected revenue based upon contractual

---

[7]National Health Statistics Group, Office of the Actuary. National Health Expenditures, 1997. Health Care Financing Review, vol 20 no. 1 HCFA pub no 03412, Washington: Health Care Financing Administration, March 1999.

[8]"Avoiding HIPAA Hype: Preparing for HIPAA Affordably," *Healthcare Financial Management*, by B. Weber, Bob Alcaro, and Vince Ciotti, August, 2001, pages 62–65.

adjustments, subsequent payor audits, and contract deductibles. These revenue adjustments generally occur long after the good or service has been provided, so there is generally no action the health care organization can take to "recover" revenue other than to raise future prices.

Capitation contracts[9] provide for a maximum (capitated) amount to be paid by the provider to the health care organization for each covered life (person) each month, and in return the health care organization agrees to provide whatever health care services are required for the covered lives. This shifts the financial risk from the third-party payor entering into the capitation contract to the health care organization. The health care organization assumes the risk that the capitated monthly payments will provide sufficient revenues to cover the expenses for goods and services provided to covered lives during the term of the capitation contract. The health care organization is implicitly making certain assumptions about the level of health care services needed based upon age and the current "wellness" of the covered lives. Capitation contracts can also provide that the health care organization pay for the cost of physician referrals, specialists, or other costs that may require establishing a liability for estimated claims.

Other third-party contracts may include a cap on the amount of increase in health care costs billed during the term of the contract. Again, this shifts risk to the health care organization and could require evaluating whether a liability should be established for contingencies if it is believed that a material liability could result.

The Health Care Finance Administration (HCFA) administers Medicare and Medicaid. Federal reimbursements from Medicare and Medicaid have complicated reimbursement systems and regulations as well. Medicare covers approximately 39 million Americans: patients 65 or older, qualified disabled parties and their dependents, certain railroad retirees, and patients with end-stage renal disease. Medicaid covers approximately 27 million Americans: primarily low-income and poor people.

Medicare pays for inpatient hospitalization based upon a prospective payment system (PPS) for inpatient operating costs that utilizes diagnosis related group (DRG) codes to authorize flat fees as payment in-full for inpatient acute care. DRGs are organized by major body or organ systems called major diagnostic categories (MDCs). The payment rates of DRGs are intended to measure resource consumption related to particular illnesses such as congestive heart failure. If the health care organization incurs expenses greater than the amount of DRG reimbursement, it will incur a loss on the patient care provided. Again, this shifts the risk of loss from Medicare to the health care organization. Special payment adjustments are made by Medicare for hospitals with higher costs such as teaching hospitals, new providers, sole community hospitals, and rural hospitals. Physician services are reimbursed by Medicare based upon resource-based, relative value scales (RBRVS) payments, which are based upon malpractice costs, physician's total workload, and other practice costs. Additional capital payments for interest and depreciation on physical plant and noncapital payments for medical education may also be made to health care organizations. Home health care, outpatient treatments, and clinical laboratory services, are also items that may qualify for Medicare reimbursement. The 1997 Balanced Budget Amendment reduced available Federal funding for Medicare and created a new Medicare + Choice menu (seven possible co-coverage choices for Medicare-eligible senior citizens to

---

[9]AICPA Audit and Accounting Guide for *Health Care Organizations* with Conforming Changes as of May 1, 2001, paragraphs 1.19–1.20.

partner Medicare coverage with private insurance products). In simpler terms, Medicare-eligible senior citizens have seven possible options to purchase "co-coverage" with Medicare; i.e., purchase private health insurance that covers the "gap" between Medicare coverage and paying it themselves. If they do not purchase the co-coverage insurance, the Medicare patient will be responsible for the "gap" in coverage that occurred as a result of Balanced Budget Act of 1997 cutbacks.

The Balanced Budget Act of 1997 outlined a new reimbursement structure shifting from the previous cost-based reimbursement structure to a PPS system of set rates for 659 clinically related groups of procedures and diagnoses under an ambulatory payment classification (APC). Obviously, a major change in reimbursement shifting from cost-based reimbursement to a defined set of procedures/diagnoses/rates can impact revenues significantly. The October 1999 Balanced Budget Relief Act had some triggers to limit the amount of "give-backs" if, for example, the health care organization "lost" more than 30% under the shift to APCs, the "give-back" is 21% prior to 2002, 13% in 2002, and 6% in 2003. This illustrates how complicated it is for health care organizations to set prices for goods and services that they can realistically expect to receive reimbursement for and to forecast their financial position. The shift to APCs can and has negatively impacted hospitals' bottom line operating net income.

Medicaid was established under Title XIX of the Social Security Act and is intended as a safety net for the indigent to obtain health care services. States design and control Medicaid programs so coverage varies from state to state. However, there are Federal guidelines that are set by HCFA, and Medicaid is often the largest single line item in a State budget and averages 15% of state spending overall. Federal funding for Medicaid is based upon state per capita incomes, so it varies from 50 to 83% across states.

Revenues and expenses

Revenues for health care services are recorded at the full established rates with an offsetting estimate for discounts, contractual adjustments to rates for third-party payors, and uncollectible accounts. The estimated adjustments to the full established rates are deducted from the gross revenues to calculate the net service revenue.[10]

Revenues for health care organizations typically arise from patient service revenue, capitation premium revenue (a capitation fee is paid that is presumed to cover all patient services required), and other service revenue.

Contributions, grants, or other support may also be received and will be classified as unrestricted, temporarily restricted, or permanently restricted depending upon restrictions placed by the external source of funds. Contributions are recorded as illustrated in Chapter 6 for not-for-profit health care organizations. Contributions for governmental health care organizations are recorded as nonexchange revenue under GASB Statement No. 33.

Other operating revenue and gains or losses of health care organizations can include:[11] investment interest; dividends and other income; investment gains and losses; educational program fees; rental of facilities to others; sale of medical/pharmaceutical supplies; fees for medical transcripts; sale of scrap; sales from auxiliary enterprises such as the cafeteria, gift shop, snack bar, newsstand, parking lot, and vending machines.

---

[10]AICPA Audit and Accounting Guide for *Health Care Organizations*, paragraph 5.03.
[11]Ibid, Paragraph 10.06.

Expenses are recorded on the accrual basis like other not-for-profit organizations or governmental proprietary funds. Charity care is a unique situation for health care organizations. It can be difficult to determine whether care provided to a patient unable to pay is charity care or bad debt expense.[12] Charity care is provided to a patient unable to pay, whereas bad debt expense is for a patient unwilling to pay. There is a very subtle distinction between charity care and bad debt expense, but the accounting is quite different. Bad debts are an expense that can be reasonably estimated as an allowance against patient service revenue receivables. Charity care is determined at initial delivery of service, and no receivable should be established as the patient is not expected to pay for care. Not-for-profit health care organizations are expected to provide a reasonable amount of charity care to the indigent as a quid pro quo for their not-for-profit tax-exempt status under Internal Revenue Code Section 501(c)(3).

Balance sheet accounts

In general, not-for-profit health care organizations record assets, liabilities and classified net assets like other not-for-profit organizations as described in Chapter 6. Governmental health care organizations would record assets, liabilities and net assets or fund balance as described in Chapter 4. Governmental health care organizations are given the option of either reporting net assets classified like not-for-profit health care organizations or fund balance reserved and unreserved like governmental entities.

Commitments and contingencies

FASB Statement No. 5 *Accounting for Contingencies* requires health care organizations to properly account for potential liabilities for which there is a reasonable estimate of loss. Health care has many contractual commitments and unique areas of risk that can create contingent liabilities[13] including, but not limited to: litigation losses, malpractice claims, third-party payor contracts, capitation contracts, major construction contracts, Federal requirements to provide uncompensated care, contractual commitments or guarantees to providers or physicians, pensions, and loans. As noted above, the unique reimbursement structure and cost pressures in health care create many areas in which financial risk is being transferred to the health care organization and could create a contingent liability. The competitive nature of the health care environment also can cause health care organizations such as hospitals to contract with physicians and guarantee a minimum level of revenues to ensure patient flow to the hospital.

Any contingent liability for which there is a reasonable likelihood of loss must be estimated and accrued for both not-for-profit and governmental health care organizations.

Health care organization financial reporting

Governmental health care organizations follow the financial reporting requirements of GASB Statement No. 34 as covered in Chapter 5. They are classified as special purpose governments engaged in business-type activities and would produce the

---

[12]Ibid, paragraph 10.03.
[13]AICPA Audit and Accounting Guide, *Health Care Organizations*, paragraph 8.01, Chapter 8.

following annual financial statements in the format required for Enterprise funds: Management Discussion and Analysis; Enterprise fund financial statements consisting of Statement of Net Assets or Balance Sheet, Statement of Revenues, Expenses, and Changes in Fund Net Assets, and Statement of Cash Flows; Notes to financial statements; and Required Supplementary Information other than MD&A, if applicable. Refer to Chapter 5 statements for proprietary funds for examples of the financial statements required for governmental health care organizations.

Not-for-profit health care organizations follow the FASB accounting for contributions and financial reporting model explained in Chapter 6. Health care organization financial statements include a Balance Sheet, Statement of Operations, Statement of Changes in Net Assets, Statement of Cash Flows and notes to the financial statements. Sample financial statements as illustrated in the *AICPA Audit and Accounting Guide* for *Health Care Organizations*[14] are shown on the following pages. Notice in the Statement of Operations (page 242) that patient service revenue is shown net of contractual adjustments, rather than displaying those contractual adjustments separately as expenses. In the Statement of Changes in Net Assets and in the Balance Sheet, the same three categories of net assets appear as seen in not-for-profit organization financial statements: unrestricted net assets, temporarily restricted net assets, and permanently restricted net assets.

A not-for-profit health care organization such as a hospital will use a Statement of Operations instead of a Statement of Activities. Patient service revenue is shown as a net revenue amount after subtracting contractual adjustments rather than displaying adjustments separately as expenses. The allowance for doubtful accounts is adjusted, and the expense account for charge-off of bad debts is called Provision for bad debts. The Provision for bad debts sounds like an allowance account but it is not; it is an expense account. The Statement of Operations lists the primary operating revenues and expenses, and then at the bottom portion of the statement nonoperating items such as unrealized gains and losses on securities, contributions, and extraordinary items are shown.

The Statement of Changes in Net Assets (page 243) shows the changes in the three basic categories of net assets: Unrestricted, Temporarily restricted, and Permanently restricted. In this statement, the hospital is doing well with $5,052,000 excess operating revenue over expenses and has actually transferred $640,000 to the parent institution. Contributions for endowment funds have fallen sharply from $411,000 to $50,000 as compared to the prior year.

The Balance Sheet (page 241) shows an increase in both current and noncurrent assets. Short-term investments have increased sharply over the previous year, and patient accounts receivable appear stable. There is an increase in unrestricted net assets of over $4 million that represents a positive increase in the bottom line for this hospital.

The Balance Sheet classifies assets and liabilities as current or noncurrent, and net assets are classified as restricted, temporarily restricted, or permanently restricted.

The Statement of Cash Flows reconciles the changes that occur between fiscal years in cash flows. Cash flows are categorized as cash flows from operating activities, cash flows from investing activities, and cash flows from financing activities. Note in the sample statement that cash flows from operating activities decreased from $11,549,000 in the first year to $9,978,000 in the second year.

---

[14]Ibid, pages 153–159. Reprinted with permission, copyright ©2001, by American Institute of Certified Public Accountants, Inc.

Sample Not-for-Profit Hospital
Balance Sheets
December 31, 20X7 and 20X6
(in thousands)

	20X7	20X6
Assets		
Current assets:		
Cash and equivalents	$ 4,758	$ 5,877
Short-term investments	15,836	10,740
Assets limited as to use	970	1,300
Patient accounts receivable, net of		
allowance for doubtful accounts of $2,500		
in 20X7 and $2,400 in 20X6	15,100	14,194
Other current assets	2,670	2,856
Total current assets	39,334	34,967
Assets limited as to use:		
Internally designated for capital acquisition	12,000	12,500
Held by trustee	6,949	7,341
	18,949	19,841
Less amount required to meet current obligations	(970)	(1,300)
	17,979	18,541
Long-term investments	4,680	4,680
Long-term investments restricted for capital acquisition	320	520
Property and equipment net	51,038	50,492
Other assets	1,695	1,370
Total assets	$115,046	$110,570
Liabilities and Net Assets		
Current liabilities:		
Current portion of long-term debt	$ 1,470	$ 1,750
Accounts payable and accrued expenses	5,818	5,382
Estimated third-party payor settlements	2,143	1,942
Other current liabilities	1,969	2,114
Total current liabilities	11,400	11,188
Long-term debt, net of current portion	23,144	24,014
Other liabilities	3,953	3,166
Total liabilities	38,497	38,368
Net assets:		
Unrestricted	70,846	66,199
Temporarily restricted	2,115	2,470
Permanently restricted	3,588	3,533
Total net assets	76,549	72,202
Total liabilities and net assets	$115,046	$110,570

Sample Not-for-Profit Hospital
Statement of Operations
Years Ended December 31, 20X7 and 20X6
(in thousands)

	20X7	20X6
Unrestricted revenues, gains and other support:		
Net patient service revenue	$85,156	$78,942
Premium revenue	11,150	10,950
Other revenue	2,601	5,212
Net assets released from restrictions used for operations	300	—
Total revenues, gains and other support	99,207	95,104
Expenses:		
Operating expenses	88,521	80,585
Depreciation and amortization	4,782	4,280
Interest	1,752	1,825
Provision for bad debts	1,000	1,300
Other	2,000	1,300
Total expenses	98,055	89,290
Operating income	1,152	5,814
Other income:		
Investment income	3,900	3,025
Excess of revenues over expenses	5,052	8,839
Change in net unrealized gains and losses on other than trading securities	300	375
Net assets released from restrictions used for purchase of property and equipment	200	—
Contributions from Sample Hospital Foundation for property acquisitions	235	485
Transfers to parent	(640)	(3,000)
Increase in unrestricted net assets, before extraordinary item	5,147	6,699
Extraordinary loss from extinguishments of debt	(500)	—
Increase in unrestricted net assets	$ 4,647	$ 6,699

Sample Not-for-Profit Hospital
Statement of Changes in Net Assets
Years Ended December 31, 20X7 and 20X6
(in thousands)

	20X7	20X6
Unrestricted net assets:		
Excess of revenues over expenses	$ 5,052	$ 8,839
Net unrealized gains on investments, other than trading securities	300	375
Contributions from Sample Hospital Foundation for property acquisitions	235	485
Transfers to parent	(640)	(3,000)
Net assets released from restrictions used for purchase of property and equipment	200	—
Increase in unrestricted net assets before extraordinary item	5,147	6,699
Extraordinary loss from extinguishments of debt	(500)	
Increase in unrestricted net assets	4,647	6,699
Temporarily restricted net assets:		
Contributions for charity care	140	996
Net realized and unrealized gains on investments	5	8
Net assets released from restrictions	(500)	—
Increase (decrease) in temporarily restricted net assets	(355)	(1,004)
Permanently restricted net assets:		
Contributions for endowment funds	50	411
Net realized and unrealized gains on investments	5	2
Increase in permanently restricted net assets	55	413
Increase in net assets	4,347	8,116
Net assets, beginning of year	72,202	64,086
Net assets, end of year	$76,549	$72,202

Sample Not-for-Profit Hospital
Statement of Cash Flows (Indirect Method)
Years Ended December 31, 20X7 and 20X6
(in thousands)

	20X7	20X6
Cash flows from operating activities:		
Change in net assets	$ 4,347	$ 8,116
Adjustments to reconcile change in net assets to net cash provided by operating activities:		
Extraordinary loss from extinguishments of debt	500	—
Depreciation and amortization	4,782	4,280
Net realized and unrealized gains on investments, other than trading	(450)	(575)
Transfers to parent	640	3,000
Provision for bad debts	1,000	1,300
Restricted contributions and investment income received	(290)	(413)
(Increase) decrease in:		
Patient accounts receivable	(1,906)	(2,036)
Trading securities	215	—
Other current assets	186	(2,481)
Other assets	(325)	(241)
Increase (decrease) in:		
Accounts payable and accrued expenses	436	679
Estimated third-party payor settlements	201	305
Other current liabilities	(145)	(257)
Other liabilities	787	(128)
Net cash provided by operating activities	9,978	11,549
Cash flows from investing activities:		
Purchase of investments	(3,769)	(2,150)
Capital expenditures	(4,728)	(5,860)
Net cash used in investing activities	(8,497)	(8,010)
Cash flows from financing activities:		
Transfers to parent	(640)	(3,000)
Proceeds from restricted contributions and restricted investment income	290	413
Payments on long-term debt	(24,700)	(804)
Payments on capital lease obligations	(150)	(100)
Proceeds from issuance of long-term debt	22,600	500
Net cash used in financing activities	(2,600)	(2,991)
Net (decrease) increase in cash and cash equivalents	(1,119)	548
Cash and cash equivalents, beginning of year	5,877	5,329
Cash and cash equivalents, end of year	$ 4,758	$ 5,877

Supplemental Disclosures of Cash Flow Information:

The Hospital entered into capital lease obligations in the amount of $600,000 for new equipment in 20X7.

Cash paid for interest (net of amount capitalized) in 20X7 and 20X6 was $1,780,000 and $1,856,000, respectively.

COLLEGES AND UNIVERSITIES

Private and public colleges and universities both followed the 1975 AICPA Accounting and Audit Guide for *Audits of Colleges and Universities* (often referred to as the AICPA college guide model) as a model for financial accounting and reporting. In 1984, GASB's creation created two separate paths for GAAP: 1) public governmental colleges and universities following GASB standards and 2) private not-for-profit colleges and universities following FASB standards. Public governmental colleges now follow GASB Statements No. 34 and 35, and private colleges now follow FASB Statements No. 115, 116, 117, and 124 for not-for-profit organizations (outlined in Chapter 6). It may not be obvious whether the college or university is governmental (public), following GASB, or private (not-for-profit), following FASB. It is common in practice to refer to colleges and universities as either public (governmental) or private (not-for-profit). The University of Michigan is a public (governmental) institution, and Harvard University is a private (not-for-profit) institution. If the answer to any of the following questions is yes, then the college or university is governmental (public):[15]

Are the officers publicly elected?
Are the officers appointed by a State or local government?
Can the government unilaterally dissolve the institution?
Can the institution levy taxes?
Can the institution issue tax-exempt debt?

All other private, not-for-profit colleges and universities follow FASB standards for accounting and financial reporting.

GASB Statement No. 35, *Basic Financial Statements—and Management's Discussion and Analysis—for the Public Colleges and Universities*, extends the provisions of GASB Statement No. 34 to public colleges and universities. This permits public colleges and universities to report as special-purpose governments engaged only in business-type activities, engaged only in governmental activities, or engaged in both governmental and business-type activities.[16] In practice, most public colleges and universities report as special-purpose governments engaged *only* in business-type activities, using the accrual method of accounting, and follow GASB standards for proprietary funds.

The National Association of College and University Business Officers (NACUBO) *Financial Accounting and Reporting Manual (FARM)* provides guidance for recording many of the transactions that are unique to colleges and universities. Guidance in the NACUBO FARM is applicable to both public and private institutions.

NACUBO is currently completely revising Chapter 300 of the *FARM* to provide guidance for accounting for public colleges engaged in only business-type activities that are implementing GASB Statements No. 34 and 35 and abandoning the superseded "college guide" model.[17] The transactions are recorded directly into the net asset classes although NACUBO recognizes many colleges and universities may elect to retain their fund accounting system internally and make adjustments at fiscal year-end to produce financial statements. Accounting for exchange and nonexchange trans-

---

[15]NACUBO *Financial Accounting and Reporting Manual*, paragraph 109.5.
[16]GASB Statement No. 35, *Basic Financial Statements—and Management's Discussion and Analysis—for Public Colleges and Universities*, paragraph 26.
[17]NACUBO issued the first of three installments of the revision of Chapter 300 of the *FARM* at the time of publication of this text.

actions following GASB Statement No. 33 is illustrated and parallels the guidance previously discussed in Chapter 3 of this text. Here are a few sample transactions that are recorded directly in the net asset classes:[18]

A college receives $1,000,000 in student tuition and fees, $50,000 from bookstore auxiliary enterprise revenue, $35,000 in unrestricted investment income, $56,000 in restricted investment income (endowments for scholarships), and issues $3,000,000 in bonds payable to construct an addition to the library. This would be recorded as follows:

Unrestricted Net Assets

Cash	1,085,000	
Revenues—Tuition and Fees		1,000,000
Revenues—Sales of Bookstore Auxiliary Enterprise		50,000
Revenues—Investment Income		35,000

Restricted Net Assets (Expendable)

Cash	56,000	
Revenues—Investment Income		56,000

Invested in Capital Assets, Net of Related Debt

Cash	3,000,000	
Bonds Payable		3,000,000

Similarly, state appropriations for general operating purposes will be recorded as revenue in unrestricted net assets, donations for specific purposes like funding a lecture series during the academic year that will be expended will be recorded in restricted net assets (expendable), and a donation to an endowment will be recorded in restricted net assets (nonexpendable).

Revenues and expenses

GASB Statements No. 34 and 35 require revenues to be reported by major source[19] (tuition and fees, research, contributions, investment, auxiliary enterprise). Revenues pledged to repay revenue bonds must be identified. Revenues, such as tuition and fees, must be reported net of discounts and allowances. Student financial aid (assistance) is considered a discount. This is a significant change from the prior model, which required that student tuition and fees revenue would be reported at the gross amount and the student financial assistance would be shown separately as an expense. In the prior method, the amount of student financial assistance was reflected in both the tuition revenue and also as an equal amount of expense. In the new method, the tuition and fee revenue is shown net of any discount (financial aid). NACUBO provides general rules to determine what tuition and fee revenue is and what a discount is:[20]

---

[18]NACUBO *Financial Accounting and Reporting Manual*, Chapter 302.3, 2001, Release 01-3.
[19]Ibid, paragraph 604.211.
[20]NACUBO Advisory Reports 97-1 and 00-5, *Accounting and Reporting Scholarship Allowances to Tuition and Other Fee Revenues by Higher Education.*

1) Amounts received to pay student tuition and fees are reported as revenue *once*.
2) Amounts received from students or third parties should be reported as revenue.
3) University resources provided to students that satisfy their tuition and fees should be reported as a scholarship allowance discount (netted from tuition and fee revenue).
4) University resources provided to students that are refunded to the student should be recorded as an expense.

Revenues are shown net of any discount (student financial assistance) or allowance accounts. This changes the reporting of gross tuition and fee revenue, which previously had drops and adds netted and financial aid was shown as a separate expense. Now, tuition and fee revenue will be reported net of student financial aid (now a discount rather than an expense) and enrollment adjustments. All institutional support provided to students in financial aid that is applied to their tuition and fee bill is reported as a discount and netted against tuition and fee revenue. However, if any financial aid in excess of the student's tuition and fee bill is refunded to the student, it should be reported as an expense.

For example, the university bills $3,750,000 and collects $3,000,000 in tuition and fees. Financial aid in the amount of $600,000 is granted to students. Several students receive $100,000 in excess refunds of financial aid after their tuition and fee bills were paid. The journal entries to record these transactions would appear as follows:

Cash	3,000,000	
Accounts Receivable	150,000	
Revenues—Tuition and Fees		3,150,000
(billing and collection of tuition and fees)		
Expenses—Scholarship Allowances	100,000	
Cash		100,000
(adjust for amount refunded directly to students)		

● **INTERPRETIVE EXERCISE**

Tuition and fee revenue is shown net of student financial aid used to pay the tuition and fee bills as well as any enrollment adjustments due to drops and adds. The financial aid used to be displayed separately as an expense in the financial report. Is the new method of netting financial aid better to show the user the true "net" tuition and fee revenue, or does it obscure the true amount the institution is spending on financial aid by "netting" it? Use the numbers in the journal entries above to evaluate this question.

If student tuition and fee revenues relate to a term or semester that bridges two fiscal years, then it should be allocated to the two fiscal years following accrual accounting concepts. In the past, the rule was to book all of the revenue in the term in which the majority of instruction took place.[21] This new allocation may result in a "tuition windfall" or tuition revenue "hit" or reduction in the year of implementation of GASB Statements No. 34 and 35 when this shift occurs as most colleges have a June

---

[21]NACUBO *Financial Accounting and Reporting Manual*, paragraphs 420.3, 444.1.

30 year-end that will require allocation. The summer tuition and fees were fully recorded in one fiscal year or the other and now it will be allocated on an accrual basis, which will cause a shift of this revenue into one fiscal year and out of another.

The following example will illustrate how to record summer tuition and fee revenue under the new rule. The college's fiscal year-end is June 30, 20x1 and it bills $2,000,000 in summer semester tuition and fees on May 15, 20x1 and collects the full amount. The summer semester bridges two fiscal years with 60% earned in fiscal year-end June 30, 20x1 and 40% in the next fiscal year based on student credit hours earned (or other rational allocation method). The college provides $200,000 of financial aid to students who use this to assist in paying their tuition and fees. The college always previously recorded this revenue in the next fiscal year. The college will record this summer tuition revenue as follows:

In fiscal year ending June 30, 20x1:

Cash	1,800,000	
Revenue—Tuition and Fees		1,080,000
Deferred Revenue—Tuition and Fees		720,000

In fiscal year ending June 30, 20x2:

Deferred Revenue—Tuition and Fees	720,000	
Revenue—Tuition and Fees		720,000

This is an example of how many unique transactions and classifications that previously existed under the AICPA "college guide model" were superseded as that AICPA "college guide" no longer exists. Public governmental colleges now follow GASB Statements Nos. 31, 33, 34 and 35 and private not-for-profit colleges now follow FASB Statements 115, 116, 117 and 124, for example.

Both public and private colleges and universities follow many of the same not-for-profit accounting rules such as the accounting for contribution revenues outlined in Chapter 6. Why? GASB decided to adopt the same standards for accounting for contributions that FASB had previously adopted. The guidance and sample journal entries for recognition of contributions that appear in Chapter 6 are not repeated here.

The classification of revenues and expenses as operating or nonoperating is important for all colleges and universities. Under GASB Statement No. 35, all state appropriations (operating monies as well as capital outlay) are nonoperating revenues. Normally, revenue items such as investment income, grants, taxes, and gains and losses are considered nonoperating revenues. All expenses are operating expenses except for interest on capital-related debt, which is classified as nonoperating. Revenues and expenditures or expenses are generally shown by function or activity. Three primary functional classifications are **academic support, institutional support**, and **student services.**

Academic support includes expenses for the primary mission: instruction, research, and public service. Institutional support includes expenses for 1) executive management activity, 2) fiscal management, 3) data processing/information systems, 4) facilities management, 5) human resources, 6) logistical support including purchasing, storage, security, printing, etc., 7) faculty and staff support that are not auxiliary enterprises, and 8) community development and fund-raising.

Student services includes expenses for services that promote students' emotional and physical health outside of the normal instructional program such as student newspapers, registration, student organizations, intramural athletics, health services (if not operated as an auxiliary activity), career guidance, advising (not including academic counseling by faculty), and student activities such as concerts and speakers.

Expenditures have been used within college and university fund groups, which were explained in Chapter 6. However, both public and private colleges and universities use the term *expenses* in their external financial reports as illustrated in Chapters 6 and 7 Basic Financial Statements.

Mandatory versus nonmandatory transfers

Mandatory[22] and nonmandatory transfers are resources being shifted within the college or university from one fund to another. Such transfers do not affect overall equity for the institution. **Mandatory transfers** are required due to some external restriction such as a donor restriction, legal contract, or grant. For example, a federal grant might require a matching amount to be appropriated from the Unrestricted current funds and transferred to current, restricted for the grant's purpose. **Nonmandatory transfers** are at the discretion of the governing board and may be changed at a later date. For example, the governing board could decide to transfer funds from the Unrestricted current fund to create a quasi-endowment or transfer realized gains from endowment under the "total return" method. For example, a debt payment of $200,000 to repay principal and interest on a bond issue for a classroom building would be recorded as follows:

Unrestricted current fund:

Mandatory Transfer for Principal and Interest— Education and General	200,000	
Due to Funds for the Retirement of Indebtedness		200,000
Due to Funds for the Retirement of Indebtedness	200,000	
Cash		200,000

Plant fund: Retirement of Indebtedness:

Due from Unrestricted current fund	200,000	
Fund Balances—Restricted Mandatory Transfer from Current Funds for Principal and Interest		200,000
Cash	200,000	
Due from Unrestricted current fund		200,000

Endowment return

Some college or universities use a "total return" method[23] for calculating endowment return that uses a formula for authorized spending that may combine interest, dividends, and realized and unrealized appreciation of endowments. If the "total return" method is used, interest and dividends earned on endowments should be reported as income as

---

[22]Ibid, paragraph 602.33.
[23]Ibid, paragraph 602.313.

specified by the donor. If the donor did not restrict use, the income will be Unrestricted current, for example. If dividends and interest are earned in excess of the spending rate, the excess will be returned to the Endowment as a nonmandatory transfer.

College and university financial reporting

Private colleges and universities follow the not-for-profit financial reporting model established by FASB Statement No. 117 described in Chapter 6. GASB Statement No. 35 *Basic Financial Statements—and Management's Discussion and Analysis for Public Colleges and Universities* requires public colleges and universities to utilize the GASB Statement No. 34 financial reporting model. GASB decided that public colleges and universities need not adapt to the governmental fund structure but would follow the GASB Statement No. 34 guidance for special-purpose governments involved in business-type activities. Remember that business-type activities generally are financed by or charge fees to external parties. Tuition from students and sponsored research are two exchange relationships that are primarily business-type activities. Most public colleges and universities receive significant resources from tuition from students and sponsored research. Therefore, most public colleges and universities will utilize the special-purpose government model illustrated in this chapter. The special-purpose government model requires an operating/nonoperating format for the Statement of Revenues, Expenses, and Changes in Net Assets. Although several respondents to the GASB Statement No. 35 exposure draft strongly suggested that state appropriations should be reported as operating revenues rather than nonoperating revenues, GASB concluded that appropriations should be labeled as nonoperating to avoid industry-specific guidance.[24] The reporting model for special-purpose governments also requires segment information and comments responding to the exposure draft noted this could result in excessive disclosure if multicampus locations were considered segments. Multicampus locations do *not* require segment disclosure. GASB concluded that note disclosure for any segment is required if there is an identifiable revenue stream pledged to repay revenue bonds.[25] The direct method of presenting cash flows is required.

The following sample financial statements for ABC University illustrate GASB Statement No. 35 Basic Financial Statements for a public college or university engaged only in business-type activities. Note in the Statement of Revenues, Expenses, and Changes in Net Assets that student tuition and fees are operating revenues but the state appropriation is a nonoperating revenue. The Basic Financial Statements include: Statement of Net Assets, Statement of Revenues, Expenses and Changes in Net Assets, and Statement of Cash Flows. The segment information for identifiable revenue streams supporting auxiliary activities such as dormitory revenue bonds and bookstore revenue bonds is not included in this illustration but would be required.

The financial statements that appear next for ABC Community College illustrate the GASB Statement No. 34 Basic Financial Statements for a public college or university engaged in both governmental and business-type activities. The Basic Financial Statements include: Government-wide Statement of Net Assets and Statement of Activities (by function/program) and Fund Financial Statements; Governmental Fund Balance Sheet and Statement of Revenues, Expenditures and Changes in Fund Balance for the governmental-type activities; Proprietary Fund Statement of Net Assets, Statement of Revenues, Expenses, and Changes in Fund Net

---

[24]GASB Statement No. 35, paragraph 52.
[25]Ibid, paragraph 55.

Assets, and Statement of Cash Flows for business-type activities. The Statement of Net Assets segregates the Assets, Liabilities, and Net Assets into two columns for Governmental versus Business-type activities.

ABC University
Statement of Net Assets
June 30, 2002

	Primary Institution	Component Unit Hospital
ASSETS		
Current assets:		
Cash and cash equivalents	$ 4,571,218	$ 977,694
Short-term investments	15,278,981	2,248,884
Accounts receivable, net	6,412,520	9,529,196
Inventories	585,874	1,268,045
Deposit with bond trustee	4,254,341	—
Notes and mortgages receivable, net	359,175	—
Other assets	432,263	426,427
Total current assets	31,894,372	14,450,246
Noncurrent assets:		
Restricted cash and cash equivalents	24,200	18,500
Endowment investments	21,548,723	—
Notes and mortgages receivable, net	2,035,323	—
Other long-term investments	—	6,441,710
Investments in real estate	6,426,555	—
Capital assets, net	158,977,329	32,602,940
Total noncurrent assets	189,012,130	39,063,150
Total assets	220,906,502	53,513,396
LIABILITIES		
Current liabilities:		
Accounts payable and accrued liabilities	4,897,470	2,911,419
Deferred revenue	3,070,213	—
Long-term liabilities—current portion	4,082,486	989,321
Total current liabilities	12,050,169	3,900,740
Noncurrent liabilities:		
Deposits	1,124,128	—
Deferred revenue	1,500,000	—
Long-term liabilities	31,611,427	2,194,236
Total noncurrent liabilities	34,235,555	2,194,236
Total liabilities	46,285,724	6,094,976
NET ASSETS		
Invested in capital assets, net of related debt	126,861,400	32,199,938
Restricted for:		
Nonexpendable:		
Scholarships and fellowships	10,839,473	—
Research	3,767,564	2,286,865
Expendable:		
Scholarships and fellowships	2,803,756	—
Research	5,202,732	—
Instructional department uses	938,571	—
Loans	2,417,101	—
Capital projects	4,952,101	913,758
Debt service	4,254,341	152,947
Other	403,632	—
Unrestricted	12,180,107	11,864,912
Total net assets	$174,620,778	$47,418,420

ABC University
Statement of Revenues, Expenses, and Changes in Net Assets
For the Year Ended June 30, 2002

	Primary Institution	Component Unit Hospital
Operating expense may be displayed using either object or functional classification.		
REVENUES		
Operating revenues:		
Student tuition and fees (net of scholarship allowances of $3,214,454)	$ 36,913,194	$ —
Patient services (net of charity care of $5,114,352)	—	46,296,957
Federal grants and contracts	10,614,660	—
State and local grants and contracts	3,036,953	7,475,987
Nongovernmental grants and contracts	873,740	—
Sales and services of educational departments	19,802	—
Auxiliary enterprises:		
Residential life (net of scholarship allowances of $428,641)	28,079,274	—
Bookstore (net of scholarship allowances of $166,279)	9,092,363	—
Other operating revenues	143,357	421, 571
Total operating revenues	88,773,343	54,194,515
EXPENSES		
Operating expenses:		
Salaries:		
Faculty (physicians for the hospital)	34,829,499	16,703,805
Exempt staff	29,597,676	8,209,882
Nonexempt wages	5,913,762	2,065,267
Benefits	18,486,559	7,752,067
Scholarships and fellowships	3,809,374	—
Utilities	16,463,492	9,121,352
Supplies and other services	12,451,064	7,342,009
Depreciation	6,847,377	2,976,212
Total operating expenses	128,398,803	54,170,594
Operating income (loss)	(39,625,460)	23,921
NONOPERATING REVENUES (EXPENSES)		
State appropriations	39,760,508	—
Gifts	1,822,442	—
Investment income (net of investment expense of $87,316 for the primary institution and $19,823 for the hospital)	2,182,921	495,594
Interest on capital asset-related debt	(1,330,126)	(34,538)
Other nonoperating revenues	313,001	321,449
Net nonoperating revenues	42,748,746	782,505
Income before other revenues, expenses, gains, or losses	3,123,286	806,426
Capital appropriations	2,075,750	—
Capital grants and gifts	690,813	711,619
Additions to permanent endowments	85,203	—
Increase in net assets	5,975,052	1,518,045
NET ASSETS		
Net assets—beginning of year	168,645,726	45,900,375
Net assets—end of year	$174,620,778	$47,418,420

ABC University
Statement of Cash Flows
For the Year Ended June 30, 2002

The direct method of reporting cash flows is required.

	Primary Institution	Component Unit Hospital
CASH FLOWS FROM OPERATING ACTIVITIES		
Tuition and fees	$33,628,945	$ —
Research grants and contracts	13,884,747	—
Payments from insurance and patients	—	18,582,530
Medicaid and Medicare	—	31,640,524
Payments to suppliers	(28,175,500)	(13,084,643)
Payments to employees	(87,233,881)	(32,988,044)
Loans issued to students and employees	(384,628)	—
Collection of loans to students and employees	291,642	—
Auxiliary enterprise charges:		
Residence halls	26,327,644	—
Bookstore	8,463,939	—
Other receipts (payments)	1,415,502	(997,502)
Net cash provided (used) by operating activities	(31,781,590)	3,152,865
CASH FLOWS FROM NONCAPITAL FINANCING ACTIVITIES		
State appropriations	39,388,534	—
Gifts and grants received for other than capital purposes:		
Private gifts for endowment purposes	85,203	—
Net cash flows provided by noncapital financing activities	39,473,737	—
CASH FLOWS FROM CAPITAL AND RELATED FINANCING ACTIVITIES		
Proceeds from capital debt	4,125,000	—
Capital appropriations	1,918,750	—
Capital grants and gifts received	640,813	711,619
Proceeds from sale of capital assets	22,335	5,066
Purchase of capital assets	(8,420,247)	(1,950,410)
Principal paid on capital debt and lease	(3,788,102)	(134,095)
Interest paid on capital debt and lease	(1,330,126)	(34,538)
Net cash used by capital and related financing activities	(6,831,577)	(1,402,358)
CASH FLOWS FROM INVESTING ACTIVITIES		
Proceeds from sales and maturities of investments	16,741,252	2,843,124
Interest on investments	2,111,597	70,501
Purchase of investments	(17,680,113)	(4,546,278)
Net cash provided (used) by investing activities	1,172,736	(1,632,653)
Net increase in cash	2,033,306	117,854
Cash—beginning of year	2,562,112	878,340
Cash—end of year	$ 4,595,418	$ 996,194

(continued)

ABC University
Statement of Cash Flows
For the Year Ended June 30, 2002
(continued)

	Primary Institution	Component Unit Hospital
Reconciliation of net operating revenues (expenses) to net cash provided (used) by operating activities:		
Operating income (loss)	$(39,625,460)	$ 23,921
Adjustments to reconcile net income (loss) to net cash provided (used) by operating activities:		
Depreciation expense	6,847,377	2,976,212
Change in assets and liabilities:		
Receivables, net	1,295,704	330,414
Inventories	37,284	(160,922)
Deposit with bond trustee	67,115	—
Other assets	(136,229)	75,456
Accounts payable	(323,989)	(75,973)
Deferred revenue	217,630	—
Deposits held for others	(299,428)	—
Compensated absences	138,406	(16,243)
Net cash provided (used) by operating activities	$(31,781,590)	$ 3,152,865

Note: The required information about noncash investing, capital, and financing activities is not illustrated.

In the Statement of Net Assets for ABC Community College there are two columns for the governmental and business-type activities. Notice the Property taxes receivable in the governmental activities column as compared to Other receivables and Inventories in the business-type activities column.

In the Statement of Activities for ABC Community College note that the governmental activities are showing net costs such as (7,058,519) for instruction while the business-type activity has net income for the college bookstore of 138,320. The general revenues such as property taxes and state appropriations are shown below in the Statement of Activities.

ABC Community College also has separate fund financial statements for the governmental funds which are illustrated to show a net excess of revenues of $6,656,949 over expenditures in the General fund. Some citizens might argue that ABC Community College should charge a lower rate for property taxes given this excess as compared to total revenues of $33,261,624. Similarly, the proprietary funds have separate fund financial statements and show net income for the business-type activities of $341,104.

ABC Community College
Statement of Net Assets
June 30, 2002

	Governmental Activities	Business-type Activities	Total
ASSETS			
Cash	$ 5,117,496	$ 490,441	$ 5,607,937
Investments	19,889,916	3,150,000	23,039,916
Property taxes receivable	7,981,008	—	7,981,008
Tuition and fees receivable	758,521	—	758,521
Other receivables	635,039	63,468	698,507
Internal balances	167,692 ←——→	(167,692)	—
Inventories	—	463,424	463,424
Prepaid items	137,120	—	137,120
Land	4,889,818	—	4,889,818
Capital assets, net of			
accumulated depreciation	62,975,781	868,750	63,844,531
Total assets	102,552,391	4,868,391	107,420,782
LIABILITIES			
Accounts payable	289,606	1,933	291,539
Accrued payroll	1,435,038	60,974	1,496,012
Deferred tuition and fees revenue	2,431,551	—	2,431,551
Other deferred revenue	102,868	—	102,868
Bonds payable:			
Due within one year	580,000	—	580,000
Due in more than one year	9,840,000	—	9,840,000
Total liabilities	14,679,063	62,907	14,741,970
NET ASSETS			
Invested in capital assets,			
net of related debt	57,445,599	868,750	58,314,349
Unrestricted	30,427,729	3,936,734	34,364,463
Total net assets	$ 87,873,328	$4,805,484	$ 92,678,812

Alternatively, the internal balances could be reported on separate lines as assets and liabilities. A notation would need to be added to inform the reader that the "Total" column is adjusted for those amounts.

ABC Community College
Statement of Activities
For the Year Ended June 30, 2002

> Indirect expenses are presented in a separate column to enhance comparability (of direct expenses by function) between institutions that allocate indirect expenses and those that do not. Allocation of support activities is optional.

Functions/Programs	Expenses	Expense Allocation
Primary institution:		
Governmental activities:		
Instruction	$13,810,090	$6,325,073
Academic support	860,032	919,058
Student services	3,734,433	2,804,118
Public service	1,368,526	—
General administration	1,785,692	—
Operations and maintenance	3,522,463	(3,522,463)
Institutional support	4,541,687	—
Interest	870,320	(870,320)
Unallocated depreciation	5,655,466	(5,655,466)
Total governmental activities	36,148,709	0
Business-type activities:		
College bookstore	2,945,641	—
Food service	1,753,369	—
Industrial training	321,825	—
Total business-type activities	5,020,835	—
Total primary government	$41,169,544	$ 0

General revenues:
  Property taxes –
  State appropriations –
  Interest –
  Miscellaneous –
Transfers –
  Total general revenues and transfers – – – – – – – – – – – – –
    Change in net assets – – – – – – – – – – – – – – – – – –
Net assets—beginning –
Net assets—ending –

| | Program Revenues | | Net Revenue (Expenses) and Changes in Net Assets | | |
| Charges for Services | | | | | |
Tuition and Fees	Sales, Services, and Other Revenues	Operating Gifts, Grants, and Contracts	Governmental Activities	Business-type Activities	Total
$12,812,745	$ —	$ 263,899	$ (7,058,519)	$ —	$ (7,058,519)
—	396,752	—	(1,382,338)	—	(1,382,338)
23,585	396,950	857,352	(5,260,664)	—	(5,260,664)
15,150	—	270,443	(1,082,933)	—	(1,082,933)
—	296,648	—	(1,489,044)	—	(1,489,044)
—	—	—	—	—	—
—	—	—	(4,541,687)	—	(4,541,687)
—	—	—	—	—	—
—	—	—	—	—	—
12,851,480	1,090,350	1,391,694	(20,815,185)	—	(20,815,185)
—	3,083,961	—	—	138,320	138,320
—	2,098,643	—	—	345,274	345,274
—	134,458	14,431	—	(172,936)	(172,936)
—	5,317,062	14,431	—	310,658	310,658
$12,851,480	$6,407,412	$1,406,125	(20,815,185)	310,658	(20,504,527)
	A separate column for tuition and fees is not required.		15,362,534	—	15,362,534
			10,959,604	—	10,959,604
			545,360	179,391	724,751
			—	147,282	147,282
			370,000	(370,000)	—
			27,237,498	(43,327)	27,194,171
			6,422,313	267,331	6,689,644
			81,451,015	4,538,153	85,989,168
			$ 87,873,328	$4,805,484	$92,678,812

ABC Community College
Balance Sheet
Governmental Funds
June 30, 2002

	General Fund	Grants and Contracts Fund	Other Governmental Funds	Total Governmental Funds
ASSETS				
Cash	$ 1,491,423	$ —	$ 3,155,721	$ 4,647,144
Investments	9,349,916	—	9,790,000	19,139,916
Property taxes receivables	6,049,682	—	1,931,326	7,981,008
Tuition and fees receivable	758,521	—	—	758,521
Interest receivable	111,895	—	164,055	275,950
Intergovernmental receivable	138,995	201,897	—	340,892
Internal receivables	1,395,629	—	—	1,395,629
Prepaid items	137,120	—	—	137,120
Total assets	$19,433,181	$ 201,897	$15,041,102	$34,676,180
LIABILITIES				
Accounts payable	$ 81,332	$ 13,991	$ 136,386	$ 231,709
Accrued payroll	1,414,199	9,757	5,035	1,428,991
Internal payables	—	75,281	1,090,115	1,165,396
Deferred tuition and fees revenue	2,431,551	—	—	2,431,551
Other deferred revenue	—	102,868	—	102,868
Total liabilities	3,927,082	201,897	1,231,536	5,360,515
NET ASSETS				
Unreserved, reported in:				
General fund	15,506,099	—	—	15,506,099
Special revenue fund	—	—	4,765,773	4,765,773
Debt service fund	—	—	3,351,013	3,351,013
Capital projects fund	—	—	5,692,780	5,692,780
Total fund balance	15,506,099	—	13,809,566	29,315,665
Total liabilities and fund balance	$19,433,181	$ 201,897	$15,041,102	

Amounts reported for *governmental activities* in the Statement of Net Assets are different because:

Capital assets used in governmental activities are not financial resources and therefore are not reported in the funds.	67,865,599
Internal service funds are used by management to charge the cost of certain activities to individual funds. The assets and liabilities of the internal service funds are included in the statement of net assets.	1,112,064
Bonds payable are not due and payable in the current period and therefore are not reported in the funds.	(10,420,000)
Net assets of governmental activities	$87,873,328

ABC Community College
Statement of Revenues, Expenditures, and Changes in Fund Balance
Governmental Funds
For the Year Ended June 30, 2002

	General Fund	Grants and Contracts Fund	Other Governmental Funds	Total Governmental Funds
REVENUES				
Tuition and fees	$12,851,480	$ —	$ —	$12,851,480
Property taxes	11,761,887	—	3,600,647	15,362,534
State appropriations	7,999,822	1,743,130	1,216,652	10,959,604
Federal appropriations	—	1,127,795	—	1,127,795
Interest	237,224	—	289,939	527,163
Other revenues	411,211	16,643	926,395	1,354,249
Total revenues	33,261,624	2,887,568	6,033,633	42,182,825
EXPENDITURES				
Current:				
Instruction	12,683,945	1,571,117	—	14,255,062
Academic support	820,110	39,750	172	860,032
Student services	1,613,935	829,338	1,291,160	3,734,433
Public service	1,235,673	8,871	123,982	1,368,526
General administration	1,785,692	—	—	1,785,692
Operations and maintenance	3,380,016	—	142,447	3,522,463
Institutional support	3,387,430	82,519	1,220,062	4,690,011
Debt service:				
Principal	—	—	440,000	440,000
Interest	—	—	870,320	870,320
Capital outlay	1,697,874	355,973	1,293,114	3,346,961
Total expenditures	26,604,675	2,887,568	5,381,257	34,873,500
Excess of revenues over expenditures	6,656,949	—	652,376	7,309,325
OTHER FINANCING SOURCES (USES)				
Transfers in	370,000	—	1,000,000	1,370,000
Transfers out	(1,000,000)	—	—	(1,000,000)
Total other financing sources (uses)	(630,000)	—	1,000,000	370,000
Net change in fund balances	6,026,949	—	1,652,376	7,679,325
Fund balances—beginning	9,479,150	—	12,157,190	
Fund balances—ending	$15,506,099	$ 0	$13,809,566	

Amounts reported for *governmental activities* in the Statement of Activities are different because:	
Governmental activities report depreciation, whereas governmental funds do not.	(5,655,466)
Governmental funds report capital outlay as an expenditure, whereas governmental activities do not.	3,346,961
Governmental funds report debt principal repayment as an expenditure, whereas governmental activities do not.	440,000
Internal service funds are used by management to charge the costs of certain activities to individual funds. The net revenue of the internal service funds is reported with governmental activities.	611,493
Change in net assets of governmental activities	$ 6,422,313

ABC Community College
Statement of Net Assets
Proprietary Funds
June 30, 2002

	Business-type Activities—Enterprise Funds				Governmental Activities
	College Bookstore	**Food Service**	**Industrial Training**	**Totals**	**Internal Service Funds**
ASSETS					
Current assets:					
Cash and cash equivalents	$ 158,832	$ 331,609	$ —	$ 490,441	$ 470,352
Investments	3,150,000	—	—	3,150,000	750,000
Interest receivable	63,468	—	—	63,468	18,197
Inventories	388,534	74,890	—	463,424	—
Total current assets	3,760,834	406,499	—	4,167,333	1,238,549
Noncurrent assets:					
Capital assets:					
Equipment	124,439	1,083,937	—	1,208,376	—
Less accumulated depreciation	(90,843)	(248,783)	—	(339,626)	—
Capital assets, net	33,596	835,154	—	868,750	—
Total noncurrent assets	33,596	835,154	—	868,750	—
Total assets	3,794,430	1,241,653	—	5,036,083	1,238,549
LIABILITIES					
Current liabilities:					
Accounts payable	—	822	1,111	1,933	57,897
Accrued payroll	22,544	26,081	12,349	60,974	6,047
Internal payables	—	—	167,692	167,692	62,541
Total liabilities	22,544	26,903	181,152	230,599	126,485
NET ASSETS					
Invested in capital assets, net of related debt	33,596	835,154	—	868,750	—
Unrestricted	3,738,290	379,596	(181,152)	3,936,734	1,112,064
Total net assets	$3,771,886	$1,214,750	$(181,152)	$4,805,484	$1,112,064

> Funds that do not meet the definition of a major fund are not required to be shown in a separate column. However, any other fund that is believed to be particularly important to financial statement users may be reported as a major fund.

ABC Community College
Statement of Revenues, Expenses, and Changes in Fund Net Assets
Proprietary Funds
For the Year Ended June 30, 2002

	Business-type Activities—Enterprise Funds				Governmental Activities
	College Bookstore	**Food Service**	**Industrial Training**	**Totals**	**Internal Service Funds**
OPERATING REVENUES					
Charges for services	$3,083,961	$2,098,643	$ 134,458	$5,317,062	$4,090,216
Total operating revenues	3,083,961	2,098,643	134,458	5,317,062	4,090,216
OPERATING EXPENSES					
Salaries	239,118	797,747	162,616	1,199,481	78,699
Employee benefits	47,480	104,662	28,544	180,686	2,756,956
Contractual services	299,027	326,314	72,059	697,400	225,576
General material and supplies	2,346,368	387,634	55,840	2,789,842	435,689
Conference and meetings	1,204	43,905	2,766	47,875	—
Depreciation	12,444	93,107	—	105,551	—
Total operating expenses	2,945,641	1,753,369	321,825	5,020,835	3,496,920
Operating income (loss)	138,320	345,274	(187,367)	296,227	593,296
NONOPERATING REVENUES (EXPENSES)					
Interest income	179,391	—	—	179,391	18,197
Miscellaneous revenues	140,131	8,346	14,500	162,977	—
Miscellaneous expenses	—	(1,195)	(69)	(1,264)	—
Total nonoperating revenues (expenses)	319,522	7,151	14,431	341,104	18,197
Income before transfers	457,842	352,425	(172,936)	637,331	611,493
TRANSFERS OUT	(370,000)	—	—	(370,000)	—
Change in net assets	87,842	352,425	(172,936)	267,331	611,493
Total net assets—beginning	3,684,044	862,325	(8,216)	4,538,153	500,571
Total net assets—ending	$3,771,886	$1,214,750	$(181,152)	$4,805,484	$1,112,064

> Funds that do not meet the definition of a major fund are not required to be shown in a separate column. However, any other fund that is believed to be particularly important to financial statement users may be reported as a major fund.

ABC Community College
Statement of Cash Flows
Proprietary Funds
For the Year Ended June 30, 2002

CASH FLOWS FROM OPERATING ACTIVITIES
Receipts from customers
Payments to suppliers
Payments to employees
Other receipts

    Net cash provided (used) by operating activities

CASH FLOWS FROM NONCAPITAL FINANCING ACTIVITIES
Cash repaid by other funds
Cash borrowed from other funds
Transfers to other funds

    Net cash provided by noncapital financing activities

CASH FLOWS FROM CAPITAL AND RELATED FINANCING ACTIVITIES
Acquisition of fixed assets

    Net cash used by capital and related financing activities

CASH FLOWS FROM INVESTING ACTIVITIES
Purchase of investments
Sale of investments
Interest on investments

    Net cash used by investing activities

        Net increase (decrease) in cash and cash equivalents
Balances—beginning of year

Balances—end of year

Reconciliation of operating income (loss) to net cash provided (used) by operating activities:
    Operating income (loss)
    Adjustments to reconcile operating income to net cash provided (used)
      by operating activities:
        Depreciation expense
        Other income
        Other expenses
    Change in assets and liabilities:
        Inventories
        Accounts payable
        Accrued payroll
Net cash provided by operating activities

	Business-type Activities — Enterprise Funds				Governmental Activities
	College Bookstore	Food Service	Industrial Training	Totals	Internal Service Funds
	$ 3,083,961	$2,098,643	$ 134,458	$ 5,317,062	$ 4,090,216
	(2,654,610)	(862,515)	(158,242)	(3,675,367)	(3,387,569)
	(234,512)	(797,103)	(161,475)	(1,193,090)	(77,401)
	140,131	7,151	14,431	161,713	—
	334,970	446,176	(170,828)	610,318	625,246
	483,431	191,159	—	674,590	—
	—	—	167,692	167,692	62,541
	(370,000)	—	—	(370,000)	—
	113,431	191,159	167,692	472,282	62,541
	—	(305,726)	—	(305,726)	—
	—	(305,726)	—	(305,726)	—
	(3,150,000)	—	—	(3,150,000)	(750,000)
	2,650,000	—	—	2,650,000	—
	199,226	—	—	199,226	—
	(330,774)	—	—	(300,774)	(750,000)
	147,627	331,609	(3,136)	476,100	(62,213)
	11,205	—	3,136	14,341	532,565
	$ 158,832	$ 331,609	$ 0	$ 490,441	$ 470,352
	$ 138,320	$ 345,274	$(187,367)	$ 296,227	$ 593,296
	12,444	93,107	—	105,551	—
	140,131	8,346	14,500	162,977	—
	—	(1,195)	(69)	(1,264)	—
	39,482	—	—	39,482	—
	(13)	—	967	954	30,652
	4,606	644	1,141	6,391	1,298
	$ 334,970	$ 446,176	$(170,828)	$ 610,318	$ 625,246

GENERALLY ACCEPTED GOVERNMENT AUDITING STANDARDS

Generally Accepted Government Auditing Standards (GAGAS) are issued by the Comptroller General of the United States in *Government Auditing Standards*. GAGAS are commonly known and referred to as the "yellow book" because *Government Auditing Standards* has a yellow cover. GAGAS are required auditing standards for any auditor performing a governmental financial audit or a single audit for federal purposes. GAGAS (a complete version is found at http://www.gao.gov) includes the AICPA generally accepted auditing standards (GAAS). **General Standards** apply to all types of audits: **financial, compliance** or **performance. Field Work Standards** are the standards an auditor must follow in the conduct of auditing done in the field. The field work is generally conducted primarily at the auditee's place of business and involves testing documentation and records as appropriate. The **Reporting Standards** apply to the preparation of the written report on the audit. Preliminary write-up work is often done in the field and then the final report is completed in the auditor's office. Field Work and Reporting Standards are different for financial audits and performance audits, but General Standards apply to all audits. GAGAS extends GAAS required standards by adding additional General Standards such as requiring the auditor to have 24 hours of continuing professional education (out of 80 total required hours) every two years in topics directly related to the governmental environment and auditing. GAGAS has additional Field Work and Reporting Standards as well. GAGAS also includes Field Work and Reporting Standards for Performance Audits, which are unique to the governmental environment. It makes sense that auditing standards in the governmental sector would extend beyond those for the private sector due to the public monies involved. The public monies require a higher standard and duty of care by both governmental officials entrusted with these funds and auditors who will attest to the accuracy of management's representations. Again, the importance of accountability for public funds comes through in the required auditing standards for governmental units.

Auditors prepare an opinion on financial statements on whether they are fairly presented in accordance with generally accepted accounting principles (GAAP). The audit opinion can be **unqualified, qualified, adverse** or a **disclaimer of opinion.** The unqualified opinion means that the auditor found no reason to qualify the opinion that the financial statements are fairly presented in accordance with GAAP. The qualified opinion means that the auditor found that the financial statements are fairly presented in accordance with GAAP except for a specific item(s). A qualification of the opinion by the auditor will explain which item(s) are not presented fairly in accordance with GAAP. For example, a qualified opinion could be possible if governmental units do not implement the GASB Statement No. 34 requirements for reporting capital assets by the required effective date. An adverse opinion is very rare and means that the auditor is attesting that the financial statements are not fairly presented in accordance with GAAP. A disclaimer of opinion means that the auditor was unable to reach a conclusion about whether the financial statements are or are not presented fairly in accordance with GAAP. A disclaimer of opinion might occur if the books and records of the governmental unit were incomplete or in serious disarray. The audit opinion must also state that the auditor performed the audit in accordance with GAGAS.

There are three types of governmental audits: financial, compliance, and performance. The auditor provides reasonable assurance and renders an opinion that the financial statements have been fairly presented in accordance with GAAP. In a governmental financial audit, it is common that auditors will also have to perform compliance auditing to ensure that the government is in compliance with requirements related to material items of revenue such as grants or contracts. Financial audits determine if financial information is presented in accordance with GAAP, has complied with financial requirements, and if the internal control structure is suitable. A performance audit independently assesses the economy and efficiency of the governmental unit and often examines if the legislative intent was met in the performance of duties and execution of the program. Performance audits independently assess performance to provide public information and make the information available to the governmental unit.

GAGAS consists of the following General Standards, Field Work Standards, and Reporting Standards:[26]

General Standards

1. The staff assigned to conduct the audit should collectively possess adequate professional proficiency for the tasks required. Continuing professional education is required to complete 24 of 80 hours every two years on subjects directly related to government auditing or the governmental environment.
2. In all matters relating to the audit work, the audit organization and the individual auditors, whether government or public, should be free from personal and external impairments to independence, should be organizationally independent, and should maintain an independent attitude and appearance.
3. Due professional care should be used in conducting the audit and in preparing related reports.
4. Each audit organization conducting audits in accordance with these standards should have an appropriate internal quality control system in place and undergo an external quality control review.

Field Work Standards for Financial Audits

1. The work is to be adequately planned and assistants, if any, are to be properly supervised.
2. A sufficient understanding of internal control is to be obtained to plan the audit and to determine the nature, timing, and extent of tests to be performed.
3. Sufficient, competent, evidential matter is to be obtained through inspection, observation, inquiries, and confirmations to afford a reasonable basis for an opinion regarding the financial statements under audit.
4. The work is to be properly planned, and auditors should consider materiality, among other matters, in determining the nature, timing, and extent of auditing procedures and in evaluating the results of those procedures.
5. Auditors should communicate information to the auditee, the individuals contracting for or requesting the audit services, and the audit committee regarding the nature and extent of planned testing and reporting on compliance with laws and regulations and internal control over financial reporting.
6. Auditors should follow up on known material findings and recommendations from previous audits.

---

[26]*Government Auditing Standards*, as of 8/18/99.

7. Auditors should design the audit to provide reasonable assurance of detecting fraud that is material to the financial statements.

8. Auditors should design the audit to provide reasonable assurance of detecting material misstatements resulting from direct and material illegal acts.

9. Auditors should be aware of the possibility that indirect illegal acts may have occurred. If specific information comes to the auditors' attention that provides evidence concerning the existence of possible illegal acts that could have a material indirect effect on the financial statements, the auditors should apply audit procedures specifically directed to ascertaining whether an illegal act has occurred.

10. Auditors should design the audit to provide reasonable assurance of detecting material misstatements resulting from noncompliance with provisions of contracts or grant agreements that have a direct and material effect on the determination of financial statement amounts. If specific information comes to the auditors' attention that provides evidence concerning the existence of possible noncompliance that could have a material effect on the financial statements, auditors should apply audit procedures specifically directed to ascertaining whether that noncompliance has occurred.

11. Auditors should obtain a sufficient understanding of internal control to plan the audit and determine the nature, timing, and extent of tests to be performed.

12. In planning the audit, auditors should document in the working papers (a) the basis for assessing control risk at the maximum level for assertions related to material account balances, transaction classes, and disclosure components of financial statements when such assertions are significantly dependent upon computerized information systems, and (b) consideration that the planned audit procedures are designed to achieve audit objectives and to reduce audit risk to an acceptable level.

13. A record of the auditors' work should be retained in the form of working papers.

14. Working papers should contain sufficient information to enable an experienced auditor having no previous connection with the audit to ascertain from them the evidence that supports the auditors' significant conclusions and judgments.

Reporting Standards for Financial Audits

1. Audit reports should state that the audit was made in accordance with generally accepted government auditing standards.

2. The report on the financial statements should either (a) describe the scope of the auditors' testing of compliance with laws and regulations and internal control over financial reporting and present the results of those tests or (b) refer to the separate report(s) containing that information. In presenting the results of those tests, auditors should report fraud, illegal acts, other material noncompliance, and reportable conditions in internal control over financial reporting. In some circumstances, auditors should report fraud and illegal acts directly to parties external to the audited entity.

3. If certain information is prohibited from general disclosure, the audit report should state the nature of the information omitted and the requirement that makes the omission necessary.

4. Written audit reports are to be submitted by the audit organization to the appropriate officials of the auditee and to the appropriate officials of the organizations requiring or arranging for the audits including external funding organizations, unless legal restrictions prevent it. Copies of the reports should also be sent to

other officials who have legal oversight authority or who may be responsible for acting on audit findings and recommendations and to others authorized to receive such reports. Unless restricted by law or regulation, copies should be made available for public inspection.

Field Work Standards for Performance Audits

1. Work is to be adequately planned.
2. Staff are to be properly supervised.
3. When laws, regulations, and other compliance requirements are significant to audit objectives, auditors should design the audit to provide reasonable assurance about compliance with them. In all performance audits, auditors should be alert to situations or transactions that could be indicative of illegal acts or abuse.
4. Auditors should obtain an understanding of management controls that are relevant to the audit. When management controls are significant to audit objectives, auditors should obtain sufficient evidence to support their judgments about those controls.
5. Sufficient, competent, and relevant evidence is to be obtained to afford a reasonable basis for the auditors' findings and conclusions. A record of the auditors' work should be retained in the form of working papers. Working papers should contain sufficient information to enable an experienced auditor having no previous connection with the audit to ascertain from them the evidence that supports the auditors' significant conclusions and judgments.

Reporting Standards for Performance Audits

1. Auditors should prepare written audit reports communicating the results of each audit.
2. Auditors should appropriately issue the reports to make the information available for timely use by management, legislative officials, and other interested parties.
3. Auditors should report the audit objectives and the audit scope and methodology.
4. Auditors should report significant audit findings, and where applicable, auditors' conclusions.
5. Auditors should report recommendations for actions to correct problem areas and to improve operations.
6. Auditors should report that the audit was made in accordance with generally accepted government auditing standards.
7. Auditors should report all significant instances of noncompliance and all significant instances of abuse that were found during or in connection with the audit. In some circumstances, auditors should report illegal acts directly to parties external to the audited entity.
8. Auditors should report the scope of their work on management controls and any significant weaknesses during the audit.
9. Auditors should report the views of responsible officials of the audited program concerning auditors' findings, conclusions, and recommendations, as well as corrections planned.
10. Auditors should report noteworthy accomplishments, particularly when management improvements in one area may be applicable elsewhere.
11. Auditors should refer significant issues needing further audit work to the auditors responsible for planning future audit work.

12. If certain information is prohibited from general disclosure, auditors should report the nature of the information omitted and the requirement that makes the omission necessary.
13. The report should be complete, accurate, objective, convincing, and as clear and concise as the subject permits.
14. Written audit reports are to be submitted by the audit organization to the appropriate officials of the auditee and to the appropriate officials of the organizations requiring or arranging for the audits, including external funding organizations, unless legal restrictions prevent it. Copies of the reports should also be sent to other officials who have legal oversight authority or who may be responsible for acting on audit findings and recommendations and to others authorized to receive such reports. Unless restricted by law or regulation, copies should be made available for public inspection.

FEDERAL SINGLE AUDIT

The Single Audit Act of 1984 as amended by Office of Management and Budget (OMB) Circular A-133 requires that all governmental or not-for-profit organizations that *expend* $300,000 or more annually in federal funds will obtain a single audit of compliance with federal program requirements. This provision was designed to eliminate duplication in audits and to ensure that the vast majority of federal funding was being audited on a timely basis. Commonly, a government or not-for-profit organization will engage an independent accountant such as a CPA to perform both their annual financial audit and single audit and issue one combined report that serves both purposes. The single audit must be performed in accordance with GAGAS. Initially, when the Single Audit Act of 1984 was enacted, only state and local governments that received over $100,000 in federal funds were required to have a single audit. The successful implementation of this requirement led to the single audit requirement being extended to include not-for-profit organizations as well. The threshold for the single audit requirement has been raised to $300,000 from $100,000.

Circular A-133 requires that the auditor rely upon the work of others to the extent possible, perform a review and evaluation of internal control, perform a risk assessment of major programs to determine the amount of testing for compliance that is necessary, and render an opinion on compliance as well as the financial statements.

Governmental auditing is an exciting and interesting field given the size of the governmental and not-for-profit sector. There are many more specific requirements in GAGAS and in Office of Management and Budget Circular A-133 for the single audit beyond the scope of this brief summary.

SUMMARY

Chapter 7 had the following learning objectives:

- Demonstrate an understanding of accounting and reporting for health care organizations
- Demonstrate an understanding of accounting and reporting for colleges and universities
- Explain basic *Government Auditing Standards* auditing principles
- Explain basic requirements of the single audit

The unique financial challenges facing health care organizations due to limitations in reimbursement from third-party payors for patient services can negatively impact net income. The complicated reimbursement and pricing systems for health care create additional challenges for health care financial managers. Public (governmental) colleges and universities engaged in business-type activities are considered special-purpose governments under GASB Statement No. 34 and are subject to the financial reporting requirements of GASB Statement No. 35. Private not-for-profit colleges and universities are subject to FASB not-for-profit financial reporting requirements.

Governmental and not-for-profit organizations face additional scrutiny on utilization of funds due to the public funding or donated monies. As a result, auditing requirements extend beyond basic Generally Accepted Auditing Standards (GAAS) and are Generally Accepted Governmental Auditing Standards (GAGAS) that include GAAS and have additional standards. The federal single audit is required of all governmental or not-for-profit organizations expending more than $300,000 annually in federal monies. The federal single audit must be conducted in accordance with GAGAS and OMB Circular A-133.

APPENDIX 1

Implementation of GASB Statement No. 35

The requirements of GASB Statement No. 35 are effective as follows:

Phase 1: Public institutions with annual revenues of $100 million or more must implement for periods beginning after June 15, 2001.

Phase 2: Public institutions with annual revenues of $10 million or more but less than $100 million must implement for periods beginning after June 15, 2002.

Phase 3: Public institutions with total annual revenues less than $10 million must implement for periods beginning after June 15, 2003.

To compute the phase-in threshold, all revenues of the primary institutions except investment in plant, other financing sources, and extraordinary items should be included in the determination of annual revenues. The implementation of the capital asset reporting provisions for general infrastructure assets as prescribed in GASB Statement 34 is slightly different from the above dates. Prospective reporting of infrastructure assets is required at the effective implementation date for Phase 1, 2, and 3 public colleges and universities. Phase 1 and Phase 2 institutions are required to go back and retroactively capitalize and report all major general infrastructure assets that have been acquired or had major capital improvements since July 1, 1980, in fiscal years beginning after June 15, 2005, for Phase 1 and after June 15, 2006, for Phase 2. Phase 3 institutions may retroactively capitalize and report all major general infrastructure assets but are not required to do so.

QUESTIONS

1. Do health care organizations follow FASB or GASB standards?
2. What is a capitation agreement?
3. What was the impact of the 1997 Balanced Budget Amendment on health care revenues?
4. Why is accounting for contingencies an important issue for health care organizations?
5. What impact will implementation of HIPPA have on health care organizations?
6. What is the difference between charity care and bad debt expense?
7. Will auxiliary enterprise revenue from the hospital cafeteria be subject to UBIT?
8. Do colleges and universities follow FASB or GASB standards?
9. What is the difference between college operating and nonoperating expenses?
10. What is a mandatory versus nonmandatory transfer?
11. Explain the difference between the three types of governmental audits.
12. What is the difference between GAAS and GAGAS?
13. GAGAS requires that illegal acts may sometimes have to be directly reported to outside parties by the auditor. In what circumstance would you consider this appropriate?
14. Performance audit standards under GAGAS require that the audited officials' views regarding the auditors' conclusions and recommendations be included in the report. Why should these views be included in the actual audit report?
15. When is a single audit required of a governmental or not-for-profit unit?

EXERCISES

Exercise 7-1

Multiple Choice—Select the best answer for each of the following:

1. Capitation means:
   a. the amount of premium is fixed regardless of level of services rendered
   b. the amount of premium is set at a maximum for each service required
   c. the amount of premium can rise with services rendered
   d. none of the above
2. Health care expenditures in America are:
   a. declining
   b. increasing
   c. erratic (up some years, down others)
   d. none of the above
3. Which of the following activities would be subject to UBIT?
   a. hospital gift shop
   b. college bookstore
   c. public hospital pharmacy
   d. hospital chapel
4. HIPPA will establish:
   a. uniform coding for Federal health care programs
   b. uniform payment rates for all health care in America
   c. maximum profit levels for hospitals
   d. a minimum amount hospitals must provide for charity care
5. The 1997 Balanced Budget Act:
   a. cut funding for Medicare
   b. placed tremendous revenue pressure upon hospitals' net profit
   c. caused hospitals to increase prices to non-Medicare clients
   d. did all of the above

6. Other operating revenue of a health care organization includes:
   a. fees for an educational weight-loss program
   b. capitation premiums
   c. patient service revenue
   d. Medicare reimbursement

7. Other operating revenue of a hospital includes:
   a. sale of a old x-ray machine for scrap
   b. cafeteria sales
   c. investment gains and losses
   d. all of the above

8. Charity care is recorded as:
   a. contra allowance account to patient service revenue
   b. expense
   c. bad debt expense
   d. none of the above

9. The Basic Financial Statements for a hospital include:
   a. Statement of Changes in Net Assets
   b. Statement of Cash Flows
   c. Statement of Operations
   d. all of the above

10. A hospital has an increase in market value of its investments at fiscal year-end. The hospital should:
    a. disclose this in the footnotes
    b. recognize the gain
    c. record the gain as deferred revenue
    d. do none of the above

Exercise 7-2

Multiple Choice—Select the best answer for each of the following:

1. A college or university is considered governmental if the governing board:
   a. can levy taxes
   b. can issue tax-exempt debt
   c. is publicly elected
   d. has all of the above

2. Public colleges and universities report revenue by major sources that include all of the following *except*:
   a. contributions
   b. academic support
   c. auxiliary enterprise
   d. tuition and fees

3. Which of the following expenses are academic support?
   a. faculty salaries
   b. faculty travel
   c. research expenses
   d. all of the above

4. Which of the following are *not* institutional support?
   a. information systems expenses
   b. president's salary
   c. chief financial officer's salary
   d. professor's salary

5. Which of the following are institutional support?
   a. chief financial officer's salary
   b. president's salary
   c. facility manager's salary
   e. all of the above

6. A mandatory transfer would occur if:
   a. the governing board designated funds
   b. the governing board set up a quasi-endowment
   c. legally required debt service is transferred from current fund to plant fund
   d. none of the above occurs

7. Auditors conducting audits in accordance with *Government Auditing Standards* must:
   a. read the "blue book"
   b. follow the "yellow book" standard
   c. have 80 hours of CPE in governmental accounting and audit every two years
   d. do none of the above

8. An auditor conducting a single audit finds a material item of noncompliance with the terms of the Federal grant that could require that the funds be returned to the Federal government. This amount has a material impact upon the financial statements. The auditor will issue:
   a. an unqualified opinion
   b. a qualified opinion
   c. an adverse opinion
   d. a disclaimer of opinion

9. An auditor renders an opinion that the governmental financial statements are presented fairly in accordance with GAAP except for the reporting of capital assets. The auditor will be issuing:
   a. an unqualified opinion
   b. a qualified opinion
   c. an adverse opinion
   d. a disclaimer of opinion

10. Staff assigned to work on governmental audits must:
   a. be certified governmental auditors
   b. pass an exam administered by the GAO on governmental auditing
   c. obtain 24 hours of CPE on governmental auditing or the governmental environment every two years
   d. report all instances of impropriety to the local newspaper

Exercise 7-3

Multiple Choice—Select the best answer for each of the following:

(Internet case: Single audit) Go to http://www.whitehouse.gov/OMB/circulars/a133/a133.html to find the Office of Management and Budget Circular A-133, which provides guidance on single audits of states, local governments, and not-for-profit organizations. Using this reference, answer the following questions:

1. A single audit for federal purposes would include:
   a. an opinion on the financial statements
   b. an opinion on major program compliance
   c. a single audit of major programs once every five years
   d. a and b

2. In a single audit, the auditor must identify major programs by:
   a. determining which programs are the most important to the public
   b. the amount of money involved to categorize programs as Type A or Type B
   c. any program over $300,000
   d. none of the above

3. In a single audit, the auditor must, at a minimum, audit as major programs all Federal programs that:
   a. comprise at least 60% of the total Federal awards expended
   b. are all high-risk Type B programs
   c. are all high-risk Type A programs
   d. are none of the above

4. A state or local government or nonprofit organization that receives Federal financial assistance must have a single audit performed if the entity receives:
   a. more than $100,000 in Federal financial assistance
   b. more than $1,000,000 in Federal financial assistance
   c. more than $300,000 in Federal financial assistance
   d. none of the above
5. A state or local government or nonprofit organization that receives Federal financial assistance is responsible for compliance with Federal requirements by:
   a. "for-profit" subrecipients of the Federal financial assistance
   b. vendors paid from the Federal financial assistance
   c. all Medicaid payments to a subrecipient
   d. none of the above
6. Factors to be considered in selecting an independent auditor to perform the single audit include:
   a. external quality control reviews
   b. staff professional qualifications and technical abilities
   c. price
   d. all of the above
7. The schedule of expenditures of Federal awards required in a single audit does not include:
   a. an estimate of Federal programs expenditures for the next fiscal year
   b. CFDA number for each Federal program
   c. Federal awards expended by program
   d. a list of individual programs by Federal agency
8. The data collection form submitted with a Federal single audit does not include:
   a. noncompliance that is material to the financial statements
   b. a signature of a senior executive officer such as the CFO, Treasurer, or Comptroller verifying the form is accurate and complete
   c. all weaknesses in internal control noted
   d. an opinion on compliance in major programs
9. In a single audit, a cognizant agency will be assigned:
   a. for all recipients expending more than $20 million in a year
   b. based upon the Federal agency with the most important program
   c. to inform and work directly with Federal agencies or law enforcement officials to prosecute all incidents that involve irregularities or illegal acts
   d. coordinate clearance of audit findings among all Federal agencies
10. The single audit report does *not* include:
    a. a schedule of findings and questioned costs
    b. a report on compliance with all major and minor Federal financial assistance programs
    c. internal control findings
    d. fraud findings

Exercise 7-4

GAGAS

Does *Government Auditing Standards*, GAGAS, extend beyond GAAS (generally accepted auditing standards)? If so, why aren't the auditing standards for private firms adequate?

Exercise 7-5

Capitation

Explain the advantages and disadvantages of capitation agreements for a health care organization. Why would actuarial advice about the prospective "covered lives" be important before a health care organization entered into the capitation agreement?

Exercise 7-6   **Expense classification**

Explain the difference between academic and institutional support expenses.

Exercise 7-7   **Expense classification**

Student services does not include academic counseling by faculty. Where would academic counseling by faculty be charged as an expense?

Exercise 7-8   **Performance audit**

Joe is conducting a performance audit of a revenue department that processes individual income tax returns. Joe observes that the password for the confidential individual income tax database is prominently taped to every terminal in the department. Should Joe wait to include this finding in his report or is action required before then? If so, what action should Joe take?

Exercise 7-9   **Performance audit**

Frank is conducting a performance audit of a governmental agency. He submits a preliminary draft of the findings to the agency and they advise him that they will have a response ready in 10 days for him to incorporate into the final report. Frank is astonished at this reply and runs to his supervisor saying: "Can you believe this? They actually think we are going to put their comments in our report." What does Frank's supervisor reply?

Exercise 7-10   **Performance audit**

Sandra is planning to tell her manager at a small CPA firm located in a remote rural area that it would be a great idea if they began conducting single audits for governmental entities. What cost to qualify staff to conduct the audits should Sandra consider in her proposal along with the benefits of additional audit revenue?

Exercise 7-11   **Performance audit**

Milly is conducting a performance audit of a governmental agency. She detects an employee who is embezzling public funds and has documentation to prove this crime has occurred. What reporting standard applies in this case and what must Milly do immediately?

Exercise 7-12   **Performance audit**

A city receives $500,000 in Federal funds for local road construction and expends $250,000 during the year. Will the city be required to have a single audit for federal purposes for this year?

PROBLEMS

Problem 7-1   **Conceptual: Reimbursement**

The current reimbursement climate for health care organizations shifts much of the financial risk to the health care entity. Why does this result in different prices for the same health care services for different patients?

Problem 7-2

Conceptual: charity or bad debt

Two large hospitals located within a mile of each other compete fiercely for market share of patient care in a city with an 800,000 population. One hospital provides 5% of its total patient care as charity care, whereas the other hospital provides less than 0.5% of its total patient care. A local member of Congress has started speaking out about this fact to the press and complaining that the tax-exempt status of the hospital only providing one-half a percent of total patient care as charity care should be revoked. The hospital responds and says the member of Congress is mistaken because it writes off 8% of patient care revenues every year as bad debts compared to the other hospital that only has 3% bad debts, so actually both provide the same level of charity care. One has 5% charity care and 3% bad debt expense, and the other has 8% as bad debt expense. What is your opinion about this matter?

Problem 7-3

Conceptual: operating or nonoperating revenue

GASB decided that appropriation support to a public university should be shown as nonoperating revenues because they do not want to make industry-specific rules. As a result, in the financial statements, the state appropriation, which is a significant amount of money, appears in the nonoperating section and can even make it appear that the institution is operating at a deficit. (See ABC University deficit of $39,625,460 in the Statement of Revenues, Expenses, and Changes in Net Assets.) Do you agree with GASB's guidance in this matter?

Problem 7-4

Journal entries

Record the following transactions for a hospital:
   a. Patient services are billed to third-party payors and patients for $6,000,000; 10% is estimated to be uncollectible due to contractual adjustments and bad debts.
   b. Capitation premiums of $500,000 are received.
   c. Utility expenses of $300,000 are paid.
   d. A malpractice lawsuit against the hospital is settled out of court for $300,000 to be paid within 9 months.

Problem 7-5

Journal entries

Record the following transactions for a hospice:
   a. Contributions of $500,000 are pledged in a phonathon.
   b. Volunteers contribute 500 hours of patient care; only one volunteer is a skilled nurse that the hospice would have had to hire. The skilled nurse donated 100 hours that normally would be paid at $38 an hour.
   c. Pledges of $200,000 are paid in cash.
   d. A patient makes a $1,000,000 donation with a life-income agreement.

Problem 7-6

Journal entries

Record the following transactions for a hospital:
   a. Capitation monthly premiums of $2,000,000 are received.
   b. Payroll expenses of $3,000,000 are paid.
   c. Auxiliary enterprises generate revenue of $300,000.
   d. Inventory is purchased for medical supplies and pharmaceuticals of $500,000.
   e. Unrestricted contributions of $250,000 are received.

| Problem 7-7 | **Journal entries** |

Record the following transactions for a private university:
  a. Contribution of $3,000,000 for construction of a building
  b. Sale of $10,000,000 in bonds for construction of the same building
  c. Issuance of a construction contract for $12,000,000 for the same building

| Problem 7-8 | **Journal entries** |

Record the following transactions:
  a. Tuition and fees of $10,000,000 were billed to students.
  b. Payments of $8,000,000 cash for tuition and fees were received.
  c. Scholarships and fellowships were awarded in the amount of $1,500,000; 80% of this amount was applied to tuition and fee bills and the remainder was refunded to students.
  d. Drops and add refunds to students totaled $300,000.

| Problem 7-9 | **Journal entries** |

Record the following transactions:
  a. Delia Donor contributes $1,000,000 to Slippery Rock University for its endowment and specifies that the annual interest earnings be utilized to provide scholarships.
  b. A year after Delia's contribution, Slippery Rock University receives $80,000 in investment income on Delia's portion of the endowment.
  c. Scholarships in the amount of $45,000 are paid.

| Problem 7-10 | **Journal entries** |

Record the following transactions:
  a. Tuition and fees of $5,800,000 are billed to students.
  b. Students receive $1,200,000 in financial aid and $1,000,000 is applied to tuition and fees and the excess is refunded to students.
  c. The tuition and fees remaining unpaid after classes start is $180,000.

| Problem 7-11 | **Journal entries** |

Record the following transactions:
  a. Summer tuition of $2,400,000 for the 12-week summer semester is collected in May. The fiscal year ends June 30. Before the fiscal year ends, 50% of the tuition and fees is expected to be earned.
  b. The fiscal year ends.

| Problem 7-12 | **Journal entries** |

Record the following transactions:
  a. Mandatory transfer of $500,000 of principal and interest on long-term debt on a university auditorium and classroom building
  b. The transfer of cash between funds occurs.
  c. The payment of principal and interest occurs.

Problem 7-13

Journal entries

Record the following transactions:
  a. Nonmandatory transfer from current fund to establish fund for future purchase of land.
  b. Tuition and fee billings of $3,000,000.
  c. Payment of tuition and fees of $2,500,000; financial aid applied was $200,000.
  d. Excess financial aid is refunded to students in the amount of $200,000.
  e. State appropriation of $3,000,000 is received.

Problem 7-14

Internet Research: Financial reporting

Go to the Internet and find a source that discusses implementation of the new HIPPA. After reviewing this, explain what some of the implementation costs appear to be and what benefits are expected in the long run to justify such costs.

Problem 7-15

Internet Research: Financial reporting

Go to the Internet and find the most recent financial report for one public university and one private university. Compare and contrast the differences in the Basic Financial Statements and financial reporting.

GLOSSARY

Academic support Instruction, research, and public service expenses at a college or university.

Accountability GASB Concepts Statement No. 1 established accountability as the "cornerstone" of financial accounting and reporting. Governmental entities must be accountable for public monies.

Accrual basis of accounting Revenues are recognized when earned and expenses when incurred, regardless of when cash is received or paid out.

Activity A specific service performed by one or more departments or organizational unit such as police protection.

Advance refunding Proceeds of new debt are irrevocably set aside to repay the old debt issue as the principal and interest is due.

Agency (or Custodian) funds Resources held on behalf of others by not-for-profit organizations are recorded in these funds.

Agency fund Monies held for others in a custodial capacity or collected on behalf of others are recorded in an agency fund. An agency fund will not record revenues, expenses or a fund balance.

American Institute of Certified Public Accountants (AICPA) A professional organization of Certified Public Accountants that issue *Audit and Accounting Guides* and other technical guidance for financial accounting, reporting, and auditing.

Amortized cost Cost of a security less the amortization of premium or plus the accretion of discount from the date of purchase to date of valuation.

Amortized cost method of accounting Investments are reported at their amortized cost and the components of investment income are interest income, accretion of discount, amortization or premium and gain or loss on sales.

Annuity and Life-income (Split interest) funds Resources donated to generate an annuity or life-income are recorded in these funds by not-for-profit organizations.

Appropriation Legal authorization to spend public monies.

Basic financial statements The fund financial statements, government-wide financial statements, and notes to financial statements that are required in a governmental or not-for-profit organization's annual financial report.

Basis of accounting The basis of accounting determines when transactions or events are recognized in the accounting system.

Bond anticipation note (BAN) A borrowing in anticipation of the issuance of long-term bonds.

Budget Master blueprint for planning, control, and evaluation of fund financial operations.

Budgetary accounts Governmental funds use budgetary accounts to track budgeted resources. Budgetary accounts start the year with a zero balance and are closed to zero at fiscal year-end.

Budgetary Fund Balance A budgetary account that functions as a surrogate for Unreserved fund balance to record budgetary activity during the fiscal year. This account is closed to Unreserved fund balance at fiscal year-end.

Business-type activities Business-like activities such as water and sewer services that are supported by fees and charges received in exchange transactions.

Capital assets Assets that have a useful life of more than one year.

Capital improvement-type special assessments Special assessments against property holders for capital improvements such as sidewalks.

Capital lease A lease that permits use of the asset and provides for the option to purchase the capital asset at the end of the lease.

Capital projects fund General government major construction and renovation projects are recorded in Capital projects funds. A separate fund is often established for each project.

Capitation A maximum rate is set for health care services; the fee is capped per covered life or capitated.

Cash Cash on hand, checks, demand deposits, and similar items.

Cash equivalents Short-term highly liquid investments that can easily be converted to cash.

Claims and judgments A reasonable estimate of probable liability for claims and judgments.

Collateral Securities pledged to cover the value of a deposit or transaction.

Collections Collections of works of art, historical treasures, or other items may not be capitalized at the discretion of the organization if the collection meets certain criteria.

Compensated absences Absences by employees for vacation or sick leave that will be compensated.

Compliance audit An independent audit to attest to the entity's compliance with laws, regulations, and external requirements.

Component units Legally separate organizations that the primary government is financially accountable for.

Composite depreciation A collection of dissimilar assets can be depreciated using a composite method that establishes an annual depreciation rate.

Comprehensive Annual Financial Report (CAFR) External annual financial report of a governmental entity as defined by GASB that includes more information than the basic financial reporting model.

Conditional contribution A contribution is conditional if it depends upon the outcome of a future or an uncertain event.

Conduit debt obligations Debt that is issued through a governmental conduit agency on behalf of a third party who is responsible for repayment rather than the issuing governmental agency.

Construction-in-progress A capital asset that represents the value of a partially constructed capital asset.

Consumption method Inventory is charged to expenditure or expense when used or consumed.

Contributed services Donated specialized services are recognized as revenue if they meet certain criteria.

Contribution An unconditional promise to give or unconditional donation or cash or other assets.

Counterparty The other party to an investment transaction.

Credit risk Risk that another party to a deposit or investment transaction will not fulfill their obligations.

Current asset Assets available to pay expenditures or liabilities or likely to be consumed or in current operating period.

Current financial resources measurement focus This measurement focus records revenues when resources flow in and can be used to pay current budgetary period expenditures and records expenditures when resources flow out to pay for them. This method of reporting is used with the modified accrual basis of accounting.

Current fund This fund accounts for general operating activity of a college or university and is divided into two parts: Unrestricted and Restricted.

Current liabilities Liabilities that are likely to be liquidated or paid within the current period with current resources.

Current refunding Debt is repaid in advance of the maturity date through issuance of new debt.

Custodial credit risk This is the risk that the party holding the security will fail to return the principal.

Debt service fund Resources set aside to pay principal and interest on general government long-term liabilities such as general obligation bonds are recorded in Debt service funds. Legal requirements often mandate a separate Debt service fund for each bond issue.

Defeasance Repayment of debt.

Deferred revenue Revenue that has been received but is not yet earned or available is recorded as a liability until it is recognized.

Defined benefit pension plan A pension plan that defines the benefits recipients will receive at retirement.

Defined contribution pension plan A pension plan that defines the contributions that will be made on behalf of recipients each year.

Demand bond A bond that must be paid upon demand of the bondholder.

Deposit Accounts such as checking, savings and non-negotiable certificates of deposit in banks and other financial institutions.

Depreciation A systematic method of allocating the cost of long-lived capital assets across the period of their useful lives.

Derived tax revenue Tax revenue that is derived from an underlying exchange transaction like a sales tax.

Designated fund balance This portion of fund balance has a self-imposed designation that the governing body can remove at will.

Economic resources measurement focus The accrual basis of accounting is based upon the economic resources measurement focus. This measurement focus records revenues, expenses, gains, losses, assets, and liabilities of exchange transactions when the exchange takes place. Nonexchange transactions are recorded according to GASB Statement No. 33. This method of reporting is used with the accrual basis of accounting.

Eligibility requirements Requirements that must be met for revenue to be recognized in government-mandated or voluntary nonexchange transactions.

Encumbrance Commitment to spend such as a purchase order or contract recorded in the governmental funds.

Endowment A permanent donation of principal that can never be expended.

Endowment fund Endowments of not-for-profit organizations are recorded in this fund.

Enterprise fund Business-type activities that charge fees to external users are recorded in Enterprise funds.

Entitlement Federally-funded program that a government chooses to voluntarily participate in.

Escheat property Unclaimed property that is returned to the government. The government will hold and publicize such property for a period of time and then sell or dispose of it and use the proceeds for purposes permitted by the appropriate escheat property law for that government.

Exchange transaction A transaction in which resources (cash, services, goods, etc.) are exchanged and the value of the resources received are approximately equal to the resources given up in the exchange.

Exchange-like transaction A transaction in which the resources received and given in the exchange are similar but not equal values.

Expenditure or Expense Decrease in financial resources recorded when incurred under the accrual basis of accounting and in an obligation of current funds under the modified accrual basis of accounting.

External investment pool The government commingles the assets of more than one legally separate entity for investment purposes. An external pool can be sponsored by a government or nongovernmental entity.

Fair value Fair market value as readily determined from a publicly available market index or information. The price a willing buyer would pay a seller in an "arm's length" transaction.

Fair value method of accounting Investments are reported at their fair value and the components of investment income are interest income, dividend income, and net increase or decrease in the fair value of investments.

Federal Accounting Standards Advisory Board (FASAB) The standard-setting body for the federal government and its agencies.

Fiduciary funds The Pension (and other employee-benefit) trust, Investment trust, Private-purpose trust, and Agency funds record transactions for monies held in a trustee or agency capacity for others and use the accrual basis of accounting.

Final budget The final budget incorporates all amendments to the budget enacted during the fiscal year by the governing body.

Financial Accounting Foundation (FAF) The Financial Accounting Foundation receives donations, provides funding for and appoints Board members of the independent standard-setting bodies: GASB and FASB.

Financial Accounting Standards Board (FASB) The standard-setting body for not-for-profit organizations and for-profit entities. (Additional information is available at www.fasb.org).

Financial audit An independent audit to review and evaluate the system of internal controls and attest to and determine if the financial statements are fairly presented in accordance with GAAP.

Financial reporting entity The primary government and component units that form the reporting entity.

Financial reporting model Information that must be included in a government's external annual financial report.

Fixed budgets The amount of funds specified for the budget is fixed.

Flexible budgets The amount of funds specified for the budget can increase or decrease based upon activity or fee levels.

Function A function is comprised of activities that relate to providing a major service or regulatory program like public safety. The government-wide financial statements can report activity by functions or programs.

Fund A self-balancing set of accounts that is considered a separate fiscal and accounting entity. Funds segregate the resources related to specific activities to enhance accountability.

Fund balance (or equity) The amount of net assets that is the difference between assets and liabilities.

Fund financial statements Financial statements that are required for the governmental, proprietary, and fiduciary funds.

General fund There is only one General fund and it is the primary fund that records general operating activities for a governmental entity.

General revenues General revenues such as property taxes, that support general governmental operations.

Generally Accepted Accounting Principles (GAAP) AICPA Auditing Standards Board Statement No. 69 established the meaning of "present fairly in accordance with GAAP" for auditor opinions on financial statements. GAAP sets minimum requirements for the fair presentation of financial data in external financial reports.

Generally Accepted Auditing Standards (GAAS) AICPA Auditing Standards Board promulgates the auditing standards that any auditor must follow to render an opinion on or attest to private financial statements.

Generally Accepted Government Auditing Standards (GAGAS) The *Government Auditing Standards* issued by the General Accounting Office are required to be followed by any auditor conducting financial, compliance, or performance audits of public or governmental entities.

Gifts-in-kind Non-cash contributions such as donations of goods or services that have a value.

Government Finance Officers Association (GFOA) A professional organization of governmental finance officers that provides a wide range of educational services and resources including publication of the "blue book," *Governmental Accounting, Auditing, and Financial Reporting,* which is a primary reference book for governmental accounting and financial reporting.

Governmental Accounting Standards Board (GASB) The standard-setting body for governmental entities including governmental not-for-profit organizations. (Additional information is available at www.gasb.org).

Governmental activities General government activities such as public safety and general administration that are primarily supported by taxes and other nonexchange transactions.

Governmental entity Government-like county, city, town, or village governed by an elected representative form of governing board. A governmental entity can also be a not-for-profit organization such as a college or university or health care organization.

Governmental funds The General, Special revenue, Capitol projects, Debt service, and Permanent funds that record general government activities and use the modified accrual basis of accounting.

Government-mandated nonexchange transaction A government provides resources to another government and requires that the resources be used for a specific purpose.

Government-wide financial statements Financial statements that provide information about the entire primary government as well as its component units. The two required statements are the government-wide Statement of Activities and Statement of Net Assets.

Grant Funding from an external party (agency, individual, foundation, etc.) that a government chooses to voluntarily accept.

Group depreciation A collection of similar assets can be depreciated using a group rate that establishes an annual depreciation rate.

Health care organization An organization that provides health care services.

Hierarchy of GAAP AICPA ranking of sources of generally accepted accounting principles to array these sources in a hierarchal chart. The ranking provides guidance as to what sources are primary authority for GAAP for governmental and nongovernmental organizations according to Statement on Auditing Standards No. 69.

Historical cost Original principal dollars invested or purchase price.

Imposed nonexchange revenue Assessment by a government that is not based upon an underlying exchange transaction such as a property tax or fine.

Individual investment account A separate account for investments of legally separate entities managed by the sponsoring government.

Inexhaustible capital assets Assets that do not waste away over time and should not be depreciated such as land, historical treasures, and rare works of art.

Infrastructure Stationary, long-lived capital assets like streets, bridges, and water and sewer systems.

Institutional support Executive, fiscal and facilities management, information systems, human resources, purchasing and fund-raising expenses at a college or university.

In-substance defeasance Monies have been irrevocably set aside to repay debt so the debt is considered to be legally satisfied or repaid.

Internal investment pool The government commingles or pools assets for investment purposes that belong to funds or component units.

Internal service funds Business-type activities that only charge fees for cost reimbursement to internal users or other governments are recorded in Internal service funds.

Interperiod equity GASB Concepts Statement No. 1 established interperiod equity as a key concept to guide financial accounting and reporting for governmental entities. Governmental entities should pay for current services with current resources and not "borrow" from future period resources to pay for current services.

Investment Securities or other investment assets purchased to provide a return on idle cash.

Investment trust funds The external portion of an investment pool is recorded in an investment trust fund by the sponsoring government. The internal portion of the investment pool is recorded in the respective funds that hold shares in the pool.

Landfill closure and postclosure costs An estimate of closure and postclosure costs for a landfill that will be allocated as the landfill is used and filled.

Loan fund This fund records college or university loans to faculty, students, or staff.

Major fund Major funds are reported in separate columns in the governmental and proprietary fund financial statement.

Management's Discussion and Analysis (MD&A) Introduction and analytical discussion of the financial statements prepared by government financial managers.

Mandatory transfers Mandatory transfers are required by some external restriction or requirement to shift resources from one fund to another of a college or university.

Market risk This is the risk that the value of an investment will rise or decline due to shifts in interest rates or other national or international market events.

Measurement focus The measurement focus refers to what is being reported upon or measured in the financial statements.

Modified accrual basis of accounting Revenues are recognized when measurable and available. Expenditures are recognized when incurred if measurable or an obligation against current budgetary resources is made.

Modified approach for reporting infrastructure Governments can choose to use the modified approach for evaluating and reporting the condition of infrastructure rather than to record depreciation.

National Association of College and University Business Officers (NACUBO) A professional organization of college and university business officers that provides technical guidance in publications like the *Financial Accounting and Reporting Manual* and educational programs.

Noncurrent asset Assets that are not liquid to pay expenditures or liabilities such as capital assets and restricted cash.

Noncurrent or long-term liabilities Liabilities that are not likely to be liquidated or paid within the current period.

Nonexchange transaction A transaction in which the value of resources (cash, services, goods, etc.) received is not equal to the value of resources (if any) given up.

Nonmajor fund Nonmajor funds can be combined in one column as "other funds" in the governmental and proprietary fund financial statements.

Nonmandatory transfers Nonmandatory transfers are made at the discretion of the governing board and shift resources from one fund to another of a college or university.

Nonoperating revenues and expenses Revenues and expenses like interest expense that are not related to operating activities of the proprietary funds.

Nonreciprocal interfund activity Nonexchange transactions between funds such as Transfers In and Transfers Out between funds such as the transfer of resources from the General fund to Debt service to pay debt service.

Notes to financial statements Disclosures of information required or suggested to be included in the annual financial report.

Not-for-profit organization Organizations that provide goods or services and whose goals are not profit-based. Resources received often include contributions.

Object An expenditure that is detailed within an activity such as salaries, supplies, etc.

On-behalf payments for fringe benefits or salaries One government pays salaries and fringe benefits for another government's employee. This might occur when the employee is on loan to another government.

Operating lease A lease that permits use of the asset but requires the asset be returned at the end of the lease.

Operating revenues and expenses Revenues and expenses related to operating activities of the proprietary funds.

Original budget Initial budget adopted by the governing body.

Other Financing Source Unusual, nonrecurring revenue.

Other Financing Use Unusual, nonrecurring expenditure.

Pension (and other employee benefit) trust funds Monies held in trust on behalf of employees and beneficiaries for pensions or other future benefits are held and recorded in Pension and other employee benefit trust funds.

Performance audit An independent audit to assess the economy, efficiency, and effectiveness of the entity.

Permanent fund Resources that are legally restricted so that only the earnings generated from the resources can be spent for general government purposes or public benefit are recorded in the Permanent fund.

Permanently restricted net assets Net assets that have donor imposed restrictions that are permanent.

Plant fund This fund accounts for capital assets and related debt of a college or university and is divided into four parts: Unexpended, Investment in Plant, Renewal and Replacement, and Retirement of Indebtedness.

Postemployment health care benefits The benefits that will be provided to employees after retirement or termination of employment.

Primary government State or general-purpose local government or special-purpose government that is legally separate and fiscally independent.

Private college or university A nongovernmental college or university that will follow FASB standards for accounting and financial reporting.

Private-purpose trust funds Resources held in trust to benefit specific individuals or groups of individuals, private organizations, or other governments.

Program The activities related to a specific purpose or objective of a government such as public welfare. The government-wide financial statements can report by functions or programs.

Program revenues Revenues that can be specifically attributed to various programs or functions.

Program service Program services deliver services or perform activities that enable a not-for-profit organization to achieve its mission.

Promise to give The promise of a contribution that is legally enforceable if there is evidence of the donor's intent.

Proprietary funds The Enterprise and Internal service funds that record business-type activities and use the accrual basis of accounting.

Public college or university A governmental-type college or university that will follow GASB standards for accounting and financial reporting.

Purchase method Inventory is charged to expenditure or expense when purchased.

Purpose restriction Restriction that limits the use of resources to a particular purpose.

Quasi-endowment Funds that have been set aside or restricted by the organization.

Quasi-external transactions Interfund transactions that are recorded as if the transaction was with an external party rather than another fund. Expenditure rather than Transfer Out is used and Revenue rather than Transfer In is used to record the transaction. A sale of power to the General fund from the Enterprise fund is an example.

Reciprocal interfund activity Exchange or exchange-like transactions between funds such as the sale of power by an Enterprise fund to the General fund or loans between funds.

Repurchase agreement An investment transaction where a government transfers cash to a broker-dealer to earn interest income on idle cash. The broker-dealer provides as collateral and agrees to repurchase those securities at some future time for an amount equal to the cash plus interest income.

Required Supplementary Information (RSI) Information required in addition to the financial statements as part of the annual financial report.

Reserved fund balance This portion of fund balance is not available to be appropriated.

Restricted assets Assets that have restrictions on their use imposed by external parties or by law.

Revenue Increase in financial resources that are recorded when available under the modified accrual basis of accounting and when earned under the accrual basis of accounting.

Revenue anticipation notes (RANS) A borrowing in anticipation of receipt of future revenues other than taxes.

Reverse repurchase agreement The government provides securities to another party in exchange for cash and agrees to repurchase those securities at some time in the future for an amount equal to the cash plus interest.

Securities lending A government may choose to lend its securities to others in return for cash or collateral securities in an investment transaction for a specified period of time as a method of generating additional income.

Serial bonds Bond issues that have an equal amount of principal due each year.

Service efforts and accomplishments GASB Concepts Statement No. 2 suggests a model for governmental entities to report information about the services provided, efforts and accomplishments for each fiscal year as a measure of the government's performance.

Service-type special assessments Special assessments against property holders for services such as garbage and snow-plowing that would normally be general government functions.

Shared revenues A government shares revenues with another government. This is commonly done for sales or property taxes according to a specified formula.

Single audit One audit that includes all federal funds expended by an entity for compliance with federal program requirements.

Special items and extraordinary items Events that are not within the control of the government such as natural disasters, etc.

Special revenue fund Resources that have some legal restriction upon their use are recorded in Special revenue funds unless they are restricted for trust or capital project purposes.

Split-interest agreements A donation of resources that has an exchange component where the donor expects something in return for the other donation component. Annuity or life-income agreements are split-interest agreements.

Student services Services that promote student's emotional and physical health outside of normal instructional expenses at a college or university.

Supporting service Supporting services include Management and general, Fund-raising, and Membership-development activities that support the program services of a not-for-profit organization.

Tax anticipation notes (TANS) A short-term borrowing in anticipation of cash to be received from tax collections.

Temporarily restricted net assets Net assets that have donor imposed restrictions that can be satisfied by time or spending for a specific purpose.

Term bonds Bonds where the entire principal is due at the end of a specified period of time.

Term endowment A donation that can be expended at the end of a fixed period of time or the occurrence of an event specified by the donor.

Third-party payors Insurance companies, HMOs, and other third parties that reimburse health care organizations for patient services provided.

Time restriction Restriction that limits the use of resources to a particular point or period in time.

Transfers In Interfund resources transferred into one fund from another for operating purposes (sometimes referred to as Operating Transfers In).

Transfers Out Interfund resources transferred from one fund into another for operating purposes (sometimes referred to as Operating Transfers Out).

Unconditional contribution A contribution that is not conditional and is recognized as revenue.

Unrelated business income tax (UBIT) An income tax charged against business income that is unrelated to the not-for-profit organizations primary mission and program activities.

Unrestricted net assets Net assets that have no donor restrictions and are available for any purpose.

Voluntary nonexchange transaction A government voluntarily accepts resources that have certain eligibility requirements imposed by legislation or donors.

INDEX